American Buildings and Their Architects

This book is the first part of the second volume of a four-volume series which, under the general title of AMERICAN BUILDINGS AND THEIR ARCHITECTS, is devoted to an architectural analysis and evaluation of American buildings from colonial times to about 1960. The volumes already published are: THE COLONIAL AND NEOCLASSICAL STYLES, PROGRESSIVE AND ACADEMIC IDEALS AT THE TURN OF THE TWENTIETH CENTURY, and THE IMPACT OF EUROPEAN MODERNISM IN THE MID-TWENTIETH CENTURY.

The second part of this volume will be published at a later time.

American Buildings and Their Architects

TECHNOLOGY AND THE PICTURESQUE

The Corporate and the Early Gothic Styles

William H. Pierson, Jr.

ANCHOR BOOKS
Anchor Press/Doubleday
Garden City, New York
1980

AMERICAN BUILDINGS AND THEIR ARCHITECTS: Technology and The Picturesque The Corporate and The Early Gothic Styles was originally published in a hardcover edition by Doubleday & Company, Inc. in 1978.

Anchor Books Edition: 1980
ISBN: 0-385-08179-0
Copyright © 1978 by William H. Pierson, Jr.
ALL RIGHTS RESERVED
Printed in the United States of America

TO MY DAUGHTERS
ELIZABETH DIXON PIERSON
AND
SARA PIERSON NOLL

Contents

List of Illustrations

Except where otherwise indicated the
photographs used for the illustrations
were made by the author.

Prefatory Remarks
and Acknowledgments

In all the volumes in this series, the ideas have been developed around a few carefully selected extant examples, each examined in depth. This raises at once the question of those countless other buildings of the period which have been left out, buildings which may be regarded by some as more important and more characteristic than those which I have chosen. In answer, I can only say that this is a very personal book, written around observations and ideas that have come together over many years of teaching and thinking about American architecture. It is not intended to be a definitive study of the subject. Rather, my objective has been to identify the larger forces and the important men who created American architecture and to illuminate these through a careful analysis of a select group of buildings. I have personally visited not once but many times every major building discussed. I have also examined in each case all the existing documents, visual materials, and architectural drawings that I have been able to find. My objective has been to get as close to the buildings as possible and to present them as they were understood by those who built them. Moreover, in communicating something of my own experience, it is my hope that the reader will be motivated to explore further on his or her own.

A work of this magnitude is never accomplished without the help of many people and I would like to acknowledge and thank those individuals and institutions which have been part of the effort. There was first the massive task of assembling the illustrations. The majority of the photographs of existing buildings are my own, and were shot specifically to illustrate ideas developed in the text. The remainder of these principally came from two sources: the Historic American Buildings Survey photographs in the Library of Congress, and the photographs made for the Carnegie Study of the Arts of the United States, which are owned by the University of Georgia and consigned to Sandak Inc. in Stamford, Connecticut. Along with these there were several individual photographers who have provided me with photographs. They are: Wayne Andrews, Tom Crane, Mary Wallace Crocker and the University and College Press of Mississippi, Louis Frohman. Various photographs were furnished by the Providence Public Library. In addition, Christopher Noll, Ernie Le Clair, Gwen W. Steege, and Anne R. Wardwell made photographs for me under my specific instructions. The photographs of English buildings were provided by the following British institutions: Country Life, Ltd., the Derbyshire Archaeological Society, and the National Monuments Record (England). Those of French buildings are the work of Whitney S. Stoddard.

Such visual material as old photographs, prints, and drawings came from the following individuals and institutions: the Avery Architectural Library, Columbia University; the Boston Athenaeum; the Boston Public Library; the Chapin Library, Williams College; the Fairmount Park Commission, Philadelphia; the Free Library of Philadelphia; Historic Harrisville, Inc., Harrisville, New Hampshire; Houghton Library and Widener Library, Harvard University; Lowell Historical Society, Lowell, Massachusetts; the Massachusetts Historical Society; the Metropolitan Museum of Art, New York City; the Museum of the City of New York; the National Gallery, London; the National Trust for Historic Preservation, Washington, D.C.; the New-York Historical Society; the New York Public Library; Old Sturbridge Village, Sturbridge, Massachusetts; the Rochester Historical Society, Rochester, New York; the Pejebscot Historical Society, Brunswick, Maine; St. Paul's Church, Brookline, Massachusetts; St. Paul's Church, Troy, New York; the Smithsonian Institution, Washington, D.C.; the Society for the Preservation of New England Antiquities, Boston, Massachusetts; Walter Knight Sturges; Trinity Church, New Haven, Connecticut; the Yale University Art Gallery; the University of Lowell, Lowell, Massachusetts.

In the course of my research the archival and rare materials of the following institutions were generously made available to me: the American Antiquarian Society, Worcester, Massachusetts; the Avery Architectural Library, Columbia University; the Edwin J. Beinecke Library, Yale University; the Boston Athenaeum; the Boston Public Library; Christ Church Cathedral, Hartford, Connecticut; the Metropolitan Museum of Art, New York City; the National Archives; the New Haven Colony Historical Society, New Haven, Connecticut; the New-York Historical Society; the New York Public Library; the Preservation Society of Newport County, Newport, Rhode Island; the Roman Catholic Dioceses of Baltimore and New York; the Vassar College Library, Poughkeepsie, New York; Yale University Library.

There are also those who have endured the invasion of their privacy by me and my camera: the Avery Architectural Library, Columbia University; Mr. and Mrs. John Bullard; Colby Museum of Art, Colby College, Waterville, Maine; John White Delafield; the Episcopal Theological Seminary, Nashotah, Wisconsin; Kingscote, Newport, Rhode Island; Lyndhurst, Tarrytown, New York; George Nathan Associates, North Providence, Rhode Island; the Old Slater Mill, Pawtucket, Rhode Island; the Church of St. James-the-Less, Philadelphia; St. John's Cathedral, Providence, Rhode Island; the Church of St. John Chrysostom, Delafield, Wisconsin; the Church of St. John in the Wilderness, Copake, New York; the Church of St. Mary's, Burlington, New Jersey; St. Patrick's Cathedral, New York City; the Church of St. Paul's, Brookline, Massachusetts; the Church of St.

Thomas, Amenia Union, New York; Mr. and Mrs. Donald Slobohm; Trinity Church, New Haven, Connecticut; the University of Lowell, Lowell, Massachusetts.

For various types of special assistance, I am indebted to Elizabeth Reed Amadon, James M. Carpenter, John Colony, Bette Copeland, Antoinette Downing, Bishop Joseph F. Flannelly, Hugh J. Gourley III, James C. Massey, John Poppeliers, Monsignor James F. Rigney, Earl G. Shettleworth, Thomas M. Slade, Eleanor Thompson.

In solving the many technical and professional problems connected with this book I have also benefited from the counsel and advice of Margo Archer, Gibson Danes, the late Richard Hale, E. J. Johnson, Gary Kulik, Donald Lehman, Howard Levitz, Charles F. Montgomery, Denys Peter Myers, John Pearce, Paul Rivard, Elizabeth Roth, Harold and Victor Sandak, Sheafe Satterthwaite, Donald S. Smith, Brooks Stoddard, William Taggart, Robert Vogel, Philip Wilder, and Karel Yasko.

A very special kind of help has come from a number of scholars who have generously shared with me the fruits of their own researches, much of it as yet unpublished. These include Richard C. Candee, Jane B. Davies, Margaret Henderson Floyd, Richard Janson, John Maass, Patrick M. Malone, Daniel Porter, Selma Rattner, Theodore Sande, and Walter Knight Sturges.

Several persons deserve special mention for their major contributions to this book. Adolf K. Placzek, the librarian of the Avery Architectural Library, has gone out of his way to make that magnificent resource available to me, and through his vast knowledge of its holdings has directed me at once to materials that I might never have found. His kindness, his patience, and his enthusiastic interest in my project have made it a joy to work at the Avery. Anne R. Wardwell, architectural consultant and former Survey Director of the Massachusetts Historical Commission, has worked as a research assistant throughout the course of this project and has been instrumental in turning up a large portion of the original materials upon which the book has been built. Elenore Selin worked with me for a year as a research assistant and typist and was responsible for developing and indexing my negative file. For the past four years Mrs. Selin's role has been filled by Gwen W. Steege. In addition, Mrs. Steege has assumed with grace and intelligence the full burden of the mechanics of the book, of collating all the material and preparing the final manuscript, and of helping me in the darkroom. She has also made all the drawings for the plans.

My colleague, William Jordy, has been of central importance in both the conception and the specifics of this book. Although Professor Jordy has completed his volumes in this series, he still remains a constant force in the development of my own thinking, and a valuable prod when the going gets slow. Along with Professor Jordy, at the core of the project, is Pyke Johnson, Jr., the Managing Editor of Doubleday. Mr. Johnson was editor of Anchor Books when this series first took serious shape. He was therefore directly involved in its early planning and he still remains the central figure in its production. Through the many and frustrating years which it has taken to bring the series this far both his civilized patience and his enthusiastic support have never wavered. For this I shall be eternally grateful.

Finally, through all of this, my wife has borne with gentle understanding the eccentric lifestyle of one who is mad enough to undertake such a project. She has also been my most severe and demanding critic.

To all I have mentioned here, and to the friendly members of the various staffs of the institutions to which I have turned for help, my most heartfelt thanks.

WILLIAM H. PIERSON, JR.

Williamstown, Massachusetts, 1976

CHAPTER I

Romanticism, Technology
and the Picturesque

*The whistle of the locomotive penetrates my woods summer
and winter.*

HENRY DAVID THOREAU

As first conceived this volume of *American Buildings and Their Architects*
was to have been a single book, the size of Volume I, and was to have
dealt with the impact of technology and the picturesque on American architecture from the beginning of the nineteenth century to the Chicago
World's Fair of 1892. This dynamic period has already been considered in
many of its parts by numerous architectural historians and critics but so
far it has never been treated as a comprehensive whole. Originally this
work was meant to do just that. As the major themes developed, however,
they proved too large and complex to be accomplished in one volume. The
intended book was therefore divided into two parts, each to be published
separately, and each conceived as a complete work in its own right. This
book is the first of these two parts.

Because of the complexity of the period such a division was not easy.
The many components of the chronicle were too intertwined to make an
inclusive horizontal cut-off in time feasible, and regardless of how the material was separated something seemed always to be left incomplete. In the
end, the most workable organization was one according to style. On this
basis, two large stylistic blocks emerged as dominant during the first two
thirds of the century. The first was the so-called "corporate style" of the
early industrial communities, a conservative and practical idiom which
continued the chaste brick architecture of early nineteenth-century Boston
into many parts of New England down to the time of the Civil War. The
second was the early Gothic Revival. This dynamic picturesque style
brought a new vitality to American religious and domestic architecture,
and at the same time introduced into this country the first architectural ingredients of the Romantic movement. Its time span, moreover, was almost
exactly the same as that of the corporate style.

What was accomplished by this division of material was a
straightforward demonstration, as first revealed in architectural form, of
two major thrusts in nineteenth-century America, technology and romanticism. But even this arrangement, with all its apparent simplicity, was not

without its problems and two of these, particularly as they relate to the second part of this volume, are of sufficient importance to be recognized. The first concerns the villa, which is a primary topic in this book. As it appeared in this country during the 1830's the villa was a new concept of the house, and one that would play a dominant role in the evolution of American domestic architecture during the entire century. Although first introduced by Alexander Jackson Davis in the Gothic style, the villa was a typological and not a stylistic concept, and during the nineteenth century was actually designed in any one of a number of picturesque styles. Among the most popular of these styles was the Italianate, and Davis, who was the first to create the Gothic villa, was also among the leaders in the development of the Italian villa. Both typologically and chronologically, therefore, it might seem logical to have included the latter in this book. On the other hand, the Italianate differed from the Gothic in that it was a round-arch, not a pointed-arch, style and thus had close connections with another important stylistic development of the period, the Romanesque. Both the Italianate and the Romanesque had much wider ramifications in the development of American architecture at mid-century than the Gothic, especially in the urban and industrial scene. They thus formed a coherent segment of architectural activity which was quite separate from the Gothic and could therefore be reasonably moved to the second part of this work; and even though this left the story of the villa incomplete it made it possible to treat with greater ease and directness the complex subject of the early Gothic Revival in America.

A second problem in the organization of material was chronology. Although the main thrust of both the corporate and early Gothic styles occurred during the same years, there were a few instances in which the Gothic was carried over to considerably later dates. Of these the most conspicuous was St. Patrick's Cathedral in New York, the largest church built in this country until very late in the century. Although dedicated in 1879 and not actually completed until early in the twentieth century, it was conceived and begun before the Civil War. Stylistically, it was the product of the attitudes toward the church which characterized the first half of the nineteenth century. Moreover, the fact that it took so long to build was simply the result of the magnitude of the task and not of any change of stylistic intention. For all these reasons, St. Patrick's quite properly belongs to the early Gothic Revival. Nevertheless, in order to give a complete account of this church, it has been necessary to reach beyond the designated time span of the book. This may disturb some readers, but as the story unfolded its coherence seemed to transcend any need for chronological neatness and the account was therefore carried through to the end.

Focusing on the corporate and early Gothic styles as the combined theme of this book offered one other considerable advantage: the time span of both developments coincided exactly with that of the Greek Revival. Thus it was possible to relate the new material to many aspects of the period already discussed in the second part of Volume I. This overlap was always intended in the design of this series, and to have the industrial and Gothic material all concentrated in one book now makes possible a richer treatment of their manifold fascinations. But to set this in motion it is necessary first to go back in time to the turn of the nineteenth century and establish the architectural situation which prevailed when technology and the doctrine of the picturesque made their appearance in this country.

CLASSICISM AND ROMANTICISM IN THE UNITED STATES

Prelude to Romanticism in the United States

The United States Treasury building by Robert Mills, begun in 1836, was in its day the most mature and expressive work of architecture yet produced by a native born American architect. It was planned to accommodate the complex functions of a growing department of the Federal Government; it was solidly built utilizing a simple but highly articulated system of vaulting, which was then an innovation. In more abstract terms, Mills's austere, geometric interpretation of the Greek style placed his work at the very center of a national enthusiasm for the architecture of ancient Greece, an enthusiasm which reached to every corner of the settled land and touched every facet of American architecture from government buildings in Washington to the smallest farmhouses on the fringes of the frontier. The Greek Revival was not only a chaste and simple style, which suited well the prevailing mood of a middle-class culture, but having originated in the democracies of ancient Greece, it was regarded by most Americans as an appropriate symbol of the political ideals upon which their own nation was based.[1]

If the Greek Revival looked forward to a new America, it nevertheless had several things in common with the colonial architecture of the eighteenth century. Both styles shared common structural methods and common building types. But more important, both were based upon classical principles of design. This meant that certain formal characteristics such as symmetrical plans and façades, the classical orders, and classical details continued after the Revolution without interruption. The Greek Revival thus carried over into the nineteenth century those qualities of serenity and quiet dignity which gave colonial architecture its special character. Indeed, the transition from colonial to Greek classical forms was accomplished with such natural ease that in some provincial areas it is only the trained observer who can immediately detect the differences. The Greek Revival appears, therefore, as a dual phenomenon. On the one hand it was an expressive architectural idiom, deliberately fashioned to fulfill the needs and aspirations of the new nation; on the other it reflected a persistent heritage with its roots in the colonial past. In spirit as well as fact it was the product of both a rising nationalism and a conservative middle-class taste. It is with good reason, therefore, that Hamlin[2] regarded the Greek Revival as the first truly national style in the United States.

But was it? Did this simple, chaste and for the most part naive mode of building have sufficient range and depth to embrace all dimensions of an emerging America? Certainly it catered both to a bourgeois nationalism and to a conservative taste. In fact, at its height it was a major medium of expression in the young nation's groping search for cultural identity. There was a quality of primitivism, too, in the bold and frequently awkward handling of the Greek forms which suggests the first hesitant stirring of a new national character. On the other hand, there were many aspects of the developing nation for which the Greek Revival was neither expressive nor appropriate. By the turn of the nineteenth century new and dynamic forces, unknown in the colonial period, were already at work adding diversity and giving new dimensions to the entire structure of American society. Its world was no longer simple, nor was it small. As the awesome vastness of the land began to unfold, the isolation and immobility of the colonials gave way to the restless impatience of a free and independent people on the move. For the bold and the aggressive the challenge no longer lay in the immediate forest or the local city street, but in the land beyond the Alleghenies. All of this energetic stirring would demand a more flexible and dynamic architecture than was possible with the serene and stable Greek idiom, however much it may have been transformed and animated by individual taste and ingenuity. To understand, therefore, precisely the relationship of the Greek Revival to the changing shapes of nineteenth-century America, and to evaluate properly the architecture which shared the stage with it and ultimately took its place, we must first review briefly the changes which occurred in architecture as the nation moved from colonialism to independence.

When the colonists arrived in the new world they found themselves in a land without an architectural heritage, so they simply adopted the conventions of the countries from which they had come. From the practical point of view this was logical; emotionally it was essential, for it brought to the frontier the visible assurances of a familiar, civilized environment. To be sure, local materials and local craftsmanship left their mark upon colonial buildings, but the degree of effect was limited and altered very little the basic character of the European styles, particularly in the English architecture which dominated the eastern seaboard. Even the seventeenth-century New England meetinghouse, the only colonial building type which seems to have had no direct ancestor in England, succumbed during the eighteenth century to the pressures of fashionable taste and took on most of the outward appearances and all the decorative paraphernalia of the London churches of Wren and Gibbs. In religion and politics the latter part of the eighteenth century was a time of rebellion, but in America's cultural affairs—particularly as revealed in the visual forms of architecture, painting, and the decorative arts—it was a period of willing and not too critical acceptance of the English example.

During the years immediately following the Revolution, American architecture continued very much as it was before the break with England; even the first phase of Neoclassicism, generally known as the Federal style, had its roots in the homeland. It is true that this new style derived from the architecture of Robert Adam rather than from that of his predecessors James Gibbs and the Palladians, but it was English nevertheless, and in general it was accepted by the Americans with the same readiness that they had shown toward the colonial styles. By the turn of the nineteenth century, however, the American attitude toward architecture began to change. Motivated initially by a growing national awareness, then stimulated by both external forces and by the more sophisticated internal needs of an increasingly complex society, American architecture became by midcentury a lively mixture of established European ideas and fresh indigenous elements unique to the land and its people.

The growing nationalism brought with it a new kind of patronage and more demanding attitudes which made it essential that American reliance on European architecture be re-examined. Passive acceptance was not enough. The anti-British sentiment released both by the Revolution and by the War of 1812 fostered, even demanded, a rejection of established English tradition in favor of new forms more expressive of the ideals of American democracy. Indeed, it was at this point that the full impact of the Neoclassical movement was felt in the United States and the Greek Revival played its major and highly nationalistic role.[3]

The gratification of national sentiment, however, did not fulfill all the aspirations of the young American republic. The individual, political and religious freedom guaranteed by the Constitution resulted in a gradual breakdown in the narrow and relatively homogeneous cultural patterns of colonial society and gave encouragement to diversity in thought and institution. Thus it was that William Ellery Channing could become a principal defender of Unitarianism in the heart of Puritan New England, and his brother-in-law, the painter Washington Allston, could challenge the established conventions of English portrait and historical painting with his own intensely personal and romantic images. In the realm of taste, too, judgment became more and more a matter of individual preference rather than accepted convention, and Robert Gilmore, caught up in the medieval romanticism of Sir Walter Scott, would reject the Greek temple altogether and commission the architectural firm of Town and Davis to design for him a Gothic castle.

With the Revolution, and the historical events which followed, colonial life with its relative simplicity came to an end, and at ever-increasing tempo a more heterogeneous, fluid society took its place. In fact, heterogeneity, which in the United States has achieved its most dynamic form in the push and pull of the American political system, has become one of the country's most formidable characteristics. Heterogeneity is, of course, inherent to the doctrine of individual liberty, but its flowering in the United States was hastened at the turn of the nineteenth century by the influx of two aggressive forces from abroad: the first was romanticism, the second, technology. Romanticism, offspring of the imagination, fed the growing self-awareness and intensifying passions of a nation seeking its own cultural destiny; technology, rooted as it was in scientific knowledge, quickened the conquest of the wilderness and laid the foundations for modern industrial America. Together they became and remained the principal protagonists in the drama of American architecture throughout the nineteenth century.

Romanticism: A Point of View

As it relates to architecture, romanticism is an evasive concept which has long posed a major challenge to architectural theorists. Such terms as Romantic Classicism, Romantic Rationalism, Romantic Eclecticism, have been used by modern critics in search of precision. Yet, each alone says something unique, and in some instances, when paired, they even seem to contradict one another. On the other hand, each is a useful concept, worked out by thoughtful scholars in an effort to clarify the complex character of nineteenth-century American architecture. We will discuss each in its proper context. Beneath these specific ideas lie the broad dimensions of the Romantic movement itself, and the question must now be asked, what is romanticism?

Wordsworth, one of the first great figures in the Romantic movement, defined poetry as "the spontaneous overflow of powerful feelings." Seen in a larger sense this is also a useful definition of romanticism itself, for a romantic statement, whether in literature, music, or art, is a product of the sensibilities rather than the intellect, of the imagination rather than reason. It revels in nostalgia, seeking forms remote in both time and distance; it identifies truth with sensory experience. Its appeal therefore is to the human emotions rather than to the mind. In strictly architectural terms, romanticism is anti-classic. Where classic forms are regular, romantic ones are irregular, where the classic are calm, the romantic are animated. Absolutes are countered by variables, the ordered by the wild, the controlled by the abandoned. Objectivity gives way to subjectivity, the universal to the individual.

A building in the romantic mode is therefore dynamic and lively. In contrast to the stability and geometric order of a classic building, it is complex and varied with its interlocked forms changing and alternating in size and shape. Instead of being balanced absolutely around a central axis, they are poised asymmetrically around an off-center fulcrum, equilibrium maintained through a resolution of tensions, weight often countered by shape, and size by space and distance. Rather than the whiteness and smoothness of the classic styles, colors in a romantic building are rich, warm and dark, textures are varied and rough. Projecting, receding and overhanging forms interrupt and shatter the illumination creating involved patterns of light and shadow. Everywhere the appeal is to the senses.

Critical Terminology

These are the contrasting visual data of the classic and romantic modes, and to consider them in opposition to one another, as we have, raises certain questions with respect to critical terminology. On the basis of their visual characteristics it is obvious that the two modes are poles apart yet, in eighteenth-century England, they flourished side by side, and sometimes were even joined in the same context. In spite of the rigid classical nature of most architecture of the period, romantic attitudes became so pervasive that even the austere Neoclassical styles have come to be regarded as part of the Romantic movement. Accordingly, some theorists have grouped them under the term Romantic Classicism.[4] There are, of course, solid and persuasive arguments for this point of view. The very act of turning to the past for direct inspiration in architecture, whether that of the classical or the medieval world, is a nostalgic act, motivated by emotion rather than rational reflection. The truths revealed in the far away and the long ago can be seen as akin to the truths found in nature itself, the ultimate source for all romantic notions. Moreover, the act of choosing from the past is an act of free will, susceptible to emotional as well as intellectual judgments. During the Greek Revival, for example, the association of the American political system with the democracy of ancient Greece was inspired by sentiment as much as by reason. The philosophical implications of all this are quite clear. The Greek Revival was, indeed, a romantic movement and "Romantic Classicism" is now a well established and useful critical term.

As applied to architectural form, however, the idea of Romantic Classicism has one major limitation: it is a judgment based on attitude and motivation *and not on the visual elements of style*. Seen as a physical object, a building in the romantic mode is the antithesis of one in the classical mode. Regarded as pure architectural form, a Greek temple can never be classified as a romantic building, or a Gothic cathedral as classical; nor were they considered as such in the nineteenth century by the proponents of the Romantic movement. As early as 1830, in a series of articles devoted to "Architecture in the United States," which appeared in *The American Journal of Science and Arts,*[5] clear distinctions were made between the various historical styles, with careful attention paid to those ingredients of form which give each style its peculiar character. Such distinctions were, in fact, the very foundation upon which the doctrine of eclecticism was to rest, and since our approach to architecture is through style we will regard the classically oriented styles as distinctly different from the romantic styles. To avoid the obvious ambiguities of "Romantic Classicism," therefore, we will use the strictly stylistic term "Neoclassicism" to define those revival styles of the first half of the century which have a classical origin,[6] and the term "Picturesque" to define those which derive from romantic sources.

PART II

ORIGINS OF THE PICTURESQUE
IN ENGLAND
AND THE UNITED STATES

The Picturesque

The "Picturesque" was the aesthetic doctrine which governed nineteenth-century design in the visual arts through its various romantic phases.[7] As a doctrine, it sanctioned and codified the anti-classical qualities of form which excited the romantic mind. Thus it not only motivated the artist in his creative efforts but also guided the critic in his attempts to evaluate the art of his own time. By the mid-nineteenth century, the word "Picturesque" had become as common as "beauty" and "truth," and because it was so useful to the period itself it can be equally useful to us. To relate the doctrine of the picturesque to the architecture which it spawned, however, we must first consider the idea picturesque as a philosphical concept.

The picturesque doctrine was a product of the Enlightenment. In an age dominated by reason, it became recognized that in the realm of human experience men came to understand the world as much through feeling as through thought. If contemplation was possible without rationalization, and observation without knowledge, then visual qualities alone were capable of stirring such sensations as delight, horror or fear, quite apart from any moral or rational values which they might convey. All this led to a renewed interest in aesthetics; and in an attempt to identify feelings, various categories of human response were established through which one sensation could be distinguished from the other. The picturesque was one of these categories.

The first major philosophical step toward the establishment of such a system was Edmund Burke's famous essay, *A Philosophical Inquiry into the Origin of Our Ideas on the Sublime and the Beautiful* (1756). In this work Burke addressed himself to a matter which had intrigued philosophers since ancient times, the definition of beauty. He differs from his predecessors, however, in that he removes the concept from the realm of pure reason and places it instead in the subjective, and more elusive, world of sensibility. Beauty, he argues, is found in the qualities of smoothness, smallness, and delicacy, all of which induce the feeling of "love, or some passion similar to it." But in arriving at this conclusion Burke was also aware that obscurity, power, and vastness affect human consciousness just as profoundly as smoothness, smallness and delicacy, but move men to terror rather than love. To accommodate this realm of experience, Burke created his second category, the sublime.

Although Burke's distinctions went a long way toward liberating visual sensations from moral and ethical values, it soon became obvious that there were yet other qualities of form which he had not taken into account. Conspicuously, irregularity and roughness did not fit into his definition of either the beautiful or the sublime, yet each was capable of arousing a pleasurable response. These two qualities would soon become the basis of "picturesque" as an aesthetic doctrine.

It is true, the term "picturesque" was fairly common in England well before Burke wrote his essay but it had not been developed as a philosophical doctrine and in general was applied loosely to those objects which had certain picture-like qualities. By the mid-eighteenth century, however, it began to have more precise meaning, largely owing to the influence of the Reverend William Gilpin. An inveterate traveler, Gilpin not only recorded his experiences in broadly rendered wash drawings of the landscape, but also was the author of numerous books. In an essay entitled "Upon Prints," published in 1768, he develops the idea that a scene or picture has beauty if it conforms with the rules of painting. He also discovered that there were numerous visual qualities in the world around him which he found altogether suitable for painting but which did not seem to be included in either of Burke's concepts. To account for these Gilpin coined the phrase "picturesque beauty."

Specific categorization of the picturesque, however, did not come until 1794 when Uvedale Price published his *Essay on the Picturesque*.[8] Here Price states his case emphatically: "The qualities which make objects picturesque, are not only as distinct as those which make them beautiful or sublime, but are equally extended to all our sensations by whatever organs they are received." He argues further that in contrast to the qualities of smoothness and gradual variation ascribed by Burke to the beautiful, "the two opposite qualities of roughness, and of sudden variation, joined to that of irregularity, are the most efficient causes of the picturesque."

Price's ideas gained immediate support from Richard Payne Knight in a didactic poem, "The Landscape," which was dedicated to Price. Although in the second edition of "The Landscape," Knight was somewhat critical of Price, his voice helped to broaden the discussion, and the lively dialogue which ensued helped to strengthen and bring into focus the picturesque system of thought. In spite of their differences, what the two men achieved was more than just another philosophical doctrine; it was also a set of working principles which could serve as a guide to architects (as well as painters, gardeners and travelers) in their search for new and more subjective forms.

The Roots of the Picturesque in Architecture

As found in the numerous architectural styles which finally emerged in nineteenth-century America, the principles of the picturesque manifest themselves in five specific qualities of form. These are: irregularity, variety, intricacy, movement, and roughness. None of these was an American invention. All five were in some way touched upon or developed by Price and Knight, as well as by other English architects and theorists of the eighteenth and early nineteenth centuries. In the midst of a burgeoning and aggressive Neoclassicism, all five qualities were anti-classical both in spirit and intent, and how this happened is one of the most intriguing aspects of the whole story.

Early in the eighteenth century, under the leadership of Richard Boyle, better known as Lord Burlington, England embarked on a course in architecture, later called the Palladian movement, which was based on the most rigid adherence to classical principles of design.[9] The hero of this movement was the sixteenth-century Italian architect and theorist Andrea Palladio, its bible was his famous publication, *I quattro libri dell' architettura,* which was first translated into English in 1714. This immensely influential work marked the beginning in architecture of more than a century of classical rule, one which was to culminate in the latter part of the century in the Neoclassical movement itself. Yet, in one of the many seeming contradictions of the Enlightenment, it was in this very climate of reason and order in architecture, that the romantic principles of the picturesque movement were formed.

That this should have happened the way it did, and at the time it did, is not so surprising as it might at first seem. Nature, after all, was one of the prime objects of eighteenth-century curiosity and some of the moral and social doctrines of the period began to assume their authority from natural rather than supernatural law. Moreover, as science began to probe ever more deeply into the mysteries of life, it became apparent that the highly structured systems of nature itself, as evidenced in the individual species of flora and fauna, produced not a world ruled by inexorable symmetry, but one of inexhaustible variety, intricacy and abandoned growth. Although all men have the same physical structure, no two are exactly alike. Since this was the organic state of nature it was not illogical, nor indeed irrational to accept and champion equally the strict immutable order of classical architecture, which was based on rhythm and relationships governed by natural law, and the wild abandoned complexity of nature which was produced by that law. The Neoclassical doctrine of variety within symmetry has its origins in precisely this point.[10]

The specific formal aspects of the picturesque were formulated not in the pragmatic controlled world of architecture, but in English landscape gardens during the first quarter of the eighteenth century; and as Pevsner has pointed out, the pioneers of the movement were not the architects or even the gardeners, but the philosophers, writers and virtuosi.[11] In the early eighteenth century Anthony Ashley Cooper, third Earl of Shaftesbury, writing for the *Moralists* (1709) and Joseph Addison in the *Spectator* (1712) complain of the rigid formality of Baroque gardens and express a preference instead for "the beautiful wildness of nature." Addison also describes with approbation the random character of the acres which surrounded his own house. In spite of their interest, however, neither he nor Shaftsbury ever designed an entire irregular garden; that would be accomplished by Alexander Pope, one of the foremost didactic poets of the eighteenth century.

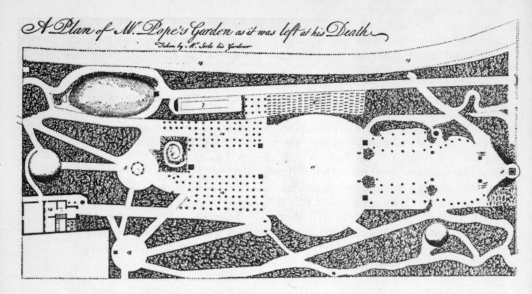

FIGURE 1. *Alexander Pope. Plan of his garden
at Twickenham, England, 1719.*

Pope was a contemporary of the leading Palladian, Lord Burlington, and both his interest in the classical past and the formality of his style make his poetry the counterpart in literature to the severely classical Palladian movement in architecture. Pope was also an enthusiastic gardener and he first expressed his remarkably picturesque theories on this subject in the *Spectator* in 1713. His attitude toward nature is similar to that of Shaftesbury and Addison. He states, for instance, "There is certainly something in the amiable simplicity of unadorned nature, that spreads over the mind a more noble sort of tranquility, and a loftier sensation of pleasure, than can be raised from the nicer scenes of art." Then, as though drawing sanction for his opinion from the classical writers who had shaped his style, he adds that "this was the taste of the ancients in their gardens, as we may discover from the descriptions extant of them."

Unlike Shaftesbury and Addison, Pope was not satisfied with the expression of theory alone, and between 1719 and 1725 he put his ideas into practice in his own garden at Twickenham (Fig. 1). Encompassing about three and one half acres, it lacked sufficient sweep to convey the impression of untouched nature (one of the objectives of many later picturesque gardens), and in its long, narrow proportions there are hints of a controlling axis. In addition, Pope utilized several Baroque devices imported from the Continent, such as the underground grotto which passed under the road and connected the house with the garden, and a series of round points from which radiated numerous straight walks. For the most part, however, the garden at Twickenham was irregular, with serpentine

FIGURE 2. *Henry Hoare. Stourhead, Wiltshire, England, landscape gardens, view over bridge to lake and Pantheon, 1741–43.*

paths winding through woods and open space, which led Horace Walpole to observe that Pope "twisted and twirled and rhymed and harmonized . . . , till it appeared two or three sweet little lawns opening and opening beyond one another, and the whole surrounded with thick impenetrable woods."

By the 1730's a number of informal gardens had appeared in England. Among the early leaders in this new approach to the landscape was William Kent, the designer of Holkham Hall.[12] An enthusiastic Palladian, Kent was one of the several architects associated with Lord Burlington. He was also a landscape gardener and in 1729 collaborated with Burlington in designing the grounds of the latter's country seat at Chiswick. Here, in the sacred precincts of high Palladianism, Burlington's austere centrally planned house, based on Palladio's Villa Rotunda in Vicenza, was deliberately combined with a vast irregular garden. Since the gardens at Chiswick have been altered so many times, very little of the original scheme is still extant. Fortunately one mid-eighteenth-century garden does remain in virtually original form, and that is the one at Stourhead (Fig. 2).

The site of Stourhead is a small valley on the southwest corner of the Salisbury Plain in Wiltshire.[13] The land was purchased in 1714 by Henry Hoare, a wealthy banker, who proceeded at once to build a new mansion. The designer was the arch-Palladian, Colen Campbell, author of *Vitruvius Britannicus,* and another of the architectural protégés of Lord Burlington.

As originally built, the house was a supreme example of English Palladianism, and one of the earliest of its type. It was a simple rectangular block with a colossal Corinthian portico; left and right of the portico single pedimented windows were set in the center of otherwise unbroken expanses of clean, dressed masonry walls.

The property was inherited by Hoare's son Henry, who, about 1745, began work on the garden that would grace Stourhead with one of the outstanding landscape designs in England. The one thousand acre tract within which it is contained lies to the southwest of the house, and is formed by two narrow valleys which join at nearly right angles and drop off in a single valley to the southwest. A dam was built where the valleys converge forming a three-armed lake about twenty acres in extent. Over the eastern end of the lake was built an arched stone bridge. The garden, with its varying stretches of wooded area and open spaces, was laid out around the lake and was penetrated by a system of meandering walks. Spaced at random along these walks are various pavilions, which range from classical temples to a rustic gothic cottage and a remarkable grotto. The last (one of the finest of its kind surviving in England) is among the most intensely picturesque features of the garden. Throughout the walk around the park, the visitor is cleverly directed to various points of outlook, each of which provides a different picture of the landscape. The view from the grotto, for instance, looks back through a cave-like opening across the lake to the stone bridge.

Stourhead's park, like the other irregular gardens of the eighteenth century, was a thoroughly romantic creation. Architectural fantasies, remote both in time and place, are skillfully combined with all the visual appearances of a wild and untouched nature. As one walks through the garden, however, one becomes increasingly aware that far from being wild and abandoned, the landscape one sees is very civilized indeed and presents an ever-changing sequence of composed vistas which have all the spatial, textural and coloristic appeal of a landscape painting.

There can be no doubt that the imitation of what Addison called "the beautiful wildness of nature" was a foremost objective of the eighteenth-century landscape gardener. The qualities of irregularity, variety, and roughness which raw nature offered were the very essence of picturesque imagery. Yet in England that imagery was also inspired by Baroque landscape painting, especially the idealized views of the Roman campagna by Claude Lorrain and Gaspard Poussin and the more intensely romantic landscapes of Salvatore Rosa. Evidence is clear and abundant that the creators of the picturesque knew the works of these masters; one of them, Richard Payne Knight, even collected the drawings of Claude Lorrain.[14] As we shall see, these same pictorial sources eventually affected certain aspects of the picturesque style in architecture. But their initial influence was on the landscape gardens, where the association of ideas was more direct.

The pictorial qualities which we have observed at Stourhead characterize all the major gardens of the period, and they were deliberately contrived. Indeed, the landscape architect came to be judged in much the

FIGURE 3. *Claude Lorrain.* Landscape, 1648 (National Gallery, London).

same way as the painter and in some instances he even received greater acclaim. The countryside was his canvas; the earth, water, foliage, open space, and sky were his pigments; the means to move, grade, plant, dam, and build were his brushes. Each vista was seen as combining foreground, middle distance and sky; woods, fields, buildings, and lakes were placed in asymmetrical but agreeable relationships with one another; trees were made to contrast with open space, hills with valleys, water with sky. Thus, Sir John Vanbrugh, when consulted about the planning of the gardens at Blenheim, prophetically summarized the spirit of the century when he suggested, "you must send for a landscape painter."

This clear relationship between the eighteenth-century English garden and landscape painting can better be understood by comparing a landscape by Claude Lorrain (Fig. 3) with one of the many vistas at Stourhead (Fig. 2). Trees, open space, water, and sky are combined in both the garden and the painting to create the appearances of abandoned variegated growth. Yet the buildings in both settings, intended presumably to be occupied by men, are unreal. They are pictorial motifs with their own special ornamental qualities, contrived to remove the image in both place and time and thereby emphasize the eternal link between man and nature. Both the painting and the garden present themselves as composed pictures, and in spite of the pervasive and evocative presence of nature, the world which each presents is not a world of random growth, but a world seen and ordered by man.

The Picturesque and the American Landscape

The romanticism which spawned the picturesque came to America from England during the last years of the eighteenth century. Here, in a flowering new society, it found fertile ground; and although it continued throughout the nineteenth century to be nourished by a steady flow of influences from abroad, the particular forms that it took in the United States were no less determined by the peculiar conditions of American society and the American environment. What these conditions were and how they affected American architecture, is a complex story. Before considering its several parts, however, it will be helpful to examine a particular aspect of the American scene which more than any other distinguished American romanticism from that of Europe and gave it a special character of its own; this is the expansiveness, beauty and wonder of the American countryside.

In both a philosophical and substantive sense, nature has always been a fundamental ingredient in the romantic attitude. Its immensity, its wild grandeur, its contrasting moods, its shadowed mysteries, its rich and variegated textures, all these have inspired romantic imagery regardless of what form that imagery has taken. But in eighteenth-century England, the major source of romantic ideals for the Americans, no untamed wilderness remained. Countless acres of land were given over to agriculture; miles of moors and mountain country provided pasture land for sheep and cattle; and much of the forest had been stripped away to provide charcoal for the blast furnaces. It was to compensate for this in part that the English landscape gardeners attempted to re-create untamed, unspoiled nature in their irregular gardens. In the United States, on the other hand, raw nature was an overwhelming reality. Beyond the settled eastern seaboard the wilderness stretched seemingly forever in endless sweeps of space which had no parallel in the over-cultivated and exploited countryside of Europe. All the qualities which the romantic mind adored—roughness, variation, irregularity—were to be found in prodigious abundance, and American romanticism could not help being affected by this awesome, pervasive presence. To understand its effect on American architecture, however, we must consider how Americans felt about their environment.

To the early settlers and to most colonials the American wilderness was an enemy, offering only danger and hardship, and the tireless ferocity with which it was subdued by the broad axe has become part of our national legend. "The axe leaps! The solid forest gives fluid utterances," sang Walt Whitman in exultant celebration of the pioneers. Through the herculean efforts of the frontiersmen the wild forest fell and was interspersed in its endless reaches with open fields and productive farms. Yet the conquest was never complete, for just beyond the edges of the fields the wilderness still remained, "daunting terrible, being full of rocky hills as thick as mole-hills in a meadow, and cloathed with the infinite thick woods."[15]

We do not know how often the wonders of nature stirred aesthetic responses in the hearts of our early settlers, but if this did happen they left no significant or collective record of the experience. The development of romantic attitudes requires a free imagination working in response to an uninhibited play of all the senses, and there was no room for such subjectivity in a strenuous and theocratic world ruled by the doctrine that "what is not useful is vicious."[16] During the early years of the new nation, however, the very fact of national independence raised questions about the character and destiny of the land and its people which had never been raised before. As the republic grew and security replaced anxiety, one of the earliest things to come under scrutiny was the natural environment itself, and it is not surprising that among the first influential Americans to recognize both the abundance and the beauty of the American landscape was Thomas Jefferson. As a political idealist committed to the agrarian way of life, he naturally responded to the infinite promise of the land. Perhaps the earliest environmental study of its kind in United States history is his *Notes on the State of Virginia*. In this descriptive and statistical account of his own state, Jefferson touched on everything from its political, economic and social conditions to its geography and climate, its flora and fauna. It is a fascinating document, a kind of guidebook,[17] which tells us much about eighteenth-century Virginia, and at the same time provides many illuminating insights into the romantic side of Jefferson's complex personality.

In examining the Virginia countryside Jefferson makes the enormously important observation that "in Europe the lands are either cultivated, or locked up against the cultivator," whereas in the United States there was "an immensity of land courting the industry of the husbandman."[18] In his recognition of the abundance of the American land, he anticipates the discovery, exploitation and celebration of the American environment which were to become such important characteristics of later nineteenth-century romanticism. Moreover, in other passages in the *Notes,* he not only reinforces the sense of abundance, but in his descriptions of the American landscape he shows extraordinary insights into the peculiar character of the American scene.[19] Indeed, his language is vivid, and in certain passages borders on the sensuous, with occasional hints of the romantic imagery conventional among eighteenth-century romantic writers in Europe. All of this was remarkable for late eighteenth-century America.

The links between Jefferson and the mainstreams of eighteenth-century European thought are, of course, well-known. But his reverence for nature gives his writing a character uniquely his own. *Notes on Virginia* is a pragmatic, semi-scientific document, written with a very practical purpose in mind. But it is also intensely personal. Jefferson saw and described the American landscape in a way that it had never been seen and described before—as a magnificent sweep of unspoiled countryside, steeped in its own special light and atmosphere and pulsing with its own visual excitement. He knew, moreover, that it was precisely these qualities which distinguished America from Europe. Not many Americans were as quick as Jefferson to understand this essential difference, and Jefferson in turn was too much of an intellectual, too steeped in eighteenth-century notions to permit his romantic impulses uninhibited freedom. But after the turn of

FIGURE 4. *Asher B. Durand.* Kindred Spirits, *1849* (New York Public Library).

the century, with the frontier moving further and further west, American writers and philosophers began to see the landscape from a native point of view, free from any eighteenth-century European conventions.

The first nineteenth-century American writers to accomplish this were the poet and journalist William Cullen Bryant and the novelist James Fenimore Cooper. Unlike Jefferson, both of these men were born well after the Revolution and came to maturity amid the surge of nationalism which followed the War of 1812. Their motivations, therefore, were from the beginning very different from Jefferson's, and in their writings America was seen for the first time with unencumbered directness and simplicity.

Bryant's appeal was for a personal and direct confrontation with nature, an appeal which he made with authority when he wandered through various parts of the Hudson Valley and the Berkshires, savoring their physical beauty, and sending back descriptions of what he saw to his own newspaper, *The Evening Post.* He did this in a deliberate attempt to open the eyes of an indifferent public to the physical wonders of their own land.[20] Nor was Bryant alone in his enthusiasm. Among his closest friends was the Hudson River School painter Thomas Cole, whose lucid paintings of the Catskill region appeared simultaneously with Bryant's writings. In celebration of this friendship Bryant and Cole are shown together in "Kindred Spirits," a remarkably revealing painting by Asher B. Durand, another member of the Hudson River School (Fig. 4). In this timely work the artist and the writer are seen standing on an overhanging ledge, discussing the view across a rocky gorge to the unbroken forest beyond. It is a clear literal statement which not only joins in an appropriate setting two of the principal creative figures of the age but, as Bryant's own writings had already done, it also records that setting directly with a joyous delight in the qualities of light, atmosphere and texture.

What we are asked to see and respond to in Durand's painting is precisely the appeal of James Fenimore Cooper. Cooper spent his childhood in the rural countryside of central New York State. His works deal with life on the frontier and are filled with the moods and physical appearances of the wild and beautiful land which he knew so well. Moreover, like the paintings of Durand and Cole, his descriptive passages are simple accounts of precisely what he had experienced; they evoke, without pretense or philosophical assumption, all the sensuous beauty of the scene: "clouds of light vapor were rising in spiral wreaths from the uninhabited woods, looking like the smokes of hidden cottages; or rolled lazily down the declivities, to mingle with the fogs of the lower land. A single, solitary, snow-white cloud floated above the valley."[21] Even the word "sublime" and "picturesque," those two constants in high romantic descriptions of nature, rarely appear in Cooper.

In the 1830's, Ralph Waldo Emerson approached nature with the same sharp vision that distinguished Bryant, Cooper and the painters of the Hudson River School, but unlike his predecessors and contemporaries he was not content simply to record what he saw. Nature to him was far more than the sum of physical facts experienced through the senses. It was the source of life itself; and hidden within its mysteries, but available to the inquiring mind, was the meaning of that life. Emerson's search for truth in nature, therefore, went beyond such immediate experiences as "clouds of white vapor rising in spiral wreaths" to "essences unchanged by man; space, the air, the river, the leaf." In short, nature for him became the object of philosophical reflection. In his essay *Nature,* published in 1836, he challenged the materialism of Puritanism and appealed instead for "a poetry and philosophy of insight and not of tradition." His call was clear and urgent. "Embosomed for a season in nature, whose floods of life stream around and through us, and invite us, by the powers they supply, to action proportioned to nature, why should we grope among the dry bones of the past, or put the living generation into masquerade out of its faded wardrobe? The sun shines today also. There is more wool and flax in the fields. There are new lands, new men, new thoughts, let us demand our own works and laws and worship."[22] This remarkable statement is probably the first clearly articulated declaration of cultural independence to be found in American literature.

The essay *Nature* also provided the assumptions about man and nature which would become the basis of American Transcendentalism; and along with Emerson's famous oration "The American Scholar," it spurred Henry David Thoreau on his lifelong search for the ultimate truths in nature. Thoreau was a junior at Harvard when *Nature* was published, and he was a senior the following year when he heard Emerson deliver his challenging address to the scholars of the Phi Beta Kappa Society. From this point on Thoreau's consuming interest was the cultural and spiritual implications of the American natural environment; and his method was to put into action what Emerson had first proposed in philosophical doctrine. In 1845, on land owned by Emerson, he built his cabin on the shores of Walden Pond and began his confrontation with nature which would result in some of the most important writings on the American environment yet produced. But even this was not enough, and in August of 1846 he took a brief furlough from the pastoral seclusion of Walden Pond and made the first of several journeys into the heart of the Maine woods. Here he encountered the American environment in its pure aboriginal state. He wrote of the experience with ecstasy: "Think of our life in nature,—daily to be shown matter, to come in contact with it,—rocks, trees, wind on our cheeks! The solid earth! The actual world! The common sense! Contact! Contact! Who are we? Where are we?"[23] The rest of Thoreau's short life was devoted to answering these questions.

Even in Thoreau's time the unspoiled simplicity which he sought and experienced was already threatened by technology. In the very years when he was writing at Walden Pond, the city of Lowell was a prosperous and booming industrial community, with satellite manufacturing towns already established on the shores of the Merrimack. The railroad, too, was cutting its first lines through the wilderness, so close indeed to Walden Pond that Thoreau could not help but respond to the intrusion. "The whistle of the locomotive penetrates my woods summer and winter, sounding like the scream of a hawk sailing over some farmer's yard, informing me that many restless city merchants are arriving within the circle of the town. Here come your groceries, country; your rations, countrymen! . . . All the Indian huckleberry hills are stripped, all the cranberry meadows are raked into the city. Up comes the cotton, down goes the woven cloth; up comes the silk, down goes the woolen; up come the books, but down goes the wit that writes them."

Even though the railroad irritates Thoreau it also fascinates him. "When I meet the engine with its train of cars moving off with planetary motion, with its steam cloud like a banner streaming behind in golden and silver wreaths, like many a downy cloud which I have seen, high in the heavens, unfolding its masses to the light . . . when I hear the iron horse make the hills echo with his snort-like thunder, shaking the earth with his feet, and breathing fire and smoke from his nostrils, it seems as if the earth had got a race now worthy to inhabit it."

With all its fascination the train still leaves Thoreau uneasy. "If all were as it seems, and men made the elements their servants for noble ends! If the cloud that hangs over the engine were the perspiration of heroic deeds, or as beneficent as that which floats over the farmers' fields, then the elements and nature herself would cheerfully accompany men on their errands and be their escort."[24]

Thoreau's picture of the railroad is vivid and compelling, but along with the excitement which he manages to communicate one senses also the doubts—the "if's—perhaps even the fear that lurking beneath the power of the machine there lies some terrifying monster, stretching to be released, and held in check by no more than reason and high purpose. Indeed, the confrontation which he so dramatically describes was a confrontation between a nature-oriented romanticism on the one hand and a burgeoning technology on the other. It was a confrontation which formed the dynamic core of nineteenth-century America.

PART III

EARLY INDUSTRIAL TECHNOLOGY
IN ENGLAND
AND THE UNITED STATES

Technology

The most fundamental attribute which distinguishes man from the animal is his capacity to command the physical world. Through his powers of reasoning he has been able to deduce from natural phenomena the laws that govern their existence and behavior. Equally important, through his manual skills, he has put those laws to work for his own benefit in an endless variety of tools, instruments, devices, and structures. This union of the mind and hand, joined in the solution of practical problems, we have come to know as technology.

Because it deals so specifically with material things, technology played a seminal role in the economic and social ferment of the eighteenth century. A changing and expanding world could only be satisfied by hard facts rigorously applied. In industry in particular, invention followed invention with a swiftness never before experienced in the western world, and the pragmatic intellectual climate which encouraged this growth would seem to have been the antithesis of romanticism. Yet, even though a responsive technology would have been impossible outside the practical application of scientific truths, the very act of invention draws heavily on the extraordinary capacity of the human intelligence to visualize the unknown. Eighteenth-century technology combined, therefore, both the passion and the reason of the era. It was as much a product of the imagination as were the irregular gardens of the eighteenth century, and in the intense human drama of its development, it was equally romantic in its appeal.

The most far-reaching contribution of eighteenth-century technology to the modern world was the power-driven machine. The story begins in the textile industry in England during the same years that saw the birth of romanticism. With the introduction of cotton as a raw material for cloth, and with the rapid growth in trade which occurred in England in the eighteenth century, the hand-operated textile machines then in use were unable to keep up with the increased demands. This was particularly true of the spinning wheel. Since each wheel operated only one spindle, it took three to five spinners to supply a single loom. Out of this situation came the first inventions which would lead to the power-driven machine.

All of the mechanical ingredients which would make up the early textile machines were already known and in general use. Some were the products of medieval technology, some had their roots even further back in the ancient world. The spinning wheel, for example, was a simple apparatus of medieval origin which was based on the principles of rotary motion. It was energized by the reciprocal motion of a treadle and crank, and accelerated by a pulley. Its productive capacity was severely limited, however, and to increase its efficiency the inventors and mechanics of the period developed a new machine in which the single spindle was replaced by a rank of spindles, all activated simultaneously by pulleys from a single rotary source. The power necessary to operate these additional spindles, however, could not easily be supplied by human energy and this led to the most decisive step of all: hand-operation gave way to an inanimate source of power.

The water wheel, which had been in use since ancient times for grinding grain, was the most readily available and the most logical choice. Although slow and cumbersome, especially when compared to the delicate high speed turning of the spindle, it nevertheless provided a rotary motion which, through the proper combination of shafts, gears, and pulleys, could be readily transmitted to the machine. The water wheel also drew its power from a reasonably reliable and steady source, the kinetic energy and weight of flowing or falling water. It was an easy matter to bring the spindle to the water wheel and by the time of the American Revolution the first power-driven textile machines in the world had been put into operation along the streams of the Midlands and the West Country.

Following the introduction of the power-driven textile machines the most dramatic technological innovation of the eighteenth century was the steam engine. Although crude steam engines had been in use for pumping purposes since the early years of the century, it was not until 1765, with the development by James Watt of the separate condensor, that the steam engine became sufficiently efficient to be used as a source of power for rotary motion. By using heat rather than kinetic energy as its source of power, the steam engine not only freed numerous industries from the geographic limitations of the water wheel, but it also offered far greater potential for the development of raw power. By 1800 in England the steam engine had joined the water wheel as a prime mover, and the spectacular industrial developments of the nineteenth century had begun.

Technology and Architecture: The Factory

The first impact of the power-driven machine on architecture was the urgent demand for buildings in which the new machines could be efficiently housed. The result was the first new building type of the modern world, the factory. To be sure, the English, as a powerful and aggressive mercantile nation, had been pioneers in the development of commercial buildings, and there is no question that certain architectural aspects of the first factories had their roots in these early building types. But the unique character which the factory ultimately assumed was even more a product of functional and structural necessity. Just as with the great cathedrals of the Middle Ages, which were the result of a sharply focused system of conditions, so it was with the factory. Instead of religious considerations, however, the determining factors were technological. For this reason, no architectural development of the nineteenth century was more organically expressive of a youthful and aggressive technology than the immense and muscular factories of England and America.

Three major architectural problems were posed by the factory: how to provide adequate space to accommodate the new machines; how to bring them into the most efficient relationship with the source of power; how to develop new structural methods which would withstand the destructive forces of machines in motion. Since the first machines were small, almost any interior space was adequate. Thus, the early English mills developed slowly from the simple utilitarian structures of the locality. According to the records many of the early machines were installed in already existing buildings. In a few instances warehouses were used, but more frequently they were set up in saw mills and grist mills, where a water wheel was already available.[25]

The practice of using existing buildings was obviously an expedient adequate as long as the machines remained simple in design and the scale of production small. But the rapid development of the machinery and the realization of its potentialities brought new and increasingly ambitious schemes which quickly outgrew the capacity of existing structures. The result was a new building type, the factory.

In its basic form the early nineteenth-century factory was a narrow rectangular block several stories high. Superficially, this would seem to be no more than an expansion of the traditional small mill. Actually, the long and narrow proportions, the height, the ranges of windows, and the arrangement in layers of large areas of relatively unbroken interior space were elements which, when combined in a single design, had no precedent in English architecture.[26]

The rectangular multi-storied form became a basic unit of factory design for the remainder of the eighteenth century and lasted throughout the nineteenth. It was a form of great functional simplicity (Fig. 5).[27] First, the required space could be achieved more cheaply in a block of several stories than in a block of one; it required less land, less foundation, less roof. Moreover, textile machines were light and lent themselves easily to this kind of arrangement. But equally important were certain limitations established by the relationship between the machine and its source of power. The closer the machine was located to the prime mover, the greater its efficiency. In England, the primary transmitting elements were both vertical and horizontal shafts and gears which, throughout most of the eighteenth century, were made of wood. Highly efficient gears could be made of this material, but the shafts presented another problem. When placed horizontally they were "subject to two forces: a force producing simple flexure, arising from their own weight, the weight of the wheels and pulleys, and the strain of the belts; and a twisting force or torsion, arising from the power transmitted."[28] Obviously, the dimensions of any given shaft had to vary in proportion to the ability of the material of which it was composed to resist these two forces. In the early mills, then, it was the strength of wood which determined the length of shafts. This in turn set the maximum length of the interior space which could be utilized. Accord-

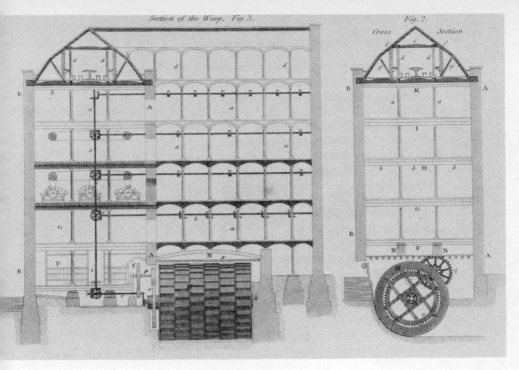

FIGURE 5. *Jedediah Strutt. North Mill, Belper, England,
section of wing and cross section, 1803.*

ingly it was found to be more efficient to arrange the machines in groups
on several floors, each served by a relatively short shaft, than to place all
the machines on a single floor, where much power would be lost in transmission by a long shaft.

The width of the mill was determined by the requirements of interior
lighting and by the necessity for keeping the machines close to the main
shaft. Since it was impossible to light from overhead in any but the top
floor of a multi-storied structure, the windows had to be kept reasonably
close to the machines. The lateral dimension of the floor area was therefore determined by whatever ceiling height permitted adequate light to
reach the central portions of the working area.[29] The machines fitted easily
into the long narrow space which resulted. They could be placed in rows
and still be at a convenient distance from the main horizontal shaft from
which each received its power.

Technology and Architecture: New Structural Techniques

In their construction, the earliest mills appear to have adhered closely to
traditional methods. Several late eighteenth-century mills still extant in
England have masonry walls and are framed on the interior in a manner
which had its roots in the Middle Ages. Since these methods were traditional and were used in all other types of utilitarian buildings there is no
reason to assume that the earliest mills differed from them in their structural characteristics. By the latter part of the century, however, dramatic

advances were being made in new structural techniques.[30] At the same time that English inventors and mechanics were pressing ahead with the factory and its power-driven machinery, the engineers and ironworkers were exploring the use of metal for building purposes. Both cast and wrought iron, which the British had long used for decorative, utilitarian and mechanical purposes, emerged during the last quarter of the eighteenth century as a promising new structural material. Because of its strength, malleability and permanence, iron offered exciting possibilities in a variety of new applications. Indeed, without it many of the most dramatic scientific and technological accomplishments of the age would never have been possible. Its most dramatic applications were in mechanics and engineering, which primarily benefited industrial machinery, bridge construction and the development of the railroad. For architecture, however, it also opened up new potentials for spanning and support, and because of its relative noncombustibility it promised relief from the ever present danger of fire. By the turn of the nineteenth century, iron trusses were being used for roof construction, and iron columns and beams for the interior framing of industrial and commercial buildings.

Technology in Colonial America

Eighteenth-century colonial America, sustained by the products of the land and the sea, was an agrarian-mercantile society. For the most part, life centered around the self-sufficient plantations of the South or the equally autonomous farming communities of the North; what urban life there was clustered in the seaport towns. Transportation was by boat along the coast and inland waterways, or by horse over poor roads and narrow trails; wood for heating came from the forest, and water from springs, streams, and private wells. What industry there was was based on conventional technology inherited from England. Even the techniques used in the design and construction of buildings, vehicles, bridges, and ships were in the tradition of the heavier crafts and were neither original to the colonies nor innovative.

The one exception to this was the application of wind and water power to various types of small mills. Here the colonials excelled. Because of the hardships of the frontier, labor-saving devices of all kinds were constantly being developed. That many of these were powered by water at a very early date is known from the testimony of French travelers who reported that power was applied to more uses in America than was generally common in Europe.[31] The American aptitude for technology was high, but the tenor of colonial life offered little incentive for its large scale development and the American genius for practical things had to wait until independence and a changing world released the forces necessary to make it flourish.

To guard her own interests England made no effort to export her new technology to the American colonies and up to the time of the Stamp Act in 1765 they remained economically dependent on the mother country. Not only were their commercial activities dominated by British capital, but also any tendency toward colonial manufacturing was vigorously opposed. British policy was to absorb colonial raw materials as much as possible and in turn to fill American markets with the products of their own factories. Manufacturing in this country was therefore carried on at the small workshop level and was almost entirely for local consumption. In the more populated areas of the middle colonies a few attempts were made to supply other than local markets.[32] But in the widespread rural and frontier districts, where the difficulties of overland transportation made commercial exchange all but impossible, mills remained small and generally dispersed.

The growth of colonial manufacturing was further retarded by legal restrictions imposed by the British themselves. England tried to check American efforts to manufacture cloth by prohibiting the exportation of any information about the latest textile machines, and as the machines and production methods were improved the laws were made more stringent. A few of the colonies made attempts to develop their own manufacturing methods and some information from abroad did filter through. It was not specific enough to be useful, however, and there was no advanced technological community on this side of the Atlantic to provide data of its own. But the potential was there, nevertheless, and after the Revolution had brought political independence the drive toward economic independence began. By the last decade of the eighteenth century the first factories were established in this country, and by the mid-nineteenth century Thoreau's vision of an unspoiled national environment had been seriously dimmed by the new and assertive pressures of an expanding technology.

CHAPTER II

The New Industrial Order: The Factory and the Factory Town

Cultivators of the earth are the most valuable citizens. They are the most vigorous, the most independent, the most virtuous . . .

THOMAS JEFFERSON

PART I

THE FIRST INDUSTRIAL DEVELOPMENTS IN RHODE ISLAND

The United States, Agrarian or Industrial

Everything that Thomas Jefferson believed and felt about the United States of America came together in his own home, Monticello (I: Fig. 214). Designed by Jefferson himself, and built under his careful supervision, this unique and beautiful place was intended by him to serve as both an instrument and symbol of the agrarian way of life.[1] Here he could live the life of productive farmer, self-sufficient in the bounties of the earth, in the manner that he wished for all Americans. Here he could find the quiet seclusion essential to contemplation and to the development of his intellectual life. Here, too, he could "ride above the storms" and savor the drama of nature as it unfolded at his feet.

In design Monticello was the first house in the United States to reject altogether the British architectural conventions which had shaped colonial architecture, and which elsewhere in the nation still ruled supreme. To be sure, the sources for Monticello were European—the books of Palladio, the architecture of ancient Rome, and the architecture of late eighteenth-century France—but they were not British, and Monticello must be

FIGURE 6. *Samuel Slater. Old Slater Mill,
Pawtucket, R.I., 1793.*

regarded as one of the first creative moments in America's struggle for cultural independence. In its comprehensive expressiveness, Monticello was the most important single house to be built in America since the first hut at Jamestown in 1607.

In 1793, the very year in which Jefferson began the building campaign which would bring Monticello to its final completion, a building of a wholly different character made its appearance in Pawtucket, Rhode Island (Fig. 6). Designed under the direction of a young Englishman, Samuel Slater, and financed and built by Almy and Brown of Providence, this simple wooden structure was in all probability the first building in the United States to be conceived from the beginning as a textile factory; and it was as unlike Monticello as it could possibly be. Even though graced with certain modest architectural amenities, it was in fact a basic utilitarian structure which would have been viewed by the sophisticated Jefferson as too lacking in elegance to serve even as an outbuilding for Monticello. Judging in terms of high style architecture, Jefferson would have been right. Architecturally, the Slater Mill was, indeed, of little consequence. Genetically, however, it was of immense importance. As a building type, it was the progenitor of the factory in the United States, and at the time of Jefferson's death the other factories which it had inspired—in the river valleys of Rhode Island and eastern Massachusetts—were already offering a serious challenge to his agrarian ideal.

The wide gulf which separates Monticello and the Slater Mill defines more than their contrast in architectural character and quality. It also marks the fundamental separation between two segments of American society, between two political and economic theories, between two ways of life which had been part of the nation since colonial time. From the very beginning the self-contained plantation society of the South was different from the community oriented society of New England. Even though all New England towns were at first agricultural in their mode of existence, those on the seaboard gradually gave way during the eighteenth century to commercial, financial and mercantile interests, and by the time of the Revolution cities such as Boston, New York and Philadelphia were thriving centers of urban activity. Before the Revolution substantial regional differences were already apparent, but were kept under control by England's jealously guarded policy of colonial decentralization. After the war, however, the very process of forming a federal government stirred controversy, and of all the issues provoked, the most sharply contested was the conflict between the agrarian South and the mercantile North.

Jefferson's principal opponent in the ensuing dialogue was the Secretary of the Treasury, Alexander Hamilton. The two men were totally unlike. Whereas Jefferson was a native born Southern aristocrat, Hamilton was born out of wedlock in the British West Indies to a drifting trader and his mistress. Where Jefferson was the master of a great Southern plantation, Hamilton was brought up in the countinghouses and commercial establishments of New York City. Whereas Jefferson believed that the future of America was in the hands of the small independent farmer, Hamilton foresaw it as belonging to the banker, merchant, and manufacturer, and his ambition was to transform the United States from an agricultural-rural to an industrial-urban society. Co-members of Washington's Cabinet, Jefferson and Hamilton disagreed at almost every level of ideology and policy. Their conflicting views, expressed at the very beginning of this nation's history as an independent republic, signaled a fundamental aspect of the American economic-political system: the eternal struggle for supremacy between the land and the machine.

All of this came to a head when they argued the question of whether or not the factory should be encouraged in the United States. Jefferson's objection, expressed as early as 1785, was sharp and to the point: "I consider the class of artificers as the panders of vice and the instruments by which the liberties of a country are generally overturned."[2] Hamilton, on the contrary, maintained that "not only the wealth; but the independence and security of a Country, appear to be materially connected with the prosperity of manufacturers."[3] In the end, the glittering promise of technology and change brought about by international events, combined in favor of Hamilton, and Jefferson was forced reluctantly to change his mind. By 1791, he was admitting that "the risk of hanging our prosperity on the fluctuating counsels & caprices of others renders it wise in us to turn seriously to manufactures."[4] After the War of 1812, his position was even more emphatic. "We must now place the manufacturer by the side of the agriculturist. . . . Experience has taught me that manufactures are now as necessary to our independence as to our comfort."[5] As a realist, Jefferson acceded to the facts, but as an idealist he never ceased to live in the fear that the "depravity of morals . . . dependence and corruption"[6] which had visited the manufacturing cities abroad would also accompany the introduction of the factory to this country.

The theoretical dialogue between Jefferson and Hamilton also bore tangible fruit. In 1791, just as Jefferson the gentleman farmer was about to begin the rebuilding of Monticello, Hamilton the ardent champion of the factory was lending his personal support to what was probably the first systematic attempt to develop extensive water power for manufacturing purposes in this country. This project was initiated in Paterson, New Jersey.[7]

The Paterson enterprise came exactly twenty years after Richard Arkwright's famous spinning frame had gone into operation in England, and it was not the only American effort at industrial development. By the end of the Revolution, news of Arkwright's success had reached America, but because of the British laws prohibiting export of technical information, no specific data about textile machinery was available. Nevertheless, and in spite of the primitive state of American technology, several attempts were made to develop textile machines. None, however, including Hamilton's project at Paterson, was completely successful.[8]

Samuel Slater's arrival from England in 1789 coincided with the most promising of these early efforts, that of Almy and Brown in Providence. Slater heard about their enterprise while in New York and immediately wrote to Moses Brown offering his services. In April of the following year a partnership between Slater and Almy and Brown was formed. Together, they designed the first efficient textile machinery in America to be powered by water.[9] It was put into operation in an old fulling mill in Pawtucket, Rhode Island, in 1790. On the fifteenth of October the following year, some of the first yarn spun by that machinery was sent to Hamilton, Secretary of the Treasury. Two months later, in his Report on Manufactures, Hamilton was able to announce that "The manufactury at Providence has the merit of being the first in introducing [into the United States] the celebrated cotton mill."[10]

The success of that first machinery of Almy, Brown and Slater was due in no small measure to Slater's first-hand knowledge of the English textile machines. As a boy of fourteen he had gone to work for Jedediah Strutt, an influential English industrialist who at one time had been a partner of Richard Arkwright. During his apprenticeship with Strutt, Slater supervised the building of at least one factory and was overseer of another. He also spent much of his time in the design and construction of textile machinery. He thus had ample opportunity to perfect his knowledge of the Arkwright machines and of English factory construction and organization.

The success of Slater's first machines set up in the fulling mill prompted the partners to expand immediately, and in 1793, on another site in Pawtucket, they built what is now known as the Old Slater Mill. At first glance there seems to be little about the architecture of this building to demand our attention. As seen today it is an extended structure with a long asym-

FIGURE 7. *Immanuel Case House, Wickford, R.I., 1786.*

metrical wing (Fig. 6). Originally, however, it was a simple box-like frame building, two and a half stories high with a modest cupola on the end. Except for its cupola, it would have looked like any of the ample wooden houses that lined the streets of Rhode Island towns in the late eighteenth century (Fig. 7). Despite its modest, conventional appearance, it was a special building with a special form, designed for a very special purpose, and it stands as the prototype for all factories that were to follow in the nineteenth century. To illustrate this, and to assess Slater's contribution to American architecture, we must go back once more to eighteenth-century England and examine some of the early factories in specific detail.

The Early Factories in England

Perhaps the earliest fully developed English factory was John Lombe's silk throwing factory built at Derby in 1718. Although it was not demolished until this century, it was apparently never photographed and few specific details are available about this remarkable building. It is known, however, that it had masonry walls, that it was 110 feet long, 39 feet wide, and five stories high. On the interior, the center line of wooden posts supported the lateral beams. An 18-foot undershot water wheel provided the power for 26,000 machine wheels.[11] It is obvious from this description that the factory form was already fully established in this building. In mid-century, its scheme was used elsewhere, and by the time Hargreaves and

FIGURE 8. *Richard Arkwright. Lower Mill,*
Cromford, England, 1777.

Arkwright had developed their respective cotton spinning machines, there
were approximately sixty silk throwing mills in England, all of which were
built on the same principles.[12] Although varying in size, they all were rectangular blocks several stories high, and had long narrow proportions,
ranges of windows, plus large areas of relatively unbroken interior space.
All these are the basic elements of the factory form as it materialized in
the nineteenth century.

The next major development in factory building occurred during the
late 1760's in response to Richard Arkwright's new cotton spinning machines. Arkwright is best known as the man who first successfully developed the spinning frame. Yet, of equal consequence was his application of
water power, not only to the spinning machines but to the whole sequence
of carding, roving, and spinning in a continuous process carried out under
one roof.[13] A man of hard will and prodigious energy, Arkwright not only
saw clearly the enormous potential of the factory, but he also had the technical and organizational skills to make the various components function
together.

The first factory built by Arkwright was the "Old Mill" at Cromford,
which was completed in 1771. It still exists, although drastically altered,[14]
and seems to have been a simple rectangular block similar to the silk
throwing factories of Lombe. Much more important, particularly in regard
to later developments in the United States, is Arkwright's second, or lower
mill at Cromford, which dates from 1777 (Fig. 8).[15] Although the form of
this building was the characteristic rectangular block it had an unusual
type of roof. Here a section of the roof plane on either side of the ridgepole was lifted to a higher level than was usual and in the space thus
created a continuous range of windows was extended the entire length of
the building. This singular device, which has something of the character of

FIGURE 9. *David Dale and Richard Arkwright.*
Mills, New Lanark, Scotland, 1785.

the clerestory windows in medieval churches, has come to be known by architectural historians as a clerestory monitor window. As far as is known Arkwright's use of it at Cromford was unique in eighteenth-century English industrial buildings, but as we shall see it was to become a dominating feature of early American factories.

Arkwright's first efforts were an immediate success, and he moved quickly to extend the scope of his operations by entering into partnership with several other ambitious industrialists. By the 1780's between fifteen and twenty textile mills operating under his patent were scattered throughout England. Of those which still survive, the ones at New Lanark in Scotland are the most impressive. Built in partnership with the entrepreneur David Dale, and begun in 1785, they were part of a remarkably coherent scheme of mills and support buildings, including housing. The unusual size of the New Lanark operation was made possible by the superb water power of the Clyde, and the most aggressive architectural feature of the complex is the monumental sequence of the mills. A contemporary engraving shows four almost identical mills arranged in a line along the banks of the river (Fig. 9). Each is a bold rectangular block five and a half stories high, and in its long dimension each story has a range of approximately twenty windows.[16] At the heart of each mill was a massive water wheel, its ponderous turning motion accelerated by the gears, and carried along the height and length of the mill by the shafts where it was further accelerated and communicated to the machines by the belts and pulleys. With its extended rectangular shape, its center accentuated by a projecting pavilion, and its ascending areas of horizontal space marked by the regular rhythm of the windows, each mill has an outward appearance that works in harmony with its inner dynamic activity. Yet, these mills are far more than unadorned utility cells. Their walls are not only large and heavy, but have a rough, varied texture that is enriched even further by the light colored stone in the quoins. In each the simple rectangular mass is broken by a pavilion, topped by a classical pediment; and one mill was once crowned with a cupola.[17] In short, the buildings combine the utilitarian simplicity of the rectangular block with certain formal architectural devices drawn from the late eighteenth-century vernacular. They thus appeal for recognition as something other than practical workshops. Indeed, the same is true of the majority of the textile factories built in England during the late eighteenth and early nineteenth centuries. These include the mills constructed by Jedediah Strutt at Belper which are of particular importance to us, because it was here that Samuel Slater served his apprenticeship. The early Strutt mills were built between 1776 and the turn of the century, but unfortunately most of them have been destroyed. The fragments which do survive, however, show them to have had architectural characteristics similar to those at New Lanark.[18] Samuel Slater was actually involved in the design and building of one of these mills.

The ambitious schemes at New Lanark and Belper were not the only ones that formed the immediate background for the early American textile mills. Equally important were the smaller mills and their attendant communities which sprang up along the streams of Yorkshire, Lancashire, and Gloucestershire, many of which would have been known to Slater. When Arkwright's patent was annulled in 1785, the expansion of the textile industry was immediate and dramatic. Scarcely three years later there were 143 cotton mills in England and Scotland, all of them powered by water.[19] A few fine late eighteenth-century examples are still to be found in the Stroud Valley in Gloucestershire. Typical is Hope's Mill at Brimscombe (Fig. 10). It is a long narrow rectangular block, four and a half stories high and built of stone. An open cupola with six columns once stood in the center of its pitched roof, but has been removed for safe keeping. On the whole, the building is more domestic in scale than the larger mills, although equally fine in its proportions.

An extremely important feature of Hope's Mill is its monitor window in the roof. We have already seen this device in the clerestory monitor in Arkwright's Mill at Cromford. Here, however, it has a different form. Instead of the entire center section of the roof being lifted to a higher level, a large section of the roof was raised to a flatter angle, as though it were a partially open trap door hinged at the top; the windows inserted here span just the opening, not the entire length of the roof. The windows on Hope's Mill are now boarded up, but they once formed a continuous row of sashes, pivoted at the center, and when open tipping in toward the top. This form of window is known as "trap-door" or "eyebrow" monitor, and like the clerestory monitor it was to become one of the most characteristic features of the earliest American cotton factories. In England, however, it seems to have appeared only in the Stroud Valley.

In viewing the mills and millworkers' houses which still survive in the Stroud Valley, one is struck by their strong utilitarian characteristics. The

FIGURE 10. *Hope's Mill, Brimscombe, England,*
late eighteenth century.

stone walls are bold and simple, and there is a supreme logic to the
directness with which mass and space have been organized. Yet one senses
here a coherent quiet beauty. The mills are not only attractive as buildings
but also as part of the environment: the materials come from it, texture
and color are in harmony with it. Situated in valleys by necessity, the mills
once received their life from the flowing waters; they worked in rhythm
with the motion of the stream. But they were also in harmony with the architectural idiom of their time. Although economy and function demanded
a reduction in the use of conventional architectural forms, those decorative elements that do appear are applied with an innate feeling for the special qualities of the surrounding architecture.

When the German architect Schinkel visited the valley of the Stroud in
the summer of 1826, he was struck by the affinity between the factories
and their natural and architectural milieu. He wrote in his diary: "The factory buildings (there are nothing but textile mills) lie hidden at a distance
under tall lindens, elms and larches and mingle with small churches, which
are equally picturesque in their settings."[20] Indeed, the beauty of these
eighteenth-century factories is in such marked contrast with the ugliness of
so much of English industrial architecture in the nineteenth century, that it
demands further comment. There can be no doubt that the primary concern of the men who built these early factories was to make them as productive as possible. Nevertheless, serious attention was also given to their
appearance. Men like David Dale and Jedediah Strutt were aggressive entrepreneurs indeed, yet as men of the eighteenth century they had an inher-

ent feeling for architectural form which was conditioned by a powerful cultural heritage. It has been argued that these early mills would have been more intrinsically beautiful if tradition had been discarded and their architectural features allowed to develop entirely from the demands of function. But this is to deny both the prolonged power of heritage and the gradual forces of evolution. The eighteenth-century industrialist could no more detach himself from his architectural environment than could the early designer of the automobile visualize its form as any other than a carriage.

The quality of these early mills was further enhanced by the fact that they were powered by water. To be near reliable sources of such power they tended to be widely dispersed along the banks of streams, in some of England's loveliest countryside. Water power was clean, of course, without smoke and soot to begrime walls, without ashes or waste to mar the landscape. Moreover, the size of a particular mill was limited by the amount of water power available. Not even the mills at New Lanark assumed the gigantic proportions that characterized the later nineteenth-century factories. Most of the earlier mills thus were domestic in scale and fitted easily into the intimate seclusion of the valleys. The relationship between architecture and nature was something with which the eighteenth-century Englishman had profound empathy. Indeed, the concept of the picturesque (first formalized in these very years) and the taste which it was intended to express (so important in the creation of the English irregular gardens) was not lost on the early mills. Samuel Sidney, in the middle of the nineteenth century, wrote of the decades-old textile mills in the Stroud Valley, "There is no more pleasant mode of investigating the process of woolen manufacture . . . than a visit to the beautiful valley of the Stroud, in Gloucestershire where the finest cloths and certain shawls and fancy goods, are manufactured in perfection in the midst of the loveliest scenery. Whitewalled factories, with their resounding water wheels, stand not unpicturesque among green wooded gorges, by the side of flowing streams."[21]

Samuel Slater and Early Industrial America:
the Old Slater Mill

It was in this world of England's early industrial success that Samuel Slater served his apprenticeship. Coming to Belper in 1782, when Jedediah Strutt's first mill was only five years old, he worked both for and with Strutt during the subsequent years of dramatic growth. With this broad experience behind him, it was with excitement and high hopes that in 1789 he made his decision to come to the United States. The primitive state of American textile machinery which he found when he arrived, and the limited resources available to him must have dampened these hopes somewhat, but with the successful operation of the first machines in Pawtucket the way was finally opened. Through his role in the designing and building of the Old Slater Mill he was able, even though on a small scale, to apply the full scope of his knowledge and skill. To evaluate the impact of this on American industrial architecture, we must now return to the mill itself and examine it in more detail.

As already noted, the original building was a wooden box-like structure, wholly domestic in character and scale. In 1801 the mill was extended westward 50 feet away from the river; during 1812–17 an identical addition was made toward the river to the east, bringing the total length to 144 feet. In both additions the height and width of the original block were maintained. The final alteration was a three-story wing extending at right angles toward the south (Fig. 6). Since it was apparently made to provide cover for a second water wheel, necessary to operate the increased number of machines, it seems probable that it was built at the time of, or shortly after, the addition of 1812–17. This south wing also contained a new interior staircase and the landing platforms. Sometime between 1823–35 a new cupola, more elaborate than the old one on the first mill, was built over the south end of this wing.[22] As seen today the original building is buried in the center of all the additions, with part of it behind the south wing and the rest extending to the west. The first addition, however, which now extends toward the river is approximately the size and shape of the original mill and if we were to place a small cupola on its westerly end we should have a good idea of how the original mill looked.

Viewing it this way, our first response would be that the Slater Mill was a modest but typical American building of its time, classically proportioned, rather delicately scaled, with a restrained application of conventional Neoclassical moldings and detail. Other aspects of the building, however, were sufficiently novel to the United States at the turn of the nineteenth century to suggest the probability that they were introduced by Slater. The first of these is the arrangement in layers of large areas of unbroken interior space. When it was a productive factory the first and second floors of the Slater Mill were open from end to end except for a single row of wooden piers down the center. This can still be seen today on the second floor of the east end of the mill, now used by the Slater Mill Historic Site as a storage area (Fig. 11). The attic was an open room beneath the rafters. The smaller English mills at this time were higher, having from four to five stories, and they were larger, but the principles of organization were the same. It has been suggested that these continuous open spaces were essential so that a single adult overseer could easily supervise the operators. This was standard practice in British mills and may have been a factor in the design here. But certainly the arrangement of machinery and problems of shafting were equally if not more important. In the Pawtucket mill the layout of the interior must have been the responsibility of Slater, and it is logical to conclude that the disposition of interior space was prompted by his experience in England.

On the exterior of the building the most conspicuous feature which suggests an English origin is the trap-door monitor window. To be sure, there is no evidence that this device was used in any of the Arkwright or Strutt mills with which Slater was actively involved. On the other hand, it was used in the mills in the Stroud Valley.[23] Since the dating of the Stroud mills is uncertain, it is impossible to say with assurance that Slater himself could have seen or even known about them before he left for America in 1789. But considering the extent of his role in industrial affairs it is incon-

FIGURE 11. *Samuel Slater. Old Slater Mill,
Pawtucket, R.I., interior, 1793.*

ceivable that he did not know of Arkwright's Mill at Cromford. It is possible, too, that there were other mills of the period which had monitor windows, mills which he could have known but which have long since disappeared. In any event, there is no example of the monitor window in American architecture before its appearance in the early mills of Rhode Island.[24] In all probability therefore the device must have come to this country from England, but actually how and when is not precisely known. Although the trap-door monitor was definitely used during the first decades of the nineteenth century in at least seven Rhode Island mills,[25] and although it has been generally credited to Slater's original mill of 1793, recent examination of the original roof rafters now suggests the strong probability that the first building had a conventional pitched roof.

This idea is supported by other known facts. First, there is an insurance document which describes the mill after the westward addition of 1801 as a *two-story* building; second, there is evidence that the addition of 1812 did have a trap-door monitor roof. The implication is clear, therefore, that the attic story was not utilized as an operational space until the addition of 1812–17, at which time the monitor window was applied to the entire roof. But was it Slater who proposed it? After all, in 1806, he had already used one in the first mill which he built on his own (in what was to become the town of Slatersville, Rhode Island). Or was it inspired by the Wilkinson Mill, built in 1810 just to the west of the Slater Mill? In any case, the monitor window did become a distinguishing feature of many early American mills and in all probability the idea came from England, either through Slater or through a general growing awareness in the United States of the English industrial scene.

FIGURE 12. *Olde Grist Mill (Perkins Mill) Kennebunkport, Me.,*
c. 1750, interior.

The principal structural features of the Old Slater Mill (Fig. 11) derive
from colonial building methods, specifically those employed in early barns,
mills and other utility structures around New England (Fig. 12). The
frame was typically heavy timber enclosed with vertical siding. The wall
posts were spaced approximately 8 feet apart with heavy lateral beams
thrown across the building between opposing posts. The floors were laid on
joists extending longitudinally between the transverse beams. The lateral
beams, however, were carried in the center by square wooden piers. This
supporting device was used during the eighteenth century both in this
country and England for warehouses where heavy weights were involved.
During the latter part of the century it also became a major characteristic
of first English and then American factory construction. Slater surely
would have known that a center pier not only gave added support but also
acted as a stiffener against the vibration and oscillation of the machines in
motion. The Englishman may have been disappointed that the walls of his
mill were wood rather than stone, but in 1793 masonry construction in the
United States was only just beginning to come into use. The fact that the
Slater Mill was made entirely of wood, therefore, gives it a peculiarly
American flavor.

Like the factories of eighteenth-century England the Slater Mill was
conceived with certain basic architectural values in mind. It was simple but
solidly built; its machinery was designed by a competent engineer and it

fulfilled its function well. This is clearly apparent when one reads the records of its continued financial success.[26] At the same time, like the barns and farms of the New England hinterland, it had substantial visual appeal. It was finely proportioned, its massing was direct and expressive, its decorative features were correct and delicately scaled. In all respects it invites comparison with the best colloquial architecture of its day.

Because of their very nature and the nature of their environment the owners of the Slater Mill would not have thought of it in any other terms. The American partners in the firm were leaders in Rhode Island business and social circles. As men of means they were culturally advantaged; as distinguished public servants, they had a genuine concern for the good of the community around them. This was particularly true of Moses Brown, whose "strong bent toward public service . . . led him to endow the New England Friends' School and the Rhode Island College which now bears his name as Brown University."[27] Moreover, his brother Joseph was not only a professor of philosophy at Rhode Island College, but a gentleman-amateur architect who designed several buildings in the Providence area, including the First Baptist Meetinghouse.[28] Although Joseph seems to have had nothing to do with the design of the Slater Mill,[29] the years of family association must certainly have left their impression upon the architectural taste of his brother. Like the eighteenth-century English industrialists, Moses was moved in his judgments by those qualitative standards which were the heritage of his time, and his factory, although functional in form and simple in detail, was nevertheless architecturally consistent and correct.

Another factor governing the appearance of the Slater Mill was the strong prejudice which existed in late eighteenth-century America against manufacturing. Ware describes the situation in the following words:

> Most people believed that industry could not add to the nation's total wealth. Those for whom land was the chief source of income thought that agriculture alone could be truly productive and were only partially persuaded by Hamilton's contention that the farmers would gain a new market for their products in the industrial centers. Commercial interests also opposed manufacturers as dangerous competitors in supplying the domestic market.
>
> The strongest and most lasting prejudice rested on a horror lest the factory system in America should degrade the worker as it had in England, and become a menace to American social and political ideals . . .
>
> In order to secure workers, the American manufacturers had to demonstrate the moral standards of the community would not be impaired.[30]

Just as in eighteenth-century England the factory, in order to overcome the prejudice against it, had to be acceptable to the public in appearance at least. Moses Brown, a Quaker and a man of the highest integrity, would have been forced by personal inclination as well as by public pressure to make sure that his industrial enterprise conformed in every way possible to the accepted and respectable standards of his time. In its simple dignity the Slater Mill is as expressive of Brown's social and business values as is Monticello of Jefferson's agrarian ideal.

Development of the Early Factory Form

The success of Almy, Brown and Slater led others to follow their example. Mechanics who had been employed by the original firm raised small amounts of capital from various sources and built factories of their own. These appeared slowly along the major streams of central Rhode Island, eastern Connecticut, and southern Massachusetts, and by 1809, the Secretary of the Treasury was able to list twenty-seven mills operating in the New England area. Most were smaller than the Slater Mill, most were made of wood,[31] and all of them were identical in basic character and organization. None survives in anything like its original form.

The second decade of the century saw a further increase in factory construction, and a change in its architectural form. The factory now became higher, longer, and wider, and thus began to assume the size and proportions of the late eighteenth-century English factories. Although the trap-door monitor continued to be a prominent feature, the clerestory monitor window made its appearance shortly after 1800[32] and offered considerable advantages. Because it raised the center part of the roof to a higher level (Fig. 30) it increased the height and illumination of the attic working space; at the same time, the clerestory monitor's broader and loftier profile gave a new vigor and monumentality to the factory, qualities which were unmatched in any other building type. Later known as the "factory roof" this type was used with increasing frequency, and by the 1830's and '40's it dominated the American industrial scene.

One of the earliest and most impressive uses of the clerestory monitor occurs in the Lippitt Mill in West Warwick, Rhode Island (Fig. 13). Built in 1810, it is a wooden structure 104 feet long by 30 feet wide; its four stories include a clerestory attic. This building is considerably larger than the Slater Mill, although the scale and general architectural character are similar. The decorative elements are somewhat richer, and the moldings framing the eaves and gable ends are more abundant and more strictly classical; the cupola remains the same size but is more delicate and is raised on a square base. Crowning this tower-like base is a cornice containing a finely scaled dentil molding. The wooden lintels over the windows flare out toward the top and have the appearance of flat masonry arches. The mill was rebuilt on the interior sometime during the nineteenth century, but there is ample evidence to indicate that its original construction was similar to that of the Slater Mill.[33] Because it represents one of the earliest known applications of the clerestory monitor, the Lippitt Mill is of great historical importance. But it is also an imposing building, far more sophisticated architecturally than the small earlier mills, and is a remarkable and exciting survival of its period.

Both in size and shape the Lippitt Mill begins to approach the classic textile mill form of the first half of the nineteenth century. But one aspect

FIGURE 13. *Lippitt Mill, Lippitt, West Warwick, R.I., 1809.*

of the building still relates it to the earlier mills and at the same time makes it of particular interest: that is the location of the cupola over one end. We are reminded at once, by the general form of the building, of Arkwright's Lower Mill at Cromford (Fig. 8), for in addition to having the only clerestory monitor that we know of in early English industrial architecture, it had a cupola at one end. The similarity between Arkwright's mill and the Lippitt Mill is, indeed, so remarkable that it seems impossible not to assume some connection between the two; and in this instance there is no question about which one came first. If such a connection did exist we may never discover what it was, but Slater must have known of Arkwright's mill, and by 1810 any number of channels of communication could have been opened up for the Americans which gave them specific information about English industrial building.

If the location of the cupola in early American mills such as the Lippitt Mill suggests an English origin there is also an equally intriguing and even more subtle relationship to the conventions of American architecture. Indeed, a source which comes immediately to mind is one of the most pervasive architectural forms of eighteenth-century America, the New England meetinghouse. Although the mill and the meetinghouse could hardly have been more different in their basic functions, each was the center of activity in its respective community and each enjoyed a position of architectural prominence which demanded special attention. In early nineteenth-century New England no architectural feature was more appropriate to that prominence than the dignified classical cupola placed over the peak of the gable, and none was more expressive of the role that each building played in the life of the community than the bell which in the meetinghouse called the congregation to worship and in the factory called the workers to their tasks. It would have been natural, until such time when economic and technical concerns made further changes in the mill essential, that the mill designers would draw their expressive forms from the familiar conventions of their own heritage. To be sure, the choice would have been intuitive, not calculated, but the similarity in basic form between the early mills and the meetinghouse is too real to be explained in pragmatic terms alone. In view of the persistent presence of a powerful tradition in early nineteenth-century architecture of the American hinterland, it is inconceivable that the forms and images which gave character to the early New England communities would not have made some impression on the intruding mills.

Although a lingering tradition was influential in the architectural character of the early American mills it could not continue forever. Changes born of necessity slowly molded the early primitive mills into a form unique to its type. The clerestory monitor was the first of these, but just about the time when it made its appearance in the Rhode Island mills another important structural innovation occurred. Shortly after 1800, masonry began to replace the wooden frame for exterior walls of factories. In Rhode Island, stone was the preferred material; in the somewhat later developments in northeastern Massachusetts the choice was brick. It is obvious that because of its greater density and weight masonry was better able to sustain the vibrations set up by machines in motion, but equally important, it was noncombustible. Under the best of circumstances fire was a constant threat and frequent reality, and in factories the friction of the many moving parts of the mechanical system, together with the lubricants and cotton waste, vastly increased the risk. Masonry walls offered at least a measure of security.

The earliest stone factories in Rhode Island were small, but in 1812[34] the material was used in a mill almost as big as the Lippitt Mill, the Nightingale Factory in Georgiaville, Rhode Island (Fig. 14). It was a substantial building 80 feet long by 36 feet wide, and three stories and an attic high; its stone walls were 2 feet thick.[35] Compared to the Lippitt Mill, with its handsome proportions and refined detail, it was a crude building. The masonry was rough, eaves and gable ends were unadorned with moldings. The windows were irregularly spaced and unequal in size. The belfry, except for the rather elegant curve of its roof and entablature, was a reduction of the classical format which could hardly be called more than a wooden frame. The interior construction was a characteristic joist floor with a row of columns down the center. A plan of the building made in 1828 shows curious discrepancies in the spacing of the transverse beams; moreover, a glance at the iron tie bolts on the side of the building (see Fig. 14) shows that this irregular spacing also varied from floor to floor. All this seems to imply lack of a comprehensive plan, decided emphasis upon economy, and inferior provincial workmanship.

This primitive but fascinating building was one of numerous mills built during the War of 1812. Because of the impetus given to the cotton industry by both the war and the somewhat earlier Embargo Act, existing mills

FIGURE 14. *Nightingale Factory, Georgiaville, R.I., 1812.*
Four bays to right added in 1828.

were swamped with orders and making enormous profits. Lured by the possibility of ready gains, hopeful new investors were drawn into the field and subsequently initiated such a flurry of mill building that there were not enough masons and mechanics available to carry out the work.[36] The Nightingale Factory was built during these hectic years, which may account in part for its somewhat jerry-built character. Nevertheless, it was a youthful, robust building altogether expressive of the experimental attitudes of the era, and because it was among the earliest mills to be constructed in stone, it was as important as the Lippitt Mill in the evolution of the early nineteenth-century factory.

The speculative and frantic expansion occasioned by the War of 1812 was followed by a decade of quiescence in factory construction. During the 1820's, however, the sporadic and small scale activity of the early years gave way to a solid steady growth which culminated in the large industrial complexes of Lowell and its satellite communities in the Merrimack Valley in Massachusetts. It was during this period, too, that the early nineteenth-century factory achieved its fully developed and characteristic form.

The Nineteenth-century Factory Form:
the Allendale Mill

One of the most important mills of the period is the Allendale Mill at Allendale in what is now North Providence, Rhode Island (Fig. 15). Built originally as a woolen mill by Zachariah Allen in 1822, it was later enlarged, and early in 1839 it was refitted for cotton manufacture. It is the

FIGURE 15. *Zachariah Allen. Allendale Mill, North Providence, R.I., 1822.*

mill in enlarged form which especially demands our attention. First, it is one of the most imposing buildings to survive from the early years and demonstrates as well as any other mill in Rhode Island the fully developed nineteenth-century factory form. But Allen's mill is also of special interest because we know so much about it, and about the man who built it. Allen's diary for 1822 not only provides a running account of the planning and building of the mill, but together with his other papers and published writings, it gives us many fascinating insights into the problems confronting the early industrialists and the ingenuity with which they were solved.

As finally completed in 1839,[37] the building measured 37 feet by 160 feet and was four stories and an attic high. In this form it must have been one of the largest factories of its kind to be built up to that time. The exterior walls are stone laid in random ashlar; the attic window was originally a clerestory monitor. Along with its unusual size and its masonry construction, the Allendale Mill has another important feature which sets it apart from most earlier mills. In the center of its long side a massive stone tower, 16 feet square at its base, rises to the level of the roof. As originally built, this tower was crowned by an octagonal cupola of sturdy proportions and simple classical detail (Fig. 15).[38]

The idea for the attached tower was not original with Allen. It appeared as early as 1816 in the second mill of the Boston Manufacturing Company in Waltham, Massachusetts (Fig. 26), and by the 1830's it was in general use, both as a means of vertical circulation and as a location for toilets. As

FIGURE 16. *Zachariah Allen. Allendale Mill,*
North Providence, R.I., dam end with buttresses, 1822.

in Allen's mill it served as a staircase outside the main block of the building. Thus in contrast to earlier mills, where an open staircase was incorporated directly in the working area (Fig. 11), the interior space was left entirely free for machinery. In addition, the stair well could be closed off from the interior of the building by heavy fire doors.[39] This, of course, greatly reduced the danger of fire spreading from floor to floor. The ample size of the tower, moreover, provided a generous amount of space for the vertical transportation of material. At each floor level was a large landing platform with a service door opening to the outside; above the tier of doors was a permanent hoist. The cupola, which fulfilled its normal function of housing the factory bell, also contained in its base a storage tank. In Allen's own mill this assured a constant supply of water for the hand sprinkler and fire hose system which he installed throughout the building.

The functional grouping of vertical circulation and fire protection within a single architectural component was one of the significant contributions to mill design during the first half of the nineteenth century and Allen was a central figure in this development. But the use of the tower in industrial building has significance far beyond the obvious practical considerations. By making it the fulcrum of the balance of the building, by conceiving it in proper proportion to the main mass of the mill, by accentuating its vertical thrust in the tapering forms of the classical cupola, Allen (and others like him) also made the tower a dynamic climax in a bold and aggressive design. In his mill at Allendale, therefore, the form of the meetinghouse, which characterized so many of the early mills, disappears altogether, and a new building type, born of necessity, and only modestly enriched by tradition, appears in its fully developed form.

In spite of its coherence, the Allendale Mill does have one curious eccentricity. Attached to the north and west corners and to the east side of the building are enormous stepped buttresses which seem anachronistic in the otherwise rectangular structural system (Fig. 16.) Since the mill was built in a period in American architecture when the romantic styles were already well entrenched, the medieval character of these unusual buttresses might be interpreted as an early appearance of Gothic forms in industrial building. However tempting this conclusion may be, such was not the case. Far from being romantic in origin the buttresses derive from the most practical reason imaginable. They were applied in an effort to stop a bizarre vibration which had developed in that end of the mill, a vibration which persisted even when the machines were not in motion. It was eventually discovered by Allen himself that the vibration frequency of the building was the same as that of the water flowing over the dam. It was ultimately stopped ". . . by fastening vertical pieces of plank, at intervals of ten feet, against the front of the dam, and projecting upwards so as to break the long sheet of water into numerous short falls, whose keynote was different from that of the whole sheet of water they displaced."[40]

This fascinating episode not only indicates the bewildering technical problems—and there were many—which confronted the pioneer industrialists, but it demonstrates, too, something of the nature of Zachariah Allen himself. Among the numerous entrepreneurs who made up the early industrial community in Rhode Island, he was outstanding. His public service alone to the city of Providence was remarkable. He was involved with hospitals and public education, served as a representative in the state legislature, and was a judge in the probate court. He was also an ingenious and knowledgeable engineer, whose contributions to the Providence water supply and fire fighting equipment were only peripheral to his major interest in the fields of textile machines, power, and power transmission. He was also the founder of the Manufacturers' Mutual Fire Insurance Company, and his mill at Allendale, with all its innovations, was the centerpiece in this undertaking. Begun at exactly the same time as Robert Mills's Fireproof Building in Charleston, South Carolina,[41] which Mills secured against fire by using vaults throughout, Allen's mill was also designed specifically with the problem of fire in mind. But rather than trying to make his building fireproof, which would have been virtually impossible with the materials available to him, Allen instead concentrated on means and methods of fire resistance and fire control. He introduced into his mill the first fire doors, the first sprinkler system, the first rotary fire pump, and the first copper-riveted hose ever used in an American textile mill. With the security of his mill against fire thus substantially increased, Allen applied to his insurance company in 1835 for a reduction in rate. He was refused. As a result, he formed the Manufacturers' Mutual Fire Insurance Company, which later grew to such proportions as to become a major influence on American factory design and construction throughout the nineteenth century.

Among the numerous fire-prevention devices developed during the late 1830's was an ingenious method of interior wooden framing. Although exterior masonry walls helped to reduce the fire hazard, they by no means eliminated it entirely. When a fire occurred in the early mills one of the greatest difficulties encountered in fighting it was the rapidity with which the wooden floors burned through and collapsed. The problem centered around the use of conventional floor joists. They were relatively light and thus quickly consumed. They were also closely spaced which created numerous hollow spaces into which it was difficult to get water to fight the fire; moreover, these joists exposed an excessive amount of wood surface to the flames. The American solution to this was practical and it was simple. The joists were eliminated. To compensate for the loss of structural strength, the large transverse beams were increased in size, and the floor, instead of remaining a single layer of plank, was increased to two layers totaling several inches in thickness. The first layer was made up of the heaviest planks running across the beams, the second, of lighter boards extending in the opposite direction. The beams, which were normally spaced about 8 feet apart, continued to be supported in the center by either wooden posts or columns, and at their ends by the masonry walls. The principal advantage of this system was the increased dimension of all its members. It would take a fire considerable time to burn through 14-inch beams and 4 inches of solid floor, thus allowing time to get water to the fire and bring it under control. Furthermore, the recessed firetraps created by the conventional joists were eliminated and the amount of exposed wood surface was cut almost in half.

The results of this system, which ultimately became known as "slow burning construction," were spectacular. Many fires which in joist construction would have burned through the floor and caused it to collapse were easily localized and brought under control. Although the number of fires was in no way affected, the number in which a mill was completely destroyed was greatly reduced. It is not known when slow burning construction first appeared in this country, but Zachariah Allen's use of it in 1839, when he made the addition to his Allendale Mill, was among the early applications.[42]

The Allendale Mill is conspicuous among those early American factories where the major problems associated with textile manufacture were dealt with coherently and solved in a practical and expressive architectural form. Except for the clerestory monitor, which generally gave way later in the century to the pitched roof and finally to the flat roof, Allen brought together in one structure the basic elements of the textile mill: masonry construction, a horizontal block comprised of layers of open interior space, and a monumental tower. Technological improvements would lead to greater size, architectural styles would take their turn under the pressure of personal taste, regional preferences and even practical concerns would modify forms, but so long as the rotary motion of the water wheel or the steam engine was communicated to the machines by shafts and pulleys, the combination of elements brought together by Allen would remain the form of the American factory. Indeed, it would dominate the American industrial scene down to the early years of the twentieth century.

FIGURE 17. *Learned Scott. Crown Mill, North Uxbridge, Mass., c. 1825.*

The Crown and Eagle mills

About the time when Allen built his mill at Allendale, stone mills with clerestory monitor roofs and monumental central towers appeared in numerous locations in Rhode Island and southern Massachusetts; the greatest concentration was in the Blackstone Valley. Several still survive in varying degrees of preservation. Until recently the most complete and impressive were the Crown and Eagle mills in North Uxbridge, Massachusetts (Fig. 19). On the night of October 2, 1975, while being rehabilitated for a housing complex, they were totally destroyed by fire in one of the most senseless acts of vandalism in modern preservation history. Built for Robert Rogerson[43] and Company in the 1820's, the blackened shells of the two mill buildings still flank each other in a line on either side of and at right angles to the Mumford River (a tributary of the Blackstone). The earlier, the Crown Mill (Fig. 17), was planned by Learned Scott of Cumberland, Rhode Island, and was finished in 1825. It is a granite structure 44 by 82 feet in its ground dimensions, and three stories and an attic high. It has a clerestory monitor roof, and in the center of its long (north) side is an attached tower of rather attenuated proportions. This tower rises through the building to the height of the ridgepole and is topped by an octagonal wooden cupola containing a belfry and having slender classical

FIGURE *18. Crown and Eagle mills, North Uxbridge, Mass.,*
from the north, c. 1825 and c. 1829.

supports and elliptical arched openings. The bearing walls and tower are
constructed of rough granite, laid in random ashlar. Window and door
openings are cleanly cut, classically proportioned and widely spaced; a
lightly scaled wooden cornice contains the various roof planes. In spite of
its obvious utilitarian character, all this gives the building a decided Neoclassical tone.

In its general massing, the Eagle Mill (Fig. 18), built in 1829, is almost
an exact replica of the Crown Mill. It is a few feet longer, however, and in
two respects it is significantly different. The masonry walls, although still
rough cut, are here coursed in *regular* ashlar, thus giving the mill a more
formal character. At the same time the tower is shorter, rising only to the
level of the clerestory window, and is thus more heavily proportioned; instead of having a cupola it terminates in a simple pitched roof. The result
is a building which in appearance is less vivacious and more basically utilitarian than its companion, the Crown Mill. Indeed, in its austere geometry, it calls to mind the rational simplicity of the granite buildings of
Alexander Parris in Boston.[44]

In 1851 the two stone mills were connected by a three story brick unit
which actually spanned the river forming one continuous building 273 feet
in length (Fig. 18).[45] Although this addition is of some engineering interest,[46] it is an architectural disaster. Not only do its brick walls introduce

FIGURE 19. *Crown and Eagle mills, North Uxbridge, Mass.,
c. 1825 and c. 1829. Print from c. 1840.*

disturbing contradictions in texture and scale, but its flat roof and squat
squarish cupola are in shattering conflict with the tapered, soaring quality
of the flanking clerestory monitor roofs. Still worse, the brick connector
destroys altogether the wide spacing of the mills, which was so essential to
their placement in the surrounding open space. To appreciate this more
fully it is essential to examine the entire scheme in some detail.

As originally built the two granite units were poised end to end in opposition to one another on either side of the river (Figs. 19, 20). Two hundred yards upstream a dam held the water back in a millpond. From here
the flow was carried to the mills by two parallel canals placed equidistant
from the river, one on either side. Between these three waterways are two
long rectangles of meadowland which stretch from the mills to a roadway.
The latter, now known as Hartford Avenue East, crosses the waterways at
a slightly oblique angle, midway between the mills and the dam, and here
forms the northern boundary of the mill compound. The vigorous granite
façades of the two mills, therefore, were originally seen as balancing cen-
terpieces in a symmetrical layout of luxuriant green open space, separated
and contained by the fiercely directional thrusts of the canals and the river.
The impression is clearly conveyed that this balanced spatial arrangement
was motivated more by formal than by practical concerns and was intended to create a monumental setting for the buildings.

This notion is supported in several interesting ways. The first is the arrangement itself: if the formal plan was not intended, then why were the
mills not placed on the same side of the stream, as they were in most other

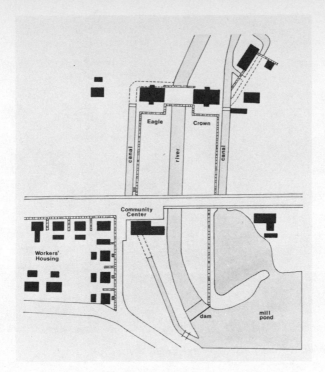

FIGURE 20. *Crown and Eagle mills, North Uxbridge, Mass.,*
plan of community.

instances, where they could be served by one canal rather than two?
Moreover, an 1830's print of the two mills in their symmetrical setting
clearly indicates a formal intent. It shows not only a continuous row of
small new trees spaced at regular intervals along the stream and canal but
also two larger trees, obviously freshly planted and sited across from each
other at that point in the grounds where the roadway crosses the river.
Carefully poised on either side of the main axis which divides the scheme,
these two matching trees are as symmetrical in their relationships with the
river and with one another as are the mills in the background. We also
know from nineteenth-century accounts that the Crown and Eagle mills
were esteemed in their day for the beauty of their planned surroundings.
One observer describes it as "one of the handsomest manufacturing establishments in the state . . . the situation is singularly beautiful, and the
grounds have been laid out and the buildings located with great taste and
regularity, and ornamented with pleasure grounds and artificial ponds."[47]

Because of its symmetrical bias the layout of the Crown and Eagle mills
is strongly Neoclassical and may therefore be fruitfully compared with two
other important Neoclassical schemes in this country. These are Thomas
Jefferson's University of Virginia, planned as early as 1810 and finished in
1826 (I: Fig. 233), and Jean Jacques Ramée's Union College in Schenec-
tady, New York, planned in 1812 (I: Fig. 238). Both were completed by
the time the Crown and Eagle mills were laid out. The arrangement in the
Jefferson and Ramée plans is axial with architectural components dis-

FIGURE 21. *Mill housing for Crown and Eagle mills,
North Uxbridge, Mass., c. 1830.*

played against symmetrically contained open spaces. Inspired by Neoclassical sources, the serene balance of both differs radically from the eccentric positioning of circles and radial avenues which marks that other major plan in our nation's early history—L'Enfant's Baroque scheme for the city of Washington (I: Fig. 283).[48]

Although there is no reason to assume a direct relationship between the Crown and Eagle mills and the university schemes of Jefferson and Ramée, the industrial plan is, nevertheless, based on the same concepts of order, and in its own way is symptomatic of the depths to which Neoclassical ideas were beginning to permeate the American consciousness. At the same time, as in the case of the University of Virginia,[49] there were in this scheme fascinating and important departures from strict classical rule. First is the simple fact that the symmetry of the scheme is not so rigid as it would first seem. As we have already noted, the two buildings themselves are not exactly the same, so that they did not oppose one another across the river in absolute reciprocal correspondence. Nor are they completely symmetrical within themselves; to be so, the doors in the stair towers would have to fall on the central axis, but instead those in the Eagle Mill are to the left of it and those in the Crown Mill to the right. This was done, no doubt, to facilitate loading, so that the symmetry in each case was sacrificed in favor of practical necessity. Furthermore, when seen from the distance the tower of each mill appears to lie on the central axis of its respective fronting meadow. But again, such is not the case. Although the buildings are in fact equidistant from the river, they are placed closer to the canals, and are therefore not centered between the waterways. Obvi-

FIGURE 22. *Community center for Crown and Eagle mills, North Uxbridge, Mass., c. 1830.*

ously, this arrangement was necessary in order to bring the wheels into the most efficient relationship with the source of power, so that again practical considerations were permitted to intrude upon formal principle. Just as in the case of Jefferson's plan for the University of Virginia, this uninhibited willingness to modify theory in favor of fact gives to Rogerson's Crown and Eagle complex, in spite of its obvious formality, an underlying urgency which is more expressive of its dynamic experimental condition than of any pretensions toward high style design.

If Rogerson's intention was to monumentalize his mills, he does not seem to have had the same attitude toward the community which he built to serve them. The two earliest housing units, which date from the 1820's, stand outside the waterway open space to the west (to the right in Fig. 19), and are arranged in a loose relationship with one another on either side of Hartford Avenue East. Both are wooden buildings. The one to the north was an old mill that was moved from its former location and converted into a boardinghouse; the one to the south was built from the beginning as a boardinghouse. To the east is another cluster of housing units which also lies outside of the open space dominated by mills. Here four small and almost identical brick tenement houses (Fig. 21) stand in a neat row along the north side of Hartford Avenue and are joined at the corner of Whitin Street, which intersects Hartford Avenue from the north, by three more similar small houses, also arranged in a row. They all date from the early 1830's. Although the houses, with their neat sequential relationships, form a coherent architectural complex, they are in no way related to the larger scheme of the mills and their waterways.

FIGURE 23. *Mill housing, Harris, R.I., c. 1850.*

One of the community buildings built by Rogerson which does fall loosely within the spatial realm of the larger design (Fig. 22) is a three-story brick building which functioned as a multipurpose community center: there was a store on the first floor, the second floor was the meetinghouse, and the third served as a tenement. It stands on the north side of Hartford Avenue and faces the Eagle Mill. Since traditionally the meetinghouse was the most important building in the early New England communities, it would seem logical that the one at North Uxbridge might have been drawn into a formal relationship with the mills. Because of its size it does, to be sure, dominate the brick tenements which it flanks. Moreover, it was built at the same time as the tenements and in both style and scale is a coherent part of the brick compound. For these very reasons it rejects the mills and is wholly identified instead with the independent sub-village of houses. Although it faces the Eagle Mill, it does not share the axis of the larger spatial environment. Nor does the refined texture of its brick walls relate to the heavier scale of the mills' stonework. Indeed, the little red brick houses and the community center all display the quiet charm of the brick vernacular architecture of hinterland New England during the first quarter of the nineteenth century; the two stone mills by contrast are large and aggressive in the circumscribed sanctum of their symmetrical enclosure. Here the mills have not only taken over completely from the meetinghouse as the center of life in the community, but they have relegated it altogether to a position of secondary importance, even to the humiliating situation of having to share the same building with other functions.

In the early industrial development of Rhode Island and the upper Blackstone Valley the Neoclassical layout of the Crown and Eagle mills was both climactic and unique. In general, the Rhode Island communities were small hamlets clustered around a single individually owned mill. The size of the community was determined by the size of the mill, the size of the mill by the amount of water power available. Moreover, in their labor

FIGURE 24. *Mill housing, Georgiaville, R.I., c. 1812.*

practices the Rhode Island mill owners, in order to take advantage of child labor, were inclined to follow the British method of hiring entire families. The workers' houses that they built, therefore, were designed for single-family occupancy (Figs. 23, 24). For the most part they were small cottages, openly spaced, and situated in pleasant rural surroundings. A number are still to be found in scattered parts of the region. Architecturally, they were minimal structures, providing only the most essential space for family living. On the other hand, they were soundly built and handsomely proportioned and a few even displayed modest ornamental features. In the majority, however, decorative ambitions were gratified by the simplest possible moldings applied to cornices and window and door surrounds. The most conservative domestic vernacular at the turn of the nineteenth century was the prevailing level of style.

One aspect of these workers' houses, however, has no precedent in the earlier architecture of New England, and that is their relationship to one another. They were equally spaced in rows or clusters, and within any given grouping the houses were all alike. Indeed, what we have in these communities is probably the first appearance in the United States of the company owned rather than the individually owned house.[50] The New England towns built during the colonial years were, to be sure, organized communities, but the objective which governed their layout was the equitable and practical distribution of the land, not mathematical repetition of units of design, and although any houses built at the same time would certainly have shown strong stylistic similarities, they were nevertheless the work of individuals, and no two were ever exactly alike. How different were the early industrial communities, such as Harris, Rhode Island (Fig. 23). There, identical cottages stood in neat ranks within walking distance of the mill, as similar in shape, size and detail as it was possible for measuring instruments and carpenter's tools to make them.

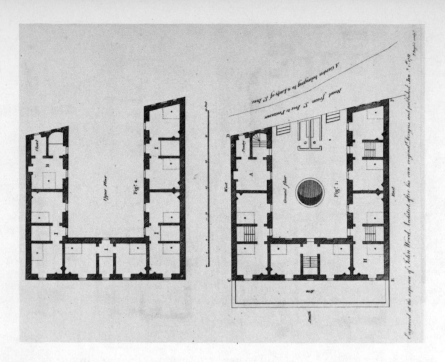

FIGURE 25. *English workers' cottages by John Wood, 1806.*

The reasons for this are obvious. It was the most economical and efficient way to provide housing for the operatives. But there was also precedence for regularized housing in England. In the small eighteenth-century communities of the Stroud Valley, for example, fragments of similar early housing clusters still exist, most of them built in stone. In size and shape the early stone houses at Georgiaville, Rhode Island (Fig. 24), which were built about the same time as the Nightingale Factory (Fig. 14) of 1812, are not unlike the English houses, and moreover, they are grouped around a central court in a manner similar to that found in an important English architectural publication of the early nineteenth century (Fig. 25).[51] In view of the predominance in Rhode Island of English manufacturing methods, it would be surprising if we did not find a corresponding English influence in the architecture of the communities themselves.

In spite of the rigid order imposed upon the housing units, there seems never to have been any desire to establish a formal relationship between the houses and the mill. The mill was placed where it could be most efficiently served by the waterway; the houses were grouped nearby, conveniently placed, but wholly independent of the position and orientation of the mill. As already noted, it was just such an arrangement which prevailed in the plan at North Uxbridge, an arrangement which makes all the more remarkable the intrusion of an axial scheme into the Crown and Eagle mill compound itself. In fact, the Crown and Eagle plan is so extraordinary in the otherwise pragmatic community planning of the Blackstone Valley that it makes it necessary to explore the possibility of new and different influences coming to the upper Blackstone from outside Rhode Island.

LOWELL AND ITS SATELLITES

The Boston Manufacturing Company; Precursor of Lowell

If Rhode Island was the birthplace of the factory in the United States, it was not the scene of its largest development. This was so primarily because of the limitations of water power. None of the rivers that fed into the Rhode Island area were very large, especially when compared to the Merrimack and Connecticut rivers, and in order to provide sustained power the water rights had to be strictly controlled. The care with which Zachariah Allen surveyed his privilege and planned his dam at Centerdale, so that he could gain maximum flowage and still not infringe upon the rights above him, is vividly revealed in his diary and leaves no question as to the critical nature of the problem.[52] Moreover, in the early days in Rhode Island, both the sources of capital and the potential markets were small. Having been indoctrinated in the technology and methods of Samuel Slater, those who controlled the Rhode Island mills were "spinners and mechanics at heart," more "intent upon the process of production"[53] than upon the problems of financing and markets. Consequently, when the time came for expansion, they tended to build new factories at new locations rather than to enlarge their existing facilities.

To meet the pressing challenge of an expanding textile industry, which seemed so far beyond the reach of the limited Rhode Island potential, a new type of industrial organization made its appearance in New England. As we have already seen, the War of 1812 together with the Embargo Act provided a stimulus to the textile mills of Rhode Island, but at the same time they dealt a disastrous blow to American commerce. In Boston the economic situation was severe enough to prompt a number of prosperous merchants to seek new fields in which to invest their capital. Impressed by the successes of the textile industry in Rhode Island, they began to see manufacturing as a potential for investment. Unlike the Rhode Islanders, however, who were mechanics and engineers, these Boston men were merchants and bankers with great executive capacity and wide experience in business organization. Their role in manufacturing, therefore, was planning, financing, and marketing, plus attention to the social problems associated with the hiring of labor. Technical and operational problems they left to the mechanics and the specialists. Out of this came a new type of factory organization which was, in fact, the prototype of the great modern corporation. It was characterized by absentee capital and the concentration of all processes of production—from raw material to finished product—under one management and in one plant.[54]

The first company organized along these lines was the Boston Manufacturing Company, established in Waltham, Massachusetts, in 1813. Its

FIGURE 26. *Boston Manufacturing Company, Waltham, Mass., first mill (left), 1813; second mill (right), 1816 (Old Sturbridge Village).*

promoter was Francis Cabot Lowell, a wealthy Boston merchant. Lowell went to England in 1811 with the specific intention of learning whatever he could about methods of cotton manufacturing. While there he made many careful mental notes on British machines and methods, giving particular attention to the power loom, which was still unknown in the United States. Immediately following his return to Boston he acquired the assistance of a brilliant young mechanic, Paul Moody; and on the basis of Lowell's recollections together they built the first power loom in the United States.

While in England Lowell had also observed that spinning and weaving were done in separate establishments. But his plan was to combine the entire process of making cloth in a single plant. This was realized in 1813 when he formed the Boston Manufacturing Company from among his business associates, and then proceeded to build its first mill in Waltham (Fig. 26).

The building was somewhat similar to those in Rhode Island. It was a rectangular block 90 by 40 feet, and four stories high with an attic and basement. Unlike the Rhode Island mills, however, it was made of brick rather than stone, and its large octagonal cupola, instead of rising above the end of the mill, was placed over the center of the clerestory monitor roof.

Between 1816 and 1818 a second mill was built directly down stream from the first (Fig. 26). It had exactly the same configuration as its predecessor except that it was 60 feet longer and had no cupola. Furthermore,

FIGURE 27. *Boston Manufacturing Company mill, Waltham, Mass.,
lower wall, 1813; top floor, added 1873.*

attached to the center of the long side was a narrow wooden tower which
rose to the level of the clerestory window and was crowned by a pitched
roof and pediment. This seems to be among the earliest appearances of the
outside tower, a feature which would become standard in the fully developed nineteenth-century factory. In this case, however, the motivation appears to have been more practical than aesthetic: it was on the stream side
of the mill and it may have contained primitive toilets on each floor.

With its completion, the second mill at Waltham, along with the earlier
mill, became a coherent part of a continuous manufacturing process. Thus
it marks the first time in America that two individual factory units were
combined in a larger industrial organism.[55] Up to this time in Rhode Island, as we have already seen, each mill had been thought of as an independent productive unit, its size determined by the limitations of the
power and transmitting elements, which in turn established its maximum
productive capacity. Yet Lowell's intention to manufacture cloth from the
raw material to the finished product in one plant far exceeded the capacity
of a single mill building. It was necessary, therefore, to build an additional
unit. To assure the greatest possible efficiency, this unit had to be brought
into close relationship with the original mill and with the source of power.
Accordingly, the second mill was built directly in line with the first but located about 80 feet down-river. The headrace for each mill fed from a
canal which passed behind the mills on the side away from the river, the
tailraces flowed back into the stream. Thus, the respective wheels received
their water from the same head with a minimum length of canal and pen-

stock. The wide spacing of the two units was maintained in order to reduce the danger of fire spreading from one to the other. In 1843, however, after the introduction of wrought iron high speed shafting and more fire resistant methods of construction, the gap between the two buildings was closed, thus making a continuous mill approximately 323 feet long.

The arrangement of the Waltham mills in a line and parallel to the principal waterway is of particular significance. In Rhode Island, where a single mill was served by a single headrace, the building was generally oriented at right angles to the stream. This was logical. The water wheel was almost always at the center of the mill and with the side of the building facing the dam the headrace could be brought directly to the wheel house in a straight line. If more than one mill was to be served, however, it was necessary, as at Waltham, to provide a feeder canal, generally parallel to the stream, from which a headrace could flow to each mill. With the water brought in this way, a right angle orientation of the mill would make it necessary to extend the headrace halfway down its length and then make a right angle turn to the wheel. This not only complicated construction, it also impeded the flow. On the other hand, with the mills arranged in a line parallel to the canal, the headrace to each water wheel was reduced to a short, straight run. Looking back at the Crown and Eagle mills, which were built approximately ten years after Waltham, it is this very point which argues so strongly for a formal rather than practical conception in the planning of the Uxbridge cluster. Each of the mills at Uxbridge received its water from its own canal.

The architectural character of the Waltham mills is exceptionally fine (Fig. 27). The main walls of the two original buildings still survive and show that the brickwork in particular is of unusual quality; its use at Waltham represents the first major application of the material to industrial building, and thus establishes an early date for the type of masonry which was to become characteristic of the nineteenth-century factory. The bricks are uniform in size and shape, but vary in color from a warm red-orange to a lighter and more neutral tone of the same hue. They are slightly coarse in texture and are laid in wide mortar with precise regularity. This clean masonry gives a crisp linear definition to the walls and window openings. The latter are more generous in size than those in the Rhode Island mills, and tend to be proportioned in the best Neoclassical manner; mullions and frames are delicately scaled. The windows themselves rather than being deeply or moderately recessed are set close to the wall, thus tending to reaffirm the flat continuity of the wall plane. In contrast, the heavier and rougher stone masonry of the Rhode Island mills stressed the thickness and density of the walls.

The unadorned, geometric simplicity of the walls at Waltham is remarkably similar to that of the best contemporary architecture in Boston (Fig. 53). Thus, just as the Slater Mill reflected the taste and environment of Moses Brown, so the mills of the Boston Manufacturing Company reflect those of the Boston industrialists. Progressive in their administrative and technological thinking, these men were also knowledgeable in architectural matters.[56] In Boston during the second decade of the century, the mature style of Charles Bulfinch was the modern New England idiom. Not only did its austere, refined classicism mirror contemporary taste, but its simplicity gave it a strongly utilitarian flavor which made it attractive to the hard-headed Boston associates intent on prudent investment and substantial profits. Thus, while the early Rhode Island promoters tended to rely upon the eighteenth century for their ideas about building style, the Boston group accepted the leadership of their most prominent contemporary architect. There is no indication that any architect was active in planning the Waltham mills, but Lowell and his associates were obviously aware of Bulfinch's genius, for in designing their mills, they relied heavily upon his architectural vocabulary. In building them they used the best available materials and craftsmanship.

Lowell and the Merrimack

The idea of grouping several factory units into a single architectural and technological complex was not an American innovation. We have already observed it at New Lanark in Scotland on a remarkably similar but larger scale (Fig. 9). On the other hand, its application at Waltham represents the first step in the United States toward the evolution of the modern industrial plant. It also established the system which was later used on a much larger scale in the planning of the city of Lowell. From the outset, the Boston Manufacturing Company was intended by Lowell to be the experimental laboratory for a very much larger industrial complex,[57] and by 1820 the immense success of the Waltham plant argued decisively in favor of proceeding with it. Unfortunately, Lowell died unexpectedly in 1817, but two of his partners, Nathan Appleton and P. T. Jackson, joined with another Boston merchant, Kirk Boott, to carry out the scheme.

Their first problem was to find an appropriate site. The one they finally chose was at the confluence of the Merrimack and Concord rivers in the town of Chelmsford. It was renamed Lowell in 1826. Of all of the locations available to them in New England this was probably the best. The Merrimack was one of the largest rivers in the region and at this particular point it dropped steeply in an extensive rapids. When dammed it provided a head of over thirty feet. In volume and flow, the river assured reliable quantities of water to sustain many times the number of mills possible on the streams of Rhode Island, or even on the Charles at Waltham. Around the rapids ran the Pawtucket Canal, a small waterway that was built in the late eighteenth century as a means of opening the upper Merrimack to river traffic. In addition, the Middlesex Canal, built in 1803, provided a direct transportation route from Chelmsford to Boston, twenty-six miles to the southeast.

An 1832 map of the town of Lowell shows that the Pawtucket Canal cut off from the Merrimack just above the rapids in a large loop to the south that formed a diamond-shaped island approximately three-quarters of a mile on each of its four sides (Fig. 28). This island was largely farmland and was divided into two parts by a winding road. In the first

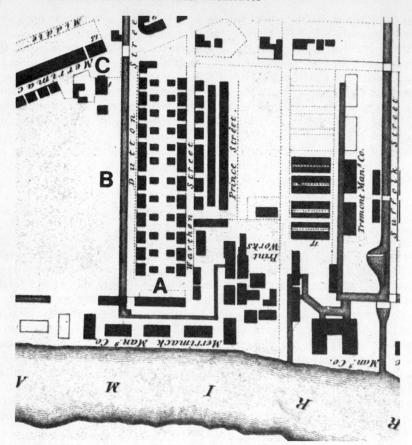

FIGURE 28. *Plan of the town of Lowell, Mass., 1832.*

distribution of land the northern area, toward the river, was reserved for the mills and mill housing; the area between the road and the canal was set aside for the community at large. The main source of water for the mills was to be the Pawtucket Canal. At a point about halfway through its course a series of radiating canals was planned that would feed back toward the river; each would carry the water to a cluster of mills.[58]

The Early Lowell Mills

The first company formed at Lowell was the Merrimack Company, incorporated by Appleton, Jackson, and Boott in 1822. Eleven years later ten different corporations were operating with a total capital of $7,450,000.[59]

An old lithographic view of Lowell made about 1833 gives us an excellent idea of the appearance of the city at that time (Fig. 29), and makes

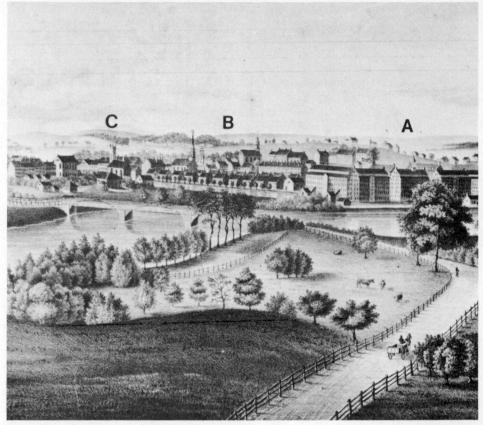

FIGURE 29. *View of Lowell, Mass., 1833.*

clear that it was a far more complex industrial community than anything we have seen up to this time. The most conspicuous elements, indeed far more conspicuous than the church steeples which appear in the background, are the mills, lined up in groups along the river. Each group was owned by a different corporation. The earliest mills, those of the Merrimack Company, may be taken as typical. They are seen to the right of center in the print, immediately behind the tree in the foreground (A, Fig. 29). We note at once that these mills are of exactly the same type that we saw at Waltham; they are about the same size and are similarly spaced from one another, each designed to make the most efficient use of the maximum power possible with the high breast wheels and transmitting elements then in use. In the Merrimack group, however, there were five mills instead of two; the arrangement is between the river and the canal, in an absolutely symmetrical scheme. Three of the mills are parallel with the river and equally spaced from one another (A, Fig. 28; A, Fig. 29); the one in the center has a cupola in the middle of its roof, accenting the fulcrum of the arrangement. All have outside stair towers similar to those seen at Waltham. The two remaining mills, which are identical to one another, cut across the main axis of the other three at right angles, one at each end of the line. They are symmetrically spaced with respect to the three center mills and form a shallow forecourt on the side away from the river. When the canal reaches this cluster it makes a sharp right angle bend and passes in front of the forecourt where it serves as the feeder for all five mills. Facing the center mill, on the other side of the canal but not quite centered on the main axis, is the countinghouse.

The 1832 map of Lowell also shows that beyond the mills, but not quite lined up with the central axis of the mill cluster, are two streets of boardinghouses, Dutton Street and Worthen Street, both of which run parallel with the main feeder canal (B, Fig. 28; B, Fig. 29). They extend from the countinghouse, just beyond the mill compound, to the main street of the city, and are joined to the mills by the embracing arms of the canal to form a complete and coherent working community. On the other side of the main street, to the south, are the elements of the city itself—the churches, stores, schools, and residences, which supported but which were not an organic part of the company community.

Perhaps the most important single fact about the planning of Lowell is the remarkable simplicity with which the rigidity of a Neoclassical scheme was made to relate to the practical problems of power and housing. In fact, it was precisely this point that seemed to fascinate Charles Dickens, the militant English critic of industrialism, when he visited Lowell in the late winter of 1842. His account of what he saw[60] takes us into the streets and the mills with a sharpness and insight that only he could provide. In one of his several observations about architecture he goes at once to the heart of the problem, the relationship between the water and the buildings; for what struck him most was that "the very river that moves the machinery in the mills (for they are all worked by water power), seems to acquire a new character from the fresh buildings of bright red brick and painted wood among which it takes its course."

Mindful of the grime and pollution of the steam-powered English industrial communities, Dickens was obviously impressed by the cleanliness of Lowell, especially since he saw it in the sharp clear light of a sparkling winter day. Water power was clean, but in the United States it was also abundant and cheap. American engineers, therefore, concentrated upon its development. Early in the century its use in this country was primitive and extravagant, but by 1850 it had changed into a systematic studied economy. Its application, in fact, became so efficient and scientific that even after the large scale introduction of steam after the Civil War water remained a major source of power until the very last years of the century.[61]

Dickens's sensitive eye saw more than the cleanliness of the scene at Lowell. He was aware, too, of the versatility of the water, even sensing its kinship with the buildings among which it flowed. The water at Lowell did, in fact, do far more than furnish power. The canals and river were highly visible space dividers, circumscribing and separating the manufacturing and living compounds; they served as reflecting pools for both the

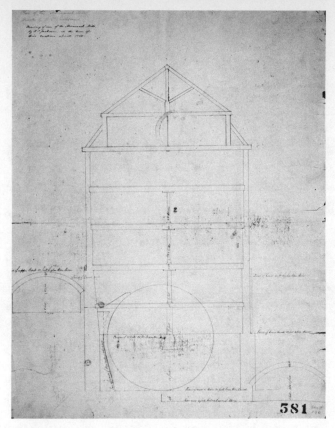

FIGURE 30. Merrimack Company mill, Lowell, Mass., original cross section, c. 1822.

mills and the housing, and when combined with freshly planted rows of elms, as they were on Dutton Street, they also brought into the controlled regular rhythms of the houses and mills something of the picturesque variety of nature itself.

The remarkable visual coherence of Lowell derived not only from the plan, but also from the architectural style. Here even more than at Waltham the red-brick and white-wood idiom of early nineteenth-century Boston, with all its refined qualities of proportion and scale, set the architectural tone of the entire company compound. As they appear in the 1833 print (Fig. 29) the early mills are seen to have been typical rectangular blocks four to five stories high, with clerestory monitor roofs. A few had cupolas, most had outside stair towers. Unfortunately, none of the early mills at Lowell survives in anything like its original form. Fragments of some are still to be seen beneath the massive piles that were heaped upon them during the enormous expansion of the city which followed the large-scale introduction of steam power after the Civil War. Those of the Merrimack Company, however, so conspicuous in the 1833 print, have disappeared altogether. Our evaluation of them as works of architecture, therefore, must be based upon one primary and one secondary piece of evidence. The primary evidence is the original cross section of one of the Merrimack mills (Fig. 30). It shows clearly both the end profile of the

FIGURE 31. *Lowell-type mill, Methuen, Mass., 1826–27.*

mill, and the method of constructing the clerestory monitor. It also shows the location and size of the great high breast wheel. The secondary evidence is an early mill in Methuen (Fig. 31) that is still sufficiently intact to make it a useful demonstration of the earliest Lowell mills. Built during 1826–27, shortly after those of the Merrimack Company, it has all the basic architectural features described above. Particularly impressive are the steep sloping profiles of the clerestory monitor roof; the clean, flat planes of the brickwork; the sharply cut window openings, so generously apportioned in relation to the wall; the elegantly proportioned stone lintels over the windows; and finally the carefully worked brick cornice which defines the planes of the roof. Although some of the contemporary Federal style buildings of Boston (Fig. 53) display more elaborate ornament, none is finer in texture, proportion and scale.

The Early Lowell Boardinghouses

The first workers' housing of the Merrimack Company, seen on Dutton Street in the Pendelton lithograph of 1833 (B, Fig. 29), was a row of seemingly identical units facing the Merrimack Canal. We know from the records that there were similar houses on Worthen Street, one block removed from the canal. Although considerable changes were made in this housing during the nineteenth century, substantial portions were still intact as late as 1966. With the help of the Pendelton lithograph, therefore, it is possible to reconstruct the original layout with reasonable accuracy. In general, the houses were large rectangular blocks, long side to the street,

FIGURE 32. *Wooden houses for Merrimack Company, Lowell, Mass., c. 1825.*

and probably most of them were double units; some of them were built of wood and some of brick forming that mixture of "bright red brick and painted wood" which attracted Dickens.

The wooden houses were ample rectangular structures, two and one-half stories high with pitched roofs and dormer windows (Fig. 32). Each of them seems to have been a duplex unit, with a double door in the center, giving access to the quarters on either side. A long wing extending to the rear contained the two dining rooms and two kitchens. Except for their double entrance doors, these wooden houses had all the characteristics of the simple domestic style found everywhere in rural New England at the turn of the nineteenth century.

Judged on the basis of those which still survive, the brick units were the same height and depth as the wooden houses, and they had identical pitched roofs. They were twice as long, however, and on the main façade were four entrances: a double one in the center, and a single one at each end (Fig. 33).

Seen as a whole, the total complex of mills and housing had extraordinary coherence. Conceived and built at the same time, its architectural components were harmoniously related through consistency of style, and further drawn together by the unifying forces of a controlled axial plan. But it was also a dynamic community, enriched by the changing profiles of its many building types, enlivened by the interweaving of buildings and waterways, and humanized both by the scale of the buildings and by the delightful contrast of brick and wood in the housing.

FIGURE 33. *Workers' boardinghouse, Merrimack Company, Dutton Street, Lowell, Mass., c. 1825.*

The Early Nineteenth-century Industrial Community: Harrisville, N.H.

The Merrimack Company's remarkable community at Lowell, which was surely one of the major achievements of the nineteenth century, was totally demolished in 1966 to make way for an urban renewal project; and the satellite communities which it spawned up the valley of the Merrimack as far as Manchester, New Hampshire, have also been so drastically altered by both growth and destruction that it is difficult to visualize their original character. In southern New Hampshire, however, there is one early factory town, Harrisville, which does survive in virtually its original form. Although substantially smaller than Lowell, this unspoiled town has qualities of style and scale which relate it directly to the more ambitious communities of the Merrimack. Harrisville began as a textile community about the same time as Lowell,[62] and by mid-century the town with its mills, houses, and other related buildings was a firmly established industrial and social entity. From then it continued as a working community right down to 1970 when economic and technological developments in the textile industry, which left no room for a family-owned, moderately scaled operation, forced the mills into bankruptcy. But because it was owned and operated by the same family[63] for one hundred and twenty years no destructive changes were made in the architectural fabric of the town,[64] and in its completeness it sheds substantial light on the whole question of the early industrial community in America.

FIGURE 34. *Harrisville, N.H., early community from the southwest.*

As it appeared in the 1850's Harrisville was both harmoniously related to, and dramatically different from Lowell. Whereas Lowell occupied a comparatively level site, Harrisville clung to a precipitous and constantly changing fall of land. Situated in the Monadnock highlands, the site was an upland plateau more than 1,000 feet above sea level, with a backdrop of gentle hills to the north, and to the south, the isolated granite massif of Mount Monadnock. Unlike the broadly flowing Merrimack which supplied Lowell, the water at Harrisville came from a series of substantial ponds which fed one into the other to form over ten square miles of watershed. The third in this chain was Harrisville Pond. From its outlet a stream fell off steeply for a vertical drop of over 100 feet in less than half a mile; it was exactly at this spot, along the lower slopes of the pond and on the steep banks of the ravine, that the town was built (Figs. 34–35).

Because of its setting the physical problems of laying out Harrisville were very different from those at Lowell. In all industrial communities the highest priority was given to locating the mill where it could make the most efficient use of the water. At Lowell the mills were placed in orderly lines along the feeder canal, parallel with the river. From the canal the water was brought easily to the wheels and then discharged back into the river. At Harrisville, the banks of the ravine were too steep to permit the construction of a canal. The mills, therefore, had to be placed astride the stream, with the water for the wheels fed directly from the stream itself.

FIGURE 35. *Harrisville, N.H., early brick village from across Goose Creek Ravine.*

The result is a dramatic visual display of the relationship between the mills and their source of power. The water was brought from Harrisville Pond by a very short extension of the pond (known locally as "the canal") to a dam which held it back on the upstream side of the upper mill in a quiet, dark pool (Fig. 36). After passing through the wheel it flowed out from under the mill and continued downstream in a tumbling cascade (Fig. 37). As it approached the lower mill it was retained by a second dam (Fig. 38). With the mills thus dominating the ravine, the rest of the community was developed naturally in response to both the life of the town and the configuration of the land (Fig. 39). The result was a loose but dynamic relationship of buildings and open space set in constantly shifting conditions of landscape, and subject to ever-changing qualities of light, shadow and reflection (Fig. 40).

The informal arrangement of the architectural components of Harrisville, which relates it so organically to the very character of the land, was born of necessity and delight, not of any preconceived formal principles of design. The controlling geometry which dominates Lowell is nowhere to be seen in Harrisville. The attitudes which made possible its open planning were already well established in New England long before either Harrisville or Lowell came into being. The early New England towns were planned communities from the very beginning.[65] Based on rigorous concepts of land apportionment, community obligation and individual rights, they were organized clusters of essential buildings unified by the single ob-

FIGURE 36. *Harris (Upper) Mill and dam,*
Harrisville, N.H., 1832.

FIGURE 37. *Harrisville, N.H.,*
up Goose Brook Ravine to Harris Mill.

FIGURE 38. Cheshire (Lower) Mill,
Harrisville, N.H., 1846–47.

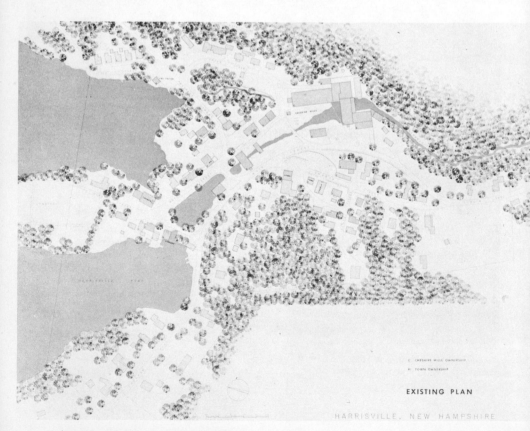

FIGURE 39. Plan of Harrisville, N.H.

FIGURE 40. *Evangelical Congregational Church,*
Harrisville, N.H., 1842.

jective of bringing order and livability to the wilderness. To be sure, the
actual physical demands imposed upon the planners of industrial communities were different from those encountered by the colonial Puritans.
In all of them the waterway rather than the common pasture was the
source of life, the mills rather than the meetinghouse dominated the site,
the owner's rather than the parson's house occupied the position of prominence. Nevertheless, Harrisville, like all other industrial communities, was
conditioned in some degree by two centuries of planning tradition which
functioned as a subtle but persistent guide to the Harrises as they developed and built their town.

But the life of Harrisville is also written in its buildings. Of the two surviving mills, the Harris or Upper Mill (Fig. 41) is the older. It was built
during 1830–32 and is situated at the head of Goose Creek Ravine immediately adjacent to the first mill dam. About a hundred yards further
downstream is the Cheshire, or Lower Mill (Fig. 42), built between 1845
and 1848.

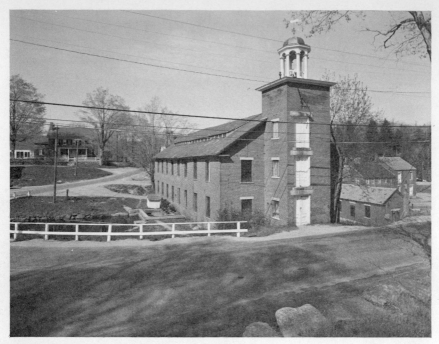

FIGURE 41. *Harris (Upper) Mill,*
Harrisville, N.H., 1832; tower, c. 1847.

Both are classic survivals of early mill building types in America. As originally built, the Harris Mill was a simple rectangular block, two stories and an attic high, with its cupola situated on the ridgepole at the south end of the building. It also had a trap-door monitor window which still exists, thus making the mill one of the rare survivals of this type. We know that the trap-door monitor first appeared in this country at an early date in Rhode Island. Moreover, we know further that the trap-door monitor was not used in any of the Lowell mills. It is obvious, therefore, that one or more Rhode Island examples must have inspired Milan Harris when he built his first mill. As it stands today the mill is an enlargement of the original building. Although its primary shape and roof line remain the same, some time after 1850 Harris extended the mill by two bays to the south, and on the end of this addition he built an outside stair tower with loading platforms. He then removed the small bell cupola from the ridgepole and crowned the new tower with a larger and more imposing cupola. The overall effect, therefore, was to increase substantially the monumentality of the building and bring it more in harmony with the towered Cheshire Mill further downstream. Since the Cheshire Mill, by this time, was owned by the Colony family, the suspicion arises that the specific shape of the new Harris cupola, which is almost identical to that on the Cheshire Mill, was not entirely motivated by practical concerns.

The Cheshire Mill is larger than the Harris Mill and also differs from it in two other important respects: it has a clerestory rather than a trap-door

FIGURE 42. *Cheshire (Lower) Mill, Harrisville, N.H.,
1846–47; brick wing, right, added 1859–60.*

monitor window in the upper story, and it is made of stone. We have already seen that by the 1830's stone mills with clerestory monitor roofs
dominated the Rhode Island scene and reached up the Blackstone Valley
as far as southern Massachusetts, the finest example being the superb
Crown Mill at North Uxbridge (Fig. 17). It seems apparent, therefore,
that the Cheshire Mill, in its form and material, also had roots in Rhode
Island. On the other hand, stone masonry was not uncommon in the
Monadnock region during the first half of the nineteenth century and a
number of interesting examples still survive. One of the best is the house
of Asa Greenwood in Marlboro (Fig. 43), only a few miles from Harrisville. Greenwood was the mason who built the Cheshire Mill, and he was
also responsible for a number of other stone buildings in the area, including his own house. We may conclude, therefore, that the use of stone in
the Cheshire Mill, although inspired by Rhode Island examples found support in an already well-developed regional craft.

Together the Harris and Cheshire mills form the monumental core of
Harrisville. They are the largest buildings in the town and from their unusual positions astride the stream they dominate the landscape. But more
than that, their strong massing, their complex roof configurations, and their
monumental towers leave no doubt as to their central authority among the
buildings which surround them. We have already observed that the very
early New England mills, especially those with frontal cupolas and towers,
bore a provocative relationship with the New England meetinghouse. At

FIGURE 43. *Asa Greenwood House, Marlboro, N.H., 1836.*

Harrisville this effect is particularly pronounced. Not only does each of the mills have very much the character of a meetinghouse, but because of their central location they have usurped from the meetinghouse the dominating role in the town; and the meetinghouse itself, which is a fine provincial Greek Revival building with sturdy proportions and superb brickwork, occupies a secondary, although lovely site on the edge of the mill canal (Fig. 40).

If the mills of Harrisville were derived from Rhode Island, the early workers' houses certainly were not. The early housing in Rhode Island was made up of small single family units many of them similar to English types (Fig. 24). At Lowell, Massachusetts, however, the majority of the housing units were boardinghouses, a provision which became standard for other mill towns of the Merrimack Valley. The Lowell system was also immensely influential elsewhere in New England, including Harrisville. Thus the Harris boardinghouse of 1852 (Fig. 44) is remarkably similar to the early brick boardinghouses on Dutton Street in Lowell (Fig. 33); and the Cheshire Mill's boardinghouse of 1851 (Fig. 45), although larger in size, also has its prototype in Lowell (Fig. 46). In view of the fact that Lowell no longer exists, the housing at Harrisville takes on special histori- cal importance.

FIGURE 44. *Harris boardinghouse, Harrisville, N.H., 1852.*

FIGURE 45. *Cheshire Mill's boardinghouse,*
Harrisville, N.H., 1851.

The core of Harrisville was built during the forty years between 1820 and 1860, and with the exception of the granite Cheshire Mill, it was all brick. Since Lowell was also largely brick, an obvious conclusion to draw would be that Harrisville was emulating Lowell. But the situation is more complicated than that. The use of brick in Harrisville does, of course, suggest a comparison with Lowell and there undoubtedly was a relationship. It is more than probable, however, that both Harrisville and Lowell drew their inspiration from a common source, the early Neoclassical architecture of New England during the first two decades of the nineteenth century. Under the leadership of Charles Bulfinch, some of the finest brick architecture in our nation's history appeared in Boston during this period.[66] From here the style spread throughout New England where it flourished for a quarter of a century in numerous local and regional variants, including the Monadnock region (Fig. 47).

But it was not just brick as a material which gave all these Neoclassical buildings in the Northeast a common character. It was brick used in a special way, with cleanly cut openings topped in most instances by stone lintels, with refined classical proportions in elegant but simple detail. What survives of the brickwork in Harrisville has a quality and consistency of architectural style which was ubiquitous throughout New England. Thus, the Milan Harris House (Fig. 48) in Harrisville has its counterpart in any of several lovely brick houses which are still to be found in neighboring towns (Fig. 47). At the same time, the boardinghouses of Harrisville (Fig. 45) like those in Lowell (Fig. 46) are comparable to the tall brick town houses on Beacon Hill (Fig. 53). Except for the greater elegance and refinement of detail of the Boston houses it is difficult to make meaningful distinctions between the industrial and the urban dwellings.

Because it was removed from the centers of culture, the architecture of Harrisville is folk architecture with a decided regional accent, and its quality is a product of time and place more than of creative genius. But it is serene, beautiful, and consistent, and it is eloquently expressive of a fascinating episode in our nation's early growth. Seen as a document of American history, the architecture of Harrisville portrays the life of a particular town, yet it is also a composite of early industrial America which has no surviving counterpart in this country. Through its heart runs the stream whose kinetic power once gave life to the machines and sustenance to the town. But the ponderous swish of the high-breast wheels and the steady muffled roaring of the turbines have long since given way to the quiet imperceptible hum of the transformers. Today, throughout our country, the machine tears away incessantly at nature, but in Harrisville the stream continues to flow as a perpetual reminder of those brief but exciting years when the machine and nature were working as one. Perhaps it is the persistent shadow of this organic relationship which still tempers the quality of life and form in Harrisville; it was certainly the relationship which once graced Lowell and, beyond that, England's Valley of the Stroud.

FIGURE 46. Workers' housing, Lowell, Mass., c. 1835.

FIGURE 47. Paul Harris House, Chesham, N.H., c. 1810.

FIGURE 48. Milan Harris House, Harrisville, N.H., 1850's.

The Corporate Style

The chaste Neoclassical style of early nineteenth-century New England, so beautifully preserved at Harrisville, reached its climax in the urban centers during the second decade of the century, and was superseded in the 1820's and '30's by the Greek Revival. In the Merrimack Valley, from Lowell to Manchester, however, and on into the more remote and smaller towns like Harrisville, this same Neoclassicism remained the architectural style right down to mid-century. The plain brick walls and stone lintels of Bulfinchian New England served both the practical needs of manufacturing and the refined but extremely conservative taste of the mill owners. Except for an increase in size, and a change from the monitor to the pitched roof in the mills, there is little to distinguish the mills and housing of mid-century from those built at Waltham in 1813. In the late 1830's, in Manchester, New Hampshire, for example, two identical mills for the Stark Company were built in a line along the banks of the canal. In 1844 the gap between them was filled in, thus making one building of very large dimensions. This ultimately became known as Stark Mill No. 1 (Fig. 49). In the final building the connecting unit was made to project on the façade as a central pavilion over which was placed an imposing pediment. Above this, in the center of the roof, was a large and handsomely proportioned classical cupola. Both the increase in size and the expanded ornamental treatment had now transformed the two earlier and simpler mills into a single unit of increased monumentality. At the same time, however, all the

FIGURE 49. *Stark Mill No. 1, Manchester, N.H., two mills built in late 1830's and joined in 1844.*

ingredients of the Federal style—the proportions, the materials, and the detailing—remained firmly in force.

At Lowell in 1846, two mills built earlier for the Hamilton Company were also transformed by a connecting unit into one large mill (Fig. 50). Here, as at Manchester, the new portion projected as a central pavilion and was crowned by a classical cupola. The following year, also at Lowell, the Merrimack Company went a step farther. Instead of combining older units to make one larger mill, the owners built a new mill planned from the beginning to be the largest and most advanced yet to appear in the city (Fig. 51). In spite of its gigantic size and improved technology, it was still cast in the familiar idiom of red brick and white painted wood, and it climaxed in a central pedimented pavilion and cupola.

As the mills became larger and more monumental, so too did the housing. The Lowell system of employing unmarried young women created a labor force which quickly outgrew the small early housing. To meet this, various companies, such as the Lawrence Company, incorporated in 1830, built large continuous front boardinghouses, three and a half stories high (Fig. 52). These newer houses were urban rather than rural in scale, and with their splendid brickwork, their clean stone linteled openings, and their towering parapeted chimneys, they were comparable in both quality and form to the long rows of town houses on Beacon Hill in Boston (Fig. 53).

FIGURE 50. *Hamilton Company, Lowell, Mass., two mills built in 1820's and joined in 1846.*

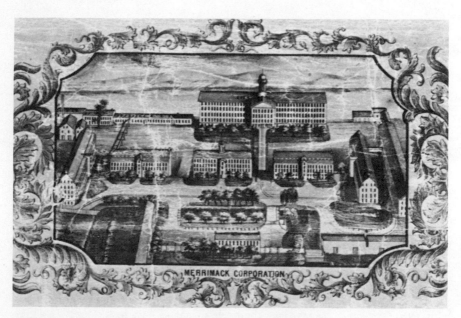

FIGURE 51. *Plant of the Merrimack Manufacturing Company, Lowell, Mass., c. 1850.*

FIGURE 52. *Lawrence Manufacturing Company, Lowell, Mass.,
general view of workers' housing, early 1830's.*

FIGURE 53. *Early nineteenth-century house
at Chestnut and Willow streets, Beacon Hill, Boston, Mass.*

FIGURE 54. *Merrimack Mill and boardinghouses,*
Lowell, Mass., 1847.

This type of boardinghouse functioned so well that even the Merrimack Company, to accommodate the additional workers necessary for its mammoth new mill, tore down half of the early houses on Dutton Street and put in their place one continuous block (Fig. 54). Known later as the New Block, it was the largest and last of the monumental Lowell boardinghouses to be built. This type of dwelling became standard in the later industrial communities of the Merrimack Valley and particularly fine examples were built across the canal from the Bay State Mills in Lawrence, Massachusetts (Fig. 55), and also in Manchester, New Hampshire (Fig. 56). Indeed, the coherence of these industrial communities set them apart for what they were, something new and unique on the New England scene. Although the architecture itself was clearly an overt and sympathetic adaptation of the Federal style, a style which was already outmoded elsewhere in New England, the elements were combined with a comprehensiveness and determination which gave these communities a character conspicuously different from that of the prevailing New England townscape. For practical reasons the style was simple and consistent; for reasons of taste it was rendered with care and grace. In every way it was a direct reflection of the technological, economic, and social aspirations of the corporations which brought it into being; and thus, as one historian has suggested, it might appropriately be called the "corporate style."[67]

The corporate style was the style of the manufacturing community, that is, the mills, utility buildings and housing. Around these working clusters

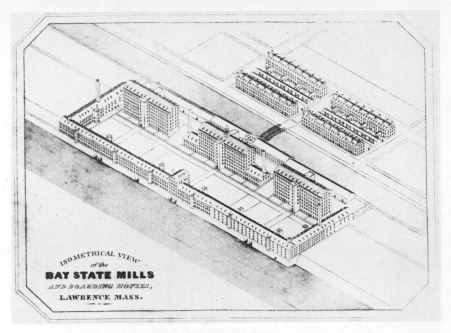

FIGURE 55. *Bay State Mills and workers' dormitories, Lawrence, Mass., isometrical view, 1846.*

FIGURE 56. *Houses of the Amoskeag Manufacturing Company, Manchester, N.H., c. 1845.*

FIGURE 57. *St. Anne's Church, Lowell, Mass., 1826.*

grew up the supporting community—the churches, public buildings and private houses. In these neighboring structures, less susceptible as they were to the constraints of corporate pragmatism, the changing tides of taste in American architecture were more directly felt. Reluctantly at first, but with increasing tempo, more aggressive and dynamic forms, consistent with emerging national attitudes, began to appear. At first the intrusions were sporadic and groping; almost always they were uncertain and frequently new forms were mixed with the old. As early as 1826, in Lowell, scarcely four years after the founding of the city, a church was completed in the Gothic style (Fig. 57). Funded by the directors of the Merrimack Company, and built in the Gothic style to satisfy the Episcopal persuasions of the company's original director, Kirk Boott, St. Anne's is a simple rectangular stone structure with pointed arch windows and entrance doors, and with a crenelated tower centered on the façade. In its conventional shape it was at once reminiscent of both the small medieval parish churches of England and the traditional New England meetinghouse, but it was Gothic nevertheless and built of stone. It was thus totally alien to the ordered red brick classicism of the corporate town. Perhaps because of this, and to keep it from upsetting the logic of the working community it-

FIGURE 58. *Milan Walter Harris House, Harrisville, N.H., c. 1852.*

self, it was placed in lonely isolation across the canal from the mill yard, on a narrow piece of land at the northeast corner of the complex (C, Fig. 28; C, Fig. 29).

In the more remote town of Harrisville, it took much longer to upset the classical tradition, and when the break did come, shortly after mid-century, it assumed a strange and amusing form. The Milan Walter Harris House, built by the eldest son of Milan Harris, is unlike all previous ones built by this family in that it is built of wood rather than brick (Fig. 58). Moreover, it is oriented in the manner of a Greek prostyle temple with its short end to the street. Four rectangular wooden posts with drastically distilled Doric capitals and detailing support what seems to be a steeply pitched pediment. But instead of the conventional triangle, formed in the typical Greek temple by the horizontal and raking cornices, the gable is open at the bottom and is framed at the eaves by a Gothic bargeboard. In addition, the windows are taller in proportion than the conventional Neoclassical windows found elsewhere in Harrisville and are crowned by Gothic hood moldings.

The presence of these Gothic forms in the otherwise ordered classical consistency of Lowell and Harrisville, was not an eccentricity of New England industrial towns. It represents rather the first intrusion into these remarkably coherent communities of the romantic attitudes which elsewhere in American architecture were already firmly established. Romanticism has been defined as "the endeavor, in the face of growing factual obstacles, to achieve, to retain, or to justify that illusioned view of the universe and of human life which is produced by an imaginative fusion of the familiar and the strange, the known and the unknown, the real and the ideal, the finite and the infinite, the material and the spiritual, the natural and the supernatural."[68] In an environment dominated by technology, where the real, the known, the familiar, the material were fundamental to life, the builders of the Milan Walter Harris House and St. Anne's were yearning for something around them that was not just good for business, not just practical, economical, efficient, plain. The growing interest in the picturesque touched even the most pragmatic hearts and the Gothic style, already an accepted idiom in certain segments of the American church community, was the most accessible picturesque style. To understand more fully how and why the Gothic style came to places like Lowell and Harrisville it is necessary now to examine the Gothic Revival movement itself.

CHAPTER III

The Early Gothic Revival

*I strive to revive not invent . . . yet how terribly do my
best efforts sink when tested by the scale of antient excellence.*

AUGUSTUS WELBY PUGIN

PART I

GOTHIC SURVIVAL
AND REVIVAL IN ENGLAND
1650–1800

The Gothic Style

The Gothic, used with such primitive charm at Lowell and Harrisville, was
the first picturesque style to challenge the classical taste of early nineteenth-century America. Appealing as it did to the stirring romanticism in
the new republic, it appeared in this country shortly before 1800, and by
mid-century Gothic buildings of all descriptions stood side by side with
Neoclassical buildings on the streets of American towns. Although the
Gothic never achieved the widespread national endorsement that the
Greek enjoyed, it actually began earlier, and by the 1840's had become a
full-fledged revival which posed a threat to the entrenched classical doctrine. When the Civil War broke out it had already begun to replace the
Greek and had opened the door for the proliferation of picturesque styles
which would mark the Romantic movement in American architecture during the second half of the century.

The Gothic style was the crowning achievement of Christian architecture during the Middle Ages. Characterized by the pointed arch and an
elaborate structural system of rib vaults and buttresses, it is a brilliant and
impassioned style in which complex volumes of space are enclosed within
a cage of stone and glass, all of it held aloft by the delicate opposition of
thrust and counterthrust. No style in the history of architecture is more
expressive of its internal dynamics. A profoundly organic style, the Gothic
seems fully capable of extension and growth, and it is precisely this quality
of being alive that ties it so closely to the world of nature itself, and made

FIGURE 59. *Cathedral of Notre Dame, Amiens, France, vault, thirteenth century.*

it so attractive to the romantic mind. Basically French in origin, the Gothic style assumed its first coherent form in the Île-de-France during the late twelfth century, and from there spread into all parts of Europe, including the British Isles. I have already discussed elsewhere certain aspects of the Gothic style in England, but only as it related to seventeenth-century colonial architecture.[1] The English Gothic, however, was also the primary source for the early Gothic Revival in America. We must therefore go back once more to the Gothic era itself and re-examine the original style in greater detail.

Gothic architecture began in England toward the end of the twelfth century, and the earliest English Gothic churches, such as Canterbury Cathedral and Westminster Abbey, have a decided French flavor. But very quickly the English developed special characteristics which clearly distinguished their work from that of the French. Their churches, for example, were much more rectilinear in plan. Whereas the French church culminated in a curved apse with similarly curved secondary chapels, the English church had a square end, and in its over-all plan the rectangle prevailed. Even the transepts became narrower in proportion and projected more prominently from the nave. Moreover, there were frequently two pairs of transepts instead of one, and this together with projecting

FIGURE 60. *Lincoln Cathedral, England,*
Angel Choir, vault, c. 1270.

side porches increased the number of rectangular connections. The effect
of extended space achieved at the east end was intensified by adding
auxiliary chapels. On the exterior, therefore, the church presented a long
descending profile toward the east end, and on the interior, the continuous
narrowing space provided a compelling visual force toward the altar, at
the same time that it made the most sacred ceremonial spaces seem far removed.

English churches were also lower than the French. Having greater emphasis on the horizontal, they lacked the soaring verticality of French
Gothic interiors, which was so eloquently articulated in the continuous
upward thrust of the clustered shafts. Vertical elements were generally
shortened in English Gothic, and often they were interrupted by strong horizontals at both the triforium and clerestory levels.

An equally distinctive characteristic of English Gothic is its tendency toward decoration, which occurs most conspicuously in the vaulting and
tracery. To the highly logical French system of structural ribs, which
crossed the center of the vault and thus formed a four-part bay (Fig. 59),
the English added secondary ribs (tiercerons). Intended primarily for decorative purposes, the tiercerons sprang from the piers and ran to the ridgepole between the diagonal ribs (Fig. 60), creating a splay effect which the

romantics of the nineteenth century were inclined to compare with the branches of a tree. To animate the vault surfaces even further, short tertiary ribs (liernes) were inserted between the main ribs and the tiercerons (Fig. 62). Although it could be argued that the tiercerons, because they ran from the spring to the ridge, performed a minor structural function, the liernes were entirely decorative. Accordingly, they could be placed in any position and made to run in any direction, thereby opening the way for an inexhaustible variety of rib patterns. Indeed, the most complex of the lierne vaults gained a fluidity not unlike that developed in the tracery, and thus enormously enhanced the effect of proliferation and growth. At the same time, however, they obscured the strong, clean articulation of structural forces, so superbly achieved in the pure four-part vaults of the French high Gothic. English love of linear complexity would reach its extreme, as we shall see, in the glorious fan vaults of the sixteenth century.

A final important characteristic which distinguishes English Gothic from French is the intensive use of the open wood-framed ceiling. Although the vast majority of the large English churches were vaulted, in the smaller churches the exact opposite was true. Using techniques ranging from conventional roof framing to the simple scissor truss, and on to the more complex forms of post and even hammer-beam trusses, the English parish churches, almost without exception, had wooden ceilings, not stone. Moreover, the numerous and relatively thin and attenuated structural members —the rafters, the tie beams, the struts, the posts, the purlins, and the braces—all made possible an even more compelling effect of interlace than did the tierceron and lierne vaults; and the British exploited this potential to the highest degree. The use of open framed ceilings is precisely what we would expect from a nation sufficiently skilled in wood construction to produce the fascinating half-timbered houses of the late Middle Ages. But in addition to this the British had a particular delight in decorative complexity. The framed ceiling in the small parish church not only was a logical solution to a straightforward structural problem, it also offered another opportunity for the development of interlocked forms, and to achieve this the British gave full play to the imagination in designing their roof trusses. Just as in the case of the lierne vaults, the specific configuration of the framing was as much effected by aesthetic as structural concerns, and in some of the more complex trusses, such as the hammer-beam, many of the members have no other purpose than decoration. Centuries later, the ingenious use of open framing, which made the English parish church so visually exciting, would become a major factor in the Gothic Revival.

As it was understood in the nineteenth century, the English Gothic was comprised of three distinct phases: the Early English, the Decorated, and the Perpendicular. The Early English style fell roughly between 1180 and 1240 and is a vigorous, even austere, mode characterized by tall thin pointed-arch windows (lancets) which are devoid of tracery. Where large windows were required they were achieved by grouping two or more lancets together. Moldings were richly carved with some of the primitive motifs from even earlier medieval periods. All surfaces were frequently broken up by numerous running arcades, sometimes set at more than one

FIGURE 61. *Salisbury Cathedral, England, from the northeast, 1225–50.*

level in depth; on other occasions they were enriched with diaper work. The use of a dark marble for colonnettes and ribs, to contrast with the lighter stone of the walls, was common. The climax of Early English may be seen in the great cathedral at Salisbury built in the second and third quarters of the thirteenth century (Fig. 61).

The Decorated phase ran from about 1240 to 1360 and can itself be divided into sub-phases: the Geometric, dating approximately between 1240 and 1300, and the Curvilinear, which spans the years 1300–60. It was during the Decorated period as a whole that the rich development of tracery and vaulting patterns first occurred. The treatment of wall surfaces quieted down and interest was focused instead on the linear and rhythmic possibilities of the structural members themselves, vaulting ribs, and tracery bars. In addition, a richer application of sculpture, particularly carvings of foliage, shifted emphasis from the primitive but vigorous forms of the early ornament to a fluid and graceful pattern of interweaving lines. Whereas tracery virtually never occurred in the early Gothic, during the Decorated period it became the crowning glory of the style, and made possible the full exploitation of the broad window, a feature which was one of

FIGURE 62. *Ely Cathedral, England,*
Lady Chapel, facing east, 1325–50.

the most distinctive characteristics of the English Gothic (Fig. 62). The expanded areas of glass were divided into multiple lights by slender vertical bars which flowered in the pointed-arch crowns as magnificent interlocks of tracery. During the Geometric phase this tracery was based on the geometry of simple curves as contained within the pointed arch and the circle. The east window of the angel choir at Lincoln Cathedral is typical (Fig. 63). Here, trefoil and quatrefoil motifs, together with an extensive use of cusps, are the primary elements.

During the Curvilinear phase of the Decorated period the sedate circle gave way to the undulating reverse curve. The tracery bars now became virtually alive, flowing into and growing out of one another in a continuous interlace. Even the pointed arch acquired new qualities of animation; the curves of the arch, rising from the spring on either side, reversed themselves at the haunch and tapered upward to a pinnacle-like crest. Known as an "ogee arch," it can be seen at the top of each of the towers of Westminster Abbey (Fig. 65). It was during the Curvilinear phase, too, that the lierne ribs became popular. Free of structural function, and therefore free to wander, they carried the qualities of interlace and movement to the structural crown of the church (Fig. 62).

The uninhibited delight in patterns of interlace which characterized the Gothic age reoccurs among the nineteenth-century revivalists. In 1844, for instance, the author of a fascinating article on "The Philosophy of Gothic Architecture" included an eloquent section on the formation of English Gothic tracery. While developing a concept which he called *"the unity of*

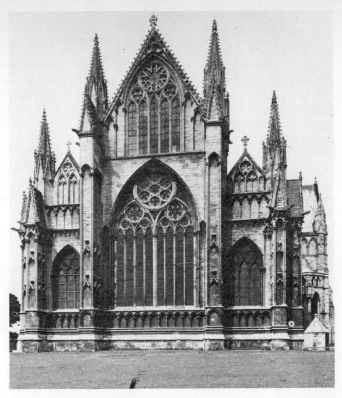

FIGURE 63. *Lincoln Cathedral, England, Angel Choir, east front, c. 1260.*

continuousness," he described the character of the Curvilinear tracery as follows: "All the trunks of the mullions, springing out of one base, rose up to a certain height and then shot themselves out into ramifications of the most intricate and delicate network, exhibiting a variety of combinations which baffles enumeration—the branches climbing and twisting one into the other in a maze full of entanglement, yet without confusion; and the whole composition, in its utmost licence and seeming extravagance of fancy, capable of being subjected to strict and inviolable laws of primary truth."[2]

Both the romantic and the genetic implications of this passage are clear. The language itself is sensuous in the extreme, using metaphors of proliferation and growth in its search for the "unity of continuousness." At the same time, the organic nature of the patterns is seen to have its origins in the "laws of primary truth," in other words in nature itself. The writer might have gone on to observe that the love of "climbing and twisting" which he recognizes as characteristic of the best English Gothic, has its roots deep in English culture itself, in the wild energy of the Anglo-Saxons and the early artistic outbursts of that energy in the fantastic illuminations of such early manuscripts as the Book of Kells.

The Perpendicular phase of the English Gothic was implicit in the Decorated phase. On the one hand it was a reasoned formalization of the ornamental richness of the earlier style, on the other it was a reassertion of both the innate verticality and the structural logic of the Gothic system. The proportions of all structural elements, including the tracery, were radically attenuated. The broad windows became even wider; and through the introduction of the depressed profile of the four-centered arch, they also became more expansive, pressing closely against the piers on either side, and pushing as far as possible into the vaults. The rising bars of the tracery were thinned and multiplied; cutting across them at widely spaced intervals, the horizontal bars subdivided the space into tall vertical panels, each topped by a small traceried arch. The piers, with their engaged colonnettes, rose unbroken from the floor to the spring of the vaults, where they then flared out in delicate tiercerons to form the fans; lierne ribs crossed the tiercerons horizontally at regular intervals to enclose tall vertical panels similar to those formed by the tracery in the windows. Carved naturalistic ornament became stylized, or gave way altogether to non-representational motifs, many of which derived from the tracery forms.

The Perpendicular style, as we shall see, would be rejected by the Ecclesiologists of the nineteenth century as debased and worldly. Nevertheless, this climactic phase of English Gothic was extremely attractive to some American Gothic Revivalists. King's College Chapel in Cambridge is a particularly expressive example (Fig. 64). Completed about 1515, this supremely beautiful building exhibits better than any other of its time the decorative and structural wonder of late English Gothic. Its walls are almost entirely of glass. Broad tall windows are crowned by four-centered arches, and divided by slender mullions into narrow vertical lights. Spreading from the slender piers, and shading each soaring window, are the chapel's magnificent fan vaults, their delicate ribs radiating like the stems of a fern in orderly splays to the crown.

Just as the unencumbered quatre-partite vaults of thirteenth-century France severely proclaim the logic of Gothic structure (Fig. 59), so the glorious fan vaults of sixteenth-century England sing of its eternal unfolding of parts. The thrusts and counterthrusts of the Gothic system are still there, subtly demonstrated in ribs of stone, but those same ribs seem also to be made of some living substance, and to multiply and grow in sheer ornamental delight. Nowhere are both the logic and the passion of Gothic architecture more vividly or gracefully combined.

Gothic and "Modern Gothick": The Early Gothic Revival in England

The English Perpendicular was the last flowering of the Gothic style. After the mid-sixteenth century the creative energy of the Gothic began to wane, and by 1600 it had all but lost its identity in the Renaissance-Gothic hybrids of the Elizabethan and Jacobean eras. We have already developed part of the story at this point and observed that one of the last buildings to descend in an unbroken line from the Gothic actually appeared in colonial America, in St. Luke's Church in Isle of Wight County, Virginia.[3] We have noted, too, that in England after 1600, the appearance of Inigo Jones on the architectural scene brought the Gothic to an end, and set the stage

FIGURE 64. King's College Chapel, Cambridge University,
England, interior toward altar, 1508–15.

FIGURE 65. *Westminister Abbey, London, England,*
west façade, designed by Christopher Wren, 1723,
executed by Nicholas Hawksmore, 1745.

for the English Renaissance.[4] We might expect, therefore, that we would
have seen the last of the Gothic until its revival in the late eighteenth century, but such is not the case. Buildings from the Gothic past were everywhere in England. Its venerable forms were rooted deeply in English tradition, and for doctrinal and other reasons it continued to assert itself. In
spite of Inigo Jones and the developing taste for classicism, shadows of the
hybrid Gothic of the late sixteenth century persisted, particularly in that
phase of early seventeenth-century domestic work which Summerson has
called "Artisan Mannerism."[5] Here Gothic forms stubbornly continued to
muddy the classical waters.

In church and collegiate architecture, where strong doctrinal traditions
prevailed, scattered examples of the more authentic forms of Gothic continued to be built. Even Christopher Wren, whose genius for the classical
idiom placed him at the very summit of the English Baroque, designed in
the Gothic when the occasion so required. His Tom Tower at Christ
Church, Oxford, built in 1681 is the earliest example; later ones include
several London churches, rebuilt after the fire of 1666, in which he used
varying forms of the Gothic.[6]

Wren actually disliked the Gothic, and his work in that style has a studied, controlled coolness which reflects his basically classical bias, but it is
competent Gothic, nevertheless, and was carried over into the eighteenth
century by Wren himself in what is perhaps the best-known and most historic of all English Gothic buildings, Westminster Abbey (Fig. 65). The
present west towers, which crown the façade, were not finished until 1745,

well after Wren's death in 1723; but they were, in fact, designed by Wren, in the last year of his life, and were carried out by his colleague Nicholas Hawksmoor.[7] Although these towers are basically Gothic in form and detail, it is a stiff classicized Gothic, all the fluidity of the style having been subdued by assertive projecting horizontal cornices, and by sharply delineated rectangular panels.

The Gothic of Wren and his followers, which came to an end with Hawksmoor, was highly individual work in which the medieval forms were subordinate to larger design intentions. It was always conceived in solid architectural terms with strong classical overtones and therefore was Gothic more in name than in spirit. Strong and coherent, it stands in marked contrast to the more decorative version used by others during the first half of the eighteenth century. Of these the arch-Palladian, William Kent, was the most unexpected. A close associate of Lord Burlington, and the architect of Holkham Hall,[8] Kent was even more steeped in classical doctrine than Wren himself; and his Gothic designs are very different from those of Wren. In his "modern Gothick," as it was called in the eighteenth century, the forms tend to be understood as applied ornament rather than as integrated parts of a coherent architectural system, and it thus has something of the quality of a pastiche.[9] At the same time, Kent went even further than Wren and Hawksmoor in his efforts to rework the Gothic elements into equivalents of classical ones.

Kent's efforts to classicize the Gothic made the style more palatable to a rigidly classical generation, and at the same time paved the way for the Gothic adventure of Batty Langley. Best-known for his architectural handbooks, Langley did much to disseminate the classical doctrine to all levels of British and colonial society. Of particular interest here, however, is a book that he devoted to the Gothic style. It was published in 1742, and its title, *Gothic Architecture improved by Rules of Proportions,* tells us much about the author's intentions. In this work Langley makes a serious effort to redesign Gothic columns and capitals into five different systems which were the equivalents of the five classical orders. On the other hand, he makes no attempt to deal with Gothic either in theoretical or in archaeological terms. As a result, the discussion becomes an essay on architectural fashion, in which Gothic motifs are presented as promising alternatives to other decorative modes, such as the Chinese and the Rococo, which were popular at the time.

Clearly, neither the Gothic of Wren and his circle nor that of Kent and Langley can be regarded as a true revival. The former was too transmuted by the imagination of powerful creative architects to be Gothic in more than the most obvious shape and characteristics. Moreover, because it was Gothic as a concession to a stubborn and tradition-minded patronage, church and university, it was still being fed, however remotely, by the main stream of the Gothic itself. It was still close to its antecedents and was therefore more a survival than a revival. The Gothic of Kent and Langley followed almost immediately that of Wren and Hawksmoor, yet in character differed even more conspicuously from its medieval forebears. Even though many of its parts were derived from the Gothic, it was too

FIGURE 66. *Horace Walpole, Strawberry Hill,
Twickenham, England, from the gardens, 1749–76.*

obsessively ornamental, too capricious, too impoverished by classical pretensions to be more than tenuously related to the Gothic itself. In the genetic sense, therefore, it is difficult to see it as a true revival form. Nevertheless, each in its time kept the Gothic alive and provided an essential if not continuous linkage between the medieval past and the first important architectural work of the Gothic Revival, Horace Walpole's Strawberry Hill.

Strawberry Hill

Strawberry Hill is a delight; it was also seriously conceived and is generally regarded as the opening essay of the Gothic Revival in architecture. It has also been shown to be an important moment in the formation of the picturesque.[10] Above all, it is an intensely personal building, as personal indeed as Jefferson's Monticello, and became in the end one of the most famous and influential works of the eighteenth century.

Horace Walpole was a dilettante who devoted what could have been a life of leisure to responsible participation in the cultural affairs of his time.[11] Although his major creative activity was writing, he was also an antiquarian and art critic with a special curiosity about the medieval past. This unusual taste led him to build his own Gothic castle at Strawberry Hill. By English eighteenth-century standards Walpole was not an architect, and in terms of the mechanics of building he did not design Strawberry Hill.[12] Yet the idea was his, and he was so closely identified with the building through every stage of its development, and provided so much of the

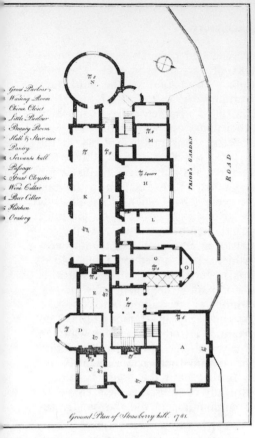

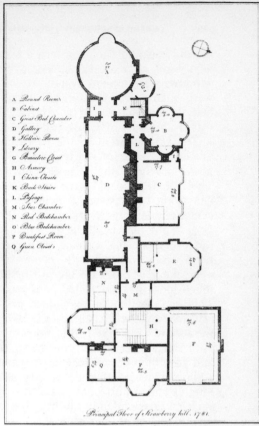

Left plan legend:
. Great Parlour
. Waiting Room
. China Closet
. Little Parlour
. Beauty Room
. Hall & Stair-case
. Pantry
. Servants hall
. Passage
. Great Cloyster
. Wine Cellar
. Beer Cellar
. Kitchen
. Oratory

Ground Plan of Strawberry hill. 1781.

Right plan legend:
A. Round Room
B. Cabinet
C. Great Bed Chamber
D. Gallery
E. Holbein Room
F. Library
G. Beaudere Closet
H. Armory
I. China Closets
K. Back Stairs
L. Passage
M. Star Chamber
N. Red Bedchamber
O. Blue Bedchamber
P. Breakfast Room
Q. Green Closets

Principal Floor of Strawberry hill. 1781.

FIGURE 67. *Horace Walpole. Strawberry Hill, Twickenham, England, ground plan, 1749–76.*

FIGURE 68. *Horace Walpole. Strawberry Hill, Twickenham, England, plan of the principal floor, 1749–76.*

thinking which produced it, that it was without question the product of his creative imagination.

Walpole had leased the property at Strawberry Hill in 1747 as a country retreat from which he could escape the growing pressures of London.[13] The site was near Twickenham, in a lovely rural setting on the Thames, and on it was a small, unpretentious cottage, which stood on a gentle rise looking across "enameled meadows" to the river. In every way the location was suited to Walpole's lifestyle and when the lease ran out in 1749 he bought the place. Shortly thereafter he decided to rebuild the cottage— and to do so in the Gothic style.

The eastern end of the house was finished first and is seen in the plan (Fig. 67B, C, D, E, F) and at the center in Figure 66. The part facing the garden (Fig. 67C, D, E) is that which incorporates the fabric of the original cottage. The shape and character of the old building, however, have been completely obliterated by Walpole's alterations. Where the original house had presented a rambling asymmetrical front to the garden, Walpole provided a symmetrical one by balancing the windows and by adding a central octagonal pavilion (Fig. 67D). Along with this, he transformed the old irregular roof line into a level crenelated parapet. The new chimneys were all medieval clustered stacks of various groupings. The new windows were topped by pointed or ogee arches; some on the third floor were quatrefoil. This section of the building, the one finished first, thus had the appearance of a carefully controlled symmetrical design which was Gothic only by virtue of certain rather flimsy applied details.

The first addition to the renovated cottage was made in 1754 at the northeast corner of the building (Fig. 67A, B). The east façade of this new block faced the Thames, and here there are hints of things to come. The river front could have been made symmetrical, to relate it to the garden front, but instead it included a projecting bay which is slightly off-center and is only two rather than three stories high; above it, on the third floor of the new block, is a vertically mullioned oriel window. At the top the level crenelated cornice of the garden front gives way to a higher parapet which is crowned in the center by a high Flemish stepped gable. Moreover, the new block on the north side is larger than that on the south, is much more heavily scaled, and has a different arrangement of windows. This new section of the house accommodated two important rooms, a refectory on the first floor (Fig. 67A), and Walpole's famous library on the second (Fig. 68F). But most important, it introduced a block which in both size and character contrasted sharply with the austere south section and gave the over-all scheme a dynamic, asymmetrical arrangement. Later additions carried this asymmetry even further until the house became a long extended horizontal mass of dynamically composed diverse elements, each more confidently Gothic, and all culminating in the thoroughly romantic towers at the west end.

The Gothic of Strawberry Hill

Walpole's use of the Gothic at Strawberry Hill not only enhances its importance in the development of the picturesque, but it also makes the building a central monument in the Gothic Revival in England. Although the eighteenth-century Gothic buildings before Strawberry Hill are of considerable interest, there was not one in which the Gothic forms were derived from specific Gothic sources. To understand the importance of this, however, we must first examine the concept of revivalism, particularly as it relates to the changing attitudes toward architecture which characterize the eighteenth century.

The idea of reviving architectural styles from the past proceeds from the assumption that those styles have been sufficiently studied and defined to make possible useful distinctions between them. Not until each can be shown, with something approaching precision, to have a life of its own can it be brought into a meaningful relationship with life in the present. This was made possible in the eighteenth century with the advent of the science of archaeology. A means of studying the past, archaeology applied methodical techniques of classification and evaluation to specific artifacts and historical data, and it is now recognized as one of the most significant contributions of the Age of Reason. The systematic efforts of the eighteenth-century archaeologists were first directed toward the classical world, and

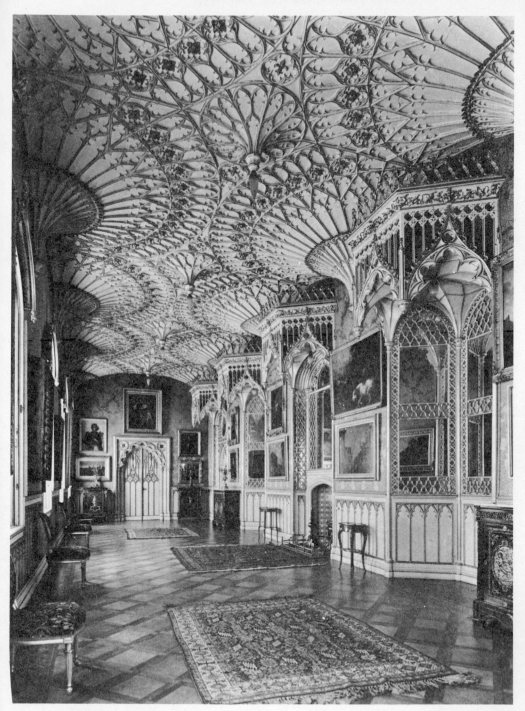

FIGURE 69. *Horace Walpole. Strawberry Hill,*
Twickenham, England,
Long Gallery, 1749–76.
(Copyright *Country Life*)

out of them came the Neoclassical movement.[14] But as the cultures of ancient Greece and Rome became better known, curiosity about other segments of history was aroused. English antiquarians in particular began to discover that their own medieval past was far more than a period of darkness. Moreover, as the facts began to accumulate, life in the Middle Ages acquired a reality with which men could identify, and to knowledge was added nostalgia, longing, and moral certainty. To sustain their romantic vision of medieval life they re-created medieval architecture in their personal surroundings, and by the second half of the eighteenth century a few books and articles appeared on the subject of Gothic architecture.[15]

Walpole was among the foremost of his contemporaries who saw the Gothic style with perceptive eyes. His enthusiasm for the Middle Ages set him clearly apart from persons having the traditional attitude, which was best exemplified by Sir Henry Wotton, who regarded the pointed arch as "natural imbecility" and the Gothic era as a "barbarous age." To eighteenth-century antiquarians like Walpole, however, the Middle Ages constituted both a fascinating and an important part of English heritage. For Walpole in particular, the Gothic had very special visual qualities which fed his own romantic notions of the era. The intricacies and irregularities of the style, unfettered by classical dogma, best suited that independent spirit which brought him from London to Strawberry Hill in the first place, and in his own words he built his house in the Gothic style "to please my own taste, and in some degree to realize my own visions."[16]

These visions became reality for Walpole at Strawberry Hill. Unlike the applied Gothicism of other eighteenth-century architects, Walpole's Gothic gained substance from the fact that it was derived from specific Gothic sources. Numerous illustrated books in Walpole's library provided the models: tombs from Westminster and Canterbury supplied motifs for the chimney piece in the library itself; one of the aisles from Henry VII's Chapel yielded details for the ceiling of the Gallery (Fig. 69); and the York chapterhouse was the source for the design of the ceiling of the apsidal room known as the Tribune. All of these Gothic features had a solid authenticity unmatched in anything that had been done in this style before. This Gothic character, which developed over a period of thirty years, was the work of Walpole and a group of special friends to whom he referred as the "Committee."[17] The searching antiquarianism with which they prowled the byways of the Gothic, both in pictorial sources and through their living experience with actual medieval buildings, only sharpened their identification with the Middle Ages. This total involvement of Walpole and his circle produced Strawberry Hill, and Strawberry Hill, in turn, led Walpole to write The Castle of Otranto, the first "Gothic novel" of the eighteenth century.

Strawberry Hill is a Gothic building precisely because it seeks to re-create the romantic visions of the era which Walpole and his friends shared, and to do so through authentic Gothic imagery. It is not, however, Gothic architecture. With all its shadowed "gloomth,"[18] narrow passages, stained-glass windows, and ribbed vaults, there is not a single instance of Gothic structure in the building. The lifeblood of Gothic architecture is the poised thrust and counterthrust contained within its stone structural system. The vaults of Strawberry Hill are wood and plaster, as devoid of that deep organic vitality which is the miracle of the Gothic as the make-believe of a stage set; and in a very real sense Strawberry Hill *is* a stage set. It was meant to create a special kind of environment, to accommodate the taste and vision of the owner. It does so with imagination and vivacity in purely visual terms, and is therefore the epitome of the picturesque.

Strawberry Hill
and the Picturesque Concept of Irregularity

The asymmetry of Strawberry Hill, which after a tentative beginning became a dominating feature of its design, also made the building seminal in the development of the picturesque in architecture; for of all the qualities of the picturesque, irregularity was the most fundamental, and in architecture it was asymmetry in plan, massing, and profile which produced the greatest effect of irregularity and provided the greatest contrast between the picturesque and classical design.

Symmetry is an obvious and static balance achieved by reciprocal correspondence of parts left and right around a central axis; asymmetry is an occult and dynamic balance arrived at through irregular distribution of weights and forces around an off-center fulcrum. It is a point of considerable historical importance that as a category of order, symmetry, with one major exception,[19] remained an overriding principle of Western architecture from ancient times through most of the eighteenth century. Even in periods such as the Middle Ages and the Baroque, when so many other qualities of the picturesque prevailed, the plan and the general massing of buildings were strictly organized around a central axis.

The first significant break with this deeply rooted condition seems to have been made not by Walpole but by the English Baroque architect Sir John Vanbrugh.[20] A leading figure in the circle of Wren, and designer of Blenheim Palace, perhaps the most aggressive and dynamic building of the English Baroque, Vanbrugh was a brilliant, urbane figure whose Flemish ancestry and natural talents made him one of the most colorful and creative personalities of his time. During the formative period of the picturesque concept, it was he who first called attention to the kinship between landscape gardening and painting, and it was also he who, in his own country house at Greenwich (Fig. 70), made the first clear gesture toward the picturesque in architecture. The original house, built shortly after 1717, was a symmetrical building. On the other hand it was anything but classical in form. The central motif was a round fortress-like tower with a corbeled top and conical roof; flanking it left and right were two tall square corner towers, also corbeled but with crenelated tops. Although the style was Romanesque rather than Gothic, the effect was of a medieval fortress and was probably inspired by Vanbrugh's knowledge of Italian stage scenery. Indeed, Vanbrugh was a distinguished dramatist as well as an architect and it may have been this, together with his own passionate nature, which engendered his romantic conception. In the development of the picturesque, however, the most important aspect of Vanbrugh's castle was not its medieval character, but the additions which he made shortly

FIGURE 70. *Sir John Vanbrugh. Vanbrugh Castle,*
Greenwich, England, 1717–19.
(Copyright *Country Life*)

after his marriage in 1719. These transformed the compact original house into a rambling asymmetrical scheme (Fig. 71).

Whatever influence Vanbrugh's rebellious asymmetrical plan might have had in England was at once suppressed by the powerful insurgence of the Palladian movement. Even in the Gothic designs of Wren, Hawksmoor, and Kent, symmetry still prevailed and it was not until mid-century, when Walpole built Strawberry Hill, that the idea of asymmetry appeared again. Since Walpole was not an architect he was less constrained by professional logic than men like Vanbrugh and Hawksmoor, and more inspired by the varied forces of romanticism already developing in England. Much is known about why he designed in the Gothic, but there is also good evidence that he shared a romantic interest in the exotic styles of far away places. As early as 1750 he wrote to Sir Horace Mann that he was "almost as fond of Sharawadgi or Chinese want of symmetry in buildings, as in grounds and gardens."[21] Walpole expressed this taste for asymmetrical form at Strawberry Hill by 1754, and of more importance, he was the first to make the connection between architecture and the picturesque gardens, where the principle of irregularity was already well established. Although Vanbrugh Castle was prophetic, it was an isolated eccentricity. Strawberry Hill, on the other hand, was decisive and influential and marked the beginning of the picturesque styles in architecture.

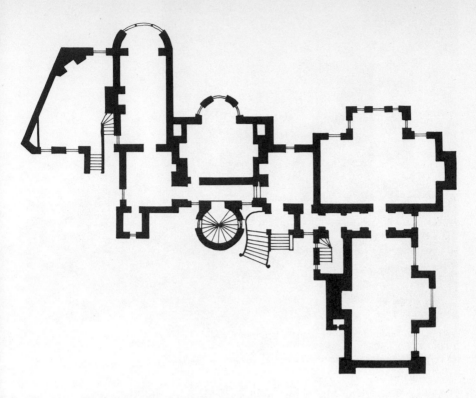

FIGURE 71. *Sir John Vanbrugh. Vanbrugh Castle, Greenwich, England, plan, 1717–19.*

Richard Payne Knight and Downton Castle

Although the actual number of houses which were directly touched by Strawberry Hill was not very great, it was one of the most famous houses of its day, and its asymmetrical plan, irregular outline, and crenelated towers were repeated in all major Gothic works that followed. Of these, two in particular demand our attention: Downton Castle, the country house of Richard Payne Knight, and the sensational Fonthill Abbey, built by James Wyatt for the romantic recluse William Beckford.

We have already encountered Richard Payne Knight as a major contributor to the philosophical definition of the picturesque.[22] He began building Downton Castle (Fig. 72), near Ludlow, in 1774 and when completed in 1778 it was the visual embodiment of his expressed belief that "houses should be irregular where all the accompaniments are irregular."[23] Like Strawberry Hill, the building is completely asymmetrical and contrasting towers are major features of the design. Unlike Strawberry Hill, which achieved its asymmetry through additions over a period of time, Downton was planned from the beginning as an irregular building. The architectural effect is thus more coherent at the same time that it is more richly varied.

FIGURE 72. *Richard Payne Knight. Downton Castle, Ludlow, England, 1774–78.* (Copyright *Country Life*)

Yet with all its architectonic medieval character, the primary source for Downton Castle was not actual buildings of wood and stone but buildings constructed of paint on artist's canvas. Writing many years after the completion of Downton, Knight tells us that "the best style for irregular and picturesque houses, which can now be adopted, is that mixed style, which characterizes the buildings of Claude and Poussin,"[24] and it is precisely those fortress-like towered buildings which cling to hillsides in the paintings of those artists which provided the inspiration for Downton Castle. Even its setting—a ridge above Downton Vale—seems to have been chosen with pictorial values in mind.

That Knight saw Downton in visual rather than architectural terms is borne out by yet another important fact. Although the exterior is indeed a solidly Gothic form, the interior is entirely Neoclassical: some of the rooms are Roman in origin, others are more elegantly Adamesque. In other words, Downton Castle is not comprehensively Gothic but is rather a mixture of classic and romantic forms in a manner and to a degree supremely characteristic of the rapidly growing eclectic attitude of the late eighteenth century. It was not a building designed by an architect as a coherent work of architecture; it was a building designed by a poet and philosopher as a demonstration of aesthetic principle. For his house in the country, where the irregularities of nature were receptive to the irregularities of building style, Knight used picturesque forms on the exterior; to preserve his personal taste for "neatness, freshness, lightness, symmetry, regularity, uniformity and propriety," he conceived the living spaces in the classical mode. It did not bother Knight and his friends that the interior

FIGURE 73. *James Wyatt. Fonthill Abbey,*
Wiltshire, England, southwest view, 1796 onward.

did not relate in style to the exterior. Indeed, he delighted in the contradiction, and thought that he had handled it very well indeed. Eclecticism in
architecture is the free use of various styles from the past and Downton
Castle is the product of eclecticism in its more overt form. The building
reflects the prodigious scholarship of the late eighteenth century and the ex-
perimentation with architectural style that followed from it. As disciplined
inquiry gave positive shape to various cultures of the past, the particulars
of their architectural styles began to emerge with clarity. The individual
builder, therefore, could now pick and choose one or several styles according to his taste and interest or even the current fashion. Walpole's eclecticism was entirely within the Gothic mode and catered to his romantic notions about the Middle Ages. Knight's eclecticism, in response to the
widening reach of eighteenth-century aesthetics and to his own direct involvement in the discourse about the Picturesque, was more comprehensive and less emotional. Downton Castle, therefore, was as much a
statement about the picturesque as it was an exercise in the Gothic style.

Fonthill Abbey

Fonthill Abbey, built in Wiltshire two decades after Downton Castle and
almost fifty years after Strawberry Hill, was a wholly different kind of
building. It was completely Gothic inside and out, although in a very personal and fantastic way, and it was designed by one of the foremost architects working in England at the turn of the nineteenth century. Conceived
in 1795 as a garden ruin, it quickly developed into a full-fledged archi-

tectural spectacular, sufficiently sensational in both size and character to accommodate the bizarre lifestyle of the willful and eccentric William Beckford for whom it was built (Fig. 73). James Wyatt, the architect, was one of the leading figures in the Neoclassical movement in England, but with the versatility that characterized so many men of the late eighteenth century he was quite capable of performing in other styles as well. Already, for example, he had designed a delightful Gothic house, the Lee Priory, which was sufficiently authentic in its medievalism to gain the approbation of Walpole.[25]

Wyatt brought to Fonthill Abbey what had been lacking at both Strawberry Hill and Downton Castle, a knowledge of Gothic architecture which, if not strictly archaeological, was at least strengthened by the insights and skills of the professional architect. In spite of its powerful elements of fantasy, Fonthill Abbey is a more coherent building than either Strawberry Hill or Downton. It was conceived from the beginnning in the Gothic style and was rendered with a more sensitive, more professional feeling for the true sculptural qualities of Gothic detail. Structurally, however, the building was no more Gothic than its predecessors. Although its walls were masonry, its vaults and many details were still executed in wood and plaster. So inadequate was the structure, in fact, that the main tower blew down during a storm in 1800. It was replaced by a second and more spectacular one 278 feet high, and in 1825 this, too, collapsed because of faulty construction.

In a sense the flimsy construction of Fonthill Abbey was indicative of its whole purpose, for it was in every way a mammoth stage set, designed with no other intent than to sustain the bizarre medieval illusions of Beckford. At the same time it offered Wyatt a superb opportunity to indulge his own Gothic enthusiasms. Previously, he had done some restoration work at Salisbury Cathedral, which lies only twelve miles away from Fonthill, and undoubtedly the soaring central tower of the Abbey was a deliberate emulation of the magnificent central tower of the Cathedral (see Fig. 61). As for Fonthill's cruciform plan, although irregular in its four arms, it was more ecclesiastical than domestic in origin. Fonthill was visually conceived and like Downton was the very essence of the picturesque. But it was also a more advanced and competent expression of the Gothic style than anything built up to that time and brought to a climax the first picturesque phase of the Gothic Revival. And, finally, it brings us to that moment in time when the Gothic first made its appearance in the United States.

THE EARLY GOTHIC REVIVAL
CHURCH
IN THE UNITED STATES
1790–1840

The Early Gothic Revival in the United States:
Trinity Parish, New York

The Gothic style of the Middle Ages was originally conceived for the church, and even though it became an international style and was used for civic and domestic buildings, it remained fundamentally an ecclesiastical one. Yet with few exceptions the early Gothic Revival in England, beginning with Strawberry Hill, was a domestic style which evolved ultimately as part of the Picturesque movement. The first phase of the Gothic Revival in the United States was just the opposite. With a few interesting exceptions, it occurred primarily in public buildings, such as the Bank of Philadelphia, designed by Benjamin Latrobe in 1807, and the Masonic Hall, also in Philadelphia, designed the following year by William Strickland, a student of Latrobe. The earliest and major thrust, however, came in churches, and for a number of important reasons. We have already noted that the Gothic Revival in England began among a small group of extremely wealthy men of the intelligentsia, and in a purely aesthetic and philosophical climate in which the church played no role whatsoever. In America the introduction of the Gothic style was associated with a period of notable expansion in the church, an expansion stimulated in part by the new religious freedom granted by the Constitution, in part by the growth of the country at large. Moreover, during the first two decades of the nineteenth century the Episcopal and Roman Catholic faiths in particular enjoyed a period of consolidation and growth which resulted in a substantial number of new churches. As we have already seen, not all of them were Gothic,[26] but an increasing number of them were, and it was via these churches that the style first made its way into American architecture.

At the turn of the nineteenth century, one of the most venerable parishes of the Episcopal Church in America was Trinity Parish in New York City; in the development of the Gothic Revival it was also one of the most influential, for in 1839 it began Richard Upjohn's Trinity Church, which proved to be a pivotal building of the movement. This famous American landmark still stands at the head of Wall Street amidst the skyscrapers of lower Manhattan, and it will be considered in detail in our next chapter. Upjohn's design, however, was preceded in the parish, and on the same site, by two earlier churches of the same dedication, both of which

FIGURE 74. *First Trinity Church, New York, 1698.*

FIGURE 75. *Second Trinity Church, New York, 1788–90.*

FIGURE *76. Batty Langley.* "An Umbrello
for the Centre or Intersection of Walks."

were also Gothic. The first of these (Fig. 74)[27] was a simple parish church
not unlike St. Luke's in Isle of Wight County, Virginia.[28] Like its counterpart in the Tidewater, therefore, it carried over into the eighteenth century
a thread of the early colonial Gothic. This building was destroyed by fire in
1776 but was not replaced until after the Revolution. The life of the second church thus began at precisely the moment when this country was
born as an independent nation. The building was begun in 1788 and was
finished in 1790. It was thus under construction, in 1789, when George
Washington was inaugurated in New York City as the first President of the
United States; moreover, in that same year the Protestant Episcopal
Church in America was first united in a General Convention.

This second Trinity Church (Fig. 75) was also Gothic, but between it
and the earlier church stood nearly a century of architecture in the Wren-
Gibbs tradition. This long period of classical hegemony brought to an end
any architecture of direct descent from medieval Gothic, a line that had
produced a handful of Gothic churches in seventeenth-century America.
The reappearance of the style in second Trinity, therefore, must make it
one of the earliest churches in America to reach back to the Gothic as a
style appropriate to church architecture. Considering the fiercely classical
disposition of the architectural climate into which it came, this in itself is
remarkable, and makes one wonder about the forces which motivated the
decision to make it Gothic. What seems most likely is that Trinity was a
conservative parish, and that having always worshipped in a Gothic
church it was determined to carry on in the same style. Within the history
of this particular parish, therefore, the second Trinity Church maintained

FIGURE 77. *Benjamin Latrobe. Gothic design for the Baltimore Cathedral, 1805.*

an unbroken line of Gothic buildings—probably the only one of its kind in America. From the colonial building, which was a survival of the late English Gothic itself, down to Upjohn's Gothic Revival church, built during the 1840's, the churches of Trinity parish were Gothic.

The second Trinity Church was a typical early Gothic building.[29] It had all the characteristics of a conventional Wren-Gibbs type church, being a simple rectangular block topped by a pitched roof and fronted by a central tower and spire. The parapet of the tower, however, had Gothic corner pinnacles and Gothic details, the tower windows were Gothic, and the semicircular porch was carried on slender Gothic colonnettes which were crowned by a Gothic parapet and pinnacles. The result was an uneasy union of a traditional colonial church and a few simple Gothic details, some of which seem to have been inspired by Batty Langley (Fig. 76).

The First Gothic Churches
in the United States:
Benjamin Latrobe

Following second Trinity in New York the first major period of Gothic church construction in the United States began shortly after the turn of the nineteenth century. A prelude to this was the alternate scheme for the Baltimore Cathedral which Benjamin Latrobe submitted in 1805 (Fig. 77). As we have already seen, the authorities of the diocese preferred Latrobe's

FIGURE 78. *Benjamin Latrobe. Christ Church,*
Washington, D.C., 1808.

second, or Roman, design, and this is the one that was built.[30] Nevertheless, Latrobe's rejected proposal did represent a Gothic scheme for an American building by a European-trained professional architect. Latrobe brought with him from Europe the eclectic attitudes of the late eighteenth century, and when he made the designs for the Cathedral he had already carried out one Gothic scheme in Sedgeley, a house in Philadelphia. This was in 1799, at the same time that he was working on his supremely classical Bank of Pennsylvania (we will consider the house further in another context). Later, as we shall see, Latrobe also did two small churches and a bank in Gothic, but he was never at home with this style. The logic of Gothic structure is in the interplay of the rib vaults and their supporting buttresses. For Latrobe the heart of structure was the bearing wall and the

FIGURE 79. *Maximilian Godefroy. St. Mary's Chapel,*
Baltimore, Md., 1806.

continuous surfaces of the spherical or cylindrical vault. This is superbly
demonstrated in his Gothic proposal for the Baltimore Cathedral, where
the windows, instead of being spaces created by piers, ribs, and tracery, are
holes cut into the wall. Indeed, they differ from those of the Roman design
only in being pointed at the top rather than round. The emphasis, therefore, is on static geometry rather than on the dynamic containment of opposing forces. On the other hand, Latrobe did not attempt to turn his
Gothic forms into equivalents of classical ones. He worked faithfully with
the basic Gothic shapes but in putting them together he was unable to forsake his own sense of structure and form. His use of the Gothic in
America, therefore, exactly matches that of Wren and Hawksmoor a century earlier in England.

This is best demonstrated in the first of his two small Gothic churches,
Christ Church in Washington, D.C. (Fig. 78), which is the only one of
Latrobe's Gothic designs which still stands in anything like its original
form.[31] Although it is smaller than the Cathedral, it is more convincing as
a Gothic design. Its massing and proportions are more authoritative, and
it lacks altogether the classicized flimsiness of the Batty Langley type. In
its austerity, Latrobe's Gothic might seem to compare favorably with the
early English lancet form of the style. But even the simplest English lancet
window is relieved by a hood molding, while Latrobe's are not. Instead,

they are cut sharply into the wall, so that the emphasis is placed on the integrity of the wall rather than on the windows as a coherent part of a Gothic structural system. It is this more than anything else which relates the building to Latrobe's Neoclassical work and makes it a rationalized form of the medieval style from which all fluidity and passion have been removed. Christ Church is a strong coherent little building, nevertheless, by one of the most talented architects of this time, and it stands conspicuously apart from the other more decoratively conceived Gothic works of the period.

Early Gothic Flimsies

In St. Mary's Chapel, built in Baltimore in 1806, the Gothic appears in a much more classicized form than that employed by Latrobe. This small church was designed by Maximilian Godefroy for a Catholic educational institution, St. Mary's College. Godefroy was a French ex-army officer who came to this country in 1805 to assume the position of professor of fine arts at St. Mary's. He was also a trained architect, although of considerably less distinction than Latrobe, but like Latrobe he was a committed Neoclassicist, and his Unitarian Church in Baltimore (1817–18) still remains as one of the most rationally conceived buildings of the period. St. Mary's Chapel (Fig. 79), which was built in medieval style obviously to satisfy a religious preference, is a curious building, as much Roman triumphal arch as Gothic chapel. Its symmetrical façade, with central door and balancing niches on either side, has a full entablature and parapet with gothicized engaged Doric columns at the corners. In its obvious classical bias it is far less architectonic than Latrobe's design for Christ Church and is strongly reminiscent of the classicized Gothic of Batty Langley.

Several Gothic churches also appeared in New England during the first decades of the nineteenth century, all of them similar in their flimsiness and stylistic uncertainties, and thus all equally different from Latrobe's more architectonic solution at Christ Church. Of these, the earliest and most hesitant was Bulfinch's Federal Street Church of 1809 (Fig. 80). Designed for his friend William Ellery Channing, who came to the Federal Street ministry in 1803, the church must have been made Gothic at Channing's request. Surely it could not have been because of Bulfinch's interest in the Middle Ages; nor could the decision have been motivated by religious preference. The church, after all, was Congregational in the heart of Federal Boston, and with the liberal Channing in the pulpit it was already leaning toward Unitarianism. It is tempting to surmise that it was Channing's personal romantic inclinations, manifest in his enthusiasm for the writings of Wordsworth, Coleridge, and Rousseau, which prompted the choice of a romantic style for his new church. In any case, as a Gothic building, Federal Street Church was a hopeless failure. Bulfinch was too much a chaste, committed Neoclassicist to think in anything other than the Wren-Gibbs formula. The building itself was a pure traditional meetinghouse with the detailing carried out in the flimsiest kind of applied Gothic ornament. Of all Bulfinch's works it is the most groping and insecure, but it was Gothic nevertheless and presaged things to come.

FIGURE 80. *Charles Bulfinch. Federal Street Church,*
Boston, Mass., 1809.

Much more interesting, and more directly related to the second Trinity
Church in New York, is John Holden Green's St. John's Church (now St.
John's Cathedral) in Providence, Rhode Island (Fig. 81). With this building, which was finished in 1810, we return to the fold of the Episcopal
Church and its growing awareness of the appropriateness of the Gothic
style to serve its traditional ends. The main form of Green's building is still
a conventional Wren-Gibbs type, consisting of a main rectangular block
fronted by a projecting central pavilion, above which rises a two-stage rectangular tower. A level classical cornice is carried around the entire building, and encloses a classical pediment above the central pavilion. Except
for the second stage of the tower, which is wood, the building is a local
Smithfield stone laid in a smooth-faced random ashlar with brown stone
quoins at the corners. In texture and color, therefore, St. John's is a ro-

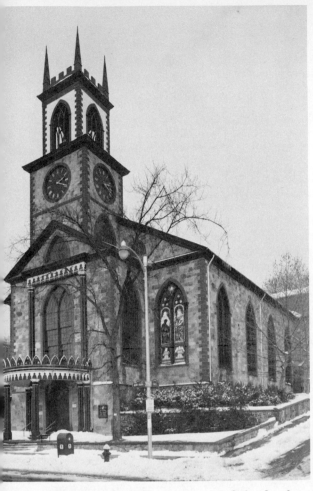

FIGURE 81. *John Holden Green. St. John's Church, Providence, R.I., 1810.*

FIGURE 82. *John Holden Green. St. John's Church, Providence, R.I., entrance portico, 1810.*

mantic building when compared with the chaste brick and white wood churches of the traditional New England scene.

Although the basic form of the building is conventional, with its roots in New England church architecture, the major detailing is Gothic. All the windows have pointed arches and are divided into two lancet-type vertical lights by a center colonnette. The openings in the wood belfry are also pointed but are divided into three vertical lights rather than two. The top of the belfry is crenelated, with tall unadorned pinnacles at the corners.

The most interesting Gothic element of St. John's Church is the entrance motif (Fig. 82). A central door is covered by a semicircular porch with Gothic clustered columns supporting a gothicized entablature. Crowning this porch is a continuous row of abutting antefixes, shaped like Gothic arches, each of them penetrated by three small trefoil openings. Above the porch, and rising to the pediment, appears what seems to be a classical tabernacle. Its flanking engaged columns, like those of the porch, are clustered, however, and the entablature is similarly gothicized. The central window between these columns is the principal one in the façade and is also Gothic.

Altogether, the Gothic paraphernalia of St. John's is remarkably similar in spirit, if not in specific detail, to the plates in Batty Langley (Fig. 76). In addition, the semicircular porch is reminiscent of that of the second Trinity Church in New York, which the Providence authorities must have known (Fig. 75). Equally interesting is the fact that although the details are Gothic, the massing, proportions, and scale of the building are absolutely consistent with the Neoclassical style which dominated the architecture of New England during these years. Even the semicircular porch was a popular device of the period; a superb example appears in the Ives House of 1806 in Providence, not very far from St. John's.[32] The only difference between the two is a superficial difference of ornament; the house is Neoclassical in the manner of Samuel McIntire, the church is Gothic; and this Neoclassical flavor is sustained by the manner in which the wooden Gothic elements are painted. The clustered colonnettes of the porch and tabernacle, and the quoins in the top stage of the tower, are brown to harmonize with the stone of the walls. Like the walls of the belfry, however, certain ornamental features are painted white, thus accentuating the purely decorative character of these applied Gothic attributes; in the same way, the white figures and ornament of Wedgwood Jasper ware contrast with the darker neutral tones of the background.

A similar Neoclassical feeling is found in the interior. The plaster ceiling of the vestibule (Fig. 83), for example, is made up of two high four-part Gothic vaults carried on clustered colonnettes. The scale of the cross ribs, however, is extremely delicate, and the moldings of the entablatures which crown the capitals have classical profiles, and are enriched by a lightly scaled bead motif. Just as on the exterior, the elegant lightness of the interior decorative elements is accentuated by contrasting tones of brown and white. The auditorium is almost square, proportioned in the manner of the conventional New England meetinghouse. Moreover, the coved circular ceiling (Fig. 84) has in the center a decorative wheel motif more Adamesque than Gothic in both detail and scale. The choir loft and organ console (Fig. 85), on the other hand, which in typical meetinghouse manner are at the entrance end of the church, are whimsically but enthusiastically Gothic. Yet even here, the taut thin character of the detailing, in spite of the overt Gothic shapes, could hardly be more Neoclassical, and with the flat sharply linear ornament boldly displayed in white against a soft brown background, the whole ensemble seems even more like Wedg-

FIGURE 83. *John Holden Green. St. John's Church,*
Providence, R.I., vestibule ceiling, 1810.

FIGURE 84. *John Holden Green. St. John's Church,*
Providence, R.I., sanctuary ceiling, 1810.

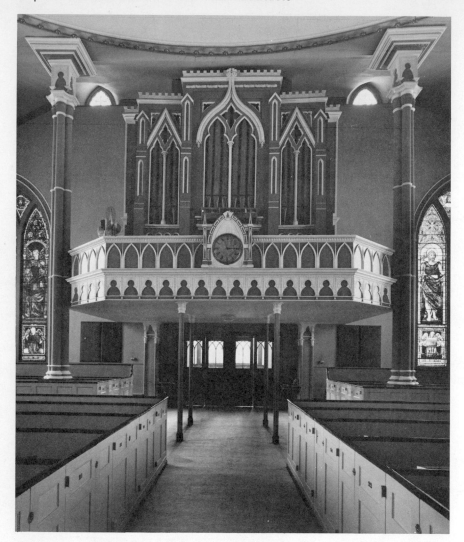

FIGURE 85. *John Holden Green. St. John's Church,*
Providence, R.I., choir loft and organ console, 1810.

wood than does the elegant two-toned portico. Indeed, John Holden
Green seems to have sensed in Gothic ornament, especially as he came to
know it through Batty Langley, a genuine kinship with Neoclassical forms,
and it is of considerable interest that he combined the two elsewhere in
Providence.[33] St. John's Cathedral, therefore, is a marvelously hybrid
building, not only striving for symbolic identification with the medieval
church tradition but—very much a part of its time and place—also reluctant to forsake in any measure the delicate grace and elegance of the
Neoclassical world in which it was built.

PART III

TOWARD AN AUTHENTIC GOTHIC

Ithiel Town
and Eclecticism as a Mode of Design

The amorphous flurry of church building which marked the earliest phase of the Gothic Revival in this country took a decisive turn during the second decade of the century in one of the remarkable churches of the period, Trinity Church in New Haven, Connecticut. The historical facts about Trinity are well documented. The architect was Ithiel Town of New Haven, whom we have encountered before both as senior partner in the firm of Town and Davis and as one of the chief proponents of the Greek Revival in America.[34] In a prelude to Trinity, Town was involved, together with his fellow Neoclassicist Isaac Damon in the building of Center Church, New Haven. Designed in the Federal style and situated on the New Haven green, it was finished in 1814. In that same year Town's Trinity Church, a Gothic design, was begun. It stood immediately next to Center Church and was finished in 1817. A third building, the Connecticut State Capitol, was designed by Town ten years later. It had the form of a pure Greek Doric temple and was located on the green immediately behind and between Trinity and Center Church (Fig. 86). The choice of

FIGURE 86. L. S. Punderson, *New Haven Green, New Haven, Conn., c. 1831.*

Gothic for Trinity therefore represented a radical departure from Town's apparent Neoclassical disposition, a departure which set him apart very early in his career as an exponent of eclectic thought which was growing so rapidly that it was beginning to dominate the architecture of America as well as Europe. Town's remarkable cluster of buildings set in the same landscape context is a vivid example of a Romantic Eclectic architect working purposefully in several different styles from the past. Although Center Church, the earliest in time, was a conventional building consistently designed in the prevailing mode, Trinity and the Capitol were mixtures of style: we will see shortly that Trinity derived from several different Gothic sources, and the Capitol, although displaying a Greek Doric order, was placed on a high Roman podium. Moreover, the fact that three such different buildings could be seen immediately adjacent to one another points up the degree to which eclecticism could be made to fulfill functional and symbolic as well as aesthetic and romantic ends. Town's work on the New Haven green was not the only instance of its kind in early nineteenth-century America,[35] but it was in every way the most dramatic and provides for us a particularly useful point of departure from which to explore the whole notion of eclecticism as a mode of design.

Eclecticism in architecture is that method of design which selects elements from a variety of stylistic sources and combines them in a new and original way. At its worst, eclecticism can be no more than the copying and combining of certain elements from the past. At its best, it can be an imaginative synthesis of ideas which accrues to a new style expressive of a new set of conditions. For one American architectural writer in 1830, a great work of architecture is the result of "a taste so well DISCIPLINED as to be able to judge with instinctive certainty as regards beauty of form, and this taste exercised with increasing industry in combining such forms and in trying their combinations. This, and nothing but this, will make an architect."[36]

As a method of design, eclecticism depends entirely upon readily available sources of stylistic data, and for the first eclectic architects these sources were books. Indeed, the eclectic movement owes its very existence to the remarkable developments in architectural literature which took place during the late eighteenth and early nineteenth centuries. From the mid-eighteenth century onward, books were of critical importance in the development of American architecture.[37] The colonial builders relied heavily on books to keep them up to date on current building modes, but these books were largely handbooks and contained no information about different historical styles. When the findings of the archaeologists began appearing in print in the late eighteenth century, however, the treasure house of historical architecture was opened to all those who had the curiosity to probe its wonders, and eclectism became a viable doctrine.[38]

In view of the general excitement which was aroused by the continuing process of discovery and revelation, it is very easy to understand why architects of the nineteenth century were attracted to the notion of eclecticism. As one segment of the past after another was brought to light, new enthusiasms were born which led to a deeper and deeper probing of the in-

FIGURE 87. *Thomas Cole*. The Architect's Dream, *1840* (*Toledo Museum of Art*).

exhaustible possibilities of historical styles as a basis of design. Although each style represented a way of life remote from the present, the romantic mind had no difficulty whatsoever in establishing fruitful associations between the past and its own objectives. This was particularly true in the United States, which, except for the narrow and exceedingly provincial idiom of its colonial years, had no architectural tradition of its own. For the Americans the newly revealed range of historical styles offered opportunities for richness and variety in architectural form which seemed altogether suitable to the restless, insecure, but immensely ambitious culture of the expanding nation.

Just how intoxicating the doctrine of eclecticism was to Americans was powerfully if naively expressed by the painter Thomas Cole in a remarkable allegorical work entitled *The Architect's Dream* (Fig. 87). Painted in 1840 for Ithiel Town, it shows in the immediate foreground an architect (presumably Town) reclining on the top of an enormous Roman Doric column. To support him in his apparent state of trance he has around and under him, as though they were a couch, a number of very large architectural books. At his feet is a portfolio of drawings, and in his hand is a plan of what seems to be a prostyle classical temple. Beyond and behind him, from his elevated position, appears his fantasy. In the distance to the right, seen brilliantly illuminated in broad sunlight, is a terraced array of Egyptian, Greek, and Roman buildings. In the middle distance to the left, and on the near side of a large placid stream, is a grove of sharply pointed trees. From this shadowed setting, as though part of its luxurious growth, rise the tapered finials and spire of a cruciform Gothic church. In contrast to the illumination of the classical world, the light in this area comes from behind the building and penetrates its interior so that the stained-glass windows are transilluminated within a deeply shadowed wall. The painting is rendered throughout with penetrating clarity.

As an allegorical statement, this work by Cole seems to convey three separate messages. The first and most obvious is that the architecture of the past holds an infinite variety of attractions for the architect of the present. He need only open his eyes to see an appropriate solution to any problem. The second makes a clear distinction between the sharply defined, directly lit geometry of classical and Egyptian architecture and the shadowed, ephemeral, and translucent qualities of the Gothic church. The statement is dramatic and unequivocal. There are two ways to see the world of architecture, either through the sharp clear light of classical antiquity or through the brooding mysteries of the Middle Ages. Each approach is valid, and has an application in the present. It is up to the architect to choose. Finally, the painting indicates that whatever style the architect may adopt for his own, his primary means of access to the knowledge he needs is through books. In this grand resource are contained all the wonder, all the specific information, indeed, even the inspiration necessary to an architect for performing his role, and it is of considerable importance to the development of eclecticism in America that Thomas Jefferson and Ithiel Town brought together two of the largest architectural libraries in the United States in their day.

As well as being an allegorical essay, Cole's painting is a brash display of erudition about architectural styles. That this erudition was acquired from books is directly implied by the architectural books he shows in the painting. We know, too, that Cole actually borrowed books from Town for use in the preparation of his work.[39] Moreover, there was nothing unusual about an exhibition of one's knowledge; in a very real sense, this was one of the main objectives of the early eclectics. For Richard Payne Knight at Downton Castle, for example, the array of various classical styles on the interior of a completely Gothic building was a deliberate flaunting of antiquarianism at the expense of architectural coherence. While to us Knight's willful juxtapositions might seem whimsical, for him Downton was a serious essay, based on patient scholarship, which brought delight to him and his friends. The house was the showplace of a poet and philosopher, designed as a release for his unbridled enthusiasm for the past. Eclecticism for Knight was the end, not the means.

For others, however, the doctrine of eclecticism offered a marvelous resource, an endless variety of forms and ideas which opened the way for new dimensions never before possible in architectural design. To understand nineteenth-century architecture we must accept this as a logical and viable premise, otherwise the work of such demanding giants as Thomas Jefferson will have no meaning. For Jefferson was an eclectic architect, perhaps the first in America, who discovered in the architecture of ancient Rome symbolic and practical qualities of relevance to the struggling new nation. We have seen his imaginative and eloquent use of Roman and French Neoclassical forms in his design for the University of Virginia; and in a more personal application his discreet and original melding of Palladian, Roman, and contemporary French ideas and motifs at Monticello.[40] Although Jefferson's wholehearted commitment to the architecture of ancient Rome had led architectural historians to identify him more as a revivalist and less as an eclectic,[41] he actually worked from a variety of Palladian and Neoclassical sources and he was the first American architect to have the intellectual curiosity, the broad erudition, and the largeness of mind necessary to make eclecticism a fruitful method of design. In the end he proved to be not only the earliest but also one of the most sensitive and skillful eclectics in American architectural history.

In spite of its urbanity, Jefferson's eclecticism was narrowly inspired by the world of classicism. Ithiel Town's, in contrast, had a broader base. In his three buildings on the New Haven green, Town went further than Jefferson by making three wholly different styles function for three equally different purposes: the Federal style of Center Church reflecting the established conventions of New England Congregationalism; the Gothic of Trinity confirming the ancient roots of the American Episcopal Church in the Church of England; and the Greek of the Capitol building celebrating the ideals of American democracy as manifest in the state. The use of a variety of styles by the same architect to satisfy the demands of a variety of functions turned out to be a productive form of eclecticism in nineteenth-century America, as we have just seen suggested in Cole's painting *The Architect's Dream*. Town's juxtaposition of the Federal, Gothic, and Greek styles, therefore, in the ambience of the New Haven green, was a dramatic realization in architectural form of precisely what Cole was trying to say in the allegorical imagery of his painting, and together they define the basic premises of eclecticism in nineteenth-century America.

Trinity Church, New Haven

Ithiel Town's Trinity Church as seen today (Fig. 88) gives the appearance of being another uneasy combination of the traditional New England meetinghouse and applied Gothic ornament. It is a simple rectangular building with an attached tower on the front. A chancel, which extends from the west end and gives the church a decided Gothic spatial character, is not part of the original structure; it was added during 1884–85. The original interior, therefore, with its balconies supported on the piers, was a simple rectangular auditorium identical to those of countless eighteenth-century New England meetinghouses. Moreover, the cornice of the eaves is extended across the building, except where interrupted by the tower; it has moldings that are classical in scale; and together with the raking cornice it forms a typical classical pediment. To all this have been added the Gothic details, and in much the same way as those at St. John's, Providence, were applied.

The Gothic of Trinity, New Haven, however, was far more persuasive and complex than that of St. John's, but to evaluate it properly, it is first necessary to recognize the degree to which Town's original design was modified over the years. The chancel just mentioned is among the changes. But our view of the New Haven green (Fig. 86) and a water color made in 1864 (Fig. 89)[42] also make it clear that the cornice line, which today seems so classical, was once crowned both along the eaves and up the raking cornice, by open (perforated) wood crenelation. Both illustrations also

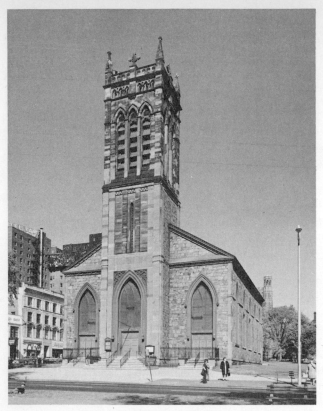

FIGURE 88. *Ithiel Town. Trinity Church,
New Haven, Conn., 1814–17, tower added, 1884–85.*

show that the tower, which was rebuilt entirely in stone during the late
nineteenth century, was originally a more intricate and lightly scaled
Gothic design in wood and was crowned by open crenelation in which the
normally solid vertical members, or crenels, were perforated instead by
tracery. Similar crenelation adorned the cornices. The original wooden
corner pinnacles, too, were much taller than those seen today. Indeed, they
stood 30 feet above the parapet line of the tower and together with the
lighter scale of the tracery gave the whole building a more tapered and
soaring character.

The fact that Town's church was more authentically Gothic than were
those churches which preceded it stems from the fact that both the open
crenelation motif on the roof line and the tower itself can be traced to
specific Gothic sources. For the tower, for example, Town turned to a
plate in one of the most influential eighteenth-century architectural books,
Gibbs's *Book of Architecture,* which shows the late Gothic Perpendicular
tower of the All Saints Church, Derby (Fig. 90).[43] The similarities between the Gibbs illustration and the original tower at Trinity leave no
question that the popular English book was Town's source. None of the
original tower ornament remains today, however, and the heavier scale of
the modification gives the present tower an obvious late nineteenth-century

FIGURE 89. *Ithiel Town. Trinity Church,*
New Haven, Conn., 1814–17. Water color dated 1864.

character. Nevertheless, Town used a complete Gothic tower as his model
and did not, as John Holden Green did in Providence, simply add Gothic
ornament to a Wren-Gibbs type tower. The vertical continuity of parts was
therefore unbroken and created a more genuine Gothic effect than the set-
back stages of St. John's. The treatment of the windows, too, although
rendered in wood, had more of the sculptural character of Gothic ornament, and the interior of the sanctuary, which in St. John's (Fig. 85) is a
typical meetinghouse space, is longer in proportion and thus oriented toward the altar. Finally at Trinity, in contrast to the circular coved ceiling
of St. John's, a rib vaulted ceiling was supported on Gothic clustered piers
(Fig. 91). Like all vaults of the early Gothic Revival in America, those at
Trinity were wood and plaster rather than masonry, and the ribs seem
originally to have been flat rather than molded in Gothic profiles. But the
splay of the non-structural ribs produced something that visually resem-
bled a Gothic vaulted ceiling, if only in its pattern effect.

Ithiel Town's own description of Trinity, New Haven,[44] written at the
time of its completion, contains many important bits of information which
help us to see it as it was when first built. But this account also gives us
two revealing insights into Town's attitude toward the problem that faced
him. The first deals with the question of why this particular church was

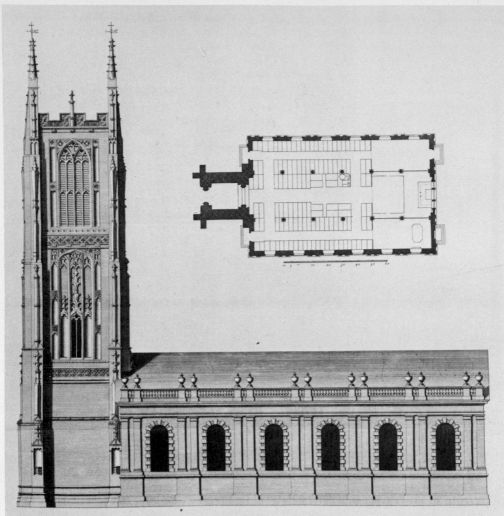

Australe latus Ecclesiæ Omnium Sanctorum, apud Derbienses, mox ab imis instaurandæ, una cum Sepulchrali Monumento inquo
Reliquiæ Prænobilis Devoniæ Prosapia conduntur, Stante adhuc Turri magnifici, quæ ad 178 pedes caput sublime attollit, Minister & Paro-
chiani ejusdem Ecclesiæ Duci Devoniensi, Viro non minus integris moribus, quam splendidis Natalitijs illustri, humillime dedicant.

Delineavit Ja: Gibbs.   Sculp: H: Hulsbergh.

FIGURE 90. *James Gibbs. All Saints Church,
Derby, England; plate showing original early sixteenth-century Gothic tower.*

built in the Gothic style. Town tells us quite simply that "the Gothic style
of architecture has been chosen and adhered to in the erection of this
Church, as being in some respects more appropriate, and better suited to
the solemn purposes of religious worship." Clearly questions were asked
about the relationship between the building and the liturgy, and the Gothic
style was recognized as the traditional Christian style and thus best suited,
both practically and symbolically, for all the requirements of the service.

Another passage in Town's description suggests that he was also aware,
however indirectly, of the growing doctrine of the picturesque; the reasons

FIGURE 91. *Ithiel Town. Trinity Church,*
New Haven, Conn., interior, 1814–17. Old print.

behind his choice of style, therefore, must also have been in part aesthetic.
In a fascinating reflection about the walls of the church Town says that
they were built of "a hard granite, quarried from a rock about two miles
northwest of the city and laid with their natural faces out, and so selected
and fitted, as to form small but irregular joints, which are pointed. These
natural faces present various shades of brown and iron-rust; and when
damp, especially, the different shades appear very deep and rich; at the
same time conveying to the mind, an idea of durability and antiquity
which may be very suitably associated with this style of architecture."

Considering that Town received his architectural training in Boston, the
fountainhead of New England Neoclassicism, this romantic response to the
sensuous appeal of materials is remarkable indeed and indicates clearly the
degree to which picturesque attitudes were already stirring in the minds of
some American architects. But it is also significant because he associates
the visual richness of the variegated stone with the antiquity of the Gothic
style. This idea of equating visual qualities with age is a subjective notion
which is at the very heart of the romantic movement. For Town to find
aesthetic pleasure in irregularity, roughness, and richness was a direct contradiction of the prevailing attitudes, which still revelled in the logical geometry of the clean unbroken wall and in the sharp pristine clarity of
white paint; and to justify his point of view the architect found sanction in

the past. Such an attitude was not only romantic, it was also the root of eclecticism, and Trinity together with the churches next to it (Fig. 86), one of them built by Town himself and starkly in contrast to Trinity, could nevertheless be acceptable to the same people, at the same time, and in the same place. Both the Gothic Revival and Romantic Eclecticism, therefore, were first unequivocally expressed in America in Town's three buildings on the New Haven green.

Other Early American Efforts in the Gothic Style

Following Trinity Church, New Haven, which was completed in 1817, the next two decades of the nineteenth century in the United States were marked by a substantial increase in church building. In part this was the result of national growth and expansion as the new country stretched farther and farther beyond the Alleghenies. In part, it was in response to growth and change in the religious community itself. Many of the new churches were Congregational, especially in New England, but also in the new lands opening up in western New York State and the Western Reserve. Almost without exception churches of this denomination were primly Neoclassical in style and rendered in the conventional materials, wood or brick. We have already examined this general development elsewhere.[45]

In the Episcopal and Catholic churches, on the other hand, quite the opposite was true. Here the vast majority were some form of Gothic, and almost all were stone. Most were small box-like structures with an attached frontal tower, pointed arch openings, and simplified Gothic detail. St. Anne's in Lowell (Fig. 57), built in 1827, was such a church. In its case, the dominating frontal tower with its crenelated top, together with the stone walls and the lack of an enclosed pediment, created the effect of an austere Gothic parish church, an effect repeated in a considerable number of urban churches in the East during the late 1820's and early 1830's. Trinity Church in Boston, built in 1829, was one of the most prominent, but as an essay in the Gothic it seemed more like a fortress than a church (Fig. 92). It was a massive squarish building with a flat roof and an enormous block tower. Built of rough granite throughout, it had crenelated parapets on both the front mass of the building and the tower. Although it had rather prim Perpendicular detailing in the windows, it was a heavy awkward building, and in spite of its dominating stone tower, was less Gothic in quality than Town's Trinity Church in New Haven.[46]

Equally ungainly is St. Stephen's Episcopal Church in Philadelphia (Fig. 93). It was built during 1822–23 and designed by the talented Neoclassical architect William Strickland, whose work we have already encountered elsewhere.[47] Strickland, like Mills, worked with Latrobe and was a much too committed Neoclassicist to have a natural feeling for the Gothic. St. Stephen's, too, with its balancing twin octagonal towers and austere flat-planed walls is Gothic only because of its tall lancet windows and crenelated top.[48] Even though he had already designed another building in the Gothic style, Strickland's use of the Gothic was decorative rather than logical. His Masonic Hall in Philadelphia[49] was a symmet-

FIGURE 92. *Trinity Church, Boston, Mass., 1829. Old print.*

FIGURE 93. *William Strickland. St. Stephen's Episcopal Church, Philadelphia, Pa., 1822–23.*

rically balanced building with a central tower and spire. Built during 1808–11, shortly after Latrobe's Bank of Philadelphia,[50] which was one of America's earliest public buildings in the Gothic style, the Masonic Hall was Gothic only by virtue of its flimsy Gothic detail. In its symmetrical massing and two-stage tower it was in every respect a conventional Neoclassical design.

In many ways more interesting than the incongruous mixtures of Neoclassical and Gothic forms which we have just examined in the urban areas are the early Gothic churches in the hinterland. Tucked away in unexpected corners of the Northeast, where urban pressures have neither altered nor destroyed them, many of these remarkable folk buildings still survive in very much their original form. Here many of the conventions of Neoclassicism are seen stubbornly to persist, and mixed with the applied Gothic details they form delightful and sometimes amusing hybrids. Two examples will suffice. St. Andrew's Church in Hopkinton, New Hampshire (1828), is a particularly charming building (Fig. 94). In spite of its rough granite walls, which suggest a romantic taste, the building has the enclosed pediment and the proportions of a Greek temple, together with the rectangular tower and open belfry of the traditional New England meetinghouse. All the openings, however, including those of the belfry, have pointed arches and the rather elegant wooden detailing is entirely Gothic.

At a still more provincial level is the beautiful little church at Riverton, Connecticut, built in 1829 (Fig. 95).[51] One of the most appealing examples of its type, it, too, has rough granite walls and pointed-arch openings. The masonry is more random than at Hopkinton, and here there is no Greek pediment. Instead, a heavy tower projects from the center of the façade, and like the walls of the building it is stone to the horizontal cornice line. Above this is a two-stage wooden spire of squarish proportions, which at first appearance is not unlike those on countless small Greek Revival churches in New England.[52] The detailing, however, is a mixture of primitive Gothic and classical forms. The cornice moldings on both stages of the spire are classical, and the upper stage has wooden quoins at the corners, but the openings have pointed arches and there are unadorned pinnacles at the corners of both stages. A parapet on the first stage is ornamented by a running pointed-arch motif. But most enchanting of all, each of the triangles formed on either side of the tower by the level cornice line and the raking roof line is screened by three flat panels of increasing height, to form the semblance of a Flemish stepped gable. On each of the two corners of this gable are flat two-dimensional pinnacles which read in their proper profile only when seen from the front.

The Influence of Trinity, New Haven

Within this climate of groping and half truths, Trinity, New Haven, stands out as a remarkable building indeed. Because it was inspired in part by an outstanding Gothic original, and because it was designed and built by a talented young architect, it was the most Gothic of all the early efforts. That it should serve, therefore, as a model for things to come, was inevitable. With the general growth of the Episcopal Church in the Northeast,

FIGURE 94. *John Leach. St. Andrew's Church, Hopkinton, N.H., 1827–28.*

FIGURE 95. *Union (Episcopal) Church, Riverton, Conn., 1829.*

several new churches were built for this denomination which were a direct outgrowth of Town's Trinity. Precisely how many there may have been cannot be accurately determined without much further exploration, but sufficient evidence is provided by three extant examples to demonstrate a substantial influence through several levels of the American architectural scene.

One of the earliest examples is St. Luke's Church, Rochester, New York, built in the years 1824–25 (Fig. 96). Here, not only was the church of substantial architectural importance, but Rochester itself was absolutely typical of the countless new towns which were coming to life as the fabric of America began to push its way westward. When first founded, shortly after the turn of the nineteenth century, Rochester was but one of several tiny hamlets along the last twelve miles of the Genesee River. But the Erie Canal, which was begun in 1817, came right through Rochester Village, and by the time it opened in 1825 the tiny hamlet had become a thriving community with a population of over seven thousand persons; by 1833 it was chartered as a city.

The first St. Luke's Church was a small wooden building erected in 1820. So rapid was the growth of the congregation, however, that by 1823 it was already too small and plans were begun for the present structure. The cornerstone was laid on May 11, 1824. The architect was Josiah R. Brady of New York City, and one of the founders was Colonel Nathaniel Rochester himself. As finished in 1825, the church building was a conventional rectangle 53 by 73 feet, with a 16-foot square central tower, 90 feet high, which projected 6 feet from the front wall. By 1828, however, the continued growth of the congregation made it necessary to add two bays to the rear of the church, giving it a much more Gothic proportion.

The top of the tower, on the other hand, has been radically changed. As in the tower of Trinity, New Haven, the top was originally square, with tall pinnacles at the corners and open crenelation between. Again as at Trinity, this crenelation was carried around the entire roof line. But the tower was completely rebuilt in 1858 into its present pointed form, and the crenelation around the roof was also later removed. With its quoined corners and enclosed pediment, therefore, the main body of the building today appears somewhat more classical than it must have looked originally (Fig. 97).

The original detailing of St. Luke's tower did not show the close affinity with the tower of All Saints, Derby, that we have noted at Trinity, New Haven. Moreover, the arches over the central door and over the tower windows of St. Luke's are ogee in shape rather than pointed, which suggests a possible origin in Batty Langley. But the three entrance doors, with their flat Tudor arches and lancet windows above, are remarkably similar to the arrangement at Trinity. Like Trinity, too, the interior of St. Luke's had a nave divided from the side aisles by clustered Gothic piers, and the suspended plaster ceiling was semi-groined although, unlike Trinity's, it does not seem to have had false Gothic ribs. This, together with the similarities already noted on the exterior, would seem to indicate that Town's church had substantial influence on architect Brady. In any case,

FIGURE 96. *Josiah R. Brady. St. Luke's Church, Rochester, N.Y., 1824–28. Old print.*

FIGURE 97. *Josiah R. Brady. St. Luke's Church, Rochester, N.Y., 1824–28.*

FIGURE 98. *St. Paul's Episcopal Church,*
Troy, N.Y., 1826–28.

the building has a convincing Gothic character. Indeed, the description of
St. Luke's which appeared in its first directory (1827) quite categorically
proclaims that "the style of the building is Gothick which has been rigidly
adhered to in every particular." In the light of what we now know about
ultimate developments in the Gothic Revival, we might find this statement
somewhat overconfident, but there is no question that St. Luke's, at least
in part, was inspired by Trinity, New Haven, and that it brought to a typical booming frontier town what was then a remarkably advanced form of
the Gothic style.

Even more interesting is a group of early nineteenth-century churches
found both on the eastern side of the Hudson River in New York state
and in adjacent western New England.

The first of these is St. Paul's Episcopal Church in Troy, New York.
Located on the Hudson River at the confluence of the Mohawk River, the
city of Troy once formed the eastern terminus of the Erie Canal. Like
Rochester, therefore, its life and growth were directly linked to that of the
canal, and from the time the waterway was begun in 1817 until it was
opened in 1825 the population of Troy more than doubled. To accommodate the increasing number of Episcopalians who had migrated to the city,
St. Paul's, the first Episcopal parish to be formed, was incorporated in

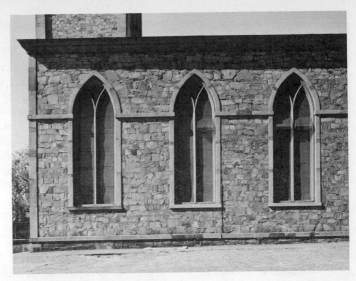

FIGURE 99. *Ithiel Town. Trinity Church,*
New Haven, Conn., partial side view, 1814–17.

FIGURE 100. *St. Paul's Episcopal Church,*
Troy, N.Y., partial side view, 1826–28.

1804. Later that same year the congregation built a church. Because of the continued expansion of the city, however, this building became obsolete in less than twenty years, and in 1826 a new and larger church was begun. It was consecrated in 1828.

An old print shows that St. Paul's began as a conventional Neoclassical building of red brick, with an open colonnaded cupola; however, an illustration of the church built in 1826 shows a Gothic structure (Fig. 102). But most important, this second building, except for a few minor details, was an almost exact replica of Trinity, New Haven. Precisely how close the relationship was is revealed by a careful comparison of the two. As originally built, both were simple rectangular boxes with classically pitched roofs, and their dimensions were within a few inches of being exactly the same size. Each had a range of five lancet windows down both flanks (Figs. 99, 100).[53] Moreover, in both buildings these windows were exactly the same height, although they varied slightly in width. Both buildings also had central frontal towers of almost the same dimensions (Figs. 89, 98).[54] In both façades, too, were three tall lancet openings, the largest in the tower, and the two balancing smaller ones in the walls on either side. The lower thirds of these openings formed the principal entrance doors and were topped by four-centered Tudor arches (they still are at St. Paul's). The upper two thirds were windows, with double lights in the ones on either side, and triple lights in the principal window in the center. At the altar end, each church had a large pointed window 40 feet high.[55] The two varied in detail but were similar in compartmentation (Figs. 91, 101).

Both buildings are stone to the top of the second stage of the tower, with the masonry laid in random ashlar between dressed pilasters at each of the four corners. Trinity, however, is a hard granite richly browned by considerable iron oxide in its content, while St. Paul's is a "dove-colored limestone." The upper stages of both towers were originally wood (St. Paul's still is). So, too, were all the cornices and the heavy Gothic moldings which cased the façade openings. Originally, both churches also had open wooden crenelation on both the horizontal and the raking cornices; in neither instance has this interesting feature survived, although it can be seen in early views of each church (Figs. 89, 102).

Most remarkable of all are the numerous similarities in detail. As seen in side views of the two churches (Figs. 99, 100), the windows are set off by plain flat fascia bands of dressed stone. These in turn are connected at the spring of the lancet arches by a horizontal stringcourse of dressed stone which is the same width as the window surrounds, but which projects more boldly from the plane of the wall. This stringcourse passes in front of and wraps around both the window surrounds and the pilasters at the corners of the building. In each instance, too, the wooden cornice is ornamented by a zigzag pattern whose elements are slightly curved in profile (Figs. 103, 104). At a distance this creates the effect of an alternating trefoil pattern; the shallow frieze below the cornice carries a continuous series of carved rosettes. Enhancing each tower, as a continuation of the horizontal cornice and frieze, is a quatrefoil band. The front face of the second stage of each tower was once adorned with wooden tracery, and here, too, the patterns were almost identical; except for minor variations in small details, the two top stages of the towers were exactly alike (Figs. 89, 98).

The extraordinary similarities between St. Paul's and Trinity leave no doubt that within the limits imposed by local materials, local craftsmanship, and distance the Troy church was a deliberate imitation of Town's design. The similarities in detail are such that St. Paul's would have been impossible without a direct knowledge of Town's church itself. Indeed, they could only have been achieved through the most careful observations, measurements, and even drawings, made on the spot. It is true that no document is known to survive which establishes a direct link with

FIGURE 101. *St. Paul's Episcopal Church,*
Troy, N.Y., chancel window, 1826–28. Old photograph.

FIGURE 102. *St. Paul's Episcopal Church,*
Troy, N.Y., 1826–28. Old print.

FIGURE 103. *Ithiel Town. Trinity Church,*
New Haven, Conn., detail of cornice, 1814–17.

FIGURE 104. *St. Paul's Episcopal Church,*
Troy, N.Y., detail of cornice, 1826–28.

Trinity. On the other hand, the rector of St. Paul's at the time of its construction was the Reverend David Butler, who had been ordained in Trinity Church, New Haven, in 1792, and had come to Troy in 1804 when the parish had been established. In view of this it would seem logical that the Reverend Butler maintained close connections with Trinity, and may even have known Town himself. However neither the name of Town, nor that of any other architect, is connected with the building of St. Paul's. For instance, an article published in the *Troy Sentinel*[56] at the time of the consecration gives no hints of possible ties with New Haven, but the statistical data, arrangement of ideas, and even the language in this article are so similar to Town's own description of Trinity that the latter must have been known in Troy and may even have been a source of vital information for the planning of the church.

Because it is a conscientious copy and not an original design, St. Paul's displays a lower level of quality than Trinity. It lacks altogether the sense of excitement and discovery so apparent in those remnants of Town's original design which still survive. At the same time, however, it is precisely the accuracy with which St. Paul's was carried out which makes it of immense historical importance; and because it is still relatively unspoiled on the exterior[57] it is here, better than anywhere else, that we can get some sense of what Trinity originally looked like. The lovely lace-like tower of St. Paul's, so like the one which formerly graced the New Haven green, makes all the more awkward the pretentious stone tower which now weighs so heavily upon Town's simple but refined design.

St. James, Arlington, Vermont

If St. Paul's Church brought to a frontier community a remarkably advanced form of the Gothic style, so did St. James Church in Arlington, Vermont (Fig. 105). The setting, of course, was very different. Arlington was not on a major transportation route to the West, and it had no industrial or commercial potential. Arlington was, and has remained, a small

FIGURE 105. *William Passman. St. James Church,*
Arlington, Vt., 1829–31.

rural community in a superb valley setting, today offering mostly serenity
and easy access to the tempting trout waters of the Battenkill. But in the
eighteenth century Arlington had one characteristic which set it apart
from other Vermont communities: it was a lonely enclave of Anglicanism
in an otherwise fiercely Congregational domain. Known at the time as
Tory Hollow, and regarded with grave suspicion because of its Anglican
persuasion, its Loyalist views, its Maypoles, and its Christmas trees, the
town was kept under constant watch by the Green Mountain Boys all
through the years of stress that surrounded the Revolution. It was in this
climate that St. James Church was founded; and when the original wooden
building was damaged by fire in 1829 the present stone Gothic church was
begun. It was consecrated in 1831.

According to a contemporary account, the new St. James was built
"strictly in the gothic style." As such, it was not only an eccentric intrusion into the world of entrenched Congregational Neoclassicism, but it

was also a very fine building, proudly conceived, eminently prophetic, and equal if not superior in quality to anything which confronted it on the main street of the town.

In form it was exactly like Trinity and St. Paul's (compare Figs. 89, 98, 105), being a simple rectangular box with an attached central tower. The walls are a lovely blue limestone laid in random ashlar to the cornice line; simple pilasters mark the corners. Above the cornice and into the tower the structure and detailing are wood. The fact that it is stone distinguishes St. James from the conventional New England meetinghouse, even though its basic shape suggests a kinship. Moreover, the over-all proportions are considerably taller. The windows, like those at Trinity, are tall and narrow with double lancet lights and pointed arch tops. But it is primarily the tower which gives the building its most conspicuous Gothic character. Although divided into three definite stages by two horizontal molding courses, the lower of which corresponds to the cornice of the building itself, the tower is clearly vertical in effect, its thin corner pilasters carrying the vertical lines through the main body of the building into the soaring taper of the pinnacles at the crown. A shorter pinnacle graces the center of each side of the tower with open crenelation between.

Immediately we are reminded of the original tower on Trinity, a similarity which is further strengthened when we examine the treatment of the belfry openings. They consist on each side of a tall lancet motif divided and subdivided by delicate strap-like tracery into a configuration of main lights and slender side panels almost identical to those on Trinity. The decoration of the second stage of St. James's tower is less like Trinity's in its specific patterns, but it is equally flat and involved; and below it is the familiar quatrefoil panel. There is no evidence that the roof line of St. James was ever graced by crenelation as it was at both Trinity and St. Paul's, but the evidence of the tower is so persuasive that it is difficult not to conclude that Trinity lies behind the Arlington church. On the whole, the building is more provincial than either of its more prominent predecessors, even though local legend attributes the design to an English architect, William Passman.[58] There is certainly nothing in the design of the church to support the idea that something distinctive was contributed by an English architect. On the contrary, logic suggests that the importance of Trinity, as an example of proper architectural form for an Episcopal church, was very great indeed, and that St. James in Arlington, like St. Paul's in Troy, was a direct result of Town's inventive genius.

St. Luke's, Lanesboro, Massachusetts

The degree to which the influence of Trinity permeated to the folk level of early Gothic building in the United States may be seen in St. Luke's Church, Lanesboro, Massachusetts (Fig. 106). Built in 1836 for a small rural parish with extremely limited means, it is more the product of a community effort than the work of skilled craftsmen under informed supervision. Even smaller than St. James, Arlington, and built of local limestone laid in rough rubble walls, this crude but delightful little building still displays coarsely filtered ingredients of Town's New Haven church—the cen-

FIGURE 106. *St. Luke's Episcopal Church,
Lanesboro, Mass., 1836.*

tral tower form with its tall pinnacled wooden upper stage, the zigzag
band below the crenelation, the double lancet windows—all combined
with awkward simplicity in a scheme which suggests as much sympathy
for the conventional New England meetinghouse as it does for the attenuated continuity and vertical thrust of the Perpendicular Gothic style.

How this particular folk version of the Gothic came to Lanesboro is of
some interest. St. Stephen's Church in neighboring Pittsfield, built in 1832,
was a stone Gothic building with a wooden tower. As shown in contemporary prints of the building,[59] this tower had a division of parts in its vertical arrangement identical to that at St. James, Arlington, which had only
just been completed. Thus, in its own remote way, St. Stephen's, too,
derived from Trinity, New Haven; and it was St. Stephen's that seems to
have been recommended in 1836 as the model for St. Luke's. On the other
hand, because of its simple rubble walls and tall lancet windows St. Luke's
is more akin to St. James, Arlington, than to St. Stephen's. But by whatever route it may have arrived, the blurred image of Trinity which appears
in St. Luke's demonstrates the extent to which Town's accomplishments
reached out to touch all levels of the aspiring and ambitious Episcopal
Church. St. Luke's brought to the isolated valleys of western Massa-

chusetts the vital seeds of contrast which were already beginning to enliven the architecture of the urban areas; for only ten years before it was finished, the Congregationalists of Lanesboro had built a new church in the heart of the town. It is a small and extremely provincial building of brick with white limestone lintels, identical in its conventional primness to numerous other red brick Neoclassical buildings which appeared in Berkshire County during the first quarter of the century. It is as different from St. Luke's as it could possibly be. On the New Haven green we have already seen a similar confrontation of styles, and in the same chronological order: Town's Center Church, which was Neoclassical, and his slightly later work in the Gothic style, Trinity Church. In the awkward vocabulary of the folk scene, St. Luke's and the Lanesboro Congregational Church were joined in the same emerging struggle between the dynamic promise of the Gothic and the tired conventions of an architectural mode whose creative impulse had long been lost in the distant past.

The Gothic authenticity of Trinity, St. Paul's, St. James, and St. Luke's, resides primarily in their towers. This is so not only because the shadow of All Saints, Derby, in varying degrees, is so conspicuous in all of them, but also because *all four were made of wood*. Since the Gothic style was a style conceived and rendered in stone, this might seem to be a contradiction in critical values. But the fact remains that to execute anything like the complex sculptural involvements of the tower of All Saints in stone would have been technically impossible at the time when these four American churches were built. There simply were no sculptors and masons available with sufficient skill and knowledge to meet the challenge. Ironically, it is this very fact which makes such churches as Trinity, Boston, which *were* built entirely of stone, so utterly *lacking* in Gothic grace. In contrast, the American skill with wood, which produced the masterful classical detailing in the churches of the colonial and Neoclassical eras, made possible in Trinity and its satellites the qualities of movement and interlace, the division and subdivision of parts, the continuity from body to arms to fingers, which are the glory of the Gothic style. These churches achieved at least the visual semblance of the Gothic, if not its organic truths. Together, they communicate something of the developing feel for the Gothic which was touched off by a new awareness within the Episcopal Church itself of the role of architecture in the Anglican tradition. Working with no firsthand knowledge of the Gothic style, and severely handicapped by the limited number of published sources, Town was able, nevertheless, to translate that awareness into architectural form. Trinity, New Haven, was, of course, meager Gothic, but it was a vigorous building with just enough authentic ingredients to give it the ring of truth, and for awhile it stood as a primary source of inspiration for the Gothic movement in this country. At the same time, by rendering his tower in wood Town evoked the special qualities of America's native building tradition, and set the stage for a form of the Gothic Revival which would have no counterpart in Europe.

CHAPTER IV

Richard Upjohn,
Trinity Church,
and the Ecclesiological
Gothic Revival

*The object is not to surprise with novelties in church Archi-
tecture, but to make what is to be made truly ecclesiastical.*
RICHARD UPJOHN

PART I

THE GOTHIC REVIVAL CHURCH
IN ENGLAND: 1800–1850
PUGIN AND
THE ECCLESIOLOGISTS

*Books about the Gothic:
Augustus Welby Pugin*

The earliest Gothic Revival buildings in England were domestic, and were
part of the Picturesque movement of the late eighteenth century. As such,
they were objects of fashion and had nothing to do with the basically religious character of the Gothic style. After 1800, however, there was a
change in the nature and objectives of the Revival, and for a number of
interesting reasons. The first was the increasing depth and accuracy of
knowledge about the Gothic, a knowledge largely disseminated through a
growing number of published works. Ranging from the antiquarian writings of John Carter at the turn of the century to the architectural polemics
of Augustus Welby Pugin in the late 1830's and early '40's,[1] these publications not only made available to architects and builders alike more authoritative information about the Gothic than had ever been known before, but

also raised serious questions about the architectural character of this style and its suitability for modern church building.

In the earliest of these publications the main thrust was literary and pictorial rather than technical. Nevertheless, they managed to stimulate an awareness of the Gothic as a truly English style, and they provided increasingly accurate details of existing Gothic buildings. Of these, the books of John Britton were the most influential,[2] particularly his *The Architectural Antiquities of Great Britain* (1804–14) and his last great work, *The Cathedral Antiquities of Great Britain* (1814–35). Especially in his later works the engravings reproduced Gothic details with greater accuracy than had ever been achieved before. These, together with Thomas Rickman's *An Attempt to Discriminate the Styles of English Architecture* (1817), which was among the earliest serious efforts to make distinctions between the various phases of the English Gothic, provided a more solid ground from which to understand and use the Gothic style.

Rickman's distinctions came closer than any previous works to describing the Gothic in purely architectural terms, but it was the moral indignation of Augustus Welby Pugin that opened the way for an understanding of the Gothic as a functional mode of building. Pugin, one of the geniuses of the nineteenth century, worked as an architect, a designer in the decorative arts, and an architectural writer and critic. He was a man of inexhaustible creative energy and the central figure in setting the tone of the Gothic Revival in England. As an architect, he is best known for his work in the Houses of Parliament, for which he designed all the Gothic detail; as a theorist and critic, he is famous for his many published works on architecture. Pugin came by his talents naturally. His father, Augustus Charles Pugin, a French émigré who came to England in 1793 to escape the Revolution, was himself an architectural draftsman and an illustrator of numerous books on architecture. The younger Pugin inherited both his ardor and his skills from this equally remarkable man. At the time of his death in 1832, the elder Pugin was at work on *Examples of Gothic Architecture,* which his son finished and published in 1838. Together with the father's *Specimens of Gothic Architecture,* published in 1821, it would become a major source for American Gothic Revival architects.

In 1835 the younger Pugin became a convert to Roman Catholicism, a commitment which intensified his feelings about the Gothic as the only true Christian style, and which led the following year to the publication of his famous *Contrasts.* This book focused attention on the Gothic not as an object of antiquarian or topological study, or even as an exercise in the rendering of accurate details, but rather as an architectural style conceived and executed in the service of the church. Pugin developed his moralistic ideas in the language of architecture, and illustrated his arguments with a vivid series of paired contrasts between specific "Christian" and "pagan" examples. It was a timely and controversial book, brought out at the very moment when serious questions were being asked about the church itself. Its influence was far-reaching.

Contrasts was followed in 1841 by *The True Principles of Pointed or Christian Architecture.* In this book, Pugin went a step further and proclaimed the Gothic as a dynamic style based on a direct relationship between structure and form. The two fundamental principles of architecture as he saw them were that "there should be no features about a building which are not necessary for convenience, construction, or propriety," and that "all ornament should consist of enrichment of the essential construction of the building." He related them to the Gothic by arguing that it was in "pointed architecture alone that these great principles have been carried out," and that "the architects of the Middle Ages were the first who turned the natural properties of the various materials to their full account, and made their mechanism a vehicle for their art."[3] For Pugin, Gothic architecture had the qualities of a living organism, as necessary to the physical and intellectual well-being of mankind as to the nourishment of the human spirit; and to return man toward high moral purpose, Pugin devoted his entire career to the revival of the Gothic style.[4]

The Commissioners' Churches

The impetus provided to the Gothic Revival in England by the growing body of architectural literature was significantly strengthened during the second and third decades of the century by a substantial increase in church building. We have already noted that during the latter part of the eighteenth century very few churches were built, and these were of no consequence in the Gothic Revival. After 1800, however, changes wrought in English society by the industrial revolution led to an unprecedented growth of cities and towns, and in the wake of this growth a need for new churches became critical. To ease the situation, a Church Building Act, passed by the government in 1818, provided a million pounds for new church construction. A group of Commissioners was appointed to oversee this program; churches built under its sponsorship were thus known as "the Commissioners' churches." Over a period of fifteen years more than two hundred were built.

Although most leading English architects submitted designs, a stringent economy in the expenditure of the funds imposed serious restrictions on what could be achieved. Because of this the Commissioners' churches were built at a minimum cost. They therefore vary in quality and for the most part are recognizable by their drabness. It is significant that the Commissioners recommended the Gothic, not because they preferred it, however, but because they considered it to be the least expensive. As a result one hundred and seventy-four of the churches were in some form of Gothic.

One of the most interesting is the London church of St. Luke's, Chelsea (Fig. 107), designed by James Savage and finished in 1824. It is an austere, flat-walled building in the Perpendicular style, with tall thin proportions, and spindly gaunt buttresses. Even though it was completely vaulted in stone on the inside, it is meager in scale, and lacks that sculptural density so characteristic of Gothic. In spite of this, it was highly regarded in its day as an accomplished Gothic design.

Altogether, the Commissioners' churches, of which St. Luke's is one of the best, do not constitute a happy episode in English architecture. Even in their time they were strongly condemned in some quarters, and they

FIGURE 107. *James Savage. St. Luke's, Chelsea, London, England, 1824.*

were to be outmoded by various events which soon followed. Regardless of motivation and quality, however, those Commissioners' churches which were built in the Gothic style represent the first major effort in church building of the English Revival. Their contemporary impact was immense, for they focused attention on the Gothic style, aroused controversy about its usefulness, and provided a convenient forum from which the fiery Pugin and more pedantic but equally adamant Ecclesiologists could develop their doctrine of purification.

The Ecclesiological movement

The influence which the Ecclesiological movement had on nineteenth-century church building was so extensive, both in England and in America, that we must examine with some care the major aspects of its architectural doctrine. Viewed in the broadest terms, Ecclesiology was a reform movement within the Anglican Church which called for a return to traditional medieval forms both in ritual and in church building. In a more specific sense, however, and certainly in the eyes of the Ecclesiologists themselves, Ecclesiology was the science of church architecture, a science, moreover, which was based on a careful and exhaustive examination of original Gothic buildings. Its first objective was to identify those features of the Gothic church and its furnishings which related to the liturgical and symbolic functions of the worship service; its second was to use that evidence for the formulation of rules which would govern church building.

In its search for what it called "sacramentality," that is the direct relationship between the church building and the demands of the worship service, the Ecclesiological movement was a rebellion against the rationalism of the eighteenth-century church. One consequence of the Reformation in England, and the powerful anti-Catholic sentiments which it ultimately released, had been a simplification of the service by stripping away all ceremonial practices that in any way suggested idolatry, or "popery." The most extreme form of this trend is found in the Separatist movement and in the religious practices of the American Puritans,[5] but by the late eighteenth century the Anglican service itself had been so rationalized that in some churches even the choir had been eliminated. The architectural results are vividly manifest in the cool simplicity and general lack of symbolic devices which one finds in such churches, particularly those in America which were built during the eighteenth and early nineteenth centuries.[6] It was to counter this condition that the Ecclesiologists sought to return richness and emotional appeal to both the worship service and the church building itself.

In part the Ecclesiological movement was motivated by the same romantic impulses which produced the Gothic novel and the picturesque Gothic in architecture. In some ways, too, it was one of the many reactions to the aggressive materialism of the Industrial Revolution. Beyond this, however, it was a profoundly theological movement, based on intensive study of historical materials on the one hand, and a high sense of moral purpose on the other. It was firmly based, drawing its stewardship from the intellectual heart of England: in Oxford from the Oxford (Tractarian) movement, touched off in 1833 by the sermons and tracts of John Keble and John Henry Newman; and in Cambridge, six years later, from the Cambridge Camden Society, founded under the leadership of John Mason Neale and Benjamin Webb.[7]

Although the Ecclesiological movement was sometimes marked by serious internal dissension and by a lack of clearly expressed goals, there was common agreement on one important issue: a liturgy based on medieval precedents could only be "decently administered" in an equally medieval ceremonial space, one "rubrically" ordered[8] and replete with appropriate symbols. Instead of viewing the Gothic style as the picturesque gothicists had done, in terms of its visual attributes—pointed arches, tracery, vaulting patterns, buttresses, crockets, and finials—the Ecclesiologists saw it for what it was, a functional architectural idiom existing in and for the church. Their views on this issue were not always entirely consistent and they changed as time went on, but they were adamantly stated and alike in their basic intent. First expressed in a flurry of pamphlets, and further developed in the *Ecclesiologist* (the monthly magazine of the Camden Society), the doctrine as it evolved was rooted in the deep conviction that all original Gothic churches had been built according to specific laws of arrangement and adornment. Moreover, the Ecclesiologists believed not only that "gothick [was] the only Christian architecture," but also that in Gothic architecture "Christian symbolism . . . found its most adequate exponent." The articles in the *Ecclesiologist* and other publications provided specific details about layout, ornamentation, and furnishings. Even the particular phase of the Gothic was specified: the so-called "Decorated or Edwardian style," which flourished between 1260 and 1360, was preferred as the purest form of Gothic. As one writer put it, "During the so-called Norman era, the Catholick Church was forming her architectural language: in the Tudor period, she was unlearning it." The elegant Perpendicular style, as found in King's College Chapel, and so popular with the early revivalists, was cast aside as debased, in favor of the Geometric and Curvilinear phases of the Decorated Gothic style.

Pugin and the Ecclesiologists

A pivotal moment in time for both the Ecclesiological movement and the Gothic Revival was the year 1841. The Camden Society's monthly magazine, *The Ecclesiologist,* was first published in that year and provided both persuasive means for disseminating the new doctrine of church building and a lively forum for an exchange of ideas on the subject. In that same year, too, the Society published the first edition of an important pamphlet, *A Few Words For Churchbuilders,* which offered useful advice for those charged with the responsibility of building and caring for churches. But 1841 also saw the publication of Pugin's *True Principles.* Pugin, whose *Contrasts* had already established his reputation as a fiery gothicist, was by this time a Roman Catholic. He was thus viewed with suspicion by the Ecclesiologists, who were as anti-Catholic as they were pro-Gothic. Pugin's views on architecture, however, were remarkably similar to those of the Ecclesiologists. Indeed, what Pugin proclaimed in broad philosophical terms was in essence what the Ecclesiologists proclaimed as dogma. The Anglican leaders did their best to reject him, but the fundamental kinship between their ideas and his was too real to be shaken, and Pugin remained a source of embarrassing inspiration for the Ecclesiologists.

More than that, one of Pugin's earliest churches, St. Oswald's, Liverpool (1839–42), was exactly the kind of small parish church which the Ecclesiological doctrine prescribed. Even though it was Roman Catholic, this seemingly unimportant little building became a seminal monument in the development of the Gothic Revival church. As Hitchcock has pointed out,[9] St. Oswald's provided a virtually new type of parish church, one so persuasively Gothic in form as to mark a decisive break with the classical mode of the Georgian era. Under the leadership of both Pugin and the Ecclesiologists, the Gothic of the Revival would no longer be conceived in terms of Gothic devices applied to a classical building type. It would become instead, as the Gothic from which it derived had been before it, a functional style organically related to the church which it served.

The architectural importance of St. Oswald's is revealed first in its irregular asymmetrical massing (Fig. 108). The main body, or nave, of the church is a horizontal mass with a steeply pitched roof; attached to it on the east end, but at a lower level, is the similarly sloping mass of the chancel. Poised against this on the west end is the vertical thrust of a solid, buttressed tower, which terminates in a broached spire of extraordinary height and taper. This tower is centrally placed, opposite the chancel, and suggests a long axis around which the building is symmetrically balanced. Actually, however, the church is not symmetrical. An entrance porch projects from the south side of the nave and adjacent to the tower, and a small sacristy projects in a similar manner from the south side of the chancel.

FIGURE 108. *Augustus Welby Pugin.*
St. Oswald's, Liverpool,
England, 1839–42.

Since neither of these units is matched by a corresponding projection on the north side, the reciprocal balance implied by the central tower gives way instead to an awkward but clear asymmetry. Even in the tower itself, the basic symmetry of its vertical mass is upset by a projecting stair turret on the southeast corner. Moreover, the heavy buttresses on both sides of the nave and the corner buttresses on the chancel combine with tall gable dormers in the spire to animate even further the contrapuntal design. In addition, the elaborate curvilinear tracery in the broad pointed window gracing the east end wall of the chancel adds a lively internal rhythm to the principal theme.

As Pugin himself recognized, the qualities of irregularity, asymmetry, and movement which he introduced at St. Oswald's were not his invention, nor, indeed, that of any other Gothic Revivalist. In 1841 in an important article,[10] "On the Present State of Ecclesiastical Architecture in England," Pugin introduced the idea of asymmetrical arrangement and defended the concept by drawing his authority from the medieval Gothic builders themselves. "To those whose ideas of architectural beauty are formed on the two and two system of modern building," he wrote, "this argument will appear very singular; but building for the sake of uniformity never entered into the ideas of the ancient designers; they regulated their plans and designs by localities and circumstances; they made them *essentially convenient and suitable to the required purpose, and decorated them afterwards.*"

Pugin's article was soon followed by *A Few Words for Churchbuilders,* an article in which the Cambridge Camden Society also argued for asymmetricality. Both Pugin and the Ecclesiologists, therefore, had very specific liturgical and symbolic reasons for the manner in which they conceived a church, and it is precisely the programmatic nature of their doctrine which makes their approach to church building more than a simple matter of taste. Rather than the rigid formality of classical design, in which function was subordinate to aesthetic principle, they preferred the flexibility of asymmetry because it made possible the "natural" disposition of parts. Each element of the church was placed where it was, not to gratify some visual whim, but rather to make the building serve its intended function. The chancel, for example, was made separate from the nave in order to identify it as the "place of sacrifice, the most sacred part of the edifice" and the principal ceremonial space. The tower, with its high tapered spire, symbolically pointed toward heaven, stood as "a beacon to direct the faithful to the house of God." The south porch served several functions, including the baptism of infants; it also contained the stoups for holy water. Attached to the chancel was the service space of the sacristy. In other words, the massing of the church was canonically and symbolically inspired so that the needs of both the worshipper and the liturgy could properly be gratified.

Although the same principles of design were applied to the interior of the church, the liturgical demands in this case produced a symmetrical rather than an asymmetrical scheme. The revival of medieval liturgy made it essential that attention be focused on the chancel, for it was here that the drama of the service unfolded. The main worship space of the church, therefore, became a sequence of two spaces, the nave and the chancel, placed end to end along a single axis. Historically, this was an arrangement which had characterized the churches of the middle ages, but in the eighteenth century, owing to the secularization of the Anglican liturgy, it had given way to the classically proportioned rectangular box of the Wren-Gibbs formula; and even though the altar still occupied a position on the east end of the church, the chancel, as a special and separate ceremonial space, had been eliminated altogether. The first item on the Ecclesiologists' lists of architectural reforms, therefore, was the restoration of the chancel. Until this was done, the service could not be rubrically celebrated.

The axial relationship of nave and chancel functioned also in another way. Ecclesiological theology held that special "high privileges" belonged to those "consecrated to the immediate service of the sanctuary," and a marked distinction was made between "Clergy" and "Laity": in architectural terms the chancel was the domain of the clergy, the nave of the laity. The chancel, therefore, was not only distinguished from the nave as a clearly articulated mass on the outside, but on the inside the division between the two was sharply defined by some architectural feature, such as an arch. Moreover, although contiguous with the nave, the space of the chancel was raised to a slightly higher level by a series of two or three steps. Finally, to emphasize still further its sacred character, a rood screen—or, if that was not possible, an altar rail—was placed at the top of the chancel steps. The altar was to be at the extreme end of the chancel; other pieces of ceremonial furniture—the lectern, the litany desk, the pulpit, even the ancient sedilia—were described and given appropriate locations. In every instance both liturgical and symbolic requirements were the deciding factors.

Another architectural concern of the Ecclesiologists was the shape of the interior spaces. The extended horizontal volume of the combined nave and chancel, which led so dramatically to the altar, also had to have an upward thrust. This was accomplished by a steeply pitched roof, an element regarded as "essential to the Christian effect of a church." In contrast, the flat or arched plaster ceiling, so brilliantly exploited by Wren and his followers, was viewed as anathema. Only exposed rafters and trusswork could properly enhance the "Christian effect," and wherever possible color was to be applied. No church, they said, would be "as it should be, till *every* window is filled with stained glass." Floors were to be polychrome encaustic tile, the rood screen and other ornaments should be "glowing with the highest tints and with gold," and ceiling and walls should be decoratively painted. It is doubtful that many of the small parish churches achieved this degree of visual splendor, although some of the larger city churches surely did,[11] but where decorative painting was impossible, trusswork and ceilings were at least stained dark tones to evoke a quiet mood appropriate to the solemnity of the medieval liturgy.

Since the qualities of asymmetry, irregularity, and surface richness proclaimed by both Pugin and the Ecclesiologists are also characteristic of the Picturesque movement, it is tempting to conclude that the doctrinaire fanaticism of the church builders was not altogether untainted by the more worldly philosophy of the picturesque aestheticians. Certainly by the time Pugin and the Ecclesiologists were making their ideas known, picturesque values were firmly established in wide areas of English architecture, and if nothing else, would have assured a sympathetic response to the notions of asymmetry and irregularity in church building, even though they might not have drawn support for the religious dogma from which the notions derived. Conversely, it would hardly have been possible for English churchmen to become so directly involved with matters of architectural design and not be touched in some measure by the prevailing doctrine of the picturesque. Even though Pugin and the Ecclesiologists disdained the picturesque as pleasure-oriented, they seemed to have had little trouble in enthusiastically embracing its formal values.

That Pugin, at least, thought in picturesque terms is clearly evident, not only in his expressed enthusiasm for asymmetry and variety but also in the highly romantic and frequently sensuous tone of his writing. Indeed, he even used the term "picturesque" in such a way as to leave little doubt that he thoroughly understood its contemporary meaning. After pressing his case for functional asymmetry in the passage quoted above, he goes on to develop the idea. "To this [asymmetry] we owe all the picturesque effects of the old buildings," he wrote, adding that "there is nothing artificial about them,—no deception—nothing built up to make a show,—no sham doors and windows to keep up equal numbers—their beauty is so striking because it is *natural. . . . This is the true spirit of pointed design, and until the present regular system of building both sides of a church exactly alike be broken up, no real good can be expected.* One of the greatest beauties of the ancient churches is this variety. It is impossible to see both sides of a building at once; how much more gratifying is it, therefore, to have two varied and beautiful elevations to examine, than to see the same thing repeated."[12]

Two things about this statement are immensely significant. First, Pugin acknowledges asymmetry and variety as qualities of the picturesque, qualities moreover which derive their beauty from their kinship with nature. Second, these qualities are not mere abstractions; the responses they evoke are the result of actual visual perception. Although each element of asymmetry may be motivated by some doctrinal concern, it is nevertheless *seen through the eyes* and appreciated for its beauty as well as its ecclesiastical connotations. Pugin's arguments may not sound exactly like those of Richard Payne Knight or Uvedale Price, but they leave little doubt that he was well aware of the picturesque doctrine.

There is yet another consequence of Ecclesiological doctrine which would prove particularly important to the American Gothic Revival: it produced what was essentially a small parish church movement. There were, of course, a number of new parish churches, more or less inspired by Ecclesiology, which were built in the heart of the great cities. Pugin's own churches make it clear that he made distinctions between the low-profiled, tall-spired country churches, which related easily and naturally to a rural setting, and the high-walled, more compact clerestoried churches for the city. For the first decade of their existence, however, the Ecclesiologists thought only in terms of the small country church and it was certainly this type which would be most useful in the American scene.

In England, the preoccupation with the small church can be explained in part by the fact that there was very little need for larger ones. The great cathedrals were already there, deeply rooted in English ecclesiastical history—Salisbury, Canterbury, Durham, Lincoln, Wells, Gloucester—all standing as eternal bastions of faith in the more or less sympathetic surroundings of the cathedral towns. On the other hand, the rapid growth of English towns made the demand for smaller parish churches very real indeed. Moreover when first built, most of the new churches, such as St. Oswald's, Liverpool, were in semi-rural areas on the fringes of the towns, and since the Ecclesiologists expressed preference for the country church in the natural setting of a secluded church yard, itself a picturesque notion, most of them were conceived and built in this way. No doubt the Ecclesiologists' position on this matter was prompted by a growing fear of the evils of the burgeoning industrial cities, a fear which found consolation in the romantic conviction that life in a small medieval town was somehow better than that in the brutal reality of a modern city. This point of view was certainly expressed in Pugin's *Contrasts*. Perhaps, too, the lively British enthusiasm for the landscape, which was so triumphantly manifest in the picturesque gardens of the eighteenth century, may also have been a contributing factor. In any case, the ideal church for the Ecclesiologist was a small richly varied building situated in an equally rich and varied natural setting. Nothing could have been more appropriate for export to the United States and it is with this in mind that we return now to the most important American church of the early Gothic Revival, Richard Upjohn's Trinity Church in New York.

RICHARD UPJOHN AND THE GOTHIC REVIVAL IN AMERICA

Trinity Church, New York

Although the activity in Gothic church building, which marked the first third of the nineteenth century in America, set the stage for Richard Upjohn's Trinity Church in New York, it had very little direct influence on the architectural character of the building itself; for Upjohn was not a native American. He was born and brought up in the hill town of Shaftsbury, in the northern part of the incomparably beautiful county of Dorset, one of the most ancient and romantic sites in England. Shaftsbury had a strong Gothic heritage of its own, and only twenty miles to the east is the cathedral town of Salisbury. In this setting, Upjohn trained and worked as a cabinetmaker, carpenter, surveyor, and draftsman, and in 1829, at the age of twenty-seven, he emigrated to America.[13] Just as Latrobe had done thirty years earlier, he came as a young man on the threshold of a career, ambitious, proud, and self-confident.[14] Upjohn was not, like Latrobe, trained from the beginning as an architect, but he did bring with him highly developed mechanical skills, a practical understanding of materials, and a sensitivity for three-dimensional construction, all of which were traditional credentials for a career in architecture. In addition, through his environment and family connections, he brought a special awareness of medieval architecture and a personal involvement in the Anglican Church, neither of which would have been possible in America. Indeed, because of his early years in England, Upjohn and Trinity Church would relate to the development of the Gothic Revival in this country in the same way that Latrobe and the Baltimore Cathedral related to American Neoclassicism; for once he proclaimed himself as an architect, he would bring to his work an awareness born of experience which no native-born architect like Ithiel Town could possibly have matched.

Richard Upjohn's association with Trinity Church began in March 1839, when he was called in as a consultant on the structural condition of the old 1790 building.[15] He was brought into the picture probably because of an earlier association with Dr. Jonathan Wainright, who had been appointed the new rector of Trinity in 1838. Before that he had served the large and important Trinity Church in Boston, a Gothic Revival church built only a few years earlier which we have already discussed. In 1835, as a young architect in Boston, Upjohn had been asked by Wainright to submit a proposal for some alterations to that church.

Upjohn first came to Boston in 1834 and for a short time worked for the Neoclassical architect Alexander Parris. His two earliest commissions, therefore, were both Neoclassical designs.[16] But his most important early

FIGURE 109. *Richard Upjohn. St. John's Church,*
Bangor, Me., 1836–39. Original drawing.

building, and one which bore directly on his later work at Trinity, was St.
John's Church in Bangor, Maine. Designed in 1836 and consecrated in
1839, it was Upjohn's first Gothic church (Fig. 109). It was a rectangular
building with a crenelated top, and except that it was made of wood it was
very much like Trinity, New Haven. Unlike Town's church, however, it
had paneled corner and wall buttresses, and tall handsomely traceried
perpendicular windows. The central tower also had corner buttresses and
was crenelated; in addition it had a tall Gothic spire. On the other hand,
the building had a low-pitched roof and no chancel, and on the inside the
extremely slender piers which ostensibly carried the four-part rib vaults,
also supported quite un-Gothic balconies along each side. Moreover, the
piers did not, in fact, carry the vaults. Like the ceilings in most conventional New England churches of the eighteenth and early nineteenth centuries, Upjohn's vaults were wood and plaster suspended from the roof
trusses above. In spite of its more consistently Gothic features, therefore,
St. John's remained a box-like building with conventional interior arrangements and was as hybrid in character as any of the Gothic churches which

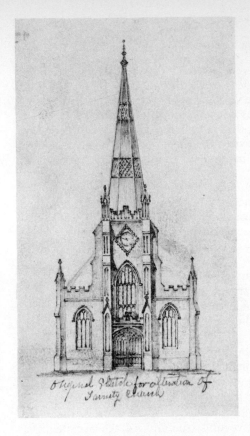

Original Sketch for alteration of / Trinity Church

FIGURE 110. *Richard Upjohn.
First sketch for alterations
of Trinity Church, N.Y., 1839.*

preceded it. Nevertheless, it had the most authentic Gothic detailing yet to appear in America, and there can be no doubt that its success must have been one of the factors which persuaded Dr. Wainright to call Upjohn to New York.

After arriving in New York, Upjohn's first assignment was to prepare plans for the renovation and enlargement of Old Trinity Church. When work was actually begun, however, it quickly became apparent that the structure of the building was too far gone to justify alteration. After much deliberation on the part of the Committee, plus the advice of other consultants, the decision was finally made to tear the old building down and replace it with a new church. Upjohn was given the commission; he submitted the first drawings to the Committee in September 1839, and the church was dedicated on May 21, 1846.

Of the many drawings that must have been made for Trinity, only a few have survived, and none of these are dated. Those that do exist, however, when combined with the evidence contained in other documents, throw interesting light on the evolution of Upjohn's design. The earliest scheme (Fig. 110), and probably the one connected with the rebuilding of the old church, was almost identical with that made by Upjohn for St. John's, Bangor. Except for the substantial character of its Gothic ornaments, it offered nothing which we have not already seen in earlier Gothic Revival churches in America. But the design for the new church submitted in September

1839 (Fig. 113)[17] was very different indeed. This building was to be much higher, with a clerestory added above the aisle roofs. It would be seven bays in length, and the entire proportional system of both the exterior mass and the interior space was conceived in the soaring vertical language of the Gothic style; and, too, the tracery and rib patterns were to be authentic and properly scaled. In every way here was a visually coherent and persuasive Gothic design, with no trace of the conventional intrusions which marred the earlier hybrids.

The transition from the fumbling uncertainities of St. John's, Bangor, to the restrained but convincing gothicism of Trinity was all accomplished within less than a decade. It represents a remarkable growth in professionalism on the part of the architect, and inevitably arouses curiosity as to how it came about. Certainly it was due in part to the flowering of a latent talent under the stimulus of an exciting and challenging major commission. Upjohn was ripe for such an assignment and he made the most of it. It must also have been due in part to his strong Anglican background, which would have quickened his understanding of the style. But the dramatic increase in his command of the Gothic forms also suggests the possibility of some outside influence.

Evidence to suggest that Upjohn did, indeed, experience such an influence is found, interestingly enough, in an article on American architecture, published in the *North American Review* at the time that Trinity was nearing completion. Its author, the young American architect Arthur D. Gilman,[18] demonstrates not only a knowledge of the current literature on the Gothic,[19] but also a perceptive understanding of the architectural character of the style. He specifically points out that since the time of such early "flimsy" Gothic efforts as Bulfinch's Federal Street Church in Boston, "a rapid advance has been made in an aquaintance with the true principles of the gothic style."[20] He then singles out Trinity as evidence of this change, and in his evaluation of the church makes extremely interesting observations which are worth quoting at some length.

> In size, in the delicacy and propriety of its decoration, and in the beauty of its general effect, we are inclined to think, that it surpasses any church erected in England since the revival of the pointed style. The new church of St. Luke, Chelsea, from the designs of Mr. Savage, minutely illustrated in Mr. Britton's descriptions and plates, will bear no comparison with the catholic propriety and finished elegance of this American structure. Governed by simple and consistent principles, the architect has conceived and finished it in the true and delicate spirit of the chastest period. It rivals the accurate taste of the best works of the fourteenth century, and is carried out upon a scale which we had deemed it impossible to adopt, in a country where architecture is in so chaotic a state. With the single exception of the Guild Chapels and private chantries introduced by Mr. Pugin in his engraving of a perfect church, it very nearly resembles that enthusiastic ideal of an ecclesiastical edifice of the Middle Ages.

FIGURE 111. Richard Upjohn. Trinity Church, New York, perspective view, 1839–46. Original water color.

The comparison which Gilman draws between Trinity (Fig. 111) and St. Luke's Chelsea (Fig. 107) puts Upjohn's church immediately into the context of the contemporary Gothic Revival; and the two buildings do have a good deal in common. They both have a nave, side aisles, a high clerestory, and a tall frontal tower, and both are in the Perpendicular style. Moreover, St. Luke's is a church that Upjohn could have known, not only from Britton's published works, as Gilman himself knew it,[21] but also from actually having seen it in London. The possibility is suggested, therefore, that St. Luke's may have been a source for Trinity.

But if St. Luke's and Trinity have much in common, they are also very different. In contrast to the cardboard-and-wire character of St. Luke's, Trinity is much richer in detailing and has a greater sculptural density. It also gives the appearance of structural solidity, and it has a soaring spire, which St. Luke's does not. As Gilman was so keenly aware, Trinity is a much more substantial Gothic building. But Gilman also knew why this was so. As an enthusiastic devotee of Pugin, he recognized that Upjohn's design was inspired not by St. Luke's but by the English gothicist himself. Pugin's *True Principles* had been published in 1841, at the very moment when critical decisions on the final nature of Trinity were being made. It

FIGURE 112. *Augustus Welby Pugin*. Ideal Church.

seems certain that Upjohn must have acquired the book immediately,[22] and equally certain that not only what he read there gave him a greater understanding of the Gothic style, but what he saw in the illustrations also provided the perfect model against which he could assess his own church.[23]

Upjohn's final design has too many things that relate to the ideal parish church illustrated by Pugin (Fig. 112)[24] to be coincidence. The massing of the nave and side aisles, the side porch,[25] and the frontal tower are all similar to those in Pugin's design. Particularly striking is the close resemblance of the upper part of Trinity's tower, with its coupled windows and ogee arches, and the soaring slender spire. In both churches, too, parapets are crenelated and wall buttresses are topped with pinnacles. Admittedly, in Trinity's spire, which rises 264 feet from the ground, the specific detailing is somewhat more simplified, especially in the buttresses at its base; and the taper of both the spire and the buttress pinnacles is also less slender. Nevertheless, the effect of verticality which results from the attenuated Gothic proportions, and the qualities of grace achieved through controlled delicate scale, are sufficiently Puginesque to leave little doubt that the Englishman's ideal church had an influence on the final form of Trinity.

All this, however, is only part of the story. Far more important is the fact that the basic form of Trinity, with its clerestory nave, side aisles, and

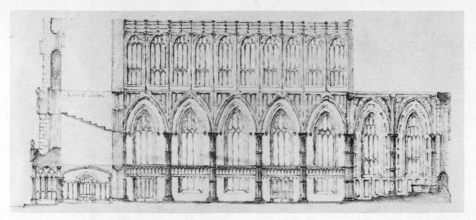

FIGURE 113. *Richard Upjohn. Trinity Church, New York,*
longitudinal section, 1839. Original drawing.

articulated chancel, *was determined before Pugin had published his ideal*
church. In his 1839 design for Trinity (Fig. 113), Upjohn shows a nave
of five bays, and a stepped chancel of two. This splendid nave, with its tall
proportions and clerestory windows, was crowned by an open timber ceiling. All this, together with the clearly defined side aisles, made it the first
truly Gothic space of the American Gothic Revival. More than that, the
chancel was continuous with the nave and at the same time precisely
differentiated from it. Unlike the nave, it was vaulted, with the crown of
the vaults at the same level as the crowns of the arches of the nave arcade.
The chancel windows, therefore, would have been the same height as the
five main windows in each flank of the nave. The sills of the chancel windows, however, were higher from the ground, and the openings themselves
were narrower than those in the nave. Thus, the independent massing of
the chancel, so firmly established by the lower roof line, was further emphasized by a difference in the character of the windows.

Upjohn's scheme with the articulated chancel was submitted to the
Committee in 1839, the very year in which the Cambridge Camden Society was founded. The scheme, therefore, is not only the first of its kind in
America, it is also one that Upjohn conceived entirely on his own, for only
later did the Cambridge Ecclesiologists express their fervent advocacy for
the liturgically designed church. The idea seems to have been too "popish"
for the Trinity Committee, however, and at first it was rejected. But Upjohn had strong Anglican convictions, and he must also have been very
persuasive, for in the end he was able to convince the church fathers that
the deep chancel was essential to the proper form of the church. It is of
considerable interest, however, that in developing his final chancel he did
not, as he had originally planned or indeed as the Pugin drawing might
have suggested, make the chancel an attached but emphatically independent architectural unit. Perhaps to make the chancel more acceptable
to the Committee, he instead made it an extension of the nave, so that the

FIGURE *114. Richard Upjohn. Trinity Church, New York,
interior, 1839–46. Anonymous drawing.*

exterior effect was one of a continuous architectural mass (Fig. 111). To achieve this, Upjohn increased the number of bays in the nave from five to seven, thus creating an even more "catholic" elongation of the space; then he added two more bays to form the chancel, making a total of nine. Because of the continuous ceiling height, these two bays appear at first to be no more than a continuation of the nave (Fig. 114). Viewed more carefully, however, they are seen to be subtly set apart to form a separate chancel. This was effected, first, by a series of steps to a level above the floor of the nave and, second, by larger piers at the line of separation, a line which is carried up and across the vaults as a heavily molded transverse arch. In the end wall, above the altar, in typical Puginesque manner, Upjohn placed a splendid Perpendicular window of fourteen major lights, each filled with stained glass.[26] Forty-four feet high and twenty-eight feet wide, it was unquestionably the finest Gothic traceried window yet to appear in America. It is one of the most thoroughly English Gothic features of the church and forms a dramatic climax to the entire design.

On the exterior, the line of division between nave and chancel is articulated by an increase in the size of the second wall buttress from the end, a point on the outside which corresponds with that within where the heavier piers begin. The aisles of the church are also terminated at this point so that the chancel, although not a completely separate entity, nevertheless is distinguished from the total width of the church, and in spite of the level roof line, projects toward the rear as a decisively articulated unit.

The second important change which Upjohn made from his original scheme was to substitute a rib-vaulted ceiling for his proposed open truss. To accomplish this it was necessary for him to fall back on the traditional American technique of lath and plaster suspended from the roof truss. There was, of course, nothing novel about this. All the early Gothic churches which attempted to imitate vaults were constructed in the same manner, and even in St. John's, Bangor, Upjohn had provided a four-part vault in lath and plaster. On the other hand, as a developing architect, Upjohn seems to have become increasingly concerned about such things as material and structure. Moreover, his professional convictions, as they grew, would surely have received important confirmation from his reading in Pugin's *True Principles*. In this book the author argues specifically against imitating masonry vaults in wood.[27] Except for the vaults, furthermore, materials were used in Trinity with genuine awareness of their peculiar properties. The primary structural material is a light brown freestone from quarries in Little Falls, New Jersey. This fine-grained stone was not only appropriate in color and texture to the growing romantic tastes of the period, but it also lent itself to precise dressing and carving. The details in Trinity have a substance and crispness which is one of the most important reasons for their authentic Gothic flavor.

Since the vast majority of Upjohn's later churches had wooden truss ceilings, and since in his original scheme for Trinity he proposed a truss, it would seem logical for him to have carried through with his early intentions. The decision to use lath and plaster, however, was not his, but was made by the Committee. This was in May of 1841. It is reasonable to assume that if he had to vault at all, Upjohn would have preferred to use stone, but this was both technically and economically impossible, and the plaster vaults, which may have caused him some professional uneasiness, obviously did not bother the Committee. They had behind them a long tradition of plaster ceilings in churches, and Upjohn had no choice but to work within the limits of that tradition. Fortunately, his understanding of Gothic vaulting systems produced an authentic lierne vault that was absolutely consistent with the restrained Perpendicular style of the rest of the church (Fig. 114). The vaults may have been plaster, but they looked like stone, skillfully carved and properly scaled, and gave the final touch of visual plausibility to the soaring Gothic space.

American Attitudes toward the Gothic before Trinity

In appearance at least, Trinity was the first church in America to demonstrate an understanding of both the architectural and the ecclesiastical characteristics of the Gothic style. Even though its vaults were plaster, and even though the development of its chancel seems to have been a compromise between the ardent high church leanings of its architect, and the reluctance of a Puritanical committee, the church is nevertheless a visually coherent structure, consistent in style, appropriate in scale and proportions, and functionally designed to serve the canons of the Episcopal service. For a Perpendicular Gothic building it is a little austere, with detailing somewhat subdued, and with areas of flat wall still vying with the windows for prominence. Nevertheless, the forms themselves, the interior spaces, and the structural elements all reveal themselves as convincingly Gothic, without the slightest residual hint of the classical tradition in American church building.

In view of the growing American interest in the Gothic, Upjohn's accomplishment at Trinity was inevitable. Although very few native-born American architects had ever seen a real Gothic building, their curiosity was being fed by an increasing flow of books from abroad. In addition to the meager offerings of James Gibbs and Batty Langley, the more comprehensive and authoritative works of such a writer as John Britton made their way to this country shortly after the turn of the century,[28] and by the 1830's the writings of Rickman, Britton, and later Pugin were frequently referred to, either directly or indirectly, in American publications. But by this time, too, the Americans themselves were beginning to react in writing to the Gothic style. The widespread appearance of Gothic buildings during the first quarter of the century presupposes some kind of exchange of ideas on the subject, and as early as 1790, at the time when the second Trinity, New York, was being completed, the Gothic style received attention in an American publication.[29] It was not until 1830, however, in an extraordinary series of articles entitled "Architecture in the United States," which appeared in two issues of *The American Journal of Science and Arts,* that the Gothic style received anything like an authoritative evaluation. The author of these articles is not known, but the editor of the journal was Benjamin Silliman of Yale, one of the leading intellectuals of his day. The articles themselves are fascinating for their scholarly erudition and for the high level of professional insights which they contain.[30]

Together, the four articles paint a broad architectural picture, including a large section on city and town planning; most relevant here is the one entitled "The Gothic Style."[31] The author begins by challenging the popular notion held by many romantics of the nineteenth century, that the idea for Gothic vaulting had its origins in the trees of the forest. "A pretty theory," he says, "but unfortunately it has no support in history," and with remarkable historical insight he goes on to point out that the Gothic vaulting system derived instead from the architecture of ancient Rome. There follows a discussion of the English Gothic in which the style is divided into three major historical periods, each defined and dated in such a way as to make it reasonably certain that the author was familiar with the writings of Rickman.

Drawing comparisons with "Grecian" architecture, the author analyzes the Gothic in considerable detail. He notes that it is an architectural idiom which "operates on all our sensations" and is emotional in its appeal. He attributes this, first, to its great height, but later also stresses its multiplicity of parts, its "irregularity and apparent disorder." "A simple Gothic build-ing," he argues, "is a contradiction of term." The problem of "lateral pres-sure" in the vaults also receives his attention, as do methods of buttressing and the advantages of the pointed arch in the resolution of thrust. He discusses the spire and argues against placing it in the center of the façade; he also mentions stained glass as belonging to the Gothic, and notes that good glass is (1830) available in Boston. Finally he discusses the difficul-ties arising from the cruciform plan of the Gothic church, which he recog-nizes as inappropriate for the Protestant form of worship, particularly in America, where the established form of church is the simple rectangular box.

It is not surprising that this brilliant article, so altogether advanced for its day, did not seem to have any influence on the church builders of the 1830's. Indeed, since *Science and Arts* was basically a scholarly journal with scientific leanings, it is unlikely that it was read by any builders or by more than a few architects. Moreover, because of its broadly philosophical tone the article itself lacked the working details necessary to make it useful for building purposes. In 1836 another article on American architecture appeared in the *North American Review*,[32] which was less analytical but dealt more specifically with a number of works of American architecture. The author was the historian Henry Russell Cleveland. On the whole, Cleveland is severely critical of most of the buildings he discusses, al-though he evaluates them in rather limited architectural terms.[33] He likes the simplicity of the Greek temple, but is also attracted to the greater vari-ety and flexibility of the Gothic, especially for buildings which required different kinds and sizes of interior space. He deplores the fact, however, that because of its complexity Gothic may be too expensive for America.

With respect to the use of the Gothic style for churches, Cleveland's ob-servations are of special interest. He recognizes that this style owed its existence to the Christian religion, and that because of this the Gothic church itself had a very special form. He notes its division into nave and side aisles, with a clerestory above; he remarks on its greater height, the prevalence of stained glass, the imposing effect of the rib vaults, and the high pitched roof. "The Gothic depends . . . for its beauty," he wrote, "on form and proportion. But churches built in this style should be much greater in length than in breadth." He goes on to put particular stress on the marked difference between the American and European churches, not-ing that "all traces of the church, as it exists in Europe, are lost in the plain and Puritanical meeting-houses of our ancestors," and he further points out that "there is not to be found . . . in the United States, a single instance of a church built in the style of the English Cathedrals, with nave and transept, and the screen parting the choir from the nave."

Cleveland complains that those churches in this country which have at-tempted to be Gothic are really "Yankee meeting-houses with Gothic or-naments on them." He demonstrates his own limited understanding of the Gothic when he approves the Gothic steeple on Bulfinch's Federal Street Church in Boston (Fig. 80). He quickly adds, on the other hand, that "there is nothing in the form of the edifice (itself) to distinguish it as

Gothic." Cleveland has particular praise for Trinity Church, Boston, the tower of which he regards as "the best Gothic in the United States," and he is also attracted to the rough-hewn stone surface of the building. Yet he recognizes the church's deficiencies, calling particular attention to the inconsistencies in style, to the short low proportions of the sanctuary, and to "the vast expanse of white-washed walls, and . . . pine painted white." His point is clear. Coherent, ecclesiastical Gothic had not yet arrived in this country. Yet there were those like Cleveland who were aware of this fact, and in its own way the country was struggling to overcome it.

Cleveland's article is particularly important because it gives us such a clear and positive contemporary opinion with respect to the state of the Gothic in this country before Upjohn's Trinity Church in New York. But just as in the case of the *Science and Arts* article it is critical rather than technical and offers no useful specific particulars about the Gothic. Indeed, the first book in this country to deal specifically with the Gothic style was John Henry Hopkins's *Essay on Gothic Architecture* published in Burlington, Vermont, in 1836; this was five years after the completion of St. James, Arlington. In 1823, Hopkins had been elected rector of Trinity Episcopal Church in Pittsburgh and two years later he designed a new church building for the parish. At the time, it was one of the largest and most important new churches in America; according to one account, it could seat one thousand people. In style, it was a crude and awkward form of Gothic, with a squat tower at each of the four corners, and a tall Perpendicular tower over the altar. There were flimsy wall and corner buttresses topped by pinnacles, and the entire building, including the towers, was crenelated.[34] The building was destroyed in the late nineteenth century.

In 1831, shortly after completing his spectacular church, Hopkins accepted the call to be assistant minister of Trinity Church, Boston, and the following year he was made the first Episcopal Bishop of Vermont. Thus he left Trinity, Boston, the year before Wainright arrived, but he was there long enough to have had his enthusiasm for Gothic architecture stimulated through the association with the Gothic church which Cleveland admired so much. Like other leading gothicists of his day, he decried "the most uncouth combinations of the gothic arch and battlement with columns, entablatures, and pediments, of the Grecian order." In order to correct this, he was beginning to assemble material for a book on Gothic architecture even while he was in Boston, and he had the lithographs for the illustrations made while he was there. He also did extensive research on the subject of Gothic architecture at the Boston Athenaeum.[35] It was not, however, until he had settled into his duties in Vermont that he finally published his book.[36] He himself recognized that it was the work of a churchman, not a professional architect, and "only intended to be of service, where better guides are not at hand . . . that it may induce our rising clergy to give attention to a subject which peculiarly concerns themselves."

Hopkins was aware that the "distinguishing features of the Gothic Style" were "the effect of the perpendicular line, and the terminating of the various parts in a point," but he embraced the idea that its origins were

Saracenic rather than Roman, and that it was brought back to Europe by the Crusaders. The weakness of Hopkins's book is that it is clearly the work of an "amateur" who had never seen a Gothic building, except as illustrated in such works as Britton's and in his own collection of "many of the best engravings of the fine English Cathedrals."

Hopkins's book offered very little to American church builders that was not already available in more authoritative form in English publications, and at present its full impact on the American Gothic Revival is still difficult to assess. It did, however, increase the awareness of Episcopal churchmen as to the appropriateness of the Gothic for church building, and was at the very least a public endorsement of the rising enthusiasm for the style. It seems also to have had some influence on a number of new churches, although this might have been greater had the book not come out on the eve of the Ecclesiological movement in England. It was overshadowed almost as soon as it appeared by the arrival in New York of Richard Upjohn, and by the almost simultaneous publication in England of the early works of A. W. Pugin. During the late 1830's and early '40's, the number of Gothic churches built in this country increased substantially, and some of them revealed a considerably greater command of the authentic medieval style. In Stanton's view they mark "the beginning of serious revivalism," and there can be little doubt that Hopkins's book was influential.[37]

Among the churches to which Stanton gives particular attention is St. John's Episcopal Church, Cleveland, Ohio. It especially attracts our attention here since the man who designed it, Hezekiah Eldridge, came to Cleveland from Rochester, New York, where, as an Episcopalian, he would have known St. Luke's very well. His Cleveland church therefore stands in a direct line of descent from the earliest phase of the Gothic Revival. Fortunately, St. John's is richly documented, and thus provides some fascinating insights into how a Gothic church of the 1830's came about.[38] Originally built in 1836, the church was considerably altered in 1867, but in its early form had a roof of much lower pitch, and was thus more like St. Luke's, Rochester. It was more substantial Gothic, however, than the earlier building. Unlike St. Luke's, which had a wooden belfry, it was stone throughout, had corner turrets and wall buttresses, and included a coherent stone tower terminated by crenelation and pinnacles.

It is against this background of searching and trying, so sharply criticized and brought into focus by a new breed of American architectural critics, and so conspicuously evident in the fumbling uncertainties of the buildings themselves, that Richard Upjohn's accomplishment at Trinity, New York, stands out with such dramatic impact. Although Trinity may be lacking in some of the niceties of Gothic grace, it is not a fumbling building, and in spite of its structural compromises, it is insistently Gothic in appearance throughout its entire fabric. There can be no doubt that the missing ingredient in the American Gothic Revival up to the time of Trinity Church was a developed sense of the Gothic style on the part of the American church builders. Upjohn, by contrast, brought to his architecture just such insights. He not only had an obvious native talent for architecture, but he had experienced actual Gothic buildings during the early years of his life in England. He did not have to interpret the involved three dimensionality of the Gothic style through the flat pages of a book. He had been inside a real Gothic church, had experienced its soaring space, its fractured light, its compelling linear movement; and all this had been seen through the eyes of a devout Anglican worshiper with high church principles. It was this two-fold perceptiveness—the architectural and the religious—that led to Trinity, and set it apart among American churches of its time as a strong and persuasive Gothic building.

PART III

RICHARD UPJOHN
AND THE ECCLESIOLOGICAL
MOVEMENT IN AMERICA

The Church of the Holy Communion, New York

The Cambridge Camden Society, which formed the spearhead of the Ecclesiological movement in England, was founded in 1839, the same year that Upjohn submitted his first designs for the new Trinity Church; and in 1841, the year in which critical decisions were being made at Trinity, the first issue of the *Ecclesiologist* appeared in Cambridge. In view of the doctrine that we have seen expressed by the Ecclesiologists, it is obvious that Trinity was a long way from being a pure Ecclesiological church. It was the "debased" Perpendicular style, it was oriented in the wrong direction, the chancel was too short in relation to the nave, the ceiling was a lath and plaster vault instead of the preferred open timber truss. Indeed, the church was criticized by the Ecclesiologists themselves for these very shortcomings.[39]

Seen in the context of the American Gothic Revival, however, Trinity did precisely what the Ecclesiologists, in their over-all objectives, strove to achieve: it introduced into the American scene an authentic Gothic church functionally designed around liturgical principles. Whatever it lacked in the way of canonical purity, it made up for in the degree to which it overcame the "prejudices and parsimony of the age." Moreover, it is highly probable that the teachings of the Ecclesiologists ultimately helped Upjohn in his struggle to achieve what he considered to be the proper form that a church should take. He owned the first volume of the *Ecclesiologist,* which he could have acquired about the same time as Pugin's *True Principles,* and might well have drawn on the arguments contained therein—especially those calling for an independent chancel—in his efforts to persuade a reluctant committee. In the same way as Trinity, New Haven, but to an even greater degree, Trinity, New York, opened a new era in the American Gothic Revival, and established a model which would serve a wide area of American church building for at least a decade. As Stanton has pointed out, "as soon as Trinity was begun, many cities acquired at least one big church in its manner."[40] Typical is James Renwick's Grace Church (Fig. 139) in New York, begun in 1843 when the walls of Trinity were already well along. Although there are substantial differences between Grace and Trinity, which will be discussed later in another context, the two buildings are similar in their basic frontal tower form.

Trinity, New York, brought to the American architectural community

FIGURE 115. *Richard Upjohn. Church of the Holy Communion, New York, 1844–45.*

what it did not have before, an authentic example of the Gothic style. In its high vaults, its pinnacled buttresses, its soaring spire, and its traceried windows, it gave three-dimensional reality to the visual character of the Gothic, which had previously been available only in books. But Trinity was a large city church, built by a wealthy parish, and except for its stylistic "truthfulness" was unsuitable for the numerous small parishes which were springing up across the expanding nation, and, for that matter, in Manhattan itself. It was for such a parish that Upjohn designed the Church of the Holy Communion in New York. Begun in 1844, and consecrated in 1846, this little church introduced into American architecture a wholly new type of church building (Fig. 115). It is still standing amid the clutter of downtown New York. Described by a contemporary observer as "an unpretending, simply beautiful parish church,"[41] it is a small completely *asymmetrical* building, with steeply pitched roofs, a crenelated tower on the northwest corner, and bold transepts of which the one to the west also served as an entrance. There is a sharply defined chancel and there are buttresses at all corners, including those of the transepts and tower. A large Geometric window graces the east end. The church was built on the southeast corner of Sixth Avenue and Twentieth Street, two and a half miles uptown from Trinity, in a part of the city which was then still largely residential, and it had all the character of a rural church. In fact, Upjohn's original perspective drawing shows it in a park-like setting;[42] so, too, does the lithograph we have chosen for our illustration. The latter was published in 1853 and is accompanied by a descriptive note which says that the "landscape scenery has been substituted for the streets of the city, as more appropriate to the character of the building.[43] In other words, the Church of the Holy Communion was visualized by its

FIGURE 116. *Richard Upjohn. Church of the Holy Communion, New York, interior, 1844–45. Original drawing.*

architect, and understood by its contemporaries, as a small rural parish church.

What Upjohn achieved in the Church of the Holy Communion is precisely the concept of the small parish church which the Ecclesiologists had foremost in their minds, especially for developing rural areas such as were on every hand in America. Moreover, there is evidence that in this case there was an indirect link between Upjohn and the Anglican community of England itself. The Reverend William Muhlenberg, who was responsible for the church, had visited England in 1843 and there made contact with the leaders of the Oxford Movement. The experience intensified his natural high church leanings, and when he returned home it was with a determination to build a church conforming with what he had learned to be the modern canonical trend in church architecture. It was logical that Upjohn, whose reputation as a church builder was by this time firmly established, should be given the commission, and this time there was no prejudice to overcome.

In preparing his design Upjohn did not, as he had at Trinity, follow a specific published model. On the other hand, it is obvious that he had read very closely the admonitions of the *Ecclesiologist* with respect to parish churches. Although the church might not have won the approval of the more doctrinaire Ecclesiologists, it certainly met the major objectives of the Society, and did so in a highly imaginative way. It was a compact little building with an overt Gothic massing of parts; detailing was handled with authority, simplicity, and restraint. The building was cruciform, and had an independent, clearly defined chancel. In the interior (Fig. 116), the high-pitched ceiling was an open wooden frame supported by curved struts which met at the center to form pointed arches. These in turn were carried on wall brackets; the spandrels between the struts and the rafters were filled with wooden tracery. A simple and authentically Gothic structure, this ceiling was the kind Upjohn had hoped to achieve at Trinity until he was forced by church authorities to resort to plaster vaults. With its dark shadowed reaches, it created precisely the effect called for by the Ecclesiologists, and both structurally and liturgically it was probably the first ceiling of its kind in nineteenth-century America. Elsewhere in the church, there were a few deviations from preferred Ecclesiological doctrine: the chancel had the same height as the nave, and the south transept substituted for the preferred south porch,[44] but these only enhanced the free, occult nature of the design.

One of the most important aspects of the Church of the Holy Communion was its asymmetry, a mode of design which encouraged greater freedom of arrangement, for whatever purpose, and made possible qualities of independence which were just as important to its success as its relationship to the Ecclesiological doctrine. To be sure, Trinity, because of its side porch, was mildly asymmetrical. Nevertheless, it was rigidly dominated by its imposing frontal tower, dominated indeed to the point where, in spite of its authentic Gothic massing, proportions and detailing, it still bore a shadowy resemblance to the conventional New England meetinghouse. The Church of the Holy Communion, on the other hand, was unlike any other church which had ever been built in the United States. It was boldly cruciform with high-pitched gables, a combination of forms based on sharp-angle relationships which was more dynamic than the depressed angles and low profile of the conventional American church. Moreover, the aggressive use of a transept in place of a porch as a major entrance was given special emphasis by a round rather than pointed window over the door. This established a motif of sufficient size and interest to counter easily the strong vertical thrust of the rather slender tower. The design, in other words, was not determined by functional concerns alone, but at times was subtly adjusted by the architect to resolve the demands of opposing visual forces. We have seen that asymmetry was embraced by both Pugin and the Ecclesiologists, but more for liturgical than visual reasons.

FIGURE *117. Richard Upjohn. St. Mary's Church, Burlington, N.J., from the northwest, 1846–48.*

The sensitivity with which Upjohn has balanced contrasting elements, however, goes beyond this basic concern. A clear aesthetic response is evident as well, and the Church of the Holy Communion, therefore, not only stands as an early milestone of Ecclesiology in America, but by virtue of its calculated "irregularity" it is also the first church in this country to reflect with certainty the doctrine of the picturesque.

St. Mary's, Burlington, New Jersey

At St. Mary's, Burlington, New Jersey (Fig. 117), Richard Upjohn had his first direct confrontation with Ecclesiology. The Right Reverend George Washington Doane, Bishop of New Jersey and rector of the church at the time it was commissioned, was elected a patron member of the Ecclesiological Society in 1841, and was the first American to be so honored. A prominent hymnologist, educator, and author, Doane was a major figure among the high church leaders of the American Episcopal Church and was also an ardent Gothic Revivalist. Indeed, his interest in church architecture may have begun very early in his career. In 1830 he had been made rector of Trinity Church in Boston, where he briefly had John Henry Hopkins as assistant minister. Since Hopkins was already working on his book on the Gothic, Doane must have known of his activity and may even have been caught up in his enthusiasm.

In 1832 Doane was called to be Bishop of New Jersey, and at the same time, to secure a living, he became rector of St. Mary's. Nine years later, shortly before his election to the Ecclesiological Society, he was invited to England to give the consecration sermon at St. Peter's at Leeds. This building was a major new achievement in the Gothic Revival in England, and for an American to be asked to preach at its consecration was a distinguished honor indeed. Moreover, it placed Doane in the limelight at the very center of the Ecclesiological movement. During the eight months that he was to remain in England he not only visited cathedrals, churches, and universities, but he also met and talked with the most important of the Ecclesiologists. This experience fired his already well-formed preference for the Gothic to new heights of intensity, and when he returned to Burlington he proceeded almost at once to make plans for a new church at St. Mary's to replace the old and simple building which had long served the parish. The commission was given to Upjohn and drawings were begun by the fall of 1846. Although the building was largely completed by 1848, it was not consecrated until 1854. Except for a few minor changes it remained as originally built until the spring of 1976 when it was entirely gutted by fire. As the church stands today, therefore, the stone walls and tower are largely original, but the interior is completely restored and, in some respects, may seem different to the visitor than the building illustrated and described in the following account.[45]

Unlike Upjohn's earlier churches, which had been designed from theoretical sources, St. Mary's, Burlington, was based on a specific English example of the early fourteenth century, the church of St. John the Baptist at Shottesbrooke, Berkshire (Fig. 118). This little Gothic church had attracted the attention of the revivalists for both its purity and its cruciform plan, and measured drawings of it by the Gothic Revival architect William Butterfield were published by the Oxford Architectural Society in 1846.[46] The text accompanying these drawings calls the church "a pure Decorated building, and a beautiful miniature of a cathedral."[47] This description was motivated no doubt by the fact that Shottesbrooke was cruciform in plan with a large central tower and spire over the crossing, a form strongly reminiscent of such great cathedrals as Salisbury (Fig. 61). The symbolic and dramatic effect of a soaring spire at the center of the church must have been attractive to Doane and his architect—both of whom were men of high church convictions. Moreover, information about this particular form of building was available to them in Butterfield's superb and accurate drawings. In every way these drawings presented the most accurate data on the Gothic parish church yet to ap-

FIGURE *118. Church of St. John the Baptist, Shottesbrooke, Berkshire, England. Old print.*

pear in the United States, and it is easy to understand why both Doane and Upjohn used Shottesbrooke for their basic model. Indeed, their motive was to improve the state of ecclesiastical architecture in the United States in precisely the way the Ecclesiologists would have them do. Ironically, their choice brought severe criticism rather than praise from the English society.[48] The men of Cambridge had their own plans for America and it was thus unthinkable that Doane should have turned to the Oxford Architectural Society rather than to them for help in planning his new church. For the same reason, and perhaps too because of his independence as a designer, Upjohn was also the subject of a condescending attack, and in the end was never completely to receive the wholehearted endorsement of the Ecclesiological Society for his achievements as a church architect. Nevertheless, in St. Mary's, Upjohn brought to the American scene a vital new church in the Gothic style, and did so with his usual fine sense of architectural form.

FIGURE 119. *Richard Upjohn. St. Mary's Church, Burlington, N.J., southeast elevation, 1846–48. Old print.*

Quite apart from the Ecclesiologists' shortsighted antagonism is the fact that St. Mary's was conscientiously conceived and became an important milestone in the development of Ecclesiological architecture in the United States (Fig. 119). It was symbolically correct, it had a south porch, it had a clearly articulated chancel inside and out. Its high-pitched roof was supported on the inside by open wooden trussing, and in the chancel the ceiling was richly decorated (Fig. 122). There was even an element of asymmetry in the positioning of the south porch counter to the prominent stair turrets on the northwest corner of the tower (Fig. 120); and, to repeat, the church was based on an authentic English model. From the architectural point of view, however, the building is exciting more for its variations on the basic theme than for its careful copying; for Upjohn took substantial and highly productive liberties with St. John's, Shottes-brooke. The English church was a squat, awkward building, with stubby transepts, a disproportionately heavy tower, and a nave that was shorter than the chancel. Moreover, the tower was squared off at the top, and the octagonal spire rose without transition from behind a crenelated parapet.

Upjohn's first major change was to extend the nave to the point where it was almost twice the length of the chancel. This brought the church to a total length of 137 feet, thereby adding a quality of grace to the flank profile that was totally lacking in the English model. Gothic vertical accents were achieved by Upjohn through the alternating but unobtrusive rhythm of the wall buttresses and the lancet windows. To make the ver-

FIGURE *120*. *Richard Upjohn. St. Mary's Church,*
Burlington, N.J., from the southwest, 1846–48.

tical thrust of the tower more emphatic, he eliminated the disruptive
crenelation of Shottesbrooke and substituted instead a simple crown molding (Fig. 120); in addition, he eased the transition from the block of the
tower to the taper of the spire by introducing an inward curving plane
which moved equally and smoothly from all four sides into the triangular
planes of the broaches on the one hand, and into the outside planes of
the spire on the other. The resulting profile flowed gracefully inward from
the horizontal crown molding and then upward to the cross at the point,
150 feet above the ground. Except for two levels of slender dormers, one
on the outer plane of the spire at the broach, the other on the diagonal
plane slightly above the middle, the spire is unadorned. This is in keeping with the austerity of the design as a whole. Upjohn replaced the Decorated windows of Shottesbrooke with simple lancets which for the most
part are devoid of tracery; the large and elaborate Curvilinear windows in
the four main gables of the English church became triple lancets in Upjohn's design, a change which appalled the Ecclesiologists. The walls of
the building are a lovely warm freestone, laid in random ashlar, and

FIGURE 121. *Richard Upjohn. St. Mary's Church, Burlington, N.J., interior, 1846–48.*

except for the regular rhythm of the simple wall buttresses and the restrained hood moldings over the windows, they are without ornamental intrusion of any kind, relying for their richness of effect upon the variegated texture and color of the masonry, and upon Upjohn's refined feeling for Gothic proportions.

The interior of St. Mary's fulfills the promise of the exterior. The major spaces—nave, transepts, and chancel—center around the four piers and arches at the crossing (Fig. 121). These massive structural supports carry the weight of the tower. They are of masonry, but their surfaces are covered with austere painted plaster and on the whole are massive and excessively geometric in their unmolded simplicity. Indeed, the almost brutal largeness of both piers and arches suggests a certain cautiousness on the part of the architect in his efforts to provide and express adequate support for the tower. Nevertheless, the heavy piers sharply articulate the equally austere spaces of the nave and transepts, which extend at right

FIGURE 122. *Richard Upjohn. St. Mary's Church,*
Burlington, N.J., chancel, 1846–48.

angles in three directions beneath the shadowed dark wood of the ham-
merbeam ceilings. All these spaces flow through the great arches into the
crossing, where they come to rest in a quiet, motionless prologue to the
contrasting visual animation of the chancel (Fig. 122). Here, all the
splendor of Gothic applied ornament, so dear to the Ecclesiologists,
enlivens structural and non-structural surfaces alike in a burst of pattern
and color, and sets the chancel apart as the sacred ceremonial space for
Upjohn's exquisite, jewel-like altar.

The nave and transepts of St. Mary's have been criticized as excessively
severe,[49] and they indeed constitute a stark and distilled sequence of

FIGURE *123. St. James-the-Less, Philadelphia, Pa., 1846–48.*

spaces. In their bold simplicity they are not unlike the severe geometry of such rational works as Mills's Treasury Building in Washington, which was brand-new at the time St. Mary's was begun.[50] There is, of course, no direct connection between the two, but in 1850 Neoclassical doctrine was still a powerful force in the formation of American taste, and it is possible that Upjohn was instinctively sensitive to this condition. Yet, like the severity of the Treasury Building, it is this same quality which makes the nave and transepts of St. Mary's more expressive of the primitive state of American society in 1846 than are the more English-bound conventions of the chancel, however lovely and appropriate they may be. By reducing the Gothic to its simplest possible terms, without sacrificing its intrinsic qualities of space, proportion, and scale, Upjohn made a statement about the Gothic at St. Mary's which was particularly expressive of the American scene and paved the way for a uniquely American understanding of the style.

St. James-the-Less, Philadelphia

At the same time that the Ecclesiologists were scolding Bishop Doane and his architect for what they regarded as the improprieties of St. Mary's, Burlington, they were announcing with some pleasure that the church of St. James-the-Less, near the Falls of the Schuylkill in Philadelphia (Fig.

FIGURE 124. St. Michael's, Longstanton,
Cambridgeshire, England, c. 1230.

123), was being built from drawings sent to the United States by the
Cambridge Camden Society. The story of how these drawings arrived in
Philadelphia, and the role of the Society in the design and construction
of St. James-the-Less, is a fascinating one which has been told by Stanton in carefully documented detail.[51] It need not concern us here. The important point, as Stanton has indicated, is that St. James-the-Less was
the first church in the United States to be built "under the direct supervision of the English Ecclesiologists."[52] In addition to receiving the drawings
the Americans responsible for the church corresponded directly with the
leaders of the Ecclesiological movement, including such prominent
figures as Benjamin Webb and the architect William Butterfield. St. James-
the-Less is historically important, therefore, because it brought to the
United States, with only minor alterations, a superb example of a small
medieval English parish church. Its architectural importance lies in the
purity and quality with which it was rendered, and in the influence which
it had on subsequent Gothic churches in the United States.

The man responsible for St. James-the-Less was Robert Ralston, a
Philadelphia merchant. The site was a spectacular enclave on a hill above
the Schuylkill, and was acquired from the adjacent Laurel Hill Cemetery.
At the time the church was built, between 1846 and '48, it was situated
in the midst of an expanding and prosperous suburban area; today, in its
sheltered courtyard, it is an island of serenity surrounded by the harsh
blight of a modern city.

The English model for St. James-the-Less was the Church of St.
Michael, Longstanton, Cambridgeshire (Fig. 124). This beautiful little

medieval church was greatly admired by the Ecclesiologists, and was one of three selected by them as appropriate in size and character for use in the "colonies."[53] Its primary architectural ingredients were those which have already been seen in Pugin's St. Oswald's, Liverpool (Fig. 108). They are a one-story nave with a high, steeply sloping roof, a smaller but similarly shaped attached chancel, and a south porch. Unlike St. Oswald's, St. Michael's does not have a frontal tower and spire. Instead, in accordance with its smaller size, it has a bell gable, or bell cote, rising directly in the plane of the west wall. Indeed, this form typifies a special group of very small English parish churches, and because of its size it was popular with the Revivalists for small rural parishes. Two characteristic examples were shown by Pugin in his *Present State* (Fig. 125).

The adoption of St. Michael's as the model for St. James-the-Less, even though brought about by curious circumstances,[54] was fortunate; for the church was exactly right in size and character for the particular situation it was built to serve. More than that, it provided the most suitable prototype yet to appear in America for the countless suburban and rural Episcopal parishes which were coming into being as the country expanded. The cruciform plan of Shottesbrooke, although eminently appropriate for the more ambitious churches such as St. Mary's, Burlington, still had hovering over it the shadow of the great cathedrals. The simple nave church, on the other hand, spoke with uncomplicated eloquence of both the aspirations and the limited means of the average small parish. Yet, in the strictest sense of the phrase, St. James-the-Less was not an American Gothic Revival church; it was rather a transplantation of an English parish church. The degree to which it was inspired and directed from England made this inevitable. Moreover, many of the incidental items in the church were made in England, including the tiles for the chancel and some of the stained glass. Even the designs for the lych gate and tombstones in the churchyard were taken from an English publication provided by Butterfield.[55] Finally, no prominent architect then practicing in America is known to have been connected with either the design or the construction of the building. Work was directed by Robert Ralston, the principal motivating figure behind the church, and actual construction has been attributed to the contractor, John E. Carver.[56]

St. James-the-Less is a pure and exquisitely beautiful Gothic church, unmatched for quality and authenticity by any other American church of its time. To achieve canonical and stylistic correctness, meticulous attention was given to the accurate rendition of the English drawings; to assure the highest order of artistry and craftsmanship, no expense was spared. Indeed the cost, initially estimated at $5,000, ended up at $30,000, a dramatic increase which seems to have been cheerfully borne by the vestry. As the church stands today on its hilltop, cloistered behind high stone walls in an expansive rustic churchyard, and surrounded by a forest of nineteenth-century gravestones, it presents the image of an ancient building in an ancient setting, as far removed from the colonial and Neoclassical conventions of the traditional American church as it could possibly be. In its sympathetic recall of an English parish church, it reminds us of

ST. ANNE'S, KEIGHLEY.

ST. MARY'S, SOUTHPORT.

FIGURE 125. *Augustus Welby Pugin. St. Anne's, Keighley, England, and St. Mary's, Southport, England.*

the seventeenth-century church of St. Luke's, in Isle of Wight County, Virginia, which we have already identified with the end of the original Gothic development in church architecture,[57] and in so doing it establishes a meaningful link between the American Gothic Revival and its origins in the Gothic past itself.

An extensive architectural analysis of St. James-the-Less is not necessary to establish its importance. It captures the specific character of the Longstanton Church as accurately as possible within the limits of the drawings, local building skills, and direction by long-range correspondence with England. Its articulated but asymmetrical massing of nave, chancel, and porch, the tapered verticality of its exterior profiles, the dy-

FIGURE 126. *St. Michael's, Longstanton,*
Cambridgeshire, England, interior, c. 1230.

namic effect of its strong stepped buttresses, even the variegated texture
and pattern of its random granite walls, all combine to fulfill the highest
expectations of Ecclesiological doctrine.

On the interior the canonical correctness with which it imitated its English Gothic model is even more starkly apparent (compare Figs. 126 and
127). Although the unbroken planes of the steeply sloping roof of the
main body of the building suggest a single interior space (Fig. 123), the
worship area is, in fact, divided into the conventional Gothic pattern of
nave and side aisles. This extremely medieval spatial arrangement is articulated on the exterior by the pair of imposing wall buttresses which press
against the west front to form the visual and structural base for the soaring
bell cote above. Within, the tripartite division is accomplished by a massive arcade running down each side of the nave; alternating round and octagonal stone piers of squat proportions support heavy Gothic ribbed
arches, which in turn carry random ashlar walls of rock-faced granite.
These walls rise to a level just below the roof, where they form the
imposts for the five-part open scissored truss of the nave ceiling; to the left

FIGURE 127. *St. James-the-Less, Philadelphia, Pa., interior, 1846–48.*

and right of the nave, in the area over the aisles, the roof is carried on simple exposed rafters which run from the nave to the outside walls. The roof of the chancel, on the other hand, which is even steeper than that of the nave and aisles, is supported by rafters that are tied slightly above their center by horizontal collar beams.

This combination of structural and spatial elements is precisely the arrangement of St. Michael's, Longstanton, and of particular importance at St. James-the-Less is the fact that all the stone elements of the interior, including the rough granite walls, were left exposed in their natural surfaces. Even though very early in the Gothic Revival the Americans discovered the expressive and picturesque qualities of stone for exterior walls, their preference was for plaster on the interiors, a preference which had its roots in the pristine geometric interiors of the colonial and Neoclassical years. Masonry walls, when they occurred inside Gothic churches, were therefore covered with plaster and painted, as at St. Mary's, Burlington. Even at St. James-the-Less there was some discussion about this point, and it was not until outside consultation gave convincing argument in favor of unplastered walls that the decision was made to leave them in their natural state.[58] This decision was, indeed, the ultimate concession to Gothic truth, and it put the crowning touch of

FIGURE 128. Richard Upjohn. St. Thomas's Episcopal Church,
Amenia Union, N.Y., 1849–51.

authenticity on the Philadelphia church, immensely enhancing its usefulness as a model for future Gothic churches in America. Of all the
American Gothic churches of the nineteenth century, St. James-the-Less
is the purest and most coherent in style, and its influence on the continuing Gothic Revival was considerable.

The Influence of St. James-the-Less

Even before St. James-the-Less was finished in 1848, churches modeled
after it made their appearance in this country, and during the 1850's the
small bell-cote type became common throughout the American Episcopal
community.[59] A brief examination of two churches based on St. James-
the-Less, both of them designed by Richard Upjohn, will illustrate this
development. We recall that Upjohn was at work on St. Mary's, Burlington, in 1847–48; these were the very years when St. James-the-Less was
also under construction. Moreover, its site was only twenty miles from
St. Mary's. It is unthinkable, therefore, that the architect did not know
of the Philadelphia church. Indeed, it is highly probable that he visited it.
In any case, in 1848, even before St. James-the-Less was completed,
Upjohn used the bell-cote form in Calvary Church, Stonington, Connec-

FIGURE 129. *Richard Upjohn. St. Thomas's Episcopal Church, Amenia Union, N.Y., interior, 1849–51.*

ticut.[60] The following year he employed it again in a more interesting way at St. Thomas's Episcopal Church, Amenia Union, New York (Fig. 128).

Remotely situated beneath the slopes of the Connecticut hills, in a rare and still unspoiled portion of eastern New York state, St. Thomas's is an utterly simple little building which represents Richard Upjohn at his very best. Refined in scale, and stripped of all non-essentials, it is both poised and pure in its massing, and exquisitely elegant in the attenuated taper of its Gothic shapes. Because it is brick rather than stone, its surfaces are plainer than the rough-cut granite walls of St. James-the-Less, and lend themselves more readily to the discreet geometry of Upjohn's modest statement. Awareness that the building was to be tiny, and that the financial means were limited, in no way inhibited the architect's inventiveness.

To the extent that St. Thomas's reflects the canonical correctness of St. James-the-Less, it is a pure Ecclesiological building. Its tall bell cote, high-pitched roof, articulated chancel, and south porch are all familiar features properly developed and related. The building stands, therefore, in a direct line of descent, through St. James-the-Less, from the English Gothic parish church. However, there are qualities of purity and primness about the building which seem to deny a medieval ancestry in favor of the traditional simplicity which characterizes the earlier churches of rural America. Of all the English-born architects practicing in this country during the Gothic Revival years, Upjohn seems to have been the most sensitive to the inherent qualities of the American architectural scene. In addition, he brought even to his smallest buildings a highly developed sense of architectural form, manifest at St. Thomas's not only in its superb scale and proportion but also in numerous internal relationships of parts. This is seen in the particular way, for example, that Upjohn reduced the weight of the façade by eliminating the heavy frontal buttresses, so conspicuous at St. James-the-Less; and having done that, the way he restored the essential vertical emphasis by projecting the bell cote slightly in front of the wall of the church as a flat attached tower; or further, the way in which he repeated the visual motif of the graceful hooded entrance in the pointed arch and high-pitched hood of the bell cote itself. All of these subtle adjustments were made specially for architectural reasons which had nothing to do with canonical correctness.

The interior of St. Thomas's (Fig. 129) is as direct and uncluttered as the exterior. The walls are unpainted plaster into which the splayed lancet openings are cut sharply without articulating surrounds. Rising from these walls, the dark pointed-arch wood brackets which support the purlins of the high-pitched roof proclaim the shape of the unadorned chancel arch, itself as austere and geometric as that of St. Mary's, Burlington (Fig. 121). Except for the chancel rail and the other pieces of liturgical furniture, the only concession to ornament in the entire interior is the simple Gothic moldings which have been cut into the feet of the main ceiling arches. Both inside and out, St. Thomas's is a coherent and austerely beautiful building, as expressive of its immediate circumstances as it is reflective of the ancient Gothic tradition from which it was born.

The second of Upjohn's many churches based on St. James-the-Less to be examined, is the Chapel of St. Mary the Virgin at Nashotah Episcopal Theological Seminary near Nashotah, Wisconsin (Fig. 130). Unlike the Amenia church, which was built to serve a small rural parish in an established part of the East, the Nashotah chapel would stand, when completed, as a bastion of Ecclesiology on the fringes of the wilderness. One of the most important thrusts of the Episcopal Church during the years of westward expansion was its domestic missionary movement. Begun in 1835, when the dynamic Jackson Kemper was chosen to be the Church's first missionary bishop, it advanced swiftly into the opening reaches of the frontier, and by mid-century had established significant outposts in numerous areas, including the rich farmlands of Wisconsin and Minnesota. In the early 1840's, a seminary was founded at Nashotah and by 1859 had grown sufficiently in strength and importance to require a new chapel. Construction began in 1859, but was not finished until after the Civil War.

The choice of Richard Upjohn as the architect for the chapel of St. Mary the Virgin was logical. The seminary at Nashotah was a center of high church sentiment, and by this time Upjohn had a solid reputation within the Episcopal Church as a professional of great skill and impecca-

FIGURE 130. *Richard Upjohn. Chapel of St. Mary the Virgin at Nashotah Episcopal Theological Seminary, Nashotah, Wis., west façade, 1859–60.*

ble canonical judgment; and he in turn showed himself to be acutely responsive to the challenge. His evocation of St. James-the-Less satisfied the liturgical aspirations of a zealous clergy, and his sensitive handling of the building as a work of architecture made the chapel particularly appropriate to the serene remoteness of its wilderness setting.

That St. Mary's, Nashotah, is based on St. James-the-Less is unequivocally clear. However, there are significant differences between the two churches. St. Mary's is both larger and more complex than its prototype, and the architect took considerable liberties with the specific character of many of its parts. Like St. James-the-Less, St. Mary's has a nave and side aisles, but Upjohn made much more of this tripartite arrangement in the exterior massing of his church. In a manner more reminiscent of St. Oswald's (Fig. 108) than St. James-the-Less, he placed a high-pitched roof over the nave, and then, with a clear break at the eave line, depressed the roof angle over each aisle. Moreover, in the façade, he permitted the frontal plane of the nave to move forward slightly but clearly beyond the walls fronting the aisles. This discreet division of space he defined even more precisely by shifting the frontal buttresses from beneath the bell cote,

FIGURE 131. *Richard Upjohn. Chapel of St. Mary the Virgin at Nashotah Episcopal Theological Seminary, Nashotah, Wis. chancel end, 1859–60.*

where they are located at St. James-the-Less, to a position coinciding exactly with the projecting corners of the nave wall. This not only strengthens the articulation of the corners of the nave, but also adds to the strong vertical thrust of the façade as a whole. To complete the canonical arrangement of the church, there was once a conventional south porch (now buried beneath the connecting corridor to a more recent seminary building), and a short but less conventional octagonal chancel abuts the east end of the nave (Fig. 131).[61]

In many ways the most exciting and original aspect of Upjohn's design is his treatment of the bell cote. At St. James-the-Less, the bell cote was continuous with the plane of the front wall; at St. Mary's, Upjohn moved it forward of the nave wall, much as he had done at St. Thomas's, Amenia Union. This created, in effect, a soaring slender tower which projects slightly and rises in a continuous frontal plane through four lateral setbacks to the triple openings of the belfry on top. The over-all result is severely geometric and bold; at the same time, however, it is exquisitely delicate. The geometry derives from the simplicity with which the walls and wall openings are treated. Although the building is rock-faced limestone laid in random ashlar, the stones are more consistently rectangular than those in the rubble masonry of St. James-the-Less, and all openings are sharply defined. Only the pointed arch of the main entrance door is articulated by a bold flat surround; all the other openings are cut directly into the wall without any ornamental definition whatsoever. The various planes of the design thus assert themselves emphatically and without interruption.

The delicacy of St. Mary's stems from both the extreme attenuation of form, and the precise linear effect created by the sharply defined intersections of planes. The extravagant verticality and taper, moreover, are enormously enhanced by the poised and rhythmic succession of wall openings. The broad pointed arch for the central door lightens the lower part of the tower, making it seem to rest on stilts; on either side, in the front wall of each aisle, is a tall narrow lancet window. Above the central door, in the face of the tower, is a pair of even taller blind lancets which, in their elongated proportions and pointed tops, imitate the shape and character of the tower itself. Still further up in the vertical line is a smaller blind lancet. Finally, as the crowning motif there appears the characteristic one-over-two lancet openings of the bell cote. The result is a graded one-two-one-two-one ascending rhythm which is comparable in its controlled relationships of shape, proportion, and interval to the most discreet designs of the Neoclassical era.

As a dedicated revivalist, Upjohn showed himself to be profoundly aware of both the dynamic excitement and the soaring grace of the Gothic style, and it is precisely these qualities of gothicism which form the very core of his work. Yet, his capacity to control and distill the Gothic forms, without destroying their intrinsic characteristics, gave his architecture an orderly simplicity which made it readily acceptable to the American mind. Although he was keenly aware of the usefulness of the small English parish church in the American scene, his particular solution in each instance went far beyond the simple functional need. Whereas St. James-the-Less had been a deliberate imitation of St. Michael's, Longstanton, as accurate in its rendition of the model as means and distance would permit, each bell-cote type church by Upjohn was a unique solution to a unique set of conditions, in a uniquely American setting. His variations on the theme of St. James-the-Less were as numerous as the churches which he built in that manner, each differing in some way from the prototype, and each as different from another as is St. Thomas's, Amenia Union from St. Mary's, Nashotah.

The Asymmetrical Church:
St. Paul's, Brookline, Massachusetts

If Richard Upjohn found the bell-cote form of St. James-the-Less useful for small and medium-sized churches, it was by no means the only type which he designed. A few of his later works were frontal-tower churches similar to Trinity, New York, although in most of these the chancel was more clearly articulated than it had been at Trinity. In a few Gothic churches which he built for denominations other than the Episcopal, the chancel was eliminated altogether. Most of his churches, however, were some form of variation on the asymmetrical tower scheme, a type first developed by the architect in the Church of the Holy Communion in New

York (Fig. 115). Because the asymmetrical tower church was to become so immensely important in the later development of the Gothic Revival in this country, it is essential that this discussion of Richard Upjohn and the Ecclesiological movement in America should include an examination of one of his masterpieces in that mode, St. Paul's Episcopal Church, Brookline, Massachusetts.

Brookline in the late 1840's was not unlike the section of Philadelphia which surrounded St. James-the-Less. It was an attractive area dominated by large country estates, and with improved transportation routes to Boston, it was becoming an exclusive residential community for the wealthy city businessmen. The story of St. Paul's, therefore, is one which was repeated over and over again in nineteenth-century America, the story of a new church, for a new parish, situated in a growing community on the outskirts of an old village. By 1848 a sufficient number of Episcopalians had established themselves in Brookline to justify the formation of a parish, and by 1850 plans for a new church were being made. The leading organizers were Augustus Aspinwall, who provided the site, and Harrison Fay. Richard Upjohn was commissioned to make the plans. The cornerstone was laid July 29, 1851, and by late 1852, except for some interior details, the building was virtually complete.[62] Ironically, in the winter of 1976, three months before St. Mary's, Burlington, St. Paul's was also gutted by fire. All that remain of the original building, therefore, are the walls and tower.[63]

Like so many of Upjohn's churches, St. Paul's was a country church when it was built, and the parish was small. It is of considerable interest, therefore, that an early drawing indicates that the original design was for a bell-cote church, very similar to St. James-the-Less in Philadelphia (Fig. 132). This modest proposal does not seem to have satisfied the larger aspirations of the Brookline parish, however, and a second drawing was submitted. It shows a similar single-roofed church with separate chancel and south porch, but with the bell cote replaced by a bold and simple tower on the northwest corner. But even this change seems not to have been acceptable and it was only in a third drawing[64] that the final scheme was achieved (Fig. 133). As seen today, therefore, St. Paul's represents a fascinating evolution in design from a simple nave church, to a much more complex building with nave and side aisles, chancel, and south porch, poised dynamically against a tall asymmetrically placed tower and a soaring broached spire.

In his final solution for St. Paul's, Upjohn treated the triple division of interior space in much the same way as at Nashotah, that is, with a second, or lower, pitch of roof over the aisles, and with wall buttresses on the west façade which define the limits of the nave within. In the progress of the design from the second to the final drawing the tower, too, was considerably changed. It was made more elegant by an increase in the height of the broached spire; it was further enriched by pilasters and corbel tabling at the belfry stage, and by the addition of simple decorated tracery in the pointed-arch openings of the belfry. In a similar vein, the

FIGURE 132. *Richard Upjohn. St. Paul's Episcopal Church,
Brookline, Mass., early design. Original water color.*

FIGURE 133. *Richard Upjohn. St. Paul's Episcopal Church,
Brookline, Mass., perspective view, 1851. Original water color.*

FIGURE 134. *Richard Upjohn. St. Paul's Episcopal Church, Brookline, Mass., 1851–52.*

treatment of the windows throughout the building was more sculptural, and thus in a sense more Gothic than the unadorned lancets at Amenia (Fig. 128) and Nashotah (Fig. 130). Moreover, the windows on the aisles are broader in proportion, are topped by a hood molding, and are divided into two lights by center bars and Decorated tracery. The west end has two balancing single-light traceried windows; above, in the point of the gable, is a hooded oculus with trefoil tracery. In typically Ecclesiological manner, the window in the east end of the chancel (Fig. 134) is the largest and most prominent in the building. It is divided into three lights with trefoil and cinquefoil patterns of tracery in the pointed arch.

On the interior of St. Paul's (Fig. 135), the division into nave and aisles is made in typical Gothic fashion by two rows of clustered piers, which carry the black walnut framing of the ceiling. Although on entering the church, one has the immediate impression that this shadowed wooden structure is complex, it is in fact extremely simple. The dominating components are the open rafters, which are carried on a series of purlin plates. As the main vertical support element in each bay, a heavy wooden post rises from the top of each pier to carry the primary plate from which all the rafters of the nave ceiling spring. The principal rafters, which abut the crowns of each post, are substantially larger than the common rafters, and act as the primary support for the two purlin plates. They also combine with a series of sweeping wooden pointed arches, which span the nave laterally from post to post to form the principal bay frames. Together

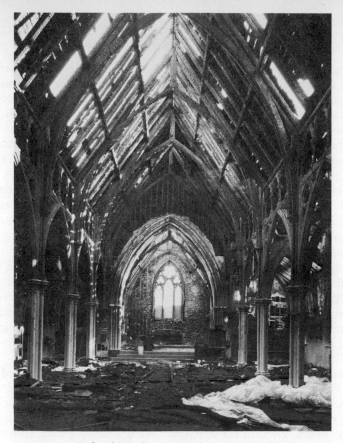

FIGURE 135. *Richard Upjohn. St. Paul's Episcopal Church, Brookline, Mass., 1851–52. Interior after fire.*

with the similar but smaller frames which support the aisle ceilings, they stiffen the total structure and help contain the lateral pressure of the rafters. The longitudinal stiffening is provided by yet another series of wooden arches which run the length of the nave between the posts. Each of these arches also carries an open Gothic arcade which acts as a filler between their crowns and the primary plate of the ceiling. Because of its position above the nave arches, this arcade has been called a triforium,[65] and it does, indeed, occupy the same position as a triforium in the conventional masonry Gothic bay. Structurally, however, it performs a very different function. The conventional triforium was an opening in the wall membrane of the Gothic bay, and it supported nothing but the tracery bars of the clerestory window above; Upjohn's arcade is an open wooden bridge which supports the primary plate of the nave ceiling. Nevertheless, its position in the structure and its visual kinship with the triforium justify its being thought of in these terms and adds substantially to the Gothic character of the nave.

Altogether, the wooden ceiling of St. Paul's is the crowning delight of the interior. Elsewhere in the worship space the architectural treatment is discreet and contained. As on the exterior, all window openings are framed by simple colonnettes and hood moldings; a deeply molded chancel arch separates the nave and chancel. Otherwise the walls are unadorned plaster. By contrast, the web-like, soaring ceiling generates a special excitement. This excitement derives in part from the directness with which the structural problem has been solved. There are no redundant hammer beams to clutter the framing, no tie beams to intercept the chancel arch or the east window. Each element is part of an interlocking system in which the structural relationships are perfectly clear, a system which would be weakened if not destroyed should any single element be removed. In the words of the *Ecclesiologist,* which preferred "unadorned rafters and braces, . . . every one of the timbers [is] exposed in all their honest nakedness."[66] At the same time, our interest in the ceiling is further aroused by the air of mystery created by its dimmed upper reaches. By virtue of the extremely high pitch of the roof and the somber tonality of the black walnut, the attenuated skeleton of the ceiling structure becomes obscured, as the Ecclesiologists hoped it would be, by the *"dark of the valley"* above.[67] The result was that ambivalent mood of reality and unreality, that evocation of "grandeur and solemnity," which was regarded by the *Ecclesiologist* as "essential to the Christian effect of a church."[68]

The frank use of materials and structure, so ardently advocated by the *Ecclesiologist,* was perfectly natural to Richard Upjohn. His sensitivity to the special qualities of stone, brick, and wood, and his intelligent understanding of the ways in which they can be made to join and adhere in a structural whole, gives to his best work an unusually poetic coherence. It is precisely this which distinguishes St. Paul's from many of the other churches of its day, and it is apparent on the outside of the building as well as within. The discreet Gothic adornment of the exterior of St. Paul's is doubly expressive since it is observed against the random rubble of the masonry. The variegated internal structure of the brown Roxbury pudding stone, laid as it is in blocks of irregular shape and size, provides a rich and contrasting foil for the controlled shapes of the moldings and tracery. But equally important, the subtle exploitation of the natural qualities of the stone also unites the building in sympathetic harmony with all the substances of nature from which it came. Indeed, Upjohn's extraordinary responsiveness to the inherent qualities of his materials is nowhere better illustrated than in the contrasting ways he handled the masonry here and at Nashotah. The limestone of the Wisconsin church, because of its consistent grain, could be readily dressed, and even though the individual blocks varied in size and were left with their outer faces rough, Upjohn had them cut for the most part in rectangular shapes. At Brookline, however, as though in response to the irregular texture of the conglomerate itself, he had the stones made up in an utterly random fashion obviously delighting in the infinite variety of their size, shape, and surface texture. The walls of St. Paul's, therefore, seem to be an organic extension of the earth upon which the building stands.

At the same time, the dynamic irregular massing of St. Paul's, made possible by the asymmetrical placement of the tower, when combined with the upward diminishing movement of its tapered forms, makes the various parts of the church appear and disappear with each change in point of view, makes them balance and rebalance as they move and change like the constantly shifting patterns of the random natural setting in which the building was made to live. Yet with all its variety and richness, there is also a poised boldness and simplicity about St. Paul's, a largeness of form and a lack of redundancy which makes the building almost austere. It is an exciting synthesis of traditional simplicity, canonical correctness, and poetic wonder. Above all, it is infused with Upjohn's own artistic will, a will shaped in large measure by the romantic values of his day, yet one which seems also to have been conditioned by many of the austere preferences of the American building tradition. In spite of the fact that he was a leading protagonist of the picturesque, the largeness and simplicity of his style gave to his work a special kinship with the prevailing American taste, and placed him in the vanguard of the nation's search for its own architectural identity.

The Ecclesiological Movement and the American Architect

The work of Richard Upjohn was a major rock in the foundation of the Gothic Revival in the United States, and was specifically influential in the spread of Ecclesiological ideas in American church architecture. This was so in spite of the fact that the Ecclesiologists were critical of Upjohn, and for a while at least were engaged with him in an unfriendly confrontation.[69] Yet with all their criticism, Upjohn remained the most popular and eminent architect in the American Episcopal community. Indeed, his reputation was one which could not be ignored and in 1849, he was invited to become an honorary member of the New York Ecclesiological Society; and in 1852, when the Society published its first list of approved architects, Upjohn's name was among them.

Because of the individuality of Upjohn's style, and because of the distinguished reputation which he enjoyed, we have chosen to develop the story of Ecclesiological Gothic in America almost entirely through his work. This does not mean, of course, that he was the only architect practicing in this country under the influence of the Ecclesiological movement. On the contrary, there were numerous others of varying degrees of competence and their combined works exceeded that of Upjohn. The most interesting among them were named along with Upjohn on the Ecclesiologists' list, and included Frank Wills and his partner Henry Dudley of New York. Of the pair, Wills was the more firmly established. Moreover, he had been associated with the New York Ecclesiological Society from its inception in 1848, and from that time onward he enjoyed recognition as its official architect. A writer as well as an architect, and an enthusiastic follower of Pugin, Wills seems to have been responsible for a number of the most searching articles on architecture which appeared in the *New York Ecclesiologist*. In the end he was more influential through his writings than he was through his actual buildings.[70]

The same can be said of John W. Priest, another of the architects endorsed by the New York group. Together with Wills, he was a major figure in articulating the architectural policy of the Society. His most influential contribution was a series of articles reviewing various English publications about architecture and aesthetics. These essays served to confirm and disseminate Ecclesiological doctrine; they also provided a vehicle through which Priest could develop his own architectural philosophy. Priest was the only native-born American in the group of approved architects, and although ardently supporting Ecclesiology, he also argued against mere copying of the past, urging instead an original "living" style. Both Wills and Priest were firm in their convictions that the Ecclesiological Gothic, when properly accommodated to the American scene (as in Upjohn's work) would produce a new form of the style, uniquely expressive of this country. From the very beginning, the New York Ecclesiological Society asserted its independence from England, and both Wills and Priest played significant roles in establishing and maintaining this point of view.

In 1853, the New York Ecclesiological Society approved another architect, John Notman of Philadelphia. As in the case of Upjohn, Notman's contribution is to be measured by his buildings rather than his writings. Born in Scotland, and eight years younger than Upjohn, he had settled in Philadelphia in the early 1830's, about the same time his fellow Britisher was getting his start in New Bedford and Boston. By the time Upjohn began work on St. Mary's in Burlington, New Jersey, Notman had already designed two buildings for Bishop Doane, his house "Riverside" (1837–39), about which we will have more to say later, and the Chapel of the Holy Innocents at St. Mary's Hall (1845–46), both of which were also in Burlington. Although Bishop Doane had turned to the highly talented Upjohn rather than to Notman for the more important church of St. Mary's, Notman was on his way to becoming a leading architect in the Philadelphia area. His St. Mark's Church in that city (1847–49) is one of the finest and earliest examples of the Ecclesiological Gothic in America (Fig. 136). Begun one year later than Upjohn's Church of the Holy Communion in New York, it, too, is an asymmetrical scheme with an off-center tower and broached spire. The design was actually inspired by the church of St. Stephen's, Westminster, London.[71] Notman modified and simplified the original, but maintained its bold dynamic massing. In its fine proportions and authoritative detail, St. Mark's is a competent building which in some ways rivals such asymmetrical tower designs as Upjohn's St. Paul's, Brookline.

St. Mark's represents Notman at his best and will serve to illustrate the general spread of the Ecclesiological doctrine in the hands of architects other than Upjohn. But to understand fully the character of the Ecclesiological movement in America we must now turn our attention to an extremely important fact about the architects approved by the New York

FIGURE 136. John Notman. St. Mark's Episcopal Church,
Philadelphia, Pa., 1847–49.

Ecclesiological Society: of the five, *four were British*.[72] Moreover, once
the Ecclesiological movement became established in this country, not a
single one of the leading native-born architects then practicing designed a
church in the Ecclesiological manner. Even architects like Town and
Strickland, who built Gothic churches during the early years when little
was known about the style, produced no Gothic churches after the
Gothic Revival became firmly established; and A. J. Davis, who was already a major figure in the American Gothic Revival, designed only a
few minor Gothic churches, none of which adhered to Ecclesiological
doctrine.

These facts about architects in particular suggest two observations of
immense importance. First, they reaffirm both the popularity and im-
pregnability of the Neoclassical movement and the dominating role which
it played in the formation of American taste during the first half of the
nineteenth century.[73] The notion that classical forms in general and Greek
architecture in particular were both symbolic of American democracy and
appropriate to the American way of life was too deeply ingrained in the
American consciousness to be easily displaced by the doctrinal strictures

of Ecclesiology. In contrast to the broad rationalism which infused the Neoclassical styles, the early Gothic Revival in church architecture was motivated by narrow and parochial values. It flourished in a sharply defined world of canonical rightness that was as far removed from the everyday sentiments of America as were Upjohn's dynamically poised and dark-toned churches from the pristine white cylinders and cubes of the Greek Revival meetinghouse. The confirmed Neoclassical architects wanted no part of the Anglican-Episcopal world. That is not to say that during the first half of the century the Gothic style did not penetrate other Protestant denominations. As we shall see it did, but even then it was almost always the Ecclesiological architects who were called in to do the work. Church architecture, therefore, at least as far as the Gothic style was concerned, became a specialty practiced with few exceptions only by those who had been properly initiated into the faith, and it was this situation that the more humanistic Neoclassicists were inclined to resist.

Recognition of this leads us to our second observation: the Ecclesiological Gothic Revival in America was not only English-inspired, it was also English in form and essence. Surely it was no accident that four out of the five architects approved by the Ecclesiologists were British. The opportunities opening up in this country would naturally have encouraged a number of British architects to migrate and those who did so brought to their work insights born of conditioning that made the Ecclesiological doctrine more readily understandable to them, and assured a greater sensitivity toward the true nature of the Gothic style. To be sure, the Englishness of American Ecclesiology was not without its conscious mutations. As in the case of Upjohn, some of the other British architects were quick to respond to their new environment, and to be influenced by American attitudes, traditions, and practices. Indeed, quite apart from stylistic considerations, a small asymmetrical parish church of stone related far more sympathetically to the countryside of rural America than did the stern, gleaming white boxes of the Greek Revival. Moreover, the New York Ecclesiological Society aggressively maintained independence from its English counterpart, and in the articles which appeared in the *New York Ecclesiologist,* the Americans avoided as far as possible the complicated byways of high Ecclesiology, dealing instead with such matters as the honest use of materials, economy, and the need to maintain actual designs within the limits of local capability. They also stressed simplicity, pointing out that it was not necessary to make a church elaborate in order to have it fulfill its doctrinal purpose.

The New York group was also acutely conscious of the need for a form of Gothic expressive of America. In reviewing one of the earliest designs by the Englishman Henry Dudley, made shortly after he joined Wills in New York in 1851, they reminded him that they did not want "the exact reproduction of the English parish church. There is a difference, both in the character of our country, and our people; and our architecture should show that difference. Let Mr. Dudley, therefore, identify himself with our church and country, if he wishes to be a great *American* architect."[74]

In spite of all this, the English stamp was firmly imprinted on the American Ecclesiological movement. Whatever modifications in style may have resulted from the pressures of the American environment, the doctrinal objectives of the American Ecclesiologists were precisely those of the English Ecclesiologists. The English parish church was still the ideal form, even if simplified to fit its new context; the majority of practitioners were Englishmen, thinking and reacting in the terms that they best understood. Because of this, the movement had a wholeness, a vitality, and a direction that gave it an identity uniquely its own, and made it a cohesive force in the American architectural scene. The Neoclassicists might choose not to be part of it, but they could not check its energy, and once established it would spill over into other developments in the Gothic, adding richness and vitality to a rapidly flowering picturesque taste. Indeed, with all its character and strength, the Ecclesiological Gothic was not the only form that the Gothic style would take in America, and to complete our picture of the early Gothic Revival church, we must now turn to one of the most commanding buildings of the period, St. Patrick's Cathedral in New York.

CHAPTER V

James Renwick, St. Patrick's Cathedral, and the Continental Gothic Revival

Every year will add to its beauty, and every turn of the setting sun will be reflected by the spires and pinnacles, and, thus forming a link with the colors of heaven, will produce the effect of carrying the mind of the beholder to the true object of the building—the worship of the maker of the universe.

JAMES RENWICK

PART I

THE CONCEPTION, THE PROGRAM, AND THE ARCHITECT OF ST. PATRICK'S CATHEDRAL

Catholicism and American Church Architecture

The impact of the Reformation on the cultural destiny of America was nowhere more immediately visible than in its ecclesiastical architecture. During the eighteenth century, the London churches of Wren, and the subsequent books of James Gibbs, so appropriate to the colonies, provided all the architectural conventions for the ubiquitous box-and-spire colonial church. Austerely plain by choice as well as environmental condition, the simple rectangular interior of the colonial church was devoid of any special ceremonial spaces, and except for the use and distribution of liturgical devices such as altars, lecterns, and pulpits, there was nothing to mark the Anglican church from the Congregational meetinghouse. In its architectural character, therefore, the colonial church was insistently

Protestant, and as a logical consequence of the Reformation, it was equally anti-Catholic. As has been shown elsewhere,[1] this form of the church prevailed after the Revolution well into the nineteenth century, changed in character only in that Adamesque and Greek details were substituted for those of the English Baroque. This continuous line of classically ornamented and proportioned churches marked the first phase of ecclesiastical architecture in America; it also represented the ultimate permeation of both Separatist and Anglican Protestant doctrine to the provincial limits of the English-speaking world.

The second major phase of American ecclesiastical architecture was the early Gothic Revival discussed in the preceding chapter. Like the classical phase, it too was a Protestant movement, but with one important difference: the primary creative drive came from the Episcopal, not the Congregational, Church. Motivated by both romantic and ecclesiastical ideals, the American Episcopal community turned to the Gothic as a style more suitable to the Episcopal service than the severe classical forms of the conventional American church. By mid-century the movement had culminated in the sharply defined architecture of Ecclesiology. In terms of American Protestantism, it might be difficult to distinguish the Gothic church advocated by the Ecclesiologists from that developed in the Catholic Middle Ages. We have observed, however, that the Ecclesiologists themselves did make such a distinction, and in stressing as they did the rural parish church, which was English and not "Romish" in origin, they evoked a form that was not only specifically conceived in terms of the Anglican liturgy, but also one which proved, in both size and character, to be particularly adaptable to the American scene. The Ecclesiological church was exclusive and smugly Anglican, and in its own subtle way was as anti-Roman Catholic as the austere Puritan churches of the colonial and Neoclassical eras.

Against the Puritan primness of the eighteenth-century colonial churches, like a glittering foil contrived to magnify their simplicity, stood the Baroque churches of the Counter Reformation. Conceived as instruments of propaganda to counteract the erosion caused by the Protestant movement, and sustained by the power and wealth of a determined Papacy, these theatrical and opulent buildings were spread across Catholic Europe in burst after burst of sensuous splendor. Coming to colonial America through Mexico, they reached their ultimate destiny in the Spanish churches of the Pacific Southwest.[2] The architecture of the Roman Catholic Church was therefore firmly established in one part of America during the colonial years. The vast reaches of wilderness which separated colonial Spain from colonial England, however, kept the two cultures entirely isolated from one another, so that neither could have influenced the other. But even if there had been contact, it would have been hostile. If for no other reason than its appeal to the senses, the Catholic Baroque was anathema on the Eastern seaboard, even to the more liturgically minded Anglicans. Already rejected by the British, who could condone no more passionate architecture than the cool intelligent churches of Wren and Gibbs, this intense and florid style stood for everything that the Reformation had denounced—sensuality and materialism, the celebration of

power and wealth, the overt appeal to the emotions. In the eyes of the colonials, the Catholic Baroque was the abyss of evil.

Even more than that, as a religious body the Roman Catholic Church
was regarded with suspicion and even hatred in the English colonies.
Here, all the animosities provoked by the bitter struggle between Protestant and Catholic in England were carried over with continuing ferocity.
Indeed, in this country the Catholics were regarded not only as the enemy
of Reformation religious doctrine, but through their allegiance to the
Pope, they appeared also as a major political conspiracy. Consequently,
throughout most of the colonies, the Catholics were restricted by law in
the practice of their religion; in some instances they were forbidden to
worship altogether. Moreover, in spite of the freedom of worship guaranteed by the Constitution, hostility toward the Catholics prevailed through
most of the nineteenth century, and isolated them as a religious community from the mainstreams of American life. Thus, in the nineteenth century, when changing conditions made it possible for them to build
churches, their work was conditioned by fiercely defensive attitudes. Occasionally, where circumstances suggested prudence, they acquiesced in
favor of prevailing American architectural conventions. In Boston, for example, when the Catholics built their first important church, the Church of
the Holy Cross (later the Cathedral of the Holy Cross), they turned for its
design to the dean of Protestant architects, Charles Bulfinch.[3] For the
most part, however, and particularly in those centers where they enjoyed a
certain amount of strength, the Catholics set a pattern which was aggressively independent. Although generally avoiding the sumptuous complexity of the Baroque, which by this time had spent its course anyway, they
nevertheless built on a scale and in styles which were quite apart from the
prevailing Protestant ecclesiastical manner.

St. Patrick's Cathedral, New York:
The Beginnings

To the extent that it can be revealed in architecture, the story of Catholicism in America comes to its climax in the nineteenth century with
the building of St. Patrick's Cathedral in New York City. The story, however, does not begin there but in Baltimore less than seven months after
Washington's inauguration. Maryland, founded by the first Lord Baltimore, a convert to Roman Catholicism, was the only one of the thirteen original colonies with sufficient religious tolerance to permit the Catholic Church to become established in any form, and during the colonial
years the Catholics clung to a precarious foothold there. After the Revolution, however, the sturdy Catholic congregation in Maryland increased
slowly but steadily and by 1789 had achieved sufficient size and strength
to be recognized as an effective religious community. Accordingly, on
November 6 of that year, the Reverend John Carroll was appointed
Bishop of Baltimore, becoming the first Roman Catholic bishop created
in this country. His see comprised the entire territory of the United States.

The elevation of Bishop Carroll, made possible by the religious free-

dom assured in the First Amendment, established the first direct link between the Catholics in this country and the Pope in Rome; the way was
then open for the power of the Papacy to be effective in consolidating the
fractured American Catholics into a coherent religious body. Moreover,
the presence of a Catholic bishop on American soil immediately raised the
issue of a cathedral to serve as the seat of his authority. In managing the
affairs of a diocese there is, in the words of one modern Catholic churchman, a "need . . . for a bishop [and] for the bishop to have a cathedral."[4]
To understand this assumption we must now explore briefly the nature of
a cathedral and its function as an instrument of Catholic doctrine. In the
broad sense of the word, a cathedral is a bishop's church. Although it can,
and frequently does, function as a parish church, this role is secondary to
its primary function, which is to provide special ceremonial and worship
facilities for the larger congregation of an entire diocese. In other words, it
is the mother church of the diocese. But a cathedral is also a center of
spiritual authority. Officially, it contains the cathedra, or bishop's chair,
which is the symbol of his authority over his diocese; and the cathedral itself then becomes the symbol of the ultimate authority of the Pope. A cathedral, therefore, is far more than a house of worship, and to meet its
many demands it must be larger and more complex in its arrangements
than the average parish church. It must also have a number of features,
such as the bishop's chair and numerous adjunct chapels, which are special to both the spiritual and the administrative activities of the diocese.

The symbolic role which the cathedral plays in the life of the Catholic
Church is clearly summarized in a letter that Archbishop Hughes wrote to
his trustees on May 29, 1858, only ten weeks before the laying of the cornerstone of St. Patrick's Cathedral in New York: "I have, myself, very
great confidence in the success of this great undertaking [the building of
St. Patrick's Cathedral], which is to be for the glory of God; the exaltation
of Our Holy Mother, the Church; the honor of the Catholic name in this
country; and as a monument of which the city of New York, either in its
present or prospective greatness, need never be ashamed."[5] In this eloquent statement it is important to recognize that the archbishop makes
only indirect reference to his proposed great church as a house of worship.
Instead, his emphasis is on the role of the cathedral as a symbol of the
spiritual power of the Catholic Church. Moreover, when viewed in the
context of the anti-Catholic sentiments which prevailed in this country
during the nineteenth century, the presence of a mighty cathedral would
help to elevate the Catholic Church in the nation at large, and do it in
such a way as to make the average American citizen proud to share in its
triumph. This was a bold expectation, especially since the cathedral, as a
building type, had never been a significant part of the American scene.
The very fact that a cathedral represented Papal authority made it abhor-
rent to the Congregationalists, and in the Anglican Church, discipline
was maintained in the colonies by commissaries sent there by the Bishop
of London. There were therefore no colonial bishops, and no need for
cathedrals. The creation of the first American bishop in the hierarchy of
the Catholic Church, however, was to change all that, and when

Bishop Carroll made plans for his new cathedral shortly after the turn of the nineteenth century, he must surely have been motivated by the same objectives as those expressed by Archbishop Hughes fifty years later.

The Cathedral of the Assumption in Baltimore, initiated by Bishop Carroll and designed by Benjamin Latrobe in 1804, was the first church in America to be conceived from the beginning as a cathedral. When completed, it was by far the most important single church of its time, and it still stands as a supreme monument to the Neoclassical movement.[6] More than that, to fulfill its role as a cathedral, it was the largest church yet to be built in America, and in form it broke completely with the Protestant tradition in church architecture. It was cruciform in plan with a dome over the crossing, it was vaulted throughout, and it had a monumental twin-tower façade. The scale of the building, especially when compared with that of even the largest contemporary American churches was colossal. In style, too, the cathedral was eccentric to the prevailing mode. Although Latrobe submitted a Gothic design, the one that was accepted was conceived in the most advanced form of the rational phase of Neoclassicism then current abroad. Finally, although the work of Latrobe as a whole was to have an enormous impact on subsequent American architecture, the Baltimore Cathedral as a type remained apart from the main developments in American church architecture, as uniquely Catholic in its character as the doctrine and aspiration which motivated it in the first place.

The Baltimore Cathedral, with all its promise, was begun in 1804. Yet during the first four years of its construction the growth of the Catholic Church in America was so rapid that a major reorganization became essential. Accordingly, on April 8, 1808, ten years before the Cathedral was completed, Pope Pius VII elevated Baltimore to an archdiocese and created four suffragan sees, three of them in the major cities of the Northeast, New York, Philadelphia, and Boston.[7] In Philadelphia and Boston, existing churches were made to serve as cathedrals,[8] but in New York plans were made at once for a new cathedral dedicated to the patron saint of Ireland, St. Patrick. Designed by the French-born engineer and architect Joseph François Mangin,[9] and begun in 1808, St. Patrick's was the second church in America intended specifically to serve the functions of a cathedral. It was a curious half-Gothic, half-classical building, similar in many ways to Godefroy's St. Mary's Chapel in Baltimore (Fig. 79). Like St. Mary's, its façade was a Roman triumphal arch motif with both classical and Gothic ornament applied. Unlike St. Mary's, it was initially intended to have twin frontal towers; these, however, were never built. Nevertheless, its Gothic features caused considerable stir in New York at the time, and when dedicated in 1815 it was the largest church building in the city.[10] Old St. Patrick's, like the Baltimore Cathedral, was utterly different from surrounding churches. In New York it stood dramatically apart from nearby St. Paul's Chapel, the Gibbsian spire of which was completed only twenty years earlier. Indeed, by its very individuality and size, St. Patrick's proclaimed its role as a cathedral, and it served in this capacity for almost three quarters of a century.

St. Patrick's Cathedral:
the Building Campaign

Following the creation of the Diocese of New York, and throughout the first half of the nineteenth century, the growth of the Roman Catholic Church in the Northeast accelerated substantially and by mid-century a further reorganization was necessary. In the summer of 1850, New York, too, was elevated to an archdiocese, and Bishop John Hughes was made its first archbishop. Hughes was an able, ambitious, and controversial man who was well aware that he exercised authority over a large, strategically placed, and rapidly expanding archdiocese. At the same time, he was a militant Catholic, and as such was extremely sensitive to the hostility which surrounded his church on every side. To strengthen his own position, and that of Catholics in general, he went over to the offensive, and one of his first aggressive acts after his elevation was the planning of a new and monumental cathedral. His dream was to build a church which in size and splendor alone would outstrip any other church in the nation, Protestant or Catholic. He envisaged a church which in the end would win for Catholics the recognition and even approbation he so passionately believed they deserved.

Archbishop Hughes's ideas about the cathedral as a symbol of the spiritual power of the church were expressed in the letter to his trustees quoted above. But the archbishop knew only too well that to achieve a spiritual symbol of the magnitude he had in mind would require massive material support and two weeks later he wrote a second letter, this time to the leading members of his diocese from whom he hoped to solicit contributions. This letter includes, of course, the same exalted references to "the dignity of our ancient and glorious Catholic name," but in addition it reveals the Bishop's pragmatic side. His intention, he wrote, was "to erect a Cathedral in the city of New York that may be worthy of our increasing numbers, intelligence, and wealth as a religious community, and, at all events, worthy, as a public architectural monument, of the present and prospective crowns of this metropolis of the American Continent."[11] In this subtle insinuation of religious and civic pride into his persuasive spiritual arguments, the Archbishop showed himself to be not only an ardent churchman but also an able politician, who was keenly aware that if certain human sentiments are stimulated the most likely results will be material generosity. In this, he seems to have been right. Within less than a month, one hundred and three persons had pledged one thousand dollars each.

The site on which the cathedral was to be built was the city block between Fifth and Madison avenues on the west and east, and Fiftieth and Fifty-first streets on the south and north. This choice of a location so far uptown drew criticism from a variety of sources, but Archbishop Hughes's decision proved to be farsighted and correct. By the time the church was completed the city was already pressing in around it. To acquire the property, however, required complex and protracted real estate negotiations, and the entire tract was not brought together until 1852. A year later, the project was sufficiently advanced that it required the services of an architect, and the New York architect James Renwick was called in to make the preliminary plans.[12] At first matters moved slowly. In October of 1854, about a year after Renwick was brought into the picture, the Archbishop went to Rome to attend a Vatican Council on church dogma, and before he left he announced to his diocese that work on the cathedral would have to be postponed.[13] In 1855, one year later, Renwick, also went abroad, accompanied by one of his other patrons, William Wilson Corcoran, to attend the International Exposition in Paris.[14] Meanwhile, the Archbishop returned from Rome. Because of dissension within his swiftly growing diocese, however, his attention seems to have been directed temporarily away from the cathedral. Indeed, in a particularly acrimonious editorial in the New York Times (July 18, 1857), he is reported to have been accused not only of "maladministration" and lack of leadership, but also of failure to produce "an architectural structure worthy of a powerful and wealthy community." The truth is, however, that the cathedral project had by no means been forgotten. As early as 1856, a year after Renwick's visit to Paris, the building was already beginning to take shape, and by 1857 its final design was largely determined. As it emerges from the fragmentary information that survives, it was a monumental scheme, far outstripping anything which had ever been conceived before in American church building (Fig. 137). As described by Archbishop Hughes, the church was "to be 322 feet long, 97 feet wide in the clere, with a transept 172 feet, and an elevation of 100 feet from the floor to the crown point of the clerestory."[15] By comparison the Baltimore Cathedral was 120 feet long, 70 feet wide, and 72 feet high at the crossing under the dome. St. Patrick's would occupy almost an entire city block, and would have an interior space of 3,613,000 cubic feet, a volume more than four times that of Upjohn's Trinity Church. With well-developed plans in hand, therefore, and with over one hundred thousand dollars either pledged or already received, the cornerstone of St. Patrick's was laid on August 15, 1858, in the presence of an estimated one hundred thousand people. Work on the foundations was begun almost at once.

Although Renwick was the architect of the cathedral from the beginning, and provided the specifications necessary to lay out the foundations, he was not officially confirmed in his post until March 5, 1859, when a formal contract was signed. It is at this point that we learn that Renwick had a partner in the cathedral project. He was William Rodrigue, a relative of Archbishop Hughes and a man who had already been associated with the cathedral as the designer of an addition to the old downtown building. Even so, there is no question that Renwick was the architect in charge, and the designer of the new cathedral. Rodrigue seems to have been brought into the picture by the Archbishop only as supervisor of construction and as a Catholic liaison with the non-Catholic Renwick. The architects were to receive $2,500 a year for eight years, but the Archbishop reserved the right to suspend construction at any time.

FIGURE 137. *James Renwick. St. Patrick's Cathedral,*
New York, c. 1877.

On March 5, 1859, a contract was also signed with Hall and Joyce Company for construction of the entire architectural fabric of the cathedral. This interesting contract, which had a remarkable clause safeguarding against the use of "spirituous liquors" anywhere on the construction site, specified that the church should be built of white marble, and fixed the cost at $850,000. The church was to be completed on or before the first of January 1867. The choice of both the marble and the Hall and Joyce Company were made on the advice of Renwick.

After the signing of the contracts, work progressed smoothly and by the summer of 1860 the building had reached the height of the first water table. The initial funds had been expended, however, and work was temporarily suspended. Announcement of this was made by the Archbishop in a letter dated August 5, 1860, and published five days later in the New York Times. The architects were also informed by letter that after August 15, 1860 they would make no additional claims for funds until further notice. Each was paid $500, presumably as a consolation fee.[16] Moreover, before efforts could be made to collect the remaining pledges of the original $100,000 raised for the cathedral, the Civil War broke out. This, together with the death of Archbishop Hughes in 1864, made it necessary to postpone indefinitely all plans for further construction.

In the fall of 1865, five years after work had been suspended, the successor to Hughes, Archbishop (later Cardinal) McCloskey revived the cathedral project. In September of that year, just five months after Lee's surrender at Appomattox, he negotiated a contract with William Joyce stipulating that he was to receive $3,000 a year for the supervision of the work.[17] Shortly after that, construction was begun again and continued steadily until 1879, when the building was completed except for the spires (Fig. 138); it was formally opened and blessed on May 25 of that year. At this point work was once again brought to a halt, this time for six years, until after the death of Cardinal McCloskey. Then, in the fall of 1885 his successor, Archbishop Corrigan, negotiated the contract for the completion of the two spires.[18] Their construction took almost three years, and in October 1888 the finial crosses were set in place. But even then the cathedral was not completed. Renwick always intended it to have a lady chapel, but this was never accomplished in his lifetime. When it was finally added in 1901, it was designed by another hand. Aside from this, the cathedral as finished in 1888 was entirely Renwick's design, and although it was seriously impaired by compromise, its completion was one of the most important architectural achievements of nineteenth-century America. For St. Patrick's is not only a monumental church by any standards, but it is also a church of compelling architectural interest and extreme historical importance. St. Patrick's has its disappointments as well as its triumphs, but it is a coherently scaled and powerful building, executed with great care down to the smallest detail, and is wholly expressive of the aggressive tenor of its place and time. To evaluate it properly, we must now turn our attention to its architect, to its sources, and to the evolution of its design.

FIGURE 138. *James Renwick. St. Patrick's Cathedral,
New York, before spires were completed.*

*James Renwick:
Prelude to St. Patrick's*

When James Renwick received the commission for St. Patrick's in the
summer of 1853, he had already designed several churches in New York.
One of these was Grace Church, which was built at the bend in Broadway and is still standing. It is of particular interest as it relates to the early
design of the cathedral. Renwick seems for the most part to have remained
aloof from the Ecclesiological movement, but he did design Grace
Church (Fig. 139) for the wealthiest and most fashionable Episcopal parish in New York, and when completed in 1846 it stood with Upjohn's
Trinity Church as an outstanding achievement of the early Gothic Revival
in the city.[19] It was Renwick's first major work and it was also one of several churches in this country built in the shadow of Trinity. Like the
others, it was conceived in the same frontal tower form as Upjohn's
church (Fig. 111). At the same time, however, Grace differs from
Trinity in two important respects: it has prominent transepts, and also a
greater proliferation of highly authentic lace-like Gothic ornament. In general, the style is English Perpendicular, expressed by open crenelated
parapets, high pinnacles, and large windows between the buttresses.

FIGURE 139. *James Renwick. Grace Church,
New York, 1843–46.*

The tracery, however, is Curvilinear, and the high freestanding gables
over both the doors and windows of the tower are more French than English. In other words, the style of Grace is mixed, and suggests in Renwick a wide-ranging curiosity about the Gothic, at once more naive and
probing than Upjohn's orthodox and somewhat austere point of view.[20]

All this is particularly surprising when we realize that Renwick was only
twenty-three when he won the competition for the design of Grace
Church; furthermore, there is no specific evidence that he had engaged in
any professional architectural activity before this time. On the other
hand, enough is known about his early life to suggest a number of interesting reasons for his precociousness. Unlike Upjohn, who began life
as a craftsman in a small English town, Renwick was born in New York
City to a socially prominent family of comfortable means. His mother was
Margaret Brevoort, the daughter of a cultured, well-established New
York family; his father was one of the extraordinary men of his time. Bril-

liant, urbane, and widely traveled, James, Sr., had graduated from Columbia College at the top of his class when he was only fifteen, and by the age of twenty had begun a lifelong career as professor of natural philosophy at Columbia College. Although primarily an engineer, James, Sr., was at the same time a man of wide-ranging talents, which included an aptitude for architecture. In fact, the year after his academic appointment, he called the attention of Columbia's authorities to the inadequacy of the college's physical plant, and made designs for three proposed new buildings. None of these was ever built, but all were in the Gothic style, which in 1813 made Professor Renwick one of the early enthusiasts for the Gothic Revival. As in the case of so many early Gothic buildings, these designs have been shown to have come from Britton's *Architectural Antiquities of Great Britain,*[21] but the elder Renwick's enthusiasm for architecture was not derived from books alone. In 1815 he took a walking trip in England with his close friend Washington Irving, and made numerous sketches of the many buildings which he saw. From England he moved on to France and Holland, still sketching as he went. His book knowledge of architecture, therefore, which was very considerable, was enormously enhanced by firsthand observation, and brought to the Renwick household a level of commitment and expertise which must surely have been a powerful incentive for the young aspiring James. In any case, following in his father's footsteps, he studied at Columbia, and after graduation at the age of seventeen he began his professional career as a structural engineer with the Erie Railroad. Later he received his first experience with building as construction superintendent for one of the reservoirs connected with the Croton Aqueduct System. He thus came to architecture with well-formed attitudes and with professional experience as an engineer.

Renwick's knowledge of architectural style unquestionably came from association with his father, and from an intelligent and careful examination of the literature available on the subject. During the 1840's, well-illustrated and increasingly sophisticated books on architecture were coming from abroad in a steady flow, to form what was described by Renwick's friend, the American architectural critic, Robert Dale Owen, as "that literary storehouse of common property of which every art has its own" and one known "to every well-read student."[22] James Renwick's cultural conditioning would have assured that he was well-read, and the books were available to him, if not at Columbia, then at home. His approach to architecture, therefore, was very different from that of Upjohn. Where the Englishman's was doctrinal and intuitive, Renwick's was that of the scholar and connoisseur. His alert curiosity and cultivated taste led him into the manifold byways of style with cool assurance, and in the end made him one of the most accomplished eclectic architects of his time.

Renwick's eclectic methods are revealed in two New York churches that he designed before receiving the commission for St. Patrick's. The first, built in 1846, was the Church of the Pilgrims on Union Square. It was Romanesque in style, which in itself made the building unusual, for interest in the Romanesque, as an alternative to the Gothic, was only just

FIGURE 140. *James Renwick. Calvary Church,*
New York, 1847.

beginning in the 1840's. Renwick's use of this style, therefore, made him a leader in what turned out to be a fascinating episode in nineteenth-century American architecture, an episode which will be discussed in detail in the second part of this volume. There is one feature of the Church of the Pilgrims, however, which is of special interest with respect to St. Patrick's, and that is its matching tower façade. The architect's drawing shows identical two-stage towers, of which only the one on the south has a spire.[23] As built, however, neither tower had a spire; furthermore, the north tower was only carried through its first stage, although it was brought to the height of the south tower by a sloping pointed roof. Whether this change was a deliberate attempt at asymmetry in response to the general trend in contemporary Ecclesiological work, or whether the height of the north tower was reduced to cut costs, is not known, but the fact that Renwick originally designed two identical towers shows him to have been experimenting with the twin-tower façade.[24]

Renwick's interest in this formal device was even more emphatically developed in Calvary Church (Fig. 140), which still stands on the northeast corner of Park Avenue South and Twenty-first Street. Finished in 1847, this aggressive but austere building was cruciform in plan with independent high-pitched roofs over the aisles, and a soaring but decisively tripartite façade; the whole culminated in identical octagonal towers having spires of extreme height and taper. The style of the building was early English, with tall sharply pointed lancet windows cut into the otherwise unadorned wall. Because of this, and because of the bold massing, Stanton quite rightly discerns the strong influence of Pugin.[25] At the same time, however, the building has obvious eccentricities which give it a tenuous quality quite unlike anything associated with Pugin. The side wall buttresses, for example, instead of terminating in pinnacles, are cut off at the eaves by a horizontal corbel table which is more Romanesque than Gothic; and the transition from square to octagon in the tower is accomplished by bizarre freestanding pinnacles of extraordinarily slender proportions which rise from the four corners of the square base to a height almost equal to the octagonal stage of the tower itself. The effect is an uneasy sense of dissolution, as the forms diminish in a slender reed-like fashion toward the tapering spires above. In spite of the bold massing of the building the end result is an instability born of a separateness of parts.

In contrast to the elegant controlled Gothic of Grace Church, Calvary is awkward and unorthodox, and is clearly the work of a young architect probing the potential of style. Although numerous components of the design reveal Renwick's admiration of Pugin, the way in which they are put together suggests something which is not only unlike Pugin but even un-English. The twin-tower façade in particular was not characteristic of the English Gothic, and rarely appeared in the work of either Pugin or the Ecclesiologists. Indeed, of the twenty-four of his own designs for churches which Pugin shows in the frontispiece of his *Apology,* only one, St. Chad's, Birmingham, has twin towers;[26] the rest have either central, frontal, or assymetrical towers. Moreover, the eccentricity of St. Chad's was recognized even in its day as "continental"[27] and not English. The very fact that in his frontispiece Pugin placed St. Chad's as far to the side as possible, half hidden behind the prominently displayed asymmetrical tower of St. Marie's, Newcastle-on-Tyne, indicates where his natural preference lay. The introduction of continental ideas in Calvary Church, therefore, is another clear indication of Renwick's early experimental attitudes. Out of these came the highly developed eclectic skills which he would demonstrate in the design for St. Patrick's.

PART II

THE EARLY DESIGNS
OF ST. PATRICK'S CATHEDRAL

*The Early Design for St. Patrick's
and Renwick's Description of the Church*

Little is known of the development of St. Patrick's in its very early phase, but among the drawings preserved at the Avery Library at Columbia there is one small pencil sketch which seems to be a very early stage in the design (Fig. 141).[28] The drawing shows two flank views, one above the other, of a cruciform church with a frontal tower. In the lower view, the building is clearly in the Perpendicular style, with a square frontal tower, high pinnacles, and crenelated transept walls. All are combined in a manner strongly reminiscent of Grace Church. In the view at the top of the page, however, the tower above the base is octagonal, and there are no pinnacles, thus the effect is a slimmer, more tapered shape, particularly as the tower relates to the spire above. In the transept, instead of crenelation there is a tall Gothic gable and broad window with flying buttresses on either side. At the ground level, a high gabled door has been cut into the center of the wall. Together, these differences, particularly in the transept, constitute a design that clearly anticipates the finished building (Fig. 145).

It is impossible to date Renwick's drawing with any degree of certainty, but the fact that it presents two solutions, each based in part at least on Grace Church, suggests strongly that it represents an early stage in the architect's thinking, perhaps even the very first. Beyond this sketch we have no specific document or drawing from Renwick himself to throw light on the evolution of the design until we get to his description of the proposed cathedral which was published at the time of the laying of the cornerstone. It appeared in the *New York Times* on August 16, 1858. This description provides a detailed picture of the major aspects of the church, and is therefore worth quoting almost in its entirety.

The building is to be a Gothic structure, on the plan of a Latin cross, 328 feet long and 175 feet wide.[29] On each corner of the west front there are to be towers, the north tower to be capped with a high pointed roof, and the southern one to bear a lofty openwork spire 333 feet in height from the pavement to the cross. A noble porch, deeply recessed, and fringed with long pendants, will occupy the space between the towers; above this will rise the gable, to the height of 150 feet from the ground, ornamented with a large rose window.

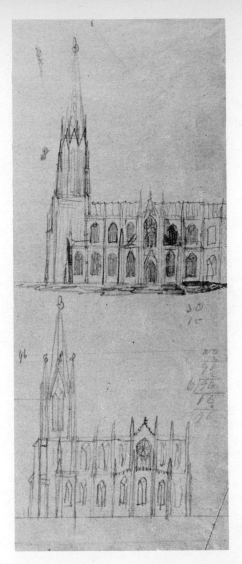

FIGURE 141. *James Renwick.*
St. Patrick's Cathedral, New York,
undated early designs.

At a distance of twenty-three feet from the centre, immense buttresses will rise on the sides and rear; these are to be constructed of solid masonry, and will sustain the arches and vaulted roof; they are to terminate with foliated pinnacles and support the walls of the clerestory with graceful flying buttresses. Between each buttress in the side aisles and clerestory will be richly traceried windows. The church is to be entered by several flights of marble steps. . . .

Entering the church by the western porch, a forest of tall marble columns will meet the eye. Fifty-seven clustered shafts will support the groined roof and bear the arches which divide the aisles. Nothing will intercept the view, and from the door to the apse which terminates the church, the high altar, approached by three flights of steps, will be the only conspicuous object to break the perspective. On either side of the altar there are to be chapels large enough to seat any ordinary congregation, and between each of the buttresses of the nave, which project outwards sixteen feet, will be small chapels, giving a larger and more airy appearance to the church.

The vault of the roof will be of masonry—the only one of any size in the United States. . . . Behind the high altar is to be a chapel of Our Lady; there will be no cellar or crypt. The building rests on one solid rock, and the floor will be simply leveled off and paved with marble.

The Avery Drawings for St. Patrick's

The major facts reported in Renwick's description of the cathedral are confirmed graphically by a set of fifteen finished drawings made by Renwick when the cathedral was almost complete, and now archived in the Avery Library.[30] The drawings, which constitute a coherent record of the history of the design, are handsomely rendered on a heavy white Whatman paper in black ink; in all plans, the lines of the vaults are rendered in red ink. Mounted on muslin, they are protected at the edges by a stitched blue linen border; a secondary border, in ink, frames them internally, and all titles and descriptive material are shown in a bold Gothic script. The style is graphic rather than pictorial, with emphasis on a precise, linear definition of parts; the results are eminently architectonic, and professional in the highest degree.

When given to Columbia University in 1957 by the descendants of James Renwick, these drawings were initially regarded as the original designs for the cathedral. Close examination of them, however, reveals that this could not be the case. First, they can be definitely dated between 1876, the date of the watermark on some of the paper,[31] and 1886, the year when seven of the fifteen drawings were published in Building.[32] Moreover, the consistency and care with which they are rendered, inscribed, and bordered, together with the precise data which they present, suggest very strongly that they were intended by Renwick not as presentation drawings for the church authorities, but rather as a demonstration piece for a wider audience. They would seem, indeed, to be an attempt on his part to set the record straight as to what he had originally planned and what, because of circumstances beyond his control, he had been forced to build.

Of the fifteen drawings, six show the cathedral as it was built, and are the ones that give three-dimensional reality to Renwick's description of the church which appeared in the Times. They comprise a ground plan, the front, side, and rear elevations, and longitudinal and transverse sections (Figs. 143–146, 148, 151, 153, 154, 156). Basically, the building which emerges from both the Times article and the drawings is a classic high Gothic cruciform church with aisles and full clerestory. It is, in one sense, more or less an enlarged version of the earlier sketch (Fig. 141). Yet it also has a number of significant differences, and to interpret them it is necessary to take into account a trip which Renwick made to Paris in 1855, and examine briefly some of the experiences he had there which may later have influenced the planning of St. Patrick's.

Renwick's Trip to Paris, 1855

When Renwick arrived in Paris in 1855 he found there a world of architecture which was utterly different from anything he had experienced before. By the mid-nineteenth century the city was rapidly becoming the artistic capital of Europe, and was on the threshold of one of its most dramatic periods of architectural growth and change. Under the patronage of Napoleon III, the powerful Baron Haussmann had just completed his work on the Rue de Rivoli, the first of his several schemes for the rebuilding of Paris, and already had his mind set on even more ambitious efforts. Nearby, Visconti's and Lefuel's additions to the Louvre were under construction, a project which was to have considerable influence on the later work of Renwick. Far more important in regard to St. Patrick's, however, was the extensive Gothic Revival activity which was being carried out in Paris, and in fact, on the Continent in general. Just as in England, where Pugin and the Ecclesiologists provided both motivation and documentation for the Gothic Revival, so too on the continent of Europe, there was a corresponding group of medieval enthusiasts who provided the intellectual base for the study and revival of the architecture of medieval France and Germany.[33] There were, however, a number of significant differences between the attitudes expressed in England and those developed on the Continent: in England the chief spokesmen were churchmen and church-oriented architects, on the Continent they were architects, archaeologists, and critics; in England the primary arguments for the revival of the Gothic were liturgical and doctrinal, on the Continent they were structural and architectural; in England the Gothic was held to be the only true Christian style, on the Continent the Christian origins of the Gothic were clearly recognized, but equal emphasis was placed on its national characteristics. Indeed, France and Germany each jealously regarded the Gothic as its own national style. In England the principal concern was for new churches and the small parish church was the recommended model. On the Continent the medieval cathedrals also served as sources of inspiration, and as much attention was given to the completion, restoration, and preservation of existing Gothic buildings as to new construction.

Like the Ecclesiologists, the continental gothicists had publications in which their ideas were discussed and disseminated. That in France was called the *Annales archéologiques;* that in Germany, the *Kölner Domblatt.* In contrast to the *Ecclesiologist,* which was sponsored by the Ecclesiological Society, the two continental periodicals were privately published. The former was edited by Adolphe-Napoleon Didron, a journalist, iconographer, and dealer in devotional objects; the latter by the lawyer August Reichensperger. The policies of both, therefore, were more independent than those journals dominated by the church. Both Didron and Reichensperger traveled widely and maintained close contact not only with one another but also with the editors of the *Ecclesiologist*. Despite their common enthusiasm for the Gothic, these English, French, and German publishers differed considerably in their ideas. Both the continental publications put less emphasis than the *Ecclesiologist* on liturgical functionalism and symbolism, and more on questions of the history of the Gothic style, archaeology, and structure. Particularly important were the articles contributed to the *Annales* by the famous nineteenth-century French architect, archaeologist, and restorer, Viollet-le-Duc. The first was a series entitled *Entretiens sur l'architecture,* which dealt both with the history of medieval architecture, and with the maintenance and conservation of historical buildings. Another series by Viollet-le-Duc, devoted to the construction of medieval buildings in France, led ultimately to his *Dictionnaire raisonné de l'architecture française du XIe au XVIe siècle.* This ten-volume work was one of the most important contributions to the knowledge of French medieval architecture to be published in the nineteenth century. Along with the other publications on the Continent, it presented a rational and scientific point of view toward the Gothic which was radically different from the impassioned efforts of the Ecclesiologists to express religious truth in architectural form.

There is no documented reason to assume that Renwick knew anything of this professional discourse. On the other hand, he read French easily and in view of his natural talents and educated attitudes he may also have read German. Moreover, his visit in Paris occurred when his design for St. Patrick's was still being developed, thus he would naturally have been on the alert for new ideas and the current literature on the Gothic would have been a primary source. But to feed his curiosity even further, the actual results of Gothic Revival activity were all around him to be seen. There was, for example, the restoration and preservation work being carried out on actual medieval buildings in France. Because of the rational approach of the French, this work was executed with greater attention to archaeological matters than were the liturgically inspired efforts of the English, and it set the tone for the Gothic Revival in nineteenth-century France. Specific projects seen by Renwick would certainly have included the restoration of the Cathedral of Notre Dame in Paris, which was then in progress under the direction of Viollet-le-Duc. Far more important than Notre Dame, however, particularly as it relates to St. Patrick's, was a very different project which was then being carried out in Germany, the restoration and completion of Cologne Cathedral. This undertaking, which carried through to its intended final form one of the greatest Gothic churches of Europe, was among the spectacular architectural achievements of the nineteenth century. It aroused the interest of Gothic Revivalists as did nothing else in its time, and although there is no evidence that Renwick visited Cologne before he began work at St. Patrick's, it is absolutely certain that he was very much aware of what was going on there.

FIGURE 142. *Cathedral of Notre Dame,*
Amiens, France, thirteenth century.

Cologne Cathedral

Like so many of the Gothic churches of Europe, Cologne remained
only partially finished at the end of the Gothic era, and at the turn of the
nineteenth century, when the Gothic Revival began, only the choir and
part of the west front were standing. Disconnected though they were by
the absence of a nave, these two units nevertheless formed in both character and scale a stirring example of the late thirteenth-century Gothic,
that elegant soaring style which the French have called Rayonnant. This

style derives its name from its radiating tracery, which is not unlike the Decorated tracery of England, but it is also marked by extreme verticality with buttresses attenuated and opened up and windows crowned by tall freestanding gables. The choir of Amiens Cathedral (Fig. 142) is one of the most characteristic examples, and Cologne was conspicuously derived from Amiens. Yet in spite of this, the unfinished building was ardently regarded by the German gothicists of the early nineteenth century as German in origin, and as interest in its completion gained momentum, the project became more and more a matter of fierce national pride.

The preliminaries to the actual building campaign at Cologne began shortly after the turn of the century, and almost at once gained international notoriety through the discovery of a number of the original Gothic plans. The medieval antiquarian, Sulpice Boisserée, one of the leading figures behind the drive to complete the cathedral, was convinced that the medieval builders had envisaged the entire church in its finished, coherent form, and the recently discovered drawings lent some support to this point of view. A later and more discriminating examination of the cathedral proved this was not entirely the case. Nevertheless, Boisserée's careful interpretation of the original drawings, particularly as they related to the existing parts, and his adherence to Gothic structural principles, gave the church qualities of stylistic and spatial wholeness that had never been achieved even by the medieval builders themselves. Although it can be argued that the new parts were more nineteenth- than thirteenth-century Gothic, the authority of the original drawings established an indisputable link with the past, and when completed Cologne stood as the only great cathedral on the Continent to fulfill anything like its intended destiny. Its effect on the nineteenth century was immense.

Restoration work on the existing parts of Cologne was begun in 1823, but the actual construction of the nave was not started until 1842, and it took another forty years to bring the entire project to completion. It was not necessary, however, for the church to be finished before its influence on the Gothic Revival could be felt. Not only was the building widely discussed in contemporary literature, but in 1821 Sulpice Boisserée brought out the first of a series of magnificent plates which showed the cathedral, both inside and out, as it would appear when completed (Figs. 147, 149). These illustrations were published in several editions over a quarter of a century, in French as well as German, and were circulated widely throughout Europe.[34] Deriving their authority from the original designs, they presented an image of Gothic architecture which for sheer visual brilliance was unsurpassed in its day. In these large and exquisitely beautiful engravings, both the majesty and the intensity of the Gothic style were brought alive with a persuasive power that no liturgical or archaeological argument could possibly match. In a wonderful way, too, these engravings were both rational and intensely romantic: their precise linear style brought into sharp definition the smallest details of decoration and structure; at the same time, a subtly modulated system of light and shadow molded into bold sculptural relief all the complex spatial involvements of the Gothic forms. Even today, seen alongside the best modern architectural photographs, the Boisserée plates are moving; in the 1820's, when they were first produced, they must have been overwhelming.

Apart from the architectural furor which Cologne aroused, and the impetus which it gave to the Gothic Revival as a whole, there was one feature of the church which attracted particular attention and that was its monumental twin-tower façade (Fig. 149). Judging from the west fronts of such cathedrals as Laon, Paris, Rheims, and Strasbourg, it seems to have been the intention of the Gothic builders to use matching towers on the façades of all churches of cathedral scale. Not one of these medieval churches, however, ever reached the point of having matching spires, although at Strasbourg a single spire—on the north tower—was completed. In some instances, such as Chartres, both west towers did acquire their spires in Gothic times. The north tower at Chartres, however, is very different from the south, not because of some caprice of design, but because it was not finished until the very late Gothic era. Accordingly, it was not carried out in the twelfth-century style of the original church, but in the style of the early sixteenth century current at the time it was built. Moreover, what was true of Chartres was also true of the vast majority of Gothic churches, especially the larger ones which were built over long periods of time. As each new part was added, it was built in the current mode; in fact, there are a few instances where it is possible to read the whole history of Gothic architecture in a single church. It was this organic approach to design which produced much of the fascinating irregularity which in turn gave sanction to the asymmetrical notions of such Revivalists as Pugin and Richard Upjohn. It was the identical approach which made it difficult for medieval builders to achieve in a single building the coherence of style to which the original designers must surely have aspired. It is precisely at this point that Cologne assumes its importance, for to the degree possible it was completed according to the intentions of the original medieval planners. This was well known in the nineteenth century, and Cologne's coherent symmetrical façade, of which there was no surviving example from Gothic times, held particular fascination for the Gothic Revivalists on the Continent.

The Influence
of Cologne Cathedral on the Continent

The impact of Cologne was felt almost immediately in France, where another effort was being made to complete an existing Gothic church. St. Ouen in Rouen stood completed in the early nineteenth century except for its west façade. Its choir and nave were in the style of the fourteenth century, but the little which had been accomplished on the west front suggested a lively sixteenth-century flamboyant concept, with its twin towers turned at a forty-five-degree angle to the façade. In the restoration work, however, which was begun in 1845, just three years after Cologne, this unusual arrangement was destroyed and in its place was built a monumental twin-tower façade conspicuously inspired by the one at Cologne. Although denounced by Viollet-le-Duc, whose sense of archaeological continuity was offended by what he regarded as *vandalisme,* the final building brought to France a church having a twin-tower front, complete with spires, which together with Cologne served as a major source of inspiration for a number of twin-tower Gothic Revival churches. St. Patrick's was one of these, but before we can consider Renwick's design, we must first turn our attention briefly to two earlier continental Revival churches, Ste. Clotilde in Paris and the Votivkirche in Vienna. Both are important monuments in the Gothic climate which Renwick encountered when he came to Paris in 1855.

Ste. Clotilde was designed in 1839 by the German-born but French-trained architect F.-C. Gau.[35] Work did not begin, however, until 1846 and the church was not completed until 1857. It was thus still under construction while Renwick was in Paris, and as a new church in progress it must surely have aroused his curiosity. Ste. Clotilde was not the first Gothic Revival church to be built in Paris, but it was the first to derive its twin-tower façade from Cologne. There may also have been some influence from St. Ouen, which was finished in 1851. On the other hand, Ste. Clotilde was actually designed six years before the work at Rouen was begun.

In the case of the Votivkirche, the connection with Cologne is greater (compare Figs. 149–150), for the church not only had a twin-tower façade with elegant open spires, but also an octagonal crossing tower that was similar in shape and character to the one on Cologne. This interesting tower is one of the distinguishing features of Cologne, and its appearance in the Votivkirche, in combination with the twin-tower façade, leaves no doubt that the Viennese church was inspired by the German cathedral. The Votivkirche was designed by Heinrich von Ferstel, who won the competition for the commission in 1853. Construction was begun in 1856 but the church was not finished until 1879. It is therefore almost contemporary with St. Patrick's. It seems impossible that Renwick did not know of the project for it was widely discussed at the time of the competition, and Von Ferstel's drawings were actually published in 1858.[36] The final decisions with respect to the design of St. Patrick's, therefore, were being made at the very time when important churches in Europe, all of them inspired by Cologne, had either just been completed or were under construction.

The Use of Iron in Church Architecture

There was one other question which was under lively discussion while Renwick was in Paris, and that was the use of iron as a structural and decorative material in church architecture. As mentioned earlier, iron was first employed for structural purposes during the late eighteenth century in the factories of England, and by the mid-nineteenth century it was being utilized extensively throughout Europe in a variety of forms. Of these, the most dramatic and influential was the Crystal Palace at the London Exposition of 1851. In this architectural fantasy the attenuated iron frame and delicate wooden arches and mullions, which held aloft virtually acres of glass, opened the way for new concepts of scale and volume in architecture which had never been possible with the conventional framing and vaulting techniques of the past. Indeed, the Crystal Palace was a forerunner in an exciting world of experiment and change, and it was into this world that Renwick came in 1855. When he arrived, however, he was not a complete neophyte; for Renwick was a trained engineer and as such, he would surely have known that the Americans themselves were also beginning to explore the potentials of iron. A "Crystal Palace," based on the London building, for example, was built in New York for the Exposition of 1853, the same year in which Renwick was commissioned to design St. Patrick's. With a design of such magnitude confronting him his natural curiosity about iron would have become even more intense so that when he arrived in Paris such buildings as the Galerie des Machines at the International Exposition would have been among the first to attract his attention. This fantastic structure in iron and glass, one of the spectacular achievements of mid-century in metal trussing, provided an uninterrupted free space 1,200 meters long and 50 meters wide, and was an important successor to the Crystal Palace in London. At the same time, it was the first of several buildings of this type which were dominant features in the international expositions of the nineteenth century.

As so vividly demonstrated in these exposition spectaculars, iron framing offered two benefits which must have been attractive to the Gothic Revivalists, a capacity for soaring vertical interior space, and a natural accommodation to delicate, attenuated and interlacing forms. Judging from the amount of discussion which appears in the literature of the period, the Revivalists were interested, but the churchmen were fearful. An article entitled "Stone and Iron" in the *New York Ecclesiologist* (October 1853) summarizes their objections. The first was symbolic. "The Rock has been chosen by God as a symbol of His own Son," and therefore stone is the most expressive material for church building. The second objection had to do with the idea of permanence. Although iron if properly maintained was considered as permanent as stone, the latter, through its visual qualities, "impresses strongly upon the mind the ideas of firmness and durability, whereas . . . iron . . . impresses upon the mind the ideas of lightness and temporary use." Stone, therefore, was regarded as "that material which God has chosen as the especial symbol of His eternal power and duration." The third objection concerned a widespread unwillingness to accept the aesthetics of iron. To build truthfully in iron was to build in forms which were alien both to the established ecclesiastical doctrine and to nineteenth-century taste. The *Ecclesiologist* could say of the Crystal Palace, therefore, "that it is not architecture: it is engineering—of the highest merit and excellence—but not architecture."

In spite of these ecclesiastical concerns iron was used with increasing frequency, and by mid-century the notion of an "iron style" was already under discussion, even in church literature.[37] Moreover, the material was used occasionally in English churches for such things as tracery and roof trusses, and the Cambridge Camden Society even went so far as to permit the publication of a design for an iron church in Butterfield's *Instrumenta Ecclesiastica*. Some of the most interesting applications of iron to church architecture, however, occurred in France. In 1837, for example, a completely iron roof was built over the vaults of Chartres Cathedral, and shortly thereafter a similar one, inspired by that at Chartres, was planned for Ste. Clotilde. Even more significant was the use of iron for Gothic structural and decorative detail. Because of its malleability, iron could be cast into intricate shapes such as tracery, ribs, and clustered piers far more quickly and cheaply than the same forms could be carved and assembled in stone. Thus, despite the appeals for the truthful use of materials which were heard from the structural purists such as Pugin, Viollet-le-Duc, and Ruskin, iron was used extensively in the nineteenth century to imitate the forms of other materials, and there were significant instances of this during the Gothic Revival. Two of them would surely have become known to Renwick while he was in Paris in 1855. The first was the 432-foot iron spire over the crossing of Rouen Cathedral. This project was begun in 1827 but was not finished until 1877. The second was the cast-iron open-work spires on the towers of Ste. Clotilde. Both demonstrated the extraordinary capacity of cast iron to develop involved structural and decorative forms. With his broad engineering background Renwick must have been particularly responsive to the potentials of iron, in the same way that his interest in architectural styles made him acutely sensitive to the special qualities of the continental Gothic Revival. There can be no question, therefore, that his experience in Paris provided exciting new possibilities for St. Patrick's, and to assess the impact of that experience on the cathedral we must now return with him to New York, and pick up the threads of the design.

PART III

THE EVOLUTION AND
MODIFICATIONS OF THE DESIGN
OF ST. PATRICK'S CATHEDRAL

The Evolution of St. Patrick's

One of the most fascinating documents of nineteenth-century American culture is the diary of the New Yorker, George Templeton Strong.[38] Strong was a brilliant and outspoken lawyer who had been at Columbia at the same time as James Renwick, and the two seem to have established a curious relationship built as much on animosity as friendship. Strong regarded himself as a critic of the arts, including architecture, and he seems to have followed the early career of Renwick with some interest. Of the several entries in his diary which deal with this subject, two are of the utmost importance with respect to St. Patrick's. The first dates from November 18, 1856, and reads as follows:

> Verplanck tells me that Dr. Ives tells him that Bishop Hughes is about beginning his grand *duomo* so long talked of, somewhere near Fiftieth Street on Fifth Avenue, and that its dimensions are to be most grandiose. I forget the precise figures, but I think its alleged length is six hundred and eighty feet!!! 'Iron is to enter largely into the structure' (as might be expected if this generation is to witness its completion on that scale), so it'll probably be a combination of Cologne Cathedral and the Crystal Palace.

The second entry was made four months later, on March 13, 1857, and enlarges somewhat on the first:

> Anderson took me yesterday to see the designs for the Roman Catholic Cathedral on Fifth Avenue. Very ambitious; scale very grand indeed—likely to be effective. Cheap ornamentation in iron; the mullions, mouldings, pillars, open work spires all iron. . . . Will surely rack itself to pieces by expansion and contraction of its incongruous materials within five years after it's finished.

Since we have no information either from Renwick himself or from the church authorities about the progress of the cathedral during the years between the architect's preliminary sketches and his description of the church at the time of the laying of the cornerstone, these two entries are of critical importance. As brief as they are, they were obviously written by an informed and interested observer, and they give us several clues with respect to the character of the building as it began to evolve. The first entry makes it clear that Renwick must have begun reworking his designs almost at once after his return from Paris, for within a year he had produced a scheme that was so far developed that Strong could characterize it in terms of both Cologne Cathedral and the Crystal Palace. This fascinating comparison which the author draws between Renwick's proposal and two outstanding nineteenth-century works of architecture tells us something about the erudition and perceptiveness of the young lawyer. But it also throws considerable light on the impact which Renwick's experience abroad had on his thinking. Even more intriguing is Strong's emphatic statement, which he puts in quotes as coming from someone else (probably his friend Verplanck), that "iron is to enter largely into the structure." This startling information—which implies so much but provides so little detail—is slightly amplified in the entry, made the following March, in which Strong adds that "the mullions, mouldings, pillars, open work spires," will all be of iron. The architectural elements which are mentioned in this passage, that is the "pillars" or main supporting piers, the "mullions" or tracery, and the "mouldings" or ribs and colonnettes, constitute the heart of the Gothic structural system, and Strong's assertion that "iron is to enter largely into the structure" emphatically suggests that what Renwick had in mind was a complete structural cage of iron, with masonry reserved for the outer walls, buttresses, and spandrels. Moreover, the proposal of this fantastic idea came at a moment in time when the United States was on the threshold of a dramatic era in the use of cast iron. By 1856 iron was being used widely for commercial and government buildings. We know also that it was employed for columns in churches in Boston before 1830.[39] There is no evidence, however, that it was ever used to create a Gothic structural system on the scale and in the integrated manner apparently proposed by Renwick for St. Patrick's. If this idea had been carried out, it would have made this cathedral unique in America if not in the entire Gothic Revival world.

Strong's entries provide two other pertinent facts about the cathedral. First, by March of 1857 a set of drawings existed for a monumental church which the author could describe as "ambitious," "very grand" in scale, and "likely to be effective." Second, the diary specifically mentions "open work spires" which, when coupled with the earlier reference to Cologne, leaves little doubt that after his return from Paris Renwick dropped his earlier idea for a single frontal tower, like that on Grace Church, and planned instead a twin-tower façade similar to that on the German cathedral. This represents a radical shift from the English influence, which had dominated the American Gothic Revival up to this point, to that of the Continent, and it is the key to the rest of Renwick's design. It is puzzling, therefore, that when describing the church in 1858 Renwick mentions a tower "on each corner of the west front," but indicates that only the south tower will have a "lofty open work spire." The north tower, he writes, is "to be capped with a high pointed roof," a solution which would have made the west front asymmetrical in a manner reminiscent of that which we have already seen in his earlier Church of the Pilgrims.

There is no evidence to indicate why this change was made in the design Strong had seen the year before. A defensive Roman Catholic Church would hardly have made such a change merely as a concession to the asymmetry preferred by the Ecclesiologists. Moreover, because of the highly logical nature of Renwick's approach to the design, we can reasonably assume that it was not a caprice of the architect. In view of the fact, however, that what was ultimately built was the symmetrical design seen by Strong, it seems most probable that the elimination of one spire was a temporary concession to cost. Renwick was forced to make a number of modifications because of this very factor, and it is altogether possible that the north spire was, for a time at least, another such economy. Except for this, the church described by the architect at the time of the laying of the cornerstone is confirmed exactly by the Avery drawings, and it is to these priceless documents that we will now turn in our analysis of the design.

St. Patrick's: The Final Design of 1857

As revealed in all available evidence, the design presented to Archbishop Hughes in 1857 was for a monumental Gothic church occupying the major part of a city block (Fig. 137). It was to be 385 feet long and 175 feet wide at the transepts.[40] The height of the nave was to be 112 feet to the crown of the vaults. The towers of the façade were shown as 330 feet high, or only slightly less than the total length of the building (Fig. 145). This, when contrasted with the 105-foot width at the base of the towers, created a vertical proportion of more than three to one and a general effect of extraordinary height and taper. There was also to have been an octagonal tower over the crossing. This distinctive feature had pierced Rayonnant gables over its eight open windows, and was topped by a short octagonal spire. Although shorter than the frontal towers, it nevertheless was to have risen 135 feet above the ridge of the roof, and would have been a dramatic climax to the ascending curved and tapered shapes of the lady chapel and the choir clerestory. It would also have been a central crown to the building as a whole.

The plan (Fig. 143) was cruciform with nave, aisles, and transepts; there were shallow chapels between the buttresses along each of the nave aisles. The choir end of the church was circular with an ambulatory and five radiating chapel-like spaces in a manner typical of the curved apse of the French Gothic. This, in effect, became the climax of the church and was the most exciting and original spatial composition in the building. Of the five radiating spaces around the ambulatory the first two, left and right of the apse, were chapels and were hexagonal in plan and open to the choir; the next two, which were pentagonal and fully enclosed, served as sacristies. Entrance to these spaces was gained by doors both from the ambulatory and from the radiating sides of the fifth space, in the center. This center space—the lady chapel—opened out on radiating lines in the same manner as the other two chapels. It differed from them, however, in that it extended to the rear of the church a full additional

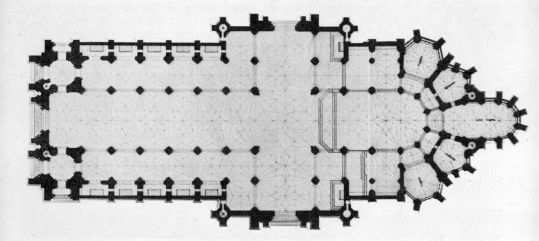

FIGURE 143. *James Renwick. St. Patrick's Cathedral,
New York, composite reconstruction
of architect's original plan.*

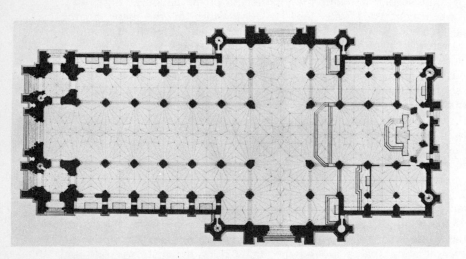

FIGURE 144. *James Renwick. St. Patrick's Cathedral,
New York, plan of the church as built.
Architect's drawing.*

FIGURE 145. *James Renwick. St. Patrick's Cathedral,*
New York, composite reconstruction
of original side elevation. Architect's drawing.

bay, and ended in a radiating, five-part apse of its own. The result was
a superb quasi-ovoid space, which flowered out on the terminus of the
main axis of the building to form a lady chapel of extreme elegance and
grace. By this ingenious and beautiful device, Renwick combined the
concept of a lady chapel, which is more characteristic of the English cathedrals than the French, with the radiating chapel of the French choir
and apse. It was eclectic but at the same time highly inventive and, as we
shall see, it set the tone for Renwick's subtle melding of English and
French elements in the rest of the building.

It is at this stage, before modifications were made, that Renwick's intended exterior design can be seen to relate most directly to his trip to
Paris in 1855. The principle features of the composition are the cruciform, clerestoried massing with the radiating apsidal choir (Figs. 143,
145), the monumental twin-towered west front (Fig. 148), and the octagonal short-spired tower over the crossing (Fig. 145). Comparing these

FIGURE 146. James Renwick. St. Patrick's Cathedral,
New York, side elevation of the church as built.
Architect's drawing.

with Cologne, and noting the number of similarities (compare Figs.
145–147 and 148, 149), it is not difficult to see the powerful and direct
influence of the German cathedral on Renwick's design. To be sure,
there are no direct quotations from Cologne in St. Patrick's. Even the crossing tower, which seems to follow the German example most closely,
has been reordered by Renwick in scale and detail to relate it to the
smaller size of St. Patrick's. But the concepts traced back to Cologne,
just as they had in Ste. Clotilde in Paris and in the Votivkirche in Vienna
(Fig. 150), and because of Renwick's highly individual variations on the
basic motif, the 1857 exterior design of St. Patrick's takes its place along
with the European churches, in the sunlight of Cologne, as a significant
example of the international Gothic Revival.

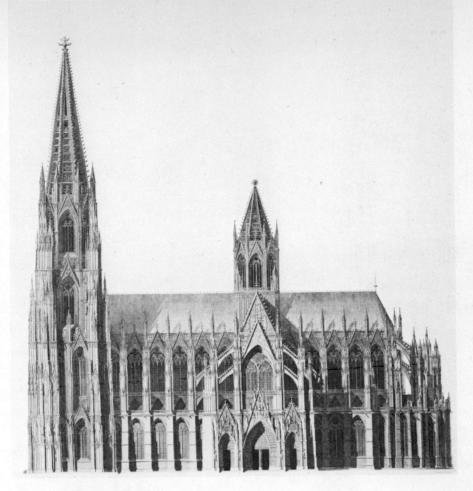

FIGURE 147. *Cologne Cathedral,*
Cologne, Germany, side elevation.

The Modifications
to the Final Design of St. Patrick's

The story which the Avery drawings tells is both fascinating and tragic. On
the one hand they reveal an American architect striving to bring to his
country's architecture the values of the continental Gothic Revival; on the
other, they dramatize the continuing American struggle between aspirations, which were always high, and the limits imposed by the conditions
of a developing society. The church that was built was simply not the
building that was originally planned; indeed, only a shadow of Renwick's
highly integrated and deeply organic scheme was ever realized. Although
the west front and the interior of the main body of the church were carried
out, visually at least, very much as the architect intended, some of the
most exciting and unique aspects of his design were stripped away in favor

FIGURE 148. *James Renwick.*
St. Patrick's Cathdral,
New York, front elevation.
Architect's drawing.

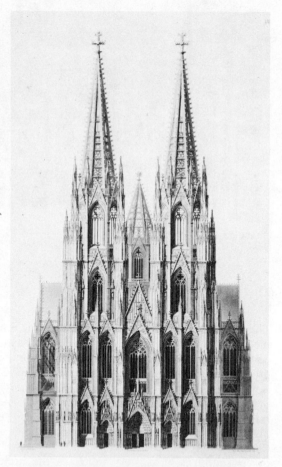

FIGURE 149. *Cologne Cathedral, Cologne, Germany,*
front elevation.

FIGURE 150. *Heinrich von Ferstel.*
Votivkirche, Vienna, Austria,
front elevation, 1856–79.

FIGURE 151. *James Renwick.*
St. Patrick's Cathedral, New York,
rear elevation. Architect's drawing.

FIGURE 152. *James Renwick. St. Patrick's Cathedral, New York, east end in 1868.*

of awkward and in some instances downright regrettable compromises. The reasons for this were both economic and technological, but the tragedy is that the necessary accommodations were made by the radical removal of essential parts of the scheme, rather than through a complete redesigning of the building in conformity with the practical means available.

The first change was the elimination of the curved east end of the building, including the ambulatory and the radial chapels. This change was ordered by Archbishop Hughes because Renwick's scheme did not leave enough room for two residential houses, one for the Archbishop and one for the Clergy, which were to be built on each of the two Madison Avenue corners of the site. To meet this condition, Renwick cut the church off at the end of the second bay of the choir, at that point where the radial chapels and ambulatory began (Figs. 143–144). He retained the apsidal end of the choir itself, however, from the piers through the clerestory, and added a third bay to each aisle in order to contain the curved shape of the choir within the new square end of the building. He then placed a straight wall across the entire east end, up to the height of the aisles (Figs. 151, 152). This permitted the curved end of the choir clerestory to show above the rear as well as above the sides. Although Renwick made an attempt, through the alternating rhythm of the windows, to relate the new east wall to the curved clerestory of the choir, the result is an awkward and uneasy union of flat and curved planes (Fig. 151). Indeed, the effect is as though the chapels had simply been ampu-

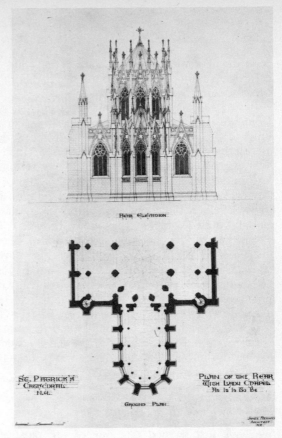

FIGURE 153. James Renwick. St. Patrick's Cathedral, New York, plan of the rear with Lady Chapel. Architect's drawing.

tated, with sufficient ends left on each side wall to bend over and cover the open wound.

On seeing the resulting square east end of the choir for the first time, one is inclined to view it with some interest as an English rather than a French type of plan (Fig. 144). But a careful examination of the drawings makes it clear that this is not what Renwick had in mind. To accomplish this, it would have been necessary for him to do two things. First, he would have had to eliminate the curved clerestory of the choir and replace it with a flat wall continuous with the lower east wall. Next, it would have been equally logical to replace the whole window arrangement with one large choir window as the English would have done (Fig. 63). The evidence of the drawings, however, makes it certain that Renwick regarded the straight east end as a temporary wall to which he would ultimately add a lady chapel. His drawing showing his alternate scheme for the lady chapel (Fig. 153) is titled "Plan of the Rear, with Lady Chapel as it is to be." So positive a statement not only signifies his intention but also implies that his proposal had the sanction of the church authorities.

Indeed, all evidence points to the fact that a lady chapel was always regarded as an essential part of the cathedral and would be built when funds became available.

Renwick's alternate scheme projected a three-bay chapel extending from the east wall and terminating in a curved apsidal end of its own (Fig. 153). It would seem, therefore, that he kept the French curved clerestory deliberately in anticipation of this new extension. If this had been carried out the church would have terminated at the ground level in an apsidal shape similar to the curved end of the choir, and would thus have resulted in a more harmonious relationship between the upper and lower levels of the choir than the unhappy flat-curved mixture which was actually built (compare Figs. 151 and 153). How strongly Renwick felt about the need for the lady chapel is borne out by the fact that throughout his career he seems to have continued his efforts to have one added to the church. That he never succeeded was one of the major disappointments of his association with the building. Ironically, the lady chapel that was finally built, after 1900, is a combination of both Renwick's original and alternate schemes. It was designed by Charles T. Matthews, who like Renwick was a graduate of Columbia, and the remarkable similarities between his scheme and the first two proposed by Renwick make it impossible to escape the notion that Matthews was thoroughly familiar with the older architect's ideas on the subject.

Modifications
in the Structure of St. Patrick's

We have just learned that one of the most spectacular aspects of Renwick's first proposal after his return from Paris was to use cast iron as a major structural and decorative material. This was a daring idea which, if carried through, would have identified the cathedral with the most advanced technology of the day. But this was not to be. Indeed, the use of iron seems to have been the first feature of the design to be dropped. Exactly why this was done is not clear but one's first reaction would be that it was because of cost. Yet, by the late 1840's, there were iron foundries in New York that were fully capable of casting the various components of Renwick's design, and architectural ornament in cast iron was already being advertised as less expensive than stone. Moreover, the technique proposed by Renwick in place of iron was stone vaulting. In view of the elaborate staging necessary to throw a Gothic rib vault, together with the general lack of American stonemasons who had the knowledge and skill to do the work, it is reasonably certain that a stone vault would have cost substantially more than one cast and assembled in iron. In the light of this, it does not seem that economy could have been the deciding factor.

It is far more probable that the decision was based on religious matters. Motivated by prevailing attitudes among churchmen which, as we have seen, saw stone as more symbolic of religious doctrine, Archbishop Hughes took the more conservative view and rejected iron as too closely associated with commercial building, and more directly subservient to engineering than to spiritual truth. In its stead he chose stone vaulting

ST. PATRICK'S CATHEDRAL
New York
ORIGINAL CROSS SECTION
WITH STONE CEILING &
CENTRE TOWER

PLAN OF CENTRE TOWER

FIGURE 154. *James Renwick. St. Patrick's Cathedral,
New York, original cross section.
Architect's drawing.*

which was the traditional technique of the Gothic builders. In view of the
state of American architecture in 1857, this was as bold a step as Renwick's
proposal to use iron. Up to this time there had been no serious effort to
construct a Gothic stone vault in the United States, and if statistics could
be compiled on structural skills which then prevailed, they would unquestionably reveal a greater expertise in iron than in Gothic vaulting
methods. Nevertheless, sometime between March 1857, when Strong saw
the drawings calling for iron, and August 1858, when the cornerstone
was laid, iron was abandoned in favor of stone.

We know of this change in building method from two primary sources.
The first is one of the four Avery drawings which show what Renwick
calls the "original" design. It is a cross section through the nave at a point
just in front of the crossing tower in which Renwick identifies a "stone
ceiling" (Fig. 154), and in this drawing the flying buttresses, necessary
to support the vaults, are clearly shown. The other source is Renwick's

FIGURE 155. *James Renwick. St. Patrick's Cathedral, New York, nave vaults from above, 1858–79.*

1858 description of the church in which he states that at 23-foot intervals "immense buttresses will rise on the side and rear; these are to be constructed of solid masonry, and will sustain the arches and vaulted roof; they are to terminate with foliated pinnacles and support the walls of the clerestory with graceful flying buttresses." In other words, the ceilings throughout the building were to have been supported by a dynamic Gothic rib system, with the thrusts of the groin vaults contained by conventional flying buttresses. Yet even here he did not abandon altogether the idea of using iron in some form. As Figure 154 clearly shows, the roof over his stone vaults was to be carried on an ingenious iron truss made up primarily of tie rods under tension. Following his idea of using iron as a major structural material, therefore, this combination of stone vaults and an iron truss for the roof was among the most daring structural proposals yet to have been made in this country, and if it had been realized it would have made St. Patrick's, as the architect's description so proudly asserts, "the only [Gothic vault] of any size in the United States."

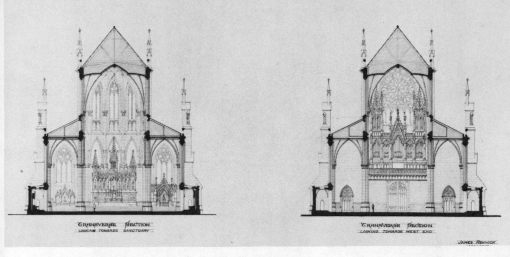

FIGURE 156. *James Renwick. St. Patrick's Cathedral,*
New York, transverse sections.
Architect's drawing.

In an article in the *New York Times* of April 5, 1868, which reports the
resumption of work on the cathedral after the Civil War, we read again
that the building will have "buttresses on the outside, terminated by pinnacles and finials, and supporting flying buttresses, which carry the
thrust of the clerestory arches to the side aisle buttresses." From this it is
clear that Archbishop McCloskey's intention was to carry out Archbishop
Hughes's scheme of vaulting in stone. Sometime before February 17,
1875, however, the decision was made to abandon stone along with
iron, and to substitute instead a lath and plaster ceiling (Fig. 155). It
was on that date that a contract was signed with Powers Brothers of New
York to carry out the work.[41] At the same time, the iron truss that was
proposed for the roof over the stone vaults was changed to a simple
wooden truss in which the only iron member was a suspension rod from
the ridge to the center of the tie beam. As we have already seen, this
technique was a well-established American practice, and if skillfully executed would have no visible effect whatsoever on the interior of the building. In fact, the same rib formations could be built up far more easily in
plaster than they could in stone, and up to the time of St. Patrick's the
vaulted ceilings in all Gothic churches in America, including Renwick's
own Grace Church, had been constructed in this manner. It was precisely because of this, therefore, that Renwick's proposal to vault in
stone was so daring and held such great promise. It would seem that at
this point in time, however, the American building trades were unable
to meet the technical challenge, at least within the limits of what the
archdiocese could afford. It was a difficult decision for all; it held em-

FIGURE 157. *James Renwick. St. Patrick's Cathedral, New York, nave buttresses, 1858–79.*

barrassing consequences for Renwick; and there can be little doubt that it was motivated primarily by cost.

The effect on the exterior of the building was disastrous. With the plaster rib system hung from the wooden truss, the entire superstructure of ceiling and roof was now carried as dead weight by the nave piers. The lateral pressure which the stone vaults would have exerted, was therefore reduced to a negligible force and with this thrust removed the concerted counterthrust of the flying buttresses, had they been built, would have pushed the building in (Figs. 156, 157). Renwick was thus forced to make the buttresses of a light rigid material, such as wood, or to eliminate them altogether; he chose the latter course. At the same time, the elimination of the stone vaults also left no sub-structure to support the octagonal crossing tower so that it, too, had to go. In this condition the building stood stripped of its dynamic structural integrity. The equipoise provided in the longitudinal massing by the crossing tower on the one hand, and by the animated grouping of the radial chapels on the other, was totally destroyed. With these essential elements gone, the frontal towers were left standing alone, with nothing but the horizontal line of the roof to counter their weight and verticality (Figs. 145, 146).

From both the structural and the visual point of view, the delicate balance of thrust and counterthrust which lies at the very heart of the Gothic rib vault system, and which is so persuasively expressed in the long and elegant reach of the flying buttresses, was utterly shattered at St. Pat-

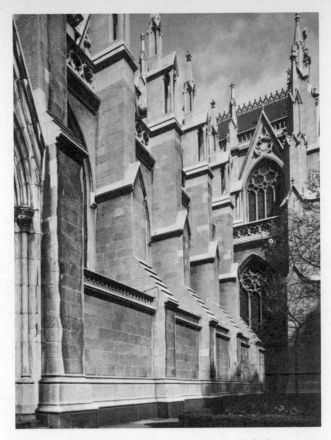

FIGURE 158. *James Renwick. St. Patrick's Cathedral, New York, nave buttresses from below, 1858–79.*

rick's. When these critical and immensely visible structural members were removed, the wall piers were left to stare helplessly across emptiness at the impotent buttress columns which they opposed (Fig. 157). Renwick did his best to lessen this effect by reducing the height of the outer buttresses by 10 feet, and by decreasing them slightly in depth. His hope was to make them seem more like pinnacles than buttresses. But no matter how much he adjusted them, it was impossible to eliminate altogether the impression of support, and with the flying arches gone the massive immobility of the buttresses (Fig. 158), so necessary to receive and contain the pressure of the vaults, was dissipated uselessly instead toward an open and ever-yielding sky.

Measured against the achievements of the European Gothic Revival, St. Patrick's as Renwick originally proposed it—vaulted in stone, and with a crossing tower and radial chapels—could have taken its place easily beside Ste. Clotilde and the Votivkirche. But the various conditions surrounding its design and construction which made possible the sacrifice of quality for economy and ease of construction, stripped the church of its organic urgency and removed it without reprieve from its enviable position among the distinguished Gothic designs of its day.

PART IV

ST. PATRICK'S CATHEDRAL
AND THE AMERICAN SCENE

What Contemporary Opinion Saw in St. Patrick's

To evaluate St. Patrick's in terms of the international Gothic Revival alone would be a grave injustice, for when it was built the cathedral was an American church designed by an American architect for an ambitious and increasingly powerful segment of the American religious community. To recognize its accomplishments as well as its shortcomings, therefore, we must also examine the building in terms of the special conditions in which it was conceived and nourished. The first and most obvious point to be made is that St. Patrick's was deliberately eccentric to the main developments in American Gothic Revival architecture. Just as the Baltimore Cathedral had been before it, the church was conceived on a scale and in a style which was unmatched by any other church of its day. This was the publicly proclaimed intention of Archbishop Hughes, and throughout the nineteenth century it remained a matter of pride in New York that St. Patrick's was the largest and most prestigious church in this country.

The official church position was clearly stated in a description of the cathedral published in 1879, at the time of the completion of the main part of the building.[42] It begins with the frank acknowledgment that there is a relationship between St. Patrick's and the continental cathedrals of Rheims, Amiens, and Cologne, but is quick to add that "though the Cathedral of New York is in this style, its design is as original and distinct as that of any of the above cathedrals." Then it goes on:

> Europe can boast larger cathedrals, but, for purity of style, originality of design, harmony of proportions, beauty of material, and finish of workmanship, New York Cathedral stands unsurpassed. It is an ornament to the city, an edifice of which every citizen of our great metropolis may feel proud; a proof that American architects and American artisans can hold their own with the architects and artisans of the Old World; and a proof, also, that the Catholics of New York, in the nineteenth century, were animated by the same spirit that, in the ages of faith, reared the sacred structures that have excited the admiration and wonder of cultivated and uncultivated minds for centuries.

In all their public statements about the cathedral, church spokesmen were pleased to point to its size, but at the same time were reticent about cost. Instead, they put their emphasis upon the more abstract notions of symbolism, design, and craftsmanship, notions which had reasonable validity, and which because they were stated with the stamp of authority were very difficult to refute. In fact, such questioning commentators as the *New York Times* were in general agreement as to the unusual magnificence of the church. As early as the laying of the cornerstone in 1858, the *Times* conceded that when completed St. Patrick's would "have no parallel on the continent."[43] Ten years later, in an article reporting on the resumption of work after the Civil War, the paper was not only more specific but in typical American manner was also quick to identify size with cost. "The building when completed," the article stated, "will be the largest, most expensive, and perhaps the most beautiful ecclesiastical building in America, worthy of the site and a fit memorial of the piety and perseverance of those by whose energy and liberality it is being erected."[44] Although cautious in its judgment about the aesthetic outcome, the *Times* was unequivocal about the cathedral's grandeur.

In its own way, too, so was the American architectural profession, even though it expressed its views with greater circumspection. In a careful but detailed description of the cathedral, published in 1878, *The American Architect and Building News* sedately demonstrated its enthusiasm by the moderate use of such expressions as "very beautiful," "very rich," "magnificent," "very striking," and "the best."[45] To be sure, some of these adjectives refer to specific parts of the cathedral, but others are more broadly applied, and the cumulative effect is one of general approbation.

In the light of all this it would seem that George Templeton Strong's earlier prediction that the cathedral was "likely to be effective," might qualify as the architectural understatement of the century. To the average American, conditioned as he was by the modest size and general austerity of the conventional American church, St. Patrick's was spectacular. Culturally insecure, and already showing a tendency to measure quality in terms of size and cost, the American public stood in uneasy awe of its grandiose magnificence. Although St. Patrick's might be small in relation to the great cathedrals of Europe, most Americans had no way of knowing this. On the other hand, they did know that there was nothing to match it in this country. The exaltation of its soaring interior space, muted by the fractured spectral light of the stained-glass windows,[46] the fascination of its Gothic interlace, the glitter and abundance of the sculptured altars that graced its many chapels, and on the exterior, the tapered vertical thrust of its many parts, all this could not help stirring even the most doubtful. Those who worshiped in the modest Gothic mysteries of Trinity and Grace Church found in the complex ceremonial spaces of St. Patrick's affirmation of their own convictions about what a church should be; and even though the severe Puritan hearts might still be suspicious of the Catholics, their plain-style meetinghouses were already giving way before the romantic pressures of the times, and with medieval forms invading their own sacred ground[47] they could not help being moved by the awesome splendor of the cathedral. There can be no doubt whatever that in terms of dramatic appeal, St. Patrick's was unique in the prevailing American scene, nor can there be any doubt that Archbishop Hughes achieved precisely what he had hoped for. The building was not only a striking symbol which exalted the Catholic Church, but it became also, in spite of continuing hostility toward the Catholics, a major architectural achievement in which New Yorkers in particular, and Americans as a whole, could and did rejoice.

If the size and splendor of St. Patrick's was something to which American popular sentiment could readily respond, it is equally true that not many Americans had either the knowledge or the critical acumen to explore very deeply its involved architectural character. Indeed, the sparsity of contemporary critical comment, even from among the professionals, seems to indicate that with all the interest and excitement the church aroused, it was sufficiently baffling to make the vast majority of observers uncertain in its presence. The remote solemnity of the Latin liturgy, which had its own impact on the architecture, was so unfamiliar to the American non-Catholic that it placed a veil of mystery between him and the cathedral itself. Except for a handful of extremely high church Episcopalians, most Americans hadn't the remotest idea of what was before them. The didactic and symbolic imagery which filled the continuous procession of chapels, stations of the cross, sculptured altars, and stained-glass windows undoubtedly was so alien that it was difficult to understand the architecture let alone evaluate its sophisticated Gothic design. Thus, those who might have spoken, were reserved and general in their commentary, avoiding altogether the complex architectural issues which were raised by the presence of a Catholic cathedral in a solidly Protestant land. Some, of course, were openly motivated by anti-Catholic sentiment and voiced their bias by ignoring the cathedral altogether.

For whatever reason nineteenth-century commentators chose to disregard St. Patrick's, the fact remains that except for several lengthy and detailed descriptions—all of which were informative rather than analytical —and except for an occasional outburst of anti-Catholic bias, we learn very little from contemporary literature about prevailing notions toward the architecture itself. The few searching observations which have come down to us, therefore, are of special importance. In this respect, there is one point which comes through clearly: there was a general awareness that the Gothic style of St. Patrick's was quite different from the Ecclesiological Gothic which was already well established in the Protestant churches of America. Although no systematic arguments were developed to sustain this point of view, tentative efforts were made to identify the specific Gothic sources from which the cathedral derived. Expressed in terms of the nomenclature then in use to describe Gothic architecture, the style of St. Patrick's was identified in the *New York Times* as early as 1868 as "the middle pointed or decorated style, which prevailed in Europe from the year 1250 to 1400, and is considered by architects as the greatest and most perfect of the three varieties of Gothic architecture."[48] In support of this view the European examples cited for the exterior were "Amiens, Rheims and Cologne," and for the interior "the nave of York, Lincoln and Westminster."

The particular combination of buildings cited is of considerable interest. The three evoked for the exterior design, Amiens, Rheims, and Cologne, are all continental churches and are in the French Rayonnant style; those for the interior are English and generally in the Decorated style. Who provided this information to the *Times* reporter is not known, although the fact that almost without exception the same examples are cited elsewhere suggests a common source.[49] The chances are it was the architect himself, or possibly the church authorities, who would also have been informed in such matters. The point is, however, that the juxtaposition of what is in fact two very different national forms of the Gothic, even though they have been cited erroneously to identify the same style (the Decorated), suggests at once the basic eclectic nature of Renwick's design. Indeed, in the *Times* article published when the church was dedicated in 1879,[50] the "decorated Gothic" is again identified as the style of the building, but in this case the author goes on to add that "Mr. Renwick, the architect, has not confined himself strictly to one style." Not that the author had any idea as to the infinite complexity of Renwick's use of the Gothic, for he quite erroneously makes reference only to the late English "perpendicular," a style which, in fact, was rejected by Renwick for St. Patrick's in favor of earlier modes. On the other hand, the author's observation does indicate a contemporary awareness at least, that Renwick was working in more than one style, and it is this point to which we must now direct our attention.

Renwick's Eclecticism:
What He Actually Did at St. Patrick's

By the time he completed the designs for St. Patrick's Cathedral, Renwick was an accomplished eclectic. He had not only designed a number of churches in a variety of Gothic and Romanesque styles, he had also won the commission for the Smithsonian Institution in Washington, for which he submitted both Gothic and Romanesque designs.[51] Brilliant and methodical by nature, with his sensibilities subtly refined by the varied stimuli of a cultured family, Renwick acquired his knowledge of architecture in numerous ways. He read intensively, collected prints and photographs,[52] and traveled widely both in this country and abroad. Because of this, and because of the demands imposed by his work for St. Patrick's, he probably had at his fingertips a more extensive body of useful knowledge about Gothic architecture than any other American architect of his day, including Richard Upjohn. More than that, he was also highly sensitive to those qualities, both structural and visual, which gave every style its special character. Finally, he had an innate sense of orderly relationships which gave to his work a high degree of internal coherence. Because of his versatility, his understanding of the Gothic was more cosmopolitan than the narrowly focused view of the Ecclesiological architects, and in every way he was the most qualified man in the country to resolve the special problems which St. Patrick's Cathedral posed.

Renwick's eclecticism at St. Patrick's is complex and refined. He has obviously ranged widely through the Gothic world in selecting his motifs, and a medieval scholar with a specialized knowledge of Gothic architecture could no doubt identify many of Renwick's sources. Indeed, one modern effort, at least, has already been made in this direction.[53] But in every instance where the sources have been pointed out the variations are so considerable that the original always loses its identity to the mutation. From the point of view of our evaluation, therefore, the overriding concern is not where the architect found his motifs, although this is of interest, but rather what he did with them after he had made his selections. It is with this in mind that we must now return to our earlier observation that Cologne Cathedral was the primary source for the exterior character and massing of St. Patrick's.

Despite a vague awareness in Renwick's own time that Cologne was the source for St. Patrick's, no specific comparisons were ever drawn. In the very late nineteenth century, however, the relationship between the two churches came under closer scrutiny when one historian pointed out that the height of the frontal spires at Cologne was exactly the same as the length of the church itself (511 feet),[54] and that a similar proportional relationship existed between height and length at St. Patrick's. Although this observation has some interest, it is actually of little importance because the measurements reported were based on the church that was built, and not on the church as originally designed. Renwick's proposed apsidal end and lady chapel would have added approximately 70 feet to the horizontal profile (Fig. 145), an increase in length which upsets the basic assumption and makes it clear that Renwick had no such arbitrary dimensional relationship in mind. In fact, there were other and more subtle concerns to command his attention. At Cologne, for example, the height of the main body of the church, when compared to the length, is considerable (Fig. 147). This effect is further enhanced by the individual bays, which are extremely tall in relation to their width. Furthermore, within these attenuated bays, the clerestory windows are taller than the aisle windows. This, together with the glazed triforium, creates a soaring vertical wall of glass in which the structural elements are reduced to the absolute minimum.

For Renwick, working in more modest dimensions and with more limited means, no such heady performance was possible. In fact, his solution was quite the opposite. At St. Patrick's the main part of the building is noticeably lower in relation to its length, and the bays less attenuated (Fig. 146). The clerestory windows, therefore, are shorter than the aisle windows, are more squat in proportions, and are separated from one another by broader and more solidly displayed structural piers. Although each window is crowned by a typical Rayonnant freestanding gable and has elegantly scaled geometric tracery, the general proportions and the relation of glass to structure are more characteristic of the high Gothic than they are of the later Rayonnant style. In contrast to the verticality of Cologne St. Patrick's is horizontal in a manner more English than French; and that this effect was intended by Renwick is confirmed by his lady chapel on the east end, which is also an English attribute. What Renwick accomplished, therefore, was to bring together two large and quite different concepts, the English and the French Rayonnant, in a single coherent design.

FIGURE 159. *James Renwick. St. Patrick's Cathedral,*
New York, 1858–79. Aerial view.

Another instance in which Renwick varied the Cologne theme is the relationship of both the central and the frontal towers with the main body of the church. Even though his central tower was very similar in its major configuration to that at Cologne, it was larger in proportion to the building itself, and was also raised above the roof line on a higher base (Figs. 145, 147). It thus assumed a position of greater prominence in the design. His frontal towers, on the other hand, are very much narrower in relation to their height than those at Cologne (Figs. 148, 149), and are more tapered from the base of the spires upward. This makes them seem higher than they actually are, particularly when compared to the more heavily proportioned towers of the German cathedral.

Renwick's variations on the major themes of Cologne can be accounted for in part by the size and proportion of the city block on which the church was built. The plot was simply too elongated to accommodate a conventional Gothic plan of the size visualized. Archbishop Hughes's ambitious scheme called for a monumental church, and Renwick therefore made the building as long as the site would permit. When this was done, however, the narrow width of the block imposed serious limitations on the lateral dimensions of the church. First, it made it impossible to develop anything like the four-bay transept of Cologne. At St. Patrick's, only two bays extend beyond the nave at the clerestory level (Figs. 158, 159). At the level of the aisle windows, the extension is only one bay; at ground level it is only far enough to accommodate a small door. On the inside at floor level, therefore, the transept of St. Patrick's is contained almost entirely within the main body of the church (Figs. 143, 144).

In addition to restricting the transept, the narrow lot also affected the width of the rest of the church. Unlike Cologne, which is a wide church with a nave and double aisles, St. Patrick's has only single aisles (Figs. 143, 144, 160). The result was a more extended plan which, because of its narrow width, drastically reduced the potential for daring vertical development of the vaults. In the frontal towers, however, the effect of the narrow lot was just the opposite. After the proper distributions of space were made on the façade to accommodate the main doors to the nave and side aisles, only 32 feet were available for the base of each of the towers, which measured 330 feet in height. Thus, even though they were shorter than the total length of the church, the towers rose in the extraordinary vertical proportion of ten to one (Fig. 148). By contrast, the proportions of the towers at Cologne, taken at corresponding points of measure, are six and one half to one (Fig. 149).

Although the narrow proportions of the site had a direct effect on Renwick's design, it would be a mistake to assume that this was the only factor that did. On the contrary, Renwick's ability as an eclectic designer and his innate sense of Gothic form were to have even more profound consequences. It was not enough to think only in terms of dimensional restrictions. It was also necessary to bring the diverse elements into a coherent and expressive whole, and this could only be done through modifications and adjustments of a much more subtle kind. In the towers, for example, the qualities of slenderness and taper which resulted from the

FIGURE 160. *James Renwick. St. Patrick's Cathedral,
New York, interior, 1858–79.*

FIGURE 161. York Minster, York, England,
first half of the fourteenth century.

enforced elongation of proportions were greatly enhanced by Renwick through a simple but imaginative compositional device. Conventionally, when an octagonal tower such as he used at St. Patrick's is placed on a square base, it is positioned so that four of its eight plane surfaces are parallel to the four sides of the base, thus bringing its other four planes to center on the corners. Renwick, on the contrary, turned his towers so that an intersection of two planes centered on each of the four sides of the base (Fig. 159).[55] This position brought the other four intersections into exact correspondence with the four angles of the base; it also placed the major vertical elements of the tower and spire in direct alignment with the main vertical elements of the base. As seen from the front, therefore, the corners of the octagonal tower became more visible than the planes, and in this unconventional relationship with the vertical lines of the base they strengthened the vertical continuity of the tower as a whole (Fig. 137). The result is unique—a soaring elegance which is unsurpassed by any other Gothic Revival church either in England or on the Continent, including the fantastic central tower and spire of the cathedral at Rouen.

Renwick's inventive variations are even more subtly apparent on the interior of St. Patrick's. Here, instead of trying to accommodate the soaring vaults of the German cathedral to his drastically restricted space, he abandoned the continental church altogether and turned instead to the interior of the English cathedral at York (Fig. 161). The early fourteenth-century nave of this beautiful church gave Renwick exactly what he was looking for. First, the width of York Minster, through the nave, was exactly the same as St. Patrick's, 105 feet. With this fundamental correspondence to work from, he proceeded to adopt many of the major elements of the English interior, including the formation of the clustered piers. But even more important, he took over almost exactly the proportional relationships between the nave arcade, triforium, and clerestory. This provided a more manageable if less spectacular arrangement than that at Cologne, an arrangement which fitted easily into his restricted area. At the same time, the results were visually and structurally Gothic; they were also thoroughly English in profile and proportion. Even more than the restrictions imposed by the lot, therefore, the shift to an English interior determined the size and shape of the clerestory windows, and gave to the exterior flank of the building, in spite of its conspicuous French Rayonnant detailing, the extended English proportions we have just observed.

If the proportional system and general arrangement of St. Patrick's nave derive from York Minster, there are a number of other things about it which Renwick specifically handled in his own way. Although the general grouping of the colonnettes which make up the piers is similar to that at York Minster, Renwick deviated from his source by setting his piers on high bases, and by making much more of the capitals both at the spring of the nave arches and at the level of the vaults (compare Figs. 160, 161). Moreover, at York Minster there is a vertical continuity between the triforium and clerestory windows which makes them seem a part of the same mullion system. At St. Patrick's, however, Renwick broke this continuity by changing the arrangement of the triforium arches, and by introducing a strong horizontal crown molding between the triforium and clerestory; in the clerestory windows, too, the interlock of tracery is uniquely his own design.

The most important deviation from York Minster is in Renwick's treatment of the main vaults (Fig. 162). Like those at York, they are lierne vaults and are thoroughly English, but the pattern of ribs is more complex, and for very interesting reasons. The liernes at York are introduced into a conventional four-part bay in which the crowns of the lateral clerestory vaults are at the same height as the crown of the longitudinal nave vault. The diagonal ribs of the four-part bay thus form the groins, with tiercerons inserted between. At St. Patrick's, on the other hand, Renwick raised the crown of the nave vault about 6 feet above the crowns of the clerestory vaults. Furthermore, the lateral profile of the nave vault is pointed, rather than rounded as at York. The clerestory vaults thus intersect the nave vault about a third of the way down on each side (Figs.

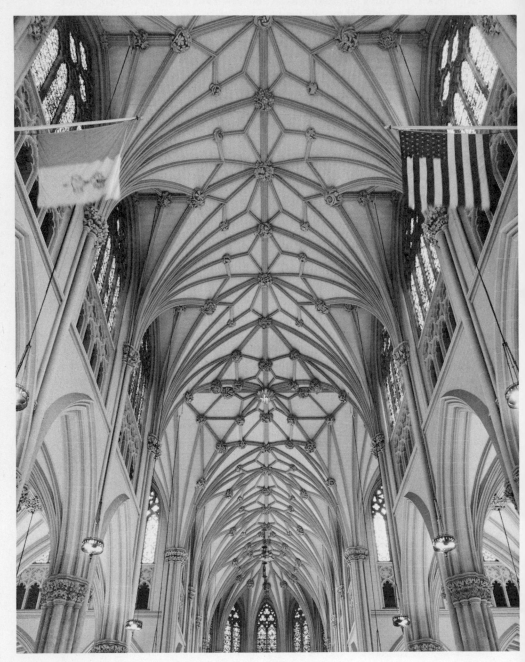

FIGURE 162. *James Renwick. St. Patrick's Cathedral,*
New York, nave vaults, 1858–79.

154a, 162). Because of this the groin ribs, which articulate the intersection of the vaults, are inside of and below the main diagonal ribs.

For this complex structural and decorative arrangement Renwick turned again to England, this time to the magnificent early fifteenth-century nave of Winchester Cathedral (Fig. 163). Here, as at St. Patrick's, the clerestory vaults penetrate the pointed nave vault below the crown, but

FIGURE 163. *Winchester Cathedral, Winchester, England, nave vaults, late fourteenth and early fifteenth centuries.*

Renwick's handling of the ribs is both simpler and more logical than Winchester, and because it is more lightly scaled, it is also more exquisitely decorative. In a moment of exceptional inspiration, Renwick extended and enriched the structural ribs by an ingenious system of tiercerons and liernes which form a lovely pattern of eight-pointed stars, just touching point to point, along the entire crown of the nave vault (Fig. 162). The effect is more open and airy than at Winchester, and because there are fewer ribs, the relationships between structure and decoration are more easily read.

Renwick's feeling for part-to-part relationships, which brought such pleasing order to his rib and tracery patterns, was coupled at St. Patrick's with a highly developed sense of scale. To be sure, the Gothic style itself is marked by a distinctive scale which sets it apart quite clearly from classical architecture, in which scale is subordinate to proportion. But Gothic scale is also flexible with both chronological and national variations frequently showing differences in scale among themselves. As he ranged through the Gothic, Renwick resolved these differences by locking the various parts together through a single overriding scale of his own. Coupled with the controlled ordering of the parts, this powerful unifying force produced a design which, in its very wholeness, was in some ways as much classical as it was Gothic.

The suggestion that there can be anything classical about a Gothic church could justifiably be viewed as a contradiction in terms. Classical architecture, as epitomized in the temples of ancient Greece, is the ultimate in reasoned stability and wholeness. The Gothic, on the other hand, is a style based on the opposition of dynamic forces, and does not submit easily to the constraints of a consciously imposed order; and St. Patrick's is Gothic from one end to the other. But in the hands of a determined synthesist even the Gothic is vulnerable, and during the process of unification at St. Patrick's some of the vital fluids of the authentic style were squeezed out. That which in Gothic times was left to the inventive hands of the individual craftsman was here predetermined by the architect, and the Gothic forms, which once rejoiced in their imperfections, were robbed of their exuberance by Renwick's unyielding drive toward perfection. To the degree that Gothic passion can be suppressed by reason, Renwick's authentic medieval fabric was stiffened by the underlying threads of rational order.

Another way to understand this aspect of Renwick's design is to compare his drawings of St. Patrick's (Figs. 143–46, 148, 154) with Upjohn's perspective of Trinity Church (Fig. 111). Renwick's renderings are geometric projections—a plan, elevations, and sections—and are precisely drawn in black ink on white paper. Color is used only as a means of clarifying structural relationships. There is no light and shade indicated and three-dimensional data can be determined only by reading all three types of projection together. Details are tendered with exquisite precision. Upjohn's water color, on the other hand, is executed in perspective in full color with light and shade. The church is seen in a graveyard against a landscape setting with a wide luminous sky. Architectural details are observed with care, but are laid on by brush rather than pen in a broader and less meticulous technique. The drawing is at once more pictorial in its intent, and more sensory in its appeal.

The extraordinary differences between these two modes of seeing and rendering are precisely those between the English and the French Gothic Revivals. The differences were recognized and widely discussed at the time. At the Paris Exposition of 1855, designs for a number of English churches were shown, and the contemporary response to these drawings is of considerable interest. In a review of the exhibition published in the

Annales archéologiques for 1855 the critic calls particular attention to the greater stress in France on geometric projections rather than perspective drawings rendered in color. He also emphasizes that the French method of presentation is graphic rather than picturesque.[56] With sharp insights into the academic tradition in French architectural education, he points out further that the Gothic buildings produced in France had greater unity and harmony than the English churches, in which function took precedence over formal principle.[57] Although Renwick never studied in France, his method of drawing indicates that he was strongly influenced by what he saw there, and something of the French preoccupation with homogeneity and balance, so clearly revealed in their exact geometric renderings, may have been a major contributing factor to the highly formal character of St. Patrick's.

It is precisely the cool perfection of St. Patrick's which has prompted certain modern critics to view the building with distaste. In the words of one it is "a dull Gothic church, consciously pure in its forms."[58] Although it is difficult to view the graceful interior of the cathedral and its elegant "star" ceiling as dull, there can be no argument about its purity. Nor can there be any doubt that this purity derives in large measure from the orderly development of its Gothic forms. Another contributing factor is the use of white marble, a material which the same critic regards as "most suitable to Gothic detail."[59] To be sure, white marble was used in Gothic churches in Italy, and at the time the decision was made to use marble Renwick cited Milan Cathedral as an example. In the minds of most mid-nineteenth-century Americans, however, who lived in a world still dominated by the white colonnaded porticoes of the Greek Revival, white marble was the material of classical architecture. Indeed, St. Patrick's had barely appeared above the ground when "the vivid brightness of [its] white marble" was criticized as being "completely at variance" with the "cloister shade" of the Gothic style.[60] In spite of its use in Italy during the Middle Ages, a practice prompted at least in part by preferences surviving from the world of ancient Rome, white marble was not the usual material for Gothic architecture. Nor was it regarded as such in the nineteenth century, particularly by romantics who rejoiced in the warmer coarser textures of the churches of the north. That Renwick chose to use marble, with all its classical overtones, is indicative of his reasoned approach to the design of St. Patrick's, and was an important factor in both the eccentricity and the "purity" of the church.

It is with respect to his struggle to achieve a unified whole that Renwick's use of plaster in the vaults is also a matter of concern. Even at the time, as in the case of Upjohn at Trinity Church, he was chastised for what was called his "plaster sham." In an article preceding the official blessing of the church in the spring of 1879, the *New York Times* was especially severe. Taking particular exception to the plaster capitals, it reminded the architect that if there had been no compromise "there would have been no sham and no shame."[61] Renwick, of course, objected to the use of plaster as much if not more than the *Times* reporter, and since he was not responsible for the decision to use it, the criticism must have been particularly galling. It might have eased his embarrassment somewhat to realize that not even the medieval builders were above "sham" techniques if circumstances made them expedient; for even in Gothic times the vaults at York Minster were no more of stone than were those at St. Patrick's. They were wood painted in imitation of stone.[62] But quite apart from this, the drive toward visual perfection which Renwick shared with his patron, and which he expressed so well through his skill as a designer, made it inevitable that he sacrifice philosophical principle for practical necessity. Moreover, in using plaster, he was performing in an established American technique whose roots were deep in the colonial years. The willingness of the Americans to place visual appearance above structural logic made it easy for the picturesque values to be accepted, even exploited, in this country, and one of the most picturesque aspects of St. Patrick's is the degree to which it relies on visual effects.

The vaults of St. Patrick's, even though of plaster, were designed and built with careful attention to their appearance. Because the structural technique is static even though it pretends to be dynamic, they lack the vigor of their robust and intricate models at Winchester, but they enclose, nevertheless, a moving and authentic Gothic space. At the same time, the light tonality of the white marble and the precisely molded ornament and controlled scale impart qualities of cool elegance which recall the balanced and refined interior spaces of such Neoclassicists as Samuel McIntire.[63] McIntire's work has the primness so characteristic of most early American architecture, and perhaps some of this quality was sufficiently residual in the impeccable Renwick to subjugate the emotional intensity of the Gothic to his own highly conditioned taste. As seen today, after a recent cleaning, the pearl gray ceiling of St. Patrick's, with its discreet touches of color in the bosses, is one of the most beautiful and because of its neatness one of the most thoroughly American Gothic interiors of the nineteenth century. At the time it was first opened in 1878 (Fig. 164), its effect upon an innocent American public must have been overwhelming; in fact, even the *New York Times,* after criticizing Renwick's use of plaster, went on to admit that except for the plaster "there is nothing to detract from the pleasure which the view of the entire grand building inspires."

The Progeny of St. Patrick's

One of the most remarkable facts in the history of St. Patrick's Cathedral is that it had little or no direct influence on other Gothic churches of its time.[64] Both as a sophisticated performance in high eclectic methods, and as a grandiose essay with its roots in the mainstream of the continental Gothic Revival, it remained an isolated spectacular outside the suburban gardens of American ecclesiology. The English parish church, with its picturesque irregularities, fitted far more sympathetically into the broad and varied American landscape than did great cathedrals. In the Catholic Church itself, from 1850 onward, rapid growth led to hundreds of new churches and several cathedrals, most of them in the metropolitan

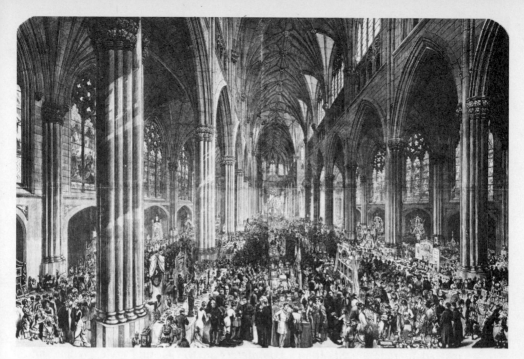

FIGURE *164*. "Grand Fair in St. Patrick's Cathedral,"
Oct. 22, 1878.

areas of the East. The majority were designed by a single architect, Patrick
C. Keely.[65] Born in Ireland, and of the Roman Catholic faith, Keely
was a trained architect who was an exact contemporary of Renwick. He
emigrated to this country in 1841 and settled in Brooklyn, New York,
where he developed a practice which ultimately became a virtual monop-
oly in Catholic Church building for more than a quarter of a century.
There are more than thirty churches by him in the Boston area alone, including the Cathedral of the Holy Cross in South Boston, a monumental
stone Gothic structure which replaced Bulfinch's earlier cathedral of the
same dedication. Keely's Gothic style, however, was based on English, not continental, sources, and was particularly reminiscent of the
work of Pugin. Related more to the Ecclesiological Gothic of Upjohn than
to the erudite eclecticism of Renwick, it set the tone for all Catholic
churches of the mid to late nineteenth century in this country. During the
same period, in the area of Protestant church building, the powerful
figures of John Ruskin and Henry Hobson Richardson were already pointing new directions toward larger and more aggressive forms. This, plus
Keely's highly popular Catholic style, tended to point up the continental
character of Renwick's cathedral and isolate it even further from the mainstreams of American church building.

It is ironical that the real architectural descendant of St. Patrick's did
not appear in this country until the early twentieth century, and then not
in a Catholic but in an Episcopal church. Rapidly growing in power and
ambition, and embarrassed by the spectacular success of St. Patrick's,
the Episcopal diocese of New York sought to reassert its pre-eminence by

announcing plans for a new cathedral of its own. Over 500 feet in length, the Cathedral of St. John the Divine would exceed St. Patrick's by 200 feet and when completed would be the fourth largest cathedral in the world. The original competition was held in 1889, the year after the spires of St. Patrick's were finished, and the winning design by Heins and Lafarge, conspicuously conceived under the influence of the great Richardson, was for an enormous pile of quasi-Gothic, Romanesque, and Byzantine forms which when built would tower above the city from the elevated crest of Morningside Heights.

Work at St. John's was begun in 1893, and by 1911 the choir and crossing were complete and in use. At this point, however, the design of the church was changed dramatically. Near the turn of the century, owing to the persuasive influence of the impassioned gothicist Ralph Adams Cram, American taste in church architecture shifted away from the Richardsonian Romanesque and toward a renewed but no less ardent enthusiasm for the Gothic. To keep pace with the times, and to reaffirm Anglicanism, the authorities of the New York diocese, in one of the most bizarre and arbitrary decisions in the history of American architecture, dismissed the original firm of Heins and Lafarge and hired Cram instead to redesign St. John's *completely* in the Gothic style. When this was done, the Episcopal cathedral was brought into obvious juxtaposition with St. Patrick's through a common style, and the analogies between the two became immediately apparent: the ambition to assert the power of the church, this time of the Episcopal Church over the Catholic, in the largest and most conspicuous visual symbol possible; the conventional high eclectic methods, this time even more highly formalized by an expansive and scientific archaeology; the plan to build a continental Gothic church in true Gothic vaulting, which this time, because of more advanced technical means, would actually be carried out. Everything that Renwick and Archbishop Hughes aspired to achieve at St. Patrick's was projected on an even larger screen at St. John's.

With the Gothic design in hand, work was renewed at St. John's in 1913 and soon the mighty nave vaults were rising to enclose a space sufficient to cover St. Patrick's, roof and all. The nave was finished in 1939 but at that point, just as on several occasions at St. Patrick's, work ceased for lack of funds. Thus the earlier crossing, which has yet to receive its new Gothic dress, remains standing in all its Byzantine splendor to mock the austere six-part vaults of the Gothic nave; and the steel centering, used to support each bay of the vaults as they were under construction, stands outside the church, rusting in the weather and waiting for that moment when it will once again be pressed into service in the rebuilding of the crossing and in the construction of the proposed transepts.

That St. Patrick's was completed at all, even in its reduced state, is one of the major administrative and architectural achievements of the nineteenth century. St. John's may never be finished, perhaps never should be. It was conceived at a time of self-confident optimism in America, when the Episcopal Church was an influential ally of a burgeoning business community. Events did not sustain the hopes, however, and the lustrous scheme began to tarnish almost as soon as it was born. The power and wealth of the new era required more arrogant symbols than the established forms of the church, however vast they may be, and at almost the same time that the style of St. John's was changed from Romanesque to Gothic, the Woolworth Building in downtown Manhattan was pushing its fifty-two stories into the sky. As the vertical thrust of one vied with the vertical thrust of the other, the kinship between the two became obvious, and to solidify this kinship it was essential that the Woolworth Building should be adorned with the tracery, pinnacles, and buttresses of the cathedral. Although the application of Gothic ornament to a steel frame made no structural sense whatever, its symbolic inferences were critical, for by establishing through the vestments of architectural style a visual identity with the cathedral, the office building gained the moral approbation it needed to sustain it in its new role.

St. Patrick's Cathedral and the Skyscraper

Although the relationship between the Cathedral of St. John the Divine and the Woolworth Building is readily apparent, the emergence of the skyscraper as the symbol of American power did not begin with that particular pair of buildings. The fact is that tall buildings first appeared in New York in the 1870's, and among the earliest was the nine-story Tribune Building designed by Richard Morris Hunt and built during 1873–75.[66] It was 260 feet high, only 70 feet shorter than the proposed towers of St. Patrick's.[67] Shortly after Renwick's towers were completed, however, another tall building, George B. Post's World Building in New York City, was challenging the cathedral for pre-eminence. Finished in 1890, the World Building was twenty-six stories high and at the time was the tallest building yet to be erected. Although its 309-foot height was still less than St. Patrick's 320 feet, it was a solid building from top to bottom, so that by sheer weight of vertical mass alone it overpowered the tapered spires of the cathedral.

At the time these early skyscrapers were beginning to appear Renwick was nearing the end of his life, and was deeply concerned that the only part of St. Patrick's still to be built was the lady chapel. To be sure, as part of the building program for the cathedral, he had designed and built in the 1870's the two residential houses that had always been planned for the bishop and the clergy (Fig. 165). These filled the Madison Avenue corners of the block, but the awkward square end of the church itself still remained to haunt him. In an effort to resolve this problem, Renwick seems to have made one final design for a lady chapel, a design which was so spectacular in its implications that it not only would have provided an unusual solution to the chapel itself, but also would have brought about a dramatic change in the character of the entire cathedral.

Renwick's sensational scheme is contained in two small drawings, a plan and an elevation which are in the Renwick collection at the Avery

FIGURE 165. *James Renwick. St. Patrick's Cathedral and residential houses, New York. Old photograph.*

Library.[68] The plan (Fig. 166) shows the proposed lady chapel, extending from the east end of the cathedral, in a form totally unlike any of the earlier schemes. Basically square in plan, it generates around a central point to which all parts relate, and is contained at the corners by four pairs of large right-angle buttresses. Between these buttresses, and facing inward toward the center, are the curved glazed walls of four identical apses. Placed as they are on axis, the one on the side of the square which joins the cathedral actually penetrates the main space of the church on a curve which is in the opposite direction to the curve of the choir. This makes a fascinating connection in the form of a single vaulted bay, and provides an easy flow between the choir and the chapel. At the same time, however, it makes the chapel an independent and clearly defined space in its own right.

The reason for maintaining the integrity of the chapel as a self-contained space becomes immediately apparent when we consider the eleva-

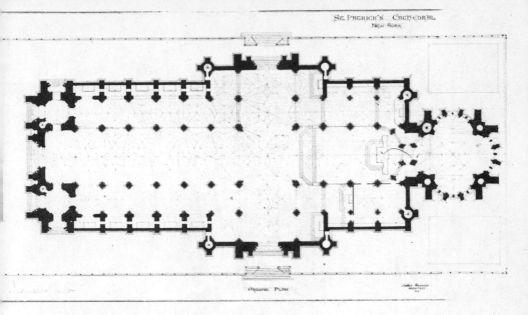

FIGURE 166. James Renwick. St. Patrick's Cathedral,
New York, ground plan showing proposed Lady Chapel.
Architect's drawing.

tion (Fig. 167). Instead of the conventional lady chapel, with a profile lower than the clerestory of the choir, Renwick proposed a free-standing Gothic tower and spire which would rise 400 feet above the pavement. Had it ever been built, this fantastic scheme, which drew its detailing, proportion, and scale from the frontal towers, would have transformed the cathedral into a double-fronted church. As such, it would have been unique in the world of Gothic Revival architecture; it would also have returned to the cathedral something of that dynamic lateral balance which was lost in the process of the various modifications.

In every way, Renwick's idea seems to have been his final effort to salvage the design, and to assert once and for all the power of his own creative genius over the administrative will of the church. At the same time, when viewed in the context of the late nineteenth century, it is difficult to resist the notion that Renwick, in his own way, was also meeting the challenge of the tall buildings that were going up all around him, buildings which ultimately would engulf his cathedral altogether (Fig. 159). Moreover, considering his ability as an engineer, one is tempted to wonder whether or not he might even have been planning to use metal in its construction. Although the solid rock upon which the cathedral is built could easily have carried a 400-foot stone tower, such events as the com-

FIGURE *167. James Renwick. St. Patrick's Cathedral,
New York, elevation showing proposed Lady Chapel.
Architect's drawing.*

pletion of the Eiffel Tower in Paris in 1889, and the increasingly sophis-ticated use of metal in the primitive tall office buildings going up in the city, would have strongly argued for metal framing as both the logical and least expensive technique. We will probably never know the truth of these matters, but the evidence of the drawings themselves makes it al-most certain that Renwick was caught up in the thrust toward vertical con-struction which characterized the last two decades of the century. If he had been able to bring his idea to fruition he would have done more than achieve one of the remarkable buildings of his time; he would also have anticipated, within the framework of ecclesiastical architecture, the dramatic exploitation of Gothic verticality which was to follow in 1911 in the Woolworth Building in New York City. If in the eyes of both nine-teenth-century and modern critics St. Patrick's falls short of expecta-tions, it was surely not entirely Renwick's fault. Considering the magni-tude of his scheme and the complex forces which shaped its destiny, St. Patrick's must stand as one of the major architectural triumphs of the nineteenth century, and as a masterpiece of Romantic Eclecticism in the United States.

Shortly after this book went into production a large and important group of original Renwick drawings was discovered, most of which seem to be-long to the early phase of the final design of St. Patrick's Cathedral. A preliminary and cursory examination makes it clear that these remarkable documents will add considerable detail to our knowledge of the evolution of the design. It is unfortunate, therefore, that their existence was un-known at the time I wrote my account. Nevertheless, I was privileged to see them soon after they were found, and my brief encounter persuades me that under careful study they will add substantial support to the evi-dence I used in developing my analysis of the design.

CHAPTER VI

Alexander Jackson Davis
and the Picturesque Villa

*To find an original man living in an original house, is as
satisfactory as to find an eagle's nest built on the top of a
mountain crag.*

ANDREW JACKSON DOWNING

PART I

ALEXANDER JACKSON DAVIS,
ARCHITECTURAL DRAFTSMAN
AND COMPOSER

Alexander Jackson Davis,
Rationalist or Romantic

The Gothic style, by its very nature, is a picturesque style. Its frag-
mented irregular shapes, its lofty tapered profiles, its constantly shifting
surfaces, its interlacing proliferous forms, all so reminiscent of the
world of natural growth, are the very qualities which form the heart of
the picturesque doctrine. It was for this reason that the first picturesque
architects sought out the Gothic style as the one most expressive of their
aspirations. It was for this reason, too, that the Picturesque movement
first flowered in this country in the early churches of the Gothic Revival,
and permeated the land in the small suburban and rural churches of mid-
century. Even St. Patrick's, with all its cool marble surfaces and
formalized conceits, was also part of the Picturesque movement.

Picturesque architecture in this country, however, was not to achieve
its most comprehensive form in the church. Indeed, the picturesque doctrine, as formulated by Uvedale Price and Richard Payne Knight, was a
philosophical argument, not a religious creed. It was an argument which
found its sanction in the relationships between man and nature, not between man and God; as we have already seen, its first impact in England
was felt in the garden and the house, not in the church. The very fact

that the critical substance of the picturesque was based on sensations derived from visual experience made nature essential to its fulfillment, and the house, with its roots both in man and nature, became a conspicuous object of its concern. If in eighteenth-century England a man-worn landscape had to be consciously manipulated to provide an appropriate picturesque setting for the house, in America a wild and abundant nature stood ready on every hand to embrace the house in its most picturesque form. All that was needed was the poetic imagination to bring the two together, and this was to come from the fertile minds of two of the most remarkable men of the period, Alexander Jackson Davis and Andrew Jackson Downing. Davis, the architect, was the older and was already well established in his profession before Downing, the landscape gardener and architectural critic, came into the picture. Once they met, however, there followed a ten-year association which would change the whole course of American domestic architecture. To develop the background of this story we will consider in this chapter Davis and his work. The next chapter will be devoted to Downing and to his productive relationship with Davis.

We have encountered Alexander Jackson Davis elsewhere[1] as the junior partner of Ithiel Town in the firm of Town and Davis of New York. There he showed himself to be a cool and reasoned designer, and we came to know him as an influential innovator in the rational phase of American Neoclassicism. In spite of his outstanding achievements as a Neoclassicist, however, Davis had too lively an imagination to have found complete gratification in the Greek temple alone. Although his methodical side —and he was an extremely methodical man—was attracted to the controlled certainties of classical doctrine, his highly tuned sensibilities made it inevitable that he would be drawn ultimately into the more abundant and shadowy world of picturesque imagery. Davis was, in fact, a true romantic and he knew it. In a sketch of himself which he wrote for Dunlap's *History of the Arts of Design in the United States*[2] he describes how, as a young man, he would "fly to his books, but not . . . to books of science and useful learning, but to works of imagination, poetry, and the drama; whence, however, he imbibed a portion of that highly imaginative spirit so necessary to constitute an artist destined to practice in the field of invention."[3] The "field of invention" for Davis was, of course, architecture, but it was architecture drawn from the world of fantasy, and nourished by intensive reading in a wide range of literature.

The degree to which Davis was motivated by his reading is revealed in part by a fascinating document which is among the Davis papers at the New-York Historical Society. Entitled *Fragments, Scraps, Etc.,* it consists of quotations taken by Davis from a variety of literary sources. The selections range over a wide spectrum of moral and philosophical issues, and when considered as a whole provide revealing insights into the breadth and quality of the architect's thinking. Among the quotations are a number which deal with creativity and taste, all of which point up

Davis's search for meaning in his profession; there are also a few which lend support to his strong feelings about the role of the imagination in the creative process. A passage from Thomas Blackwell's *Enquiry into the Life and Writings of Homer*[4] is particularly pertinent: "Mankind receive more delight from the fancy, than the understanding: few are capable of pleasures purely intellectual, and every creature is capable of being pleased or disquieted in some degree by the fancy. Hence plain, naked truth is either not perceived, or soon disrelished, but the man who can give his ideas life and colouring . . . and then weave them into a strange and passionate story: to him we listen with wonder, and greedily learn his soothing tale."

Such notions must have been heady wine for the young romantic who, in his earliest architectural adventures, spent hours "in puzzling over the plan of some ancient castle of romance, arranging the trap doors, subterraneous passages, and drawbridges, as pictorial embellishment was the least of his care, invention all his aim."[5] The idea that uninhibited imagination is more fruitful than rational thought in architectural design was, of course, not unique to Davis. It was an essential condition of all nineteenth-century romantic architecture and even in this country, by the 1830's, it was widely accepted. In an important article, "Architecture in the United States,"[6] the architect and critic Arthur D. Gilman saw the lack of creative imagination among American architects as a major obstacle to high quality building in this country. In support of his position he quotes from no less an authority than the English landscape gardener and critic J. C. Loudon.[7] The passage which he evokes reads in part: "The architect to whom architecture is not an art of imagination as well as an art of reason, can never, by any possibility, rise above the rank of an imitative builder . . . the architect of imagination [is the only one who] is entitled to be considered as an artist possessing the powers of invention, or genius."[8]

Loudon's *Architectural Magazine* was published in London between 1834 and 1839. It was widely read by architects in this country and along with other works by the same author was to have decisive influence on the writings of Andrew Jackson Downing. There can be no doubt that Loudon also had considerable impact on Davis, and the ideas which lie behind his picturesque architecture mark a dramatic departure from the rational Neoclassicism, which, in the 1830's and '40's, still dominated the American scene. Davis's "highly imaginative spirit" had little in common with Robert Mills's conviction that "beauty is founded upon order and that convenience and utility were constituent parts."[9] To be sure, the Neoclassical work which Davis produced during his early years with Town would have received Mills's hearty approval. Moreover, it was work of which Davis himself was justly proud, and for certain types of building he continued to design in the Neoclassical mode throughout his career. In his domestic work, however, his delight in "fancy" would transcend his need for "understanding" and in the end his creative urge would find its most fruitful outlets in the more provocative world of the picturesque.

Architectural Drawing
in Early Nineteenth-century America

While Davis's romantic appetite took him into the "subterraneous chambers" of fantasy, his extraordinary ability as a draftsman gave him the power to capture and develop his reveries in persuasive concrete form. His acute visual sensitivity and skill of hand produced drawings which had both the precision and the flexibility to render his complex picturesque inventions. How these drawings were to affect his architecture can best be introduced by viewing them in terms of the general state of architectural drawing at the time he began his career. Until the late eighteenth century, sophisticated architectural drawings were virtually non-existent in America. The simple box-like structures of the colonial years, with their conventionalized special features, necessitated little in the way of specific instructions to the builder. More often than not the builder himself was the designer, and if he was not, he generally knew more about building than his adviser did. With rare exception, it was the skill and knowledge of the craftsman, and not the creative genius of an architect as expressed in drawings that produced the best early buildings in this country. Even for Bulfinch and Jefferson, who were among the first American architects to use drawings in a professional way, the basic schematics, that is, the plan and elevation, were adequate to render the simple geometry of their Neoclassical schemes. It was not, in fact, until the very last years of the eighteenth century, with the arrival in this country of the European-trained architect Benjamin Latrobe, that a method of architectural drawing capable of conveying the notion of three dimensions became known to American architects.

Latrobe's technique was built around three highly specialized skills. The first was a complete command of geometric perspective. To be sure, during the eighteenth century American painters had come to understand perspective, and by the turn of the nineteenth century were handling it with impressive ease, but aside from a very primitive effort by Charles Bulfinch, no drawings have survived which indicate that perspective was ever used by an early American architect. In contrast to the two-dimensional line drawings which characterized the first American efforts, Latrobe's perspective renderings produced a dramatic three-dimensionality (Fig. 175). Thomas Jefferson's precise delineations on ruled paper, when seen against Latrobe's visually exciting drawings, seem exactly what they are—austere schematics. Schematics, of course, have always been part of the architectural design process. The plan, the section, and the elevation describe exact dimensional relationships. They are the basic visual tools of architecture, and were used by all professional architects, including Latrobe. But schematics record outline only and tell one nothing about a building as it would appear in space to a person viewing it from a fixed position. Perspective, on the other hand, is the linear demonstration of optical illusion. Through the correct construction of convergence and foreshortening it transforms the plane into the solid, and it became for architects the primary means for recording on a two-dimensional surface the appearance of an object as seen in space.

Latrobe was a master of perspective and was the first architect in America to use it in an intelligent and persuasive way, but the effects of visual reality which he was able to create were not achieved through perspective alone. Equally important was his convincing and discreet use of another powerful ingredient in optical illusion, light and shade. Like perspective, light and shade had been used by painters since the fifteenth century in Italy, and even American painters of the eighteenth century, such as John Singleton Copley, understood and utilized its powerful pictorial advantages. Like perspective, too, the effect of light and shade is to heighten the visual impression of three-dimensionality. Unlike perspective, however, which inflexibly relates to the geometry of an object itself, light and shade relates to a condition outside of the object, a condition moreover which is infinitely variable. Although light, when interrupted by solid objects, behaves consistently according to certain laws, its quality and character are also directly affected by the complexities of the environment into which it penetrates. It is absorbed, reflected, fractured, and diffused by every surface which stands in its way, and through its pervasive power of envelopment it enlivens objects not only as geometric solids but also as visual sensations in color and texture. Whereas perspective is immutable, light and shade can be modeled at the artist's will and therefore afford inexhaustible possibilities for pictorial effect. In the drawings of Latrobe (Fig. 77) form-revealing shadows made luminous by carefully placed reflected lights are rendered vividly real by an extraordinary control of tonal gradations. Thrusting some solids forward, drawing others into the obscurity of shadow, the light and shade brings into immediate recognition all of the three-dimensional relationships of the design.

The development of light and shade was made possible for Latrobe by the third of his specialized skills, the water color technique. Whether his drawings were conceived in perspective or as geometric projections, they have a vitality and lucidity which derive almost completely from his intelligent and authoritative exploitation of this medium (Fig. 175). Water color is an extremely flexible method of rendering. It can be worked in large washes to achieve a subtle control of tonal gradation: it can also be used to delineate small details. It is crisp and specific at the same time that it is lush and fluid. Thus it broadens the visual data of architectural drawing far beyond the simple recording of dimensionality, to evoke the more provocative worlds of color, texture, and luminosity. In the hands of a competent practitioner like Latrobe, water color not only made possible a more plausible presentation of three-dimensional space, but through the inexhaustible potential of tone it also opened the way for the full development of those visual qualities so essential to the picturesque—irregularity, variety, and contrast. As a rational Neoclassicist, Latrobe's use of water color was controlled, and was directed primarily toward the explicit demonstration of a large and bold geometry. But it was subtle and luminous, nevertheless, and in the work of his direct followers, particularly the sensitive and talented William Strickland, the pictorial characteristics of the medium were exploited with increasing freedom. By the time Davis began his architectural career water color was on the threshold of becoming a popular technique for American architects.

Alexander Jackson Davis, Architectural Illustrator

The precocious Davis began using drawings as a means of communication very early in his life, but his first formal training did not come until 1823 when he attended the Antique School in New York City (later called the National Academy of Design). One of the first art schools in the country, it was organized by the painter John Trumbull. Although its early offerings were modest, it gave Davis precisely what he needed, a mastery of the basic tools of pictorial representation. It was here, so he tells us, that he "applied himself to perspective, the grammar of his art," and also learned "to draw from the model." Since Trumbull was primarily a painter, the techniques and attitudes that Davis encountered at the school were directed toward pictorial rather than architectural concerns. At the same time, the versatile Trumbull also maintained a lively, semi-professional interest in architecture, and he recognized at once the younger man's special talents. In fact, it was Trumbull who "advised him to devote himself to architecture, as a branch of art most likely to meet with encouragement, and one for which, by the particular bent of his mind, he appeared to be well fitted."

Trumbull's advice was surely prompted in part by the extraordinary aptitude for architectural drawing which Davis displayed. Even while still a student at the Antique School, he was at work on a series of views of the city of New York, which were drawn on lithographic stone for the New York bookseller and publisher, A. T. Goodrich. Indeed, this kind of drawing occupied much of his time during the early years, with the major emphasis on illustrations of public buildings. He also produced material for important publishers other than Goodrich, including Pendleton and Currier. These associations were of special importance in his growth as an architect, for they brought him to the profession not as a designer, or even as a draftsman in an architectural office, but rather as an illustrator of architectural subjects.

There were several advantages to be gained by Davis from his work as an illustrator. To reproduce buildings in pictorial form with the highest degree of visual fidelity required that he be an intelligent observer as well as a highly disciplined draftsman. By examining buildings in minute detail, he came to know their many parts intimately, and to understand the complex relationships between those parts. Equally important, he came to be responsive to the more subtle considerations of proportion and scale. Above all, drawing actual buildings made him consider them in relation to their man-made and natural environment. He thus came to understand each not only in terms of its geometry, but also in terms of its texture and color and the effects of light and atmosphere. All of this quickened his artistic judgment and helped to confirm his growing conviction that architecture was to be his profession.

To make his conviction become a reality required much more of Davis than the simple recording of existing buildings, and in 1826 he went to work as a draftsman in the office of Josiah R. Brady, a New York architect. Brady himself was an ingenious draftsman, and also a thoroughly seasoned practical builder. In addition, he was among the early practitioners in the Gothic style and, as we have already seen, he was the architect of St. Paul's, Rochester. Davis spent a year with Brady and during that time strengthened his growing talents by direct experience with the practical problems of building: it was probably with Brady that he mastered the techniques of schematic and structural drawings, and learned to calculate and write specifications.

Although his association with Brady was essential to his success as an architect, Davis was by nature a restless and impatient man, and by the fall of 1827 we find him in Boston. Before leaving New York, however, he had an encounter which would change the course of his life: sometime early in that year the young architect met his future partner, Ithiel Town. We know of this meeting because one of the letters of introduction which Davis took with him to Boston was written by Town.[10] That letter is a rare document which not only establishes the beginning of the relationship between the two men, but it also tells us why Davis went to Boston. He went, Town records, "for the purpose of taking and painting perspective views of some of the best public buildings in that city." The trip, therefore, was an extension of Davis's activities as an architectural illustrator. The drawings which he produced were made for and published by Pendleton and are among the most beautiful and useful illustrations of Boston public buildings ever recorded (Fig. 168).

In regard to Davis's future as an architect, a more revealing piece of information contained in the letter is Town's expression of confidence in Davis as "an artist of talent." It is obvious that Town already admired Davis and saw in him a man of great promise. More than that, we are also told in his letter that he "offered to pay part of the expenses" of reproducing a drawing which Davis was apparently to make for him, a gesture which suggests that the younger man was already working for Town, at least on an incidental basis. There is no hint yet, however, of a formal association between the two. Indeed, Davis was not quite ready for such an association. Although he returned to New York for the summer of 1828, by fall he was back in Boston, where he remained for another two months making more drawings. He also visited the Athenaeum where he "passed a large portion of time . . . in study and reading." When he finally returned to New York, therefore, in November of 1828, he not only had behind him many months of training at the Antique School and with Brady, but he also had two years of extensive experience with historical buildings, both as objects of study in the Athenaeum and as subjects for the many drawings he made in both New York and Boston. This in itself was enough to start him on his way to an architectural career, but at this point the special opportunity finally came which would bring him at once into the forefront of his profession. During 1827–28, while dividing his time between New York and Boston,

FIGURE 168. *Charles Bulfinch. State House,*
Boston, Mass., 1795–98.
Drawing by A. J. Davis.

Davis made several drawings for Town of three of the latter's buildings. He recorded the results as follows: "Town . . . is so pleased with my drawings in perspective for the Connecticut Capitol, Hartford City Hall, and Sachem's Wood, he kindly proposes an association to practice Architecture professionally in New York, opening an office at Thirty-Two Merchant's Exchange for the transaction of business."[11] Davis accepted the offer and in the summer of 1829 the architectural firm of Town and Davis was formed.

Alexander Jackson Davis, Architectural Draftsman

It is easy to understand why Town regarded Davis as an artist of talent. Everything we can learn about the young man from his early diaries, notebooks, sketch books and letters shows him to have been a mercurial youth of sparkling inventiveness and brash self-confidence. These traits alone would have made him attractive to an architect of Town's professional acumen. But as Davis himself tells us, it was his drawings that were the ultimate magnet. In fact, drawings were to Davis what words were to his contemporary, Nathaniel Hawthorne, a vital means of bringing to life the copious outpourings of an inexhaustible imagination. From beginning to end, drawings in steady procession and infinite variety functioned for Davis in every facet of his creative life. More than that, he seems to have viewed drawing as instrumental in developing moral well-being. In a remarkable passage which he copied from Loudon we read: "Drawing has now become an essential part of polite education. The mere circumstance of familiarizing the mind with orderly arrange-

FIGURE 169. *A. J. Davis. Approach to Washington up the Potomac. Pencil drawing.*

ment, regular figures, symmetry, means adapted to the end in view, either in buildings, in furniture, or in gardens, must have influence on conduct. Order is the fundamental principle of all morals; for what is immorality but a disturbance of the order of civilized society, a disturbance of the relations between man and man? We do not say that all kinds of drawing have a tendency to produce an orderly mind, but we do affirm that architectural drawing has that tendency in an eminent degree."[12]

The equation of moral values with artistic activity was a growing concern of the nineteenth century and would culminate by mid-century in the writings of John Ruskin. Although the moral arguments which appear in the various writings of Davis are prim, stiff, and generally indignant, especially when compared to the urbane grace of Ruskin, his concern was nevertheless genuine. The idea that the discipline of architectural drawing can elevate human behavior has a fascinating Ruskinian ring, and by embracing it Davis anticipates the great English critic and shows himself to be thoroughly in tune with the main philosophical streams of his time.

Whether or not Davis's deep involvement with drawing strengthened his moral fiber, his style was versatile, expressive, and hauntingly beautiful. He made exquisite landscapes in pencil (Fig. 169), gentle in touch and distilled in substance, lovely veiled images in which solid objects dissolve in a sea of silver and light; he made swift small sketches in his Day Book using ink (Fig. 170), or ink and wash, each defining with directness and simplicity the essential elements of some architectural

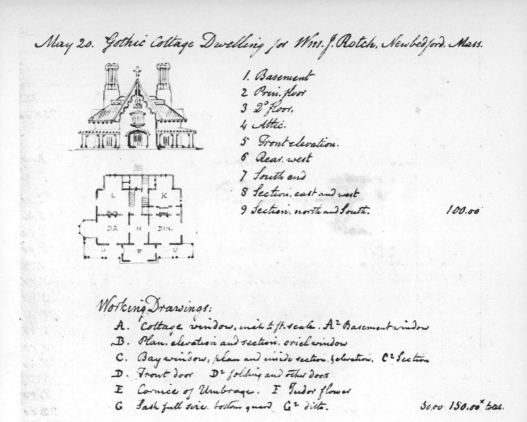

May 20. Gothic Cottage Dwelling for Wm. J. Rotch. Newbedford. Mass.

1. Basement
2. Prin. floor
3. 2° floor.
4. Attic.
5. Front elevation.
6. Rear. west
7. South end
8. Section. east and west
9. Section. north and South.

100.00

Working Drawings:

A. Cottage window. inch to ft. scale. A² Basement window
B. Plan. elevation and section. oriel window
C. Bay window, plan and inside section. ½ elevation. C² Section
D. Front door D² folding and other doors
E. Cornice of Umbrage. F Tudor flower
G. Sash full size. bottom guard G² ditto.

50.00 150.00* total.

FIGURE 170. A. J. Davis. *Entry from his Day Book,*
May 20, 1845.

scheme. Scattered through the pages of his notebooks, or drawn on the back of some cast-off advertisement, are enchanting vignettes in various media, including water color (Fig. 171), vivacious little sketches which record the probings of his intellectual and visual curiosity. But above all, Davis produced the finest architectural renderings of his generation (Fig. 211). Conceived in varying degrees of light and shade, and executed in water color with fluid ease, these drawings reveal with sureness and clarity the full-bodied substance of his designs. Through delicate precise lines they delineate the smallest elements of architectural detail; at the same time, they are richly luminous and vibrant, brought alive by an extraordinary control of tone. Indeed, the key to Davis's achievement lies in his sensitivity to the total range of values, from dark through subtly modulated middle tones to light. It is this that separates him so sharply from the other architectural draftsmen of his time, and gives his style its peculiar stillness and purity. Only Latrobe and a few other architects, trained abroad,[13] had anything like his command of tone.

Davis's highly individual handling of light through tone had another significant effect. Although some of his architectural drawings show the buildings in a landscape setting (Fig. 224), there are many which are simple elevations without any hint of surrounding land, trees, or sky (Fig. 257). Yet even in these the sense of environment is compelling.

FIGURE 171. A. J. Davis. Wildmont,
Llewellyn Park, Orange, N.J., c. 1878.

Through the magic of his luminous style, his buildings seem enveloped in an atmosphere of breathless beauty, and the essence of that atmosphere is a gentle caressing light, a light which pervades everything, modeling geometry and evoking texture. But that light is not just any light. On the contrary, it is the light of a very special place at a very special moment in time; it is the light of the architect's own environment, the light of the still unspoiled slopes of the Hudson River Valley.

A. J. Davis
and the American Creative Community

If Davis's style took something from his environment, it was also a style of the artistic climate into which he was born, and of which he was to become a significant part. The years when he first came into prominence as an architect were the very years when the American creative community was becoming aware of the unique character of the American landscape. William Cullen Bryant had already begun his descriptive essays about his travels in the Hudson River Valley and the Berkshires. In the late 1820's and early '30's, too, Thomas Cole produced some of his most beautiful landscapes of the Catskills and western New England. Both men were leaders of a group of artists and writers in which Davis was very much a part. Entries in his Day Book make it perfectly clear that he knew both Bryant and Cole intimately. Indicative of the character of the relationship is the occasion in July of 1834 when he went to Catskill with the painter Asher B. Durand and two other New York friends. Here they met Cole, who took them on a long walk through the woods. They stayed at the famous Catskill Mountain House and on the next day they went to Kaaterskill Falls (which was painted by Cole in 1826) and then down to the "Clove," one of the favorite scenes of the Hudson River School painters. There they had lunch and scaled the mountain to the north.

It seems impossible to imagine that these encounters both with the countryside and with those who came to celebrate it in poetry, prose, and painting did not leave an indelible mark on Davis's own romantic sensibilities. Bryant's essays on the Catskills and the Berkshires were intended to awaken the American public to the special qualities of their own land, and were an effective prelude to Emerson's appeal in "The American Scholar" (1837) for "insight into today," an appeal to which Davis already enthusiastically responded. But the most profound impressions must have come from the landscapes of his fellow artist Thomas Cole. Although born in England, Cole was trained in the United States and from the beginning his work showed characteristics that distinguished it from European painting of the period. Many of his paintings were direct uninhibited statements about what he saw, and as his style flowered during the 1830's and '40's it showed an increasing sensitivity to the texture and substance of the American scene. Unencumbered by convention, Cole was able to capture with beguiling innocence the translucent atmosphere so peculiar to the regions of the Northeast. Nor was he alone in his vision; for the light and haze which fills the work of both Cole and Davis is the same luminous ambience that floods so much of the writing of Hawthorne and Bryant, an ambience which Henry James was moved to describe as one of "delicious warmth," in which "the long daylight seems to pause and rest."

This common response to the American environment which marked most creative work of the period is vividly summarized in Durand's *Kindred Spirits* (Fig. 4). Painted in 1849, it was conceived as a memorial to Cole, who had died the year before. It was also intended to eulogize the artistic kinship between Cole and Bryant, who, on May 4, 1848, delivered the funeral oration honoring his friend before the National Academy of Design in New York. At the same time, through the clarity of his vision, Durand was also saying something about the special qualities of the natural world in which all the creative artists of the period lived and worked. The two friends are shown looking out upon a very particular forest scene. It is, in fact, the same scene to which Cole had guided Davis and Durand on that memorable excursion into the Catskills fourteen years earlier; and the qualities of Cole's vision which Durand celebrates in paint are the same qualities which moved Bryant to say in his funeral oration that Cole had the capacity to carry "the eye over scenes of wild grandeur peculiar to our country, over our aerial mountain-tops with their mighty growth of forest never touched by the axe, along the banks of streams never deformed by culture, and into the depth of sky bright with hues of our own climate." Davis, in his own way, was as much a part of this fresh luminous world as Cole and Bryant, and because his buildings were all conceived in the bright hues of his own climate he was the first American architect truly to be identified with the romantic naturalism of his time.

A. J. Davis,
Architectural Composer

That Davis himself was aware of the strongly pictorial nature of his design methods is borne out by the fact that from the beginning of his career he thought of himself, and advertised himself, as an "architectural composer."[14] The idea is a fascinating one, for the act of composing is one which is more generally associated with painting and music than with architecture. Davis's use of the term, therefore, suggests that he felt a generic kinship with creative artists in other fields. Davis's first job had been as a compositor for a publishing house in Alexandria, Virginia, and it is possible that the idea was prompted by that experience. On the other hand, the notion that design in architecture is in fact "composition" is one of the many philosophical outgrowths of the Picturesque movement, and as such it was a subject which came under frequent discussion during the early nineteenth century. In 1834, for example, Loudon published an article in *The Architectural Magazine* entitled "On those Principles of Composition in Architecture, which are common to all the Fine Arts," where he defines what he calls "the elementary materials of architecture" as "forms, lines, lights, shades, and colors." Loudon makes only passing reference to questions of structure and style, and centers his entire discussion around "the principles of composition in architecture, with reference to the production of beauty." These principles he defines as: "1. the principle of a whole, founded on the necessity of unity of sensation; 2. the principle of the recognition of art, founded on the immutability of truth, or the necessity of a thing appearing to be what it is; 3. the principle of regularity, including uniformity and symmetry, founded on the inherent love of order existing in the human mind; and, 4. the principle of variety, including intricacy and harmony, founded on the desire for novelty, occasioned by the activity of the human mind."[15]

Loudon deals entirely with the visual aspects of architecture, and makes it clear that the principles which he proposes are basic principles of composition, common to all the arts. That Davis was familiar with the writings of Loudon there can be no doubt. We read in his Day Book that he purchased Loudon's *Encylopaedia of Architecture* in September 1835, only two years after the book was published. We also encounter among his papers various references to *The Architectural Magazine*. But his design methods alone prove how much his point of view coincided with Loudon's. Davis showed extraordinary sensitivity to form as revealed by light, he used line with explicit facility and ease, he recognized the central importance of color in achieving effects of luminosity and texture. With good reason, therefore, he called himself an "architectural composer."

PART II

THE PICTURESQUE VILLA
AND THE GOTHIC REVIVAL

Town, Davis,
and the Picturesque

Davis joined Town as a partner on February 1, 1829, and his arrival in the office could not have been more opportune. Although Town had begun his career as an architect, and was so known and recognized throughout his lifetime, he was also a man of diversified interests, with a strong practical bent and a genuine flair for engineering. Among the fields of knowledge toward which he was to direct his attention were such things as transatlantic steam navigation and mathematics, but his greatest contribution, apart from architecture, was his invention of the Town Lattice Truss. Patented in 1820, this ingenious device was a wooden truss beam which could span distances of up to 160 feet without intermediate support. Through its strength and simplicity of construction it made possible the remarkable proliferation of wooden covered bridges which spanned so many streams in the northeastern United States during the mid to late nineteenth century. The royalties from this invention provided Town with a respectable income through a good part of his life, but the obligations which grew out of it required more and more of his professional attention, and by the late 1820's were making serious inroads in the time he had to devote to architecture.

The vital sources of creative energy which were so seriously diverted by Town's outside activities were more than renewed by Davis's arrival. His unusual skill and prolificacy as a draftsman easily met the day-by-day requirements of the office; his genius as a designer brought new levels of quality and excitement to its work. From the very beginning he assumed a commanding position in the office, so much so in fact, that in less than a year's time Town felt free to sail for Europe, leaving his young partner in complete charge. Before the first period of the partnership would end five and a half years later the work of Town and Davis would assume a wholly different character.

At the time of Davis's arrival the work of the firm was dominated by Town's classical taste. To be sure, Town was one of the important early eclectic architects in America, and stood ready to provide a Gothic design if a client wanted it—witness Trinity Church, New Haven. But like the other confirmed Neoclassicists of his time, such as Latrobe, Mills, and Strickland, men who also designed in the Gothic style, Town not only lacked a firm knowledge of the Gothic but, even more important, was emotionally committed to classical doctrine, to the stability and order of that grand tradition which had nourished him as an ar-

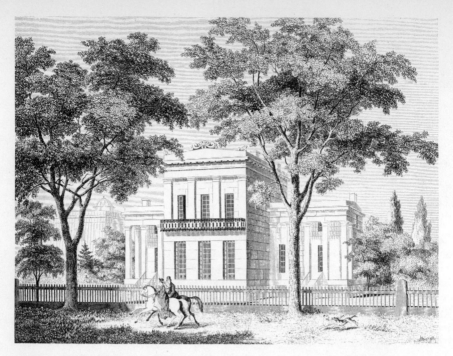

FIGURE 172. *Ithiel Town. Ithiel Town House,*
New Haven, Conn., 1836–37.

chitect, and which suited so perfectly his austere demanding intelligence.
Perhaps this is best seen in his own house on fashionable Hillhouse Avenue in New Haven, which was built between 1836 and 1838 (Fig. 172).
This building in its unyielding symmetry and distilled Greek forms was as
Neoclassical as any design of its time. Nowhere in its chaste balanced arrangements was there the slightest hint of the picturesque exuberance
which would characterize Davis's summer lodge, Wildmont (Fig. 171).
Not only was Davis's house fantastically romantic, but also its site contrasted sharply with the urban setting of Town's residence. Perched on the
edge of the cliff at Eagle Rock, above Llewellyn Park in Orange, New
Jersey, Wildmont looked out across gentle forested hills to Newark Bay
and beyond to New York City.

The contrast between these two houses exemplifies the contrast between
the two partners themselves. It is true that Davis came to Town as a disciplined classicist, and used the classical mode for certain types of buildings throughout most of his creative life. Except for its unusual grace and
urbanity, however, Davis's classical work did not reflect his natural artistic temperament. Although both men shared a refined sense of order,
their actual creative strengths lay at quite opposite poles. Davis's approach
to architecture was intuitive and visionary, Town's was practical and
reasoned. There can be no doubt, therefore, that the firm's dramatic
entrance into the field of picturesque design, which occurred in the early
1830's, was brought about by the younger man. Not that Town was opposed to the picturesque. We have already seen how he demonstrated an
awareness of its values in his use of the Gothic in Trinity Church, New

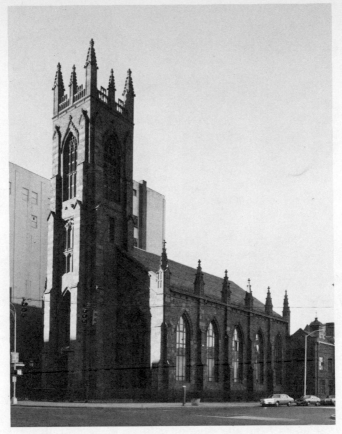

FIGURE 173. *Ithiel Town. Christ Church Cathedral, Hartford, Conn., 1827–29.*

Haven. Moreover, through his reading and wide cultural interests, he was certainly familiar with the picturesque doctrine, which was now beginning to make itself felt in the American intellectual and artistic community. But the picturesque was not Town's natural idiom. In the affairs of the firm, therefore, it was the irrepressible and imaginative Davis who provided the romantic imagery necessary to translate that doctrine into architectural form.

Town and Davis
and the Early Gothic Revival in America

If Town's first use of the Gothic in Trinity, New Haven, was motivated by pressure from within the Episcopal Church itself, precisely the same was true of his second major Gothic design, Christ Church Cathedral, in Hartford, Connecticut. The commission came in 1827 when Town was asked to submit plans. The building was consecrated on December 23, 1829. In some ways the church was a replica of Trinity (Fig. 173). It was a simple rectangular box with a central Perpendicular tower, three Gothic-arch doorways on the principal façade, and a range of Gothic

FIGURE 174. *William Buckland. Gunston Hall,
Fairfax County, Va., porch, 1755–58.*

windows down each side. It differed from Trinity, however, in that the
tower was planned from the beginning to be of stone rather than wood,
and the building had both corner and side-wall buttresses, also of stone.
It was therefore more authentically Gothic than Trinity. As in the case of
Trinity, New Haven, however, the motivation for the use of the
Gothic style came from the church and not Town. Indeed, the rector of
Christ Church, Nathaniel S. Wheaton, had traveled in England in 1823
where he saw the English Gothic at first hand. This experience seems to
have made him an ardent Gothic enthusiast, and there is strong evidence
to suggest that the final form of the church was determined as much by
him as by Town. There is no direct evidence to connect Davis with the
design. On the other hand, he was working for .Town as a draftsman at
the time, and it is possible that he could have made some of the drawings. But whether he did or not, there must have been considerable conversation around the office about the Gothic building, conversation
which could not help but stimulate the interest of an ardent young architect with romantic tendencies.

Whatever impact the experience of the Hartford church may have had
on Davis the possibilities of the Gothic as an exciting style for domestic architecture seem to have been very much in his consciousness almost from
the time he joined Town. As early as January 1830 he records[16] making a
design for a small Gothic castle, and within four months he had also designed a Gothic cottage.[17] Two years later he was deeply involved in
studying the Gothic style, giving particular attention to English publications on the subject, such as those of Britton and Rickman.[18]

FIGURE 175. *Benjamin Latrobe.*
Sedgeley, Philadelphia, Pa., 1799.
Original water color.

All of this was the prelude to the first commission for a Gothic house to be received by Town and Davis. It came from James W. Moulton of Brooklyn, New York, and is first recorded in Davis's Day Book on June 19, 1832.[19] No drawings survive to give us any notion of what it may have been like, but it seems to have been a landmark in the work of the firm and was actually claimed by Davis as the first Gothic residence in America.[20] This blunt assertion raises interesting questions about what Davis meant by a "Gothic residence," for the Moulton House was certainly not the first in this country to be treated in a Gothic manner. To understand Davis's claim we must go back briefly to the early part of the century and examine a few of the first efforts in domestic Gothic.

The Gothic Revival in American domestic architecture began at the turn of the nineteenth century, and followed very much the same course, although to a significantly lesser degree, as did the Gothic in church architecture. There were even scattered examples of "Batty Langley" Gothic in the eighteenth century, of which the octagonal porch of Gunston Hall in Fairfax County, Virginia, is one of the best known (Fig. 174). Designed by William Buckland during 1755–58, its ogee arches clearly suggest a possible source in Langley's *Gothic Architecture Improved*.[21] But the Gothic forms in the porch are framed by a sturdy classical order, and were obviously intended as a purely decorative motif. The exotic nature of both Gothic and Chinese elements appealed to eighteenth-century English and American taste, and they frequently appear not only in the architecture but also in the decorative arts of the period.

These whimsical adaptations of Gothic forms, even if taken collectively, can hardly be seen as a true Gothic Revival. Indeed, the first American house in which the use of the Gothic can be said to be architectural rather than decorative was "Sedgeley," which Benjamin Latrobe designed in 1799 for the Philadelphia merchant William Crammond. It was demolished in 1857 and is known to us only through engravings and Latrobe's own water color (Fig. 175). In the latter it is shown on a slight rise of land in an irregular park-like setting. To the left, the Schuylkill River meanders into the distance. Like Latrobe's other Gothic designs, Sedgeley is solidly geometric with widely spaced openings set in assertive wall planes. Although the plan is absolutely symmetrical, the four attached corner pavilions are more reminiscent of English late medieval house plans than they are of the more widely spaced dependencies with connecting passages which are so typical of the English Palladian plan.[22] Between these corner pavilions at Sedgeley are covered porches supported by slender Gothic posts. These appear on the river side and at the ends of the house. In contrast, the main façade on the land side, as seen in a contemporary engraving (Fig. 176), has a central entrance pavilion, is curved in plan, and is approached through a small porch, also carried on Gothic posts. All the windows on the first floor of the house, and those on the second floor on the river side, have square heads and are crowned by Gothic hood moldings. Elsewhere, the second-floor windows have Gothic pointed arches, as do the main openings in the four corner pavilions. In the center of all four sides of the hip roof was a dormer window with a pointed-arch opening; above each of these windows was a steep gable decorated by a verge board.[23] In Latrobe's water color the principal eave line which runs level around the entire house has a modillioned cornice; in the engraving, however (Fig. 176), which was based on a drawing made between 1827 and 1830, the eaves are decorated by a Gothic drip molding.

Like Latrobe's Christ Church in Washington (Fig. 78), Sedgeley is a mixed design, combining Neoclassical and Gothic elements. Like Christ Church, too, the house is not simply another flimsy. Through his keen architectural sense, Latrobe has integrated the Gothic elements into the main geometry of his design by holding them close to the wall and by permitting them to mold into and envelop the openings rather than simply surround them as a frame attached to the outer surface. Latrobe also maintained a consistent scale in the Gothic elements, thus strengthening the unity of the design, and setting it conspicuously apart from the more characteristic Gothic concoctions of the period, such as Dorsey's Gothic Mansion, built in Philadelphia about ten years after Sedgeley (Fig. 177). In Sedgeley, as in all the Gothic designs of Latrobe, the architect transcends the decorator, and this house remains the first coherent example of the Gothic Revival in American domestic architecture. It was one, however, which would not immediately inspire similar works, for in spite of Latrobe's promising design the Gothic did not gain favor as a mode of domestic building in this country during the first quarter of the century. Except for a handful of eccentric efforts, such as Dorsey's Gothic Mansion, the Greek temple dominated the scene.[24] In contrast,

FIGURE 176. Benjamin Latrobe.
Sedgeley, Philadelphia, Pa., 1799.

FIGURE 177. Dorsey's Gothic Mansion,
Philadelphia, Pa., c. 1809.

the number of Gothic churches rapidly increased during this period. Davis's claim of "first," therefore, may not be so extravagant as it might seem. If his Moulton house was not the first use of the Gothic in American domestic architecture, it did mark the beginning of a new and coherent type of Gothic house, a type which Davis himself would largely create, and one which in the end would become seminal for the more demanding romanticism of the second half of the century

Sir Walter Scott
and the American Gothic Revival

The preference for the Gothic which opened the way for the picturesque house in America was not confined to architects such as Davis. It was the taste also of a growing segment of American architectural patronage, outside of the church, a patronage which found its inspiration not so much in the architectural writings of Britton and Rickman, as in the widely read novels of the Scottish author Sir Walter Scott.[25] Although some Americans saw the Middle Ages much as the Puritans did, as an era shadowed in darkness and tainted by the sinister implications of "popery," there were others who were excited by the bright dynamic world described by Scott. Here was a challenging world in which chivalrous men prevailed through feats of extraordinary valor, and this had a familiar ring to the early nineteenth-century Americans who were already building their own legends of heroic deeds. In a very real sense, Scott glorified the medieval knight in much the same way that the emerging American dream glorified the individual. But it was not only the heroic behavior of Scott's characters that stirred the American romantic mind, it was also the fascinating ambience in which it occurred. The medieval castle in particular came through clearly in Scott's novels and with its complex chambers for living it offered intoxicating possibilities for the gathering ambitions of the literate and successful American.

Scott's vision of medieval living was not limited to his writing. Utterly captivated by his own imagined world he built for himself an actual Gothic castle, Abbotsford, in which he lived and worked (Fig. 178). One of the most remarkable Gothic Revival houses in Scotland, it ranks in importance with such other outstanding works of the period as the royal residence, Balmoral Castle.[26] Built for the author by William Atkinson during 1812–15, and considerably enlarged in 1819, Abbotsford became one of the prodigious shrines of its day, not only because it was Scott's house, but also because it gave physical substance to the medieval work in which so much of his writing was set. Pilgrims came to see it from everywhere, including America. As Carlyle put it, Abbotsford "became infested to a great degree with tourists, wonder-hunters, and all that fatal species of people," which he goes on to describe as "buzzing swarms of blue-bottles, who never fail where any taint of human glory or other corruptibility is in the wind."

Among the many "blue-bottles" who descended upon Abbotsford was the American author James Fenimore Cooper. He visited the castle in the

FIGURE 178. *William Atkinson.*
Abbotsford, Scotland, 1812–15; 1819.

early 1830's and was so impressed by it that in 1834, immediately after his return to the United States, he turned the family home in Cooperstown, New York, into a Gothic castle of his own. Before the remodeling, Otsego Hall was a typical late eighteenth-century house. Cooper made it Gothic by adding a Gothic porch, Gothic hood moldings over the windows, and a crenelated parapet along the eave line. Although there is little in such whimsical ornamentation to match the complex Gothic fantasies of Abbotsford, and although it is hard to see the wilderness world of Cooper's novels as having anything to do with the chivalric world portrayed by Scott, a high romantic spirit permeates the works of both authors, and there can be little doubt that the American was moved not only by Abbotsford but also by the writings of Scott. Cooper's intrepid forest heroes wear coonskin caps rather than visored helmets, and behave with qualities of innocence which suggest Jean Jacques Rousseau more than Scott. Yet the American's frontiersmen and the Scotsman's valiant knights, each in their own way, and in their own environment, move through the drama of life with valor toward kindred ends. This underlying correspondence of fact and fiction made Scott's novels particularly attractive to the Americans, but so, too, did the physical world in which the action was set. Because of its complexity and brilliance, it opened up new and tantalizing possibilities for living which seemed ideally suited to both the dynamics and the picturesqueness of the American environment. Indeed, Scott's impact was as great in arousing in this country a taste for the Gothic house as the writings of the *Ecclesiologist* were to be in the creation of the American Gothic Revival church.

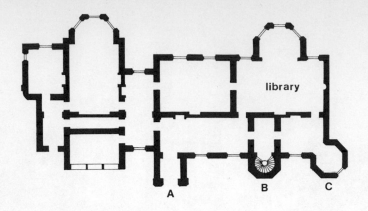

FIGURE 179. *William Atkinson. Abbotsford, Scotland, plan, 1819.*

Abbotsford and Glen Ellen

The first house in the United States to be directly influenced by Scott and Abbotsford was Glen Ellen. Designed by Town and Davis in 1832 for Robert Gilmore of Baltimore, it was the first major domestic work of the firm in the Gothic style about which solid data survives. It thus occupies a position of primary historical importance. The man who built Glen Ellen was the descendant of a line of Scottish merchants who first came to this country immediately following the Revolution. Gilmore, who broke with the family tradition and became a gentleman farmer rather than a merchant, was a cultured, literate, and intensely romantic man with a genuine taste for the exotic. After his graduation from Harvard in 1828, he went to France as attaché to the American embassy and spent several years abroad. During that time he visited his ancestral Scotland and while there made a pilgrimage to Abbotsford, where he met Sir Walter Scott.

The Abbotsford that Gilmore saw was the castle which was completed in 1825 (Fig. 179). It was an asymmetrical pile of towers, turrets, stepped gables, oriels, pinnacles, crenelated parapets, and clustered chimney stacks, all assembled with calculated irregularity. The complex and colorful Gothic interiors were rich in the trappings of the Middle Ages, and the American, fresh from the prim byways of Neoclassical Baltimore, was overwhelmed. Shortly after his return from abroad he and his brother William purchased approximately two thousand acres of land on the Gunpowder River north of Baltimore, in an area now known as Loch Raven,[27] and plans for a baronial mansion were begun.

Named for his wife Ellen Ward, daughter of Judge Ward of Baltimore, and given a special Scottish ring by the addition of "glen," Glen Ellen was conceived from the beginning as an irregular house in the Gothic style with a broken roof line and asymmetrical arrangements both inside and out. The plan was made by Town and Gilmore; the Gothic detailing was designed by Davis,[28] who also made all the drawings. As seen in one of these drawings (Fig. 180), the house was originally intended to

THE ORIGINAL DESIGN

DWELLING, EXECUTED FOR ROBT. GILMOR ESQ. NEAR BALTIMORE.

FIGURE 180. A. J. Davis.
Design for Glen Ellen, Baltimore, Md., 1833.

have two stories and a basement, but as built it was reduced by one story. In plan, the building had two rectangular parts. There was a primary section oriented north and south which contained the main entrance vestibule, a circular saloon, a library, and a parlor. Joined to this, at right angles, was a somewhat narrower wing which apparently contained a dining room, kitchen, and bedrooms.

Together these two units formed an extended plan of fascinating complexity. The fulcrum of the design was a sequence of rooms—the vestibule, saloon, and library—which fell on the primary cross axis of the building; at one end of this axis was the main door of the house, at the other the octagonal bay of the library. This formal grouping made up one side of the main section of the house; parallel with it, and stretching across the entire width of the building on the other side, was a long narrow parlor. This was the largest room in the house and had elongated proportions which were reminiscent of a medieval gallery, such as that at Strawberry Hill (Fig. 69). But unlike a medieval gallery, which was always an enclosed space, Town's parlor opened on its long side through four full-length Gothic windows onto a narrow porch. Here, seven slender Gothic posts, set on a shallow segmental curve, carried the delicately traceried eave of a similarly curved roof.

The pivotal space of the total design was the round saloon which, with its recessed curved niches, seemed more like a Roman rotunda than a Gothic chamber. The center of this circular space not only lay on the main cross axis of the building, but it also served as one terminal point for the secondary axis which ran down the hall of the wing to an outside door at the other end. It was this hall, more than the rooms themselves, which established the right-angle relationship between the wing and the main body of the building.

The asymmetry achieved by Town on the interior of Glen Ellen was not fully realized on the exterior. Although the main front of the house, with its off-center entrance door, set-back wing, corner buttresses and turrets, was asymmetrically balanced, the front facing the river (Fig. 180) was monumental in its symmetry and actually contradicted the irregular arrangement of the interior. On this side the richly traceried octagonal bay of the library, which was on axis with the off-center main door, was the central motif in a symmetrical stretch of wall, more classical than Gothic in its horizontal proportions. To complete the absolute balance identical windows were symmetrically placed left and right. This created the impression that on the interior there were identical spaces either side of the library. We know, however, that this was not the case. Behind the defiant symmetry of this wall unit were asymmetrical rooms; moreover, to achieve its symmetry the wall was forced to reach beyond that section of the interior of which it was a logical part, and to embrace as well one room of the wing. This arbitrary concession to formal principle on the outside denied the functional separation of the two basic parts of the house which the interior arrangement had so explicitly defined.

The denial of a basically asymmetrical scheme by the intrusion of an assertive and prominently placed symmetrical element clearly shows Town's uneasiness with the picturesque mode. It is revealed again both in his use of a Neoclassical rotunda as the focal point of his cross-axis arrangement and in his use of a segmental curve for the line of his porch posts. Although he conceded to Gilmore's wish to emulate Abbotsford and designed an irregular Gothic building, the classical principles were too deeply rooted in his artistic consciousness to make it possible for him to forsake them altogether. The Gothic ornament, on the other hand, which was designed by Davis, was handled with grace and ease, and shows the younger man already to be fully in command of both of its structural and decorative implications. The building, therefore, in spite of its residual Neoclassical elements, was still convincingly Gothic.

The association with Abbotsford is too deeply rooted in the legend which surrounds Glen Ellen to be denied. But beyond that, there are interesting similarities between the two buildings, particularly in the plan (compare Figs. 179 and 180). Except for its symmetry, for example, the sequence on the river front of Glen Ellen—from octagonal corner turret, to an octagonal bay, to a square corner tower—is remarkably like the sequence of elements in the southeast front of Abbotsford (Fig. 179A, B, C). Moreover, the libraries of both houses culminate in deep octagonal bays. These two similarities point to aspects of the Scottish castle that Gilmore could easily have remembered. The specific Gothic details at Glen Ellen, on the other hand, which would have been extremely difficult if not impossible to develop from Gilmore's recollections, have nothing to do with those at Abbotsford. Instead, Davis seems to have been left free to refer to his own sources, and to use his own imagination in developing the Gothic character of the house. This he did with infinite grace and skill. The superb scale and authentic Gothic treatment of the bay windows, and the elegant lace-like sweep of the gently curved porch, were unmatched in their day.

Glen Ellen not only was conspicuous because of its convincing Gothic character, it also introduced into this country a completely new concept of a house. For one thing, it was rooted in the literary romanticism of the period, both directly and to a degree that we have not encountered before. But equally important, it was an asymmetrical house. There can be no question that this aspect of the plan was motivated by Gilmore, perhaps with some enthusiastic support from Davis. But whoever was responsible, it was the first American house since the seventeenth century to be deliberately designed with an off-center balance. Both in form and intent, therefore, it can be directly associated with the Picturesque movement. It was irregular in plan and massing, Gothic in style, and was situated in the lush Maryland countryside. From its terraced knoll, it looked out across sweeping lawns through clumps of trees to the river below; and to set the mood for its abundant tracery and embattled profile, the long approach road began at a Gothic gatehouse, built from the beginning as a ruin. At Glen Ellen all the ingredients of the picturesque, in both the house and its natural setting, were intentionally combined in a single concept for the first time in American architecture.

Rural Residences and the Villa

Glen Ellen was the only Gothic house designed by Town and Davis in which the older partner played a significant role. From that point on it was Davis who handled all the Gothic work. Three houses in particular will demand our attention, all of them on the east bank of the Hudson River north of New York City: a Gothic villa for Robert Donaldson, designed in 1834, and intended for a site near Fishkill; Blithewood, also for Donaldson, designed in 1836 and located near Barrytown; and the famous Lyndhurst in Tarrytown, which was designed originally for Philip A. Paulding in 1838. Before we can put these houses in their proper relationship with one another, however, we must examine a very different kind of work by Davis, his *Rural Residences*. This remarkable book, which appeared in 1837, was intended as a means for "the improvement of American country architecture," and it is a milestone in American architectural literature. Illustrated with hand-colored lithographs from drawings by the architect, it contained designs for a variety of building types including "cottages, farm-houses, villas and village churches." Most of these were actually designed by Davis himself. Each illustration included plans, and was accompanied by a brief description, an estimate of cost, and a summary of materials and construction.

Rural Residences was privately printed, limited in its distribution, and was never completed in the form Davis envisaged.[29] Nevertheless, it was a superb document of its time and was the first book on architecture published in this country which broke with the conventional "builders' guides"; it was written instead as a "house pattern book." The builders' guides, which dominated American architectural literature up to the mid 1830's, offered technical information and stylistic details. In contrast, Davis organized his material around architectural types, and therefore offered his readers ideas about the shape a building should take rather than about how it should be ornamented. Plates illustrating the classical orders were replaced in Davis's book by plans, elevations, and three-dimensional drawings.

Many of the eighteenth-century English architectural books that circulated in this country, such as James Gibbs's *Book of Architecture* and Robert Morris's *Select Architecture,* were this type of book. The major flourishing of the house pattern books, however, occurred in England after the turn of the nineteenth century and it was these later books, led by the writings of T. F. Hunt, Robert Lugar, J. B. Papworth, and P. F. Robinson, that Davis was trying to emulate in *Rural Residences*. In spite of its limited distribution, the book opened the way for wholly new attitudes toward the character and function of the American house.

As well as containing explicit information about individual building types, *Rural Residences* provides a remarkably coherent picture of Davis's practical and philosophical views on architecture. Even though he was inspired by the early nineteenth-century English pattern books, Davis sought seriously to accommodate the English picturesque doctrine to the American scene. In the preface, he expresses a preference for the

Gothic style over the Greek not only because he finds it more appropriate for country residences, but also because "it admits of greater variety both of plan and outline;—is susceptible of additions from time to time, while its bay windows, oriels, turrets and chimney shafts, give a pictorial effect to the elevation." He deplores the general state of domestic architecture in America, both because of the prevailing classical styles, and particularly because of "the want of connection with its site." His expressed preference is for "the picturesque Cottages and Villas of England," yet he acknowledges that the large English villas "are on a scale far more extended and expressive than we can accomplish with our limited means," while England's small cottages "are too inconsiderable and humble for the proper pride of republicans." What was suitable for America was something in between, and this is precisely what his book proposes.

In both the subtitle and the text of *Rural Residences* appears the descriptive term "Villa." To the present-day reader, Davis's use of this word may seem of little importance. Actually, however, it signifies a dramatic change in American domestic architecture, and heralds the ultimate triumph of the picturesque over the rational values of the Neoclassical movement. Before the publication of Davis's book, the term does not occur anywhere in the architectural literature of this country, nor was there any reason why it should. Rural domestic architecture during the colonial years and into the early nineteenth century was dominated by one single house form, the rectangular box, with pitched, hipped, or gambrel roof, a door in the center of the long side, and windows symmetrically placed left and right. Two stories high (or very occasionally three), this form served for farmhouses, plantation houses, and suburban dwellings alike with the only major variations to be found in the quality and character of the ornamental treatment. The primary function of the American house was twofold: it provided accommodations for the day to day requirements of living, and for some persons it was one of the symbols of social prestige. The term "house," therefore, was entirely adequate to describe most American dwellings, and the term "mansion" sufficed for the larger and more ambitious residences.

To the theorists and architects of the early nineteenth century, the villa represented a very different concept of a house, a concept which Davis understood and wholeheartedly embraced. He used the term as early as 1830, and from then on it appears with increasing frequency in his papers. In this respect it is of extreme interest that he owned a copy of Loudon's *Encyclopaedia of Architecture,* for there the villa is described in detail. According to Loudon,[30] a villa is "a country residence, with land attached, a portion of which, surrounding the house, is laid out as a pleasure ground . . . with a view to recreation and enjoyment, more than profit . . . the end in view, in forming a villa, is to produce a healthy, agreeable, and elegant country residence." The form of the villa "ought to be characterized by irregularity," although "it is not necessary that the dwelling of the villa should be large, or the land surrounding it extensive; the only essential requisites are, that the possessor should be a man of some wealth, and . . . taste." A villa, in other words, for Davis as well as Loudon, was not just a house, but a country house built for a man of means and discriminating judgment, and sympathetically designed in relation to a particular natural setting. The term, therefore, embraces the house, its occupant, and its total ambience, and it is this meaning of "villa" that Davis began to explore in Donaldson's Gothic villa.

Donaldson's Gothic Villa

Robert Donaldson was a prosperous New York merchant who played a major role in Davis's early career, not only as a client but also as a patron and friend. In addition, he was a man of wide cultural interests and an art collector of some distinction. Indeed, he seems even to have been directly involved in the publication of *Rural Residences,* for in describing Donaldson's villa Davis refers to his patron as a man "to whose taste and aid, in selecting designs, the public are mainly indebted for the present publication." Donaldson maintained a town house in New York, and his villa at Fishkill was to be his country retreat. For some reason the house was never built, but we know a great deal about it from the illustration and data included in *Rural Residences* and from numerous references and drawings found among Davis's papers.

The story of Donaldson's Gothic villa begins on January 15, 1834, when Davis recorded in his Day Book that "Mr. Donaldson called to look for a Gothic villa in books, and get a design for a residence, I studied out several."[31] Within two months preliminary sketches were delivered, and on November 1 of that same year Davis went to Fishkill with Donaldson to examine the proposed site. It was apparently shortly after this that the scheme was dropped, and Davis went on to work on another project for Donaldson at Blithewood. Even though the house at Fishkill was never constructed, the design for it was sufficiently important to be published by Davis in his *Rural Residences* (Fig. 181). In fact, it was the architect's first essay in what he defined in the text as a "villa in the English Collegiate style."

It is clear that the roots of the Donaldson design are in Glen Ellen. The most obvious relationship is seen in the main façade. Like the original design for the Gilmore house, Donaldson's villa has a two-storied front symmetrically balanced around a central pavilion with turrets at the corners. In both houses the first-floor windows have pointed arches, while those on the second floor have square heads, and all of the windows are topped by Gothic hood moldings. But here the similarities end. In the over-all composition of the Donaldson house, the wing which adjoins the symmetrical central unit is to the right rather than to the left, and is lower in profile than the main part of the house. Standing alone this asymmetrical wing upsets the primary balance of the design, but the resulting instability is resolved at the left by a tall tower on the west front. The roof, too, is steeply pitched rather than almost flat, with tall gables at both ends. This gives the main part of the house a much more vertical character than Town achieved at Glen Ellen, an effect which is ac-

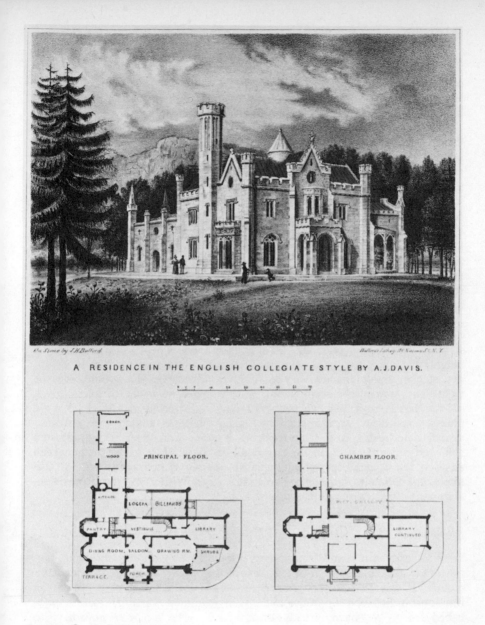

A RESIDENCE IN THE ENGLISH COLLEGIATE STYLE BY A.J.DAVIS.

FIGURE 181. A. J. Davis.
Donaldson's Gothic villa, 1834.

centuated by the piling of the central pavilion. A deep porch projects
boldly from the façade, creating a shadowed semi-enclosed space which
is seen through heavy pointed-arch openings. Corner buttresses add to the
sense of weight and intensify the vertical thrust. The porch is topped by a
crenelated parapet above which an oriel window, less bold in its projection but equally assertive in its verticality, extends the tapered massing
toward the high crocketed gable which crowns the whole. The central pavilion is thus more substantially Gothic than the extremely delicate bay
window at Glen Ellen. Moreover, it cuts vigorously through the rectangle

of the façade, and together with the tall Gothic windows, buttresses, and turrets creates a vertical effect which is quite in contrast to the classical horizontal emphasis created by Town at Glen Ellen (Fig. 180).

Davis also achieved a more logical and expressive relationship between the exterior and interior components of his design. As we have already seen, symmetry in itself was not alien to the Gothic style, although a horizontal emphasis with classical proportions was, and symmetrical sub-units appear frequently in Davis's Gothic work. It is no surprise, there-fore, to encounter symmetry in the design of Donaldson's villa. What distinguishes it from that at Glen Ellen, however, is that Davis's use of it was not contrived: the symmetry seen on the façade corresponds exactly to the arrangement of the rooms within, even though the rooms them-selves, as they balance left and right around the central axis, do not ex-actly correspond in size and shape. Throughout the design there is a direct relationship between the exterior components and the practical distri-bution of interior space.

Unlike the formal symmetrical front of the house, the rest of the design is completely irregular and asymmetrical. Because of the extensive service wing to the rear, the plan is L-shaped. The roof line varies in height; the mass moves forward and retreats; and towers, turrets, chim-ney stacks, and pinnacles vary in height and shatter the profile. On the right-hand side of the south front, in the angle between the main block of the house and the east wing, a covered porch, designed to hold plants, creates a second semi-enclosed space to match the entrance porch. The result is a lively, occult balance—an over-all equilibrium achieved through a dynamic composition of varied forces rather than through the formal correspondence of exactly matching parts. All this makes the Donaldson design more coherently picturesque than Glen Ellen, and many times more interesting as a house.

Blithewood: The House and Its Environment

With its asymmetry and irregularity, Donaldson's villa was not only im-portant in the development of the picturesque in American domestic archi-tecture. It was also the first American house for which awareness of the relationship between the house and its environment was expressed in pub-lished form. We have already discussed Davis's pictorial approach to design and how it enabled him to understand a house both as an object of high visual excitement and as an organic part of the natural world in which it was to be placed. To him a house and its setting were inseparable and one could not be understood apart from the other. Throughout his professional career, this relationship was an overriding concern, a con-cern which he would share with his friend and colleague Andrew Jackson Downing. But even before he met Downing, Davis's opinions were firm on the subject. Indeed, he expressed them publicly as early as 1837 in *Rural Residences,* specifically in regard to Donaldson's villa. In describ-ing that house, Davis reveals in one simple sentence that his conception of the villa included more than just the building itself. The design, he wrote, is "irregular and suited to scenery of a picturesque character."

FIGURE 182. *A. J. Davis. Blithewood,*
Barrytown, N.Y., 1836. Original pencil drawing.

This idea is clearly borne out by the illustration (Fig. 181). The frag-
mented, irregular mass of the building is seen across a short expanse of
flowered lawn, against a wild setting of clustered trees and a rock-faced
hill; to the left, in the foreground, two tapering spruce trees reflect the
pointed gables and pinnacles which break the roof line. In every aspect of
its varied shapes and fractured surfaces, the house identifies with the
landscape. But the landscape also identifies with the house. Further in his
description, Davis adds that the house is suitable "to an eminence commanding an extensive view." In other words, the house is not only to be
seen as an object in harmony with its natural setting, it is also a point of
vantage from which the landscape itself may be viewed and savored. The
house belongs to the landscape, but the landscape in turn belongs to the
house.

Even though it was in connection with Donaldson's villa that Davis introduced this intriguing idea, it was not there that he brought it to full architectural realization. It was rather in another project which he carried
out for Donaldson. About the same time that Davis was working on the
Fishkill villa, Donaldson purchased another property, this time above
Barrytown on the Hudson. Called "Annandale" by its previous owner,
he renamed it Blithewood and invited Davis there in June of 1836 to
make some modifications and additions to the existing house and estate.
Included was a design for a new veranda. This interesting feature appears
in several drawings,[32] most of them in pencil, which show a wide
covered porch surrounding three sides of the house (Fig. 182). The idea
of a sheltered area attached to the house and conceived as a space for living was not new to American architecture. Remote from the Hudson River
Valley, and perhaps even unknown to Davis, were the wide porches of
the plantation houses in the lower Mississippi Valley and the so-called

water & sky lightest.   *hemlock*   *pine*   *View N.W. at Blithewood.*

FIGURE 183. *A. J. Davis. Blithewood,*
Barrytown, N.Y., view northwest from veranda, 1836.
Original water color.

"single houses" in Charleston, South Carolina, both regional developments in response to local climatic conditions. More readily available to
Davis were the Dutch houses of the colonial era which still survived in
substantial numbers along the Hudson River from New York to Albany.
Many of these were characterized by an overhanging roof supported on a
line of posts which formed an open porch along one wall. These were
surely known to Davis and may have inspired him to adopt the motif.
Most important of all, however, just the year before Davis began working
at Blithewood, his friend Washington Irving, for whom he inscribed a
copy of *Rural Residences,* had remodeled an old Dutch cottage into a
quasi-Gothic irregular house which had, among other things, a low veranda. Irving was also a friend of Donaldson's and it is altogether probable that the idea of using a veranda came from that source. But whatever
its origin at Blithewood, the veranda became for Davis a major architectural component, and in the end would be a mark of distinction between the American and English houses of the Gothic Revival.

That Davis intended the veranda at Blithewood as a means of extending
the relationship between the house and the landscape is borne out by a
lovely water-color drawing, not of the house as seen from the grounds, but
of the view from the house looking toward the river (Fig. 183). The view-
point is the semi-enclosed space of the veranda as defined by the open

raftered ceiling and trellised posts. The architectural components are precisely drawn with a ruling pen, and then subtly shaded with discreet areas of wash. The landscape has no pen lines in it whatsoever; instead, it is rendered in wash with an open brush technique. The architectural space and the natural space are thus emphatically distinguished one from the other. On the other hand, the architecture accepts and rejoices in the landscape. The fine scale and small components of the trellis, together with the leaf-like shapes of the Gothic drip molding, establish an immediate relationship with the variegated patterns of the trees and shrubs. Moreover, the vertical and horizontal lines of the posts, floor, and eaves frame and compose various segments of the vista, thus creating individual landscapes, each with its own special qualities. Most important of all, the sky-lit space of the landscape flows easily through the shaded architectural space of the veranda to enfold all elements, man-made or natural, in the same translucent atmosphere.

These effects are further enhanced by Davis through the extraordinary subtlety of his color. A strong but diffuse sunlight, filtered through a veiled sky, floods the shadowless landscape with its delicate warmth. To portray the effect of this light within the veranda space, the shaded interior surfaces of the architectural components are modeled with gentle washes of a muted but transparent yellow-orange. Against the resulting pervasive warmth are set the cooler yellow-green of the lawn, the darker blue-green of the foliage, and the graded blue-violet to blue of the haze-enshrouded hills. Further to harmonize the architecture with the landscape, the Gothic drops of the drip molding are made a darker blue-green similar to that of the trees. House and landscape thus reach to embrace one another in a world of white-gold light.

Although the porch was not new to American architecture, the idea that the veranda was the link between the house and nature had picturesque connotations that had not been encountered before. The very fact that Davis frequently referred to the veranda as an "umbrage" indicates that he conceived it as an architectural space profoundly affected by light. Indeed, so directly did the veranda function for him as an outdoor living area sheltered from the sunlight that intriguing possibilities arise as to the origin of the idea.

A clue to this is found in P. F. Robinson's *Rural Architecture.* Here, what seems to be a veranda in several of his illustrations is actually called an "awning." In addition to this, Davis, in *Rural Residences,* shows a small villa designed for David Codwise (Fig. 230) which has a special kind of veranda along one side. Its roof is concave and ribbed, and sweeps in a hanging curve from its connection with the wall to a delicate eave line of open trelliswork; the slender supporting posts are also trellised. The effect in shape and scale is more that of a canvas canopy, or awning, than it is of a wooden roof covered with metal, and in support of this idea Davis says in his description of the villa that "a shelter or awning may be added to the dining-room window, where shown on the plan." Even more important, in evaluating his own design he adds that it "partakes of an oriental character, from its veranda-like porch."

The veranda at Blithewood (Fig. 184), although it was not concave, did have a broad stretching character, and was coupled in its setting with at least one outlying pavilion which was a genuine, elegant canvas canopy. (Fig. 185). In view of this, and the number of verandas in this country which show a concave profile, canopy-like hanging ornament on the eave, and slender supporting posts (Fig. 233), it is impossible to escape the conclusion that the real origin of the veranda, as a semi-enclosed outdoor space, was not architectural at all but was found rather in the ornamental canopy or tent.[33] Davis's allusion to the Orient, and the increasing knowledge of exotic parts of the world which marks the period, makes this idea altogether plausible and adds another touch of high romanticism to the growing image of the picturesque house in America.

Blithewood: The Gatehouse

While working on the veranda at Blithewood, Davis also designed a gatehouse for the estate. Dated 1836, it is preserved in several drawings and is illustrated in *Rural Residences* under the title, *Gate-house in the Rustic Cottage Style* (Fig. 186). As seen in the illustration, it is a modest little dwelling with ornamental verge boards in the gables, and a latticed porch roof carried on rough log posts. As the title claims, the building is rustic, and like the veranda, which is seen in the background, it is deliberately shaped to relate to its natural setting. Except for its considerable picturesque charm, however, it seems an unpretentious small house, similar in its general appearance to the numerous cottages illustrated in several English pattern books of the period. There is little to suggest, therefore, that it might be a work of major architectural interest. Yet, in regard to Davis's ultimate impact on American architecture, the Blithewood gatehouse is probably one of the most important designs of his entire early career; for in this little house Davis made two innovations which would be central to a major development in American architecture during the middle decades of the century.

The first of these is the introduction in the Blithewood gatehouse of the board-and-batten technique of siding for a wooden frame building. As developed by nineteenth-century Americans, the board-and-batten was a logical and simple method with strong picturesque appeal. In contrast to the horizontal clapboard, which had dominated American wooden architecture almost from the very beginning, or even the horizontal matched boards favored by the Neoclassicists, in board-and-batten siding "the superstructure is framed," as Davis put it, "and is boarded vertically. The plank is tongue and grooved with a fillet or batten covering the joint."[34] Since the batten is a narrow wood strip, it produces a fractured surface with a strong vertical emphasis, and this was much more in keeping with the over-all vertical character of the Gothic style than was the horizontality of the earlier and more conventional methods. Although the actual origins of board-and-batten are obscure in this country it was Davis, in his *Rural Residences,* who first published the idea. It was also in the Blithewood gatehouse that it was used expressively for the first time, and for several decades its impact on American architecture was enormous.

FIGURE 184. A. J. Davis. Blithewood,
Barrytown, N.Y., 1836. Old print.

FIGURE 185. A. J. Davis. Blithewood,
Barrytown, N.Y., canopied pavilion, 1836.
Original pencil drawing.

In addition to its structural interest, the Blithewood gatehouse was important in the history of American architecture as the first house to be designed and published as a "cottage." In contrast to a villa, which was a pleasure seat for a man of means and taste, a cottage was a house for the working class. It was therefore immediately attractive to the broad reach of American house builders. The architectural character of the cottage was subject to the same picturesque values as the villa, and its details were

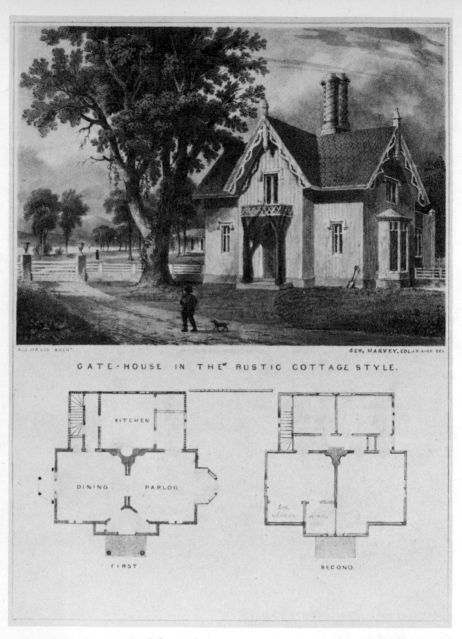

GATE-HOUSE IN THE RUSTIC COTTAGE STYLE.

FIGURE 186. A. J. Davis. Blithewood,
Barrytown, N.Y., gatehouse, 1836.

worked out with similar care. It was regarded by men like Davis as an object of quality in spite of its size, and by the 1850's it had become one of the most uniquely American developments of the nineteenth century. The full story of both the cottage and the board-and-batten will be developed in the next chapter, but there is one aspect of the "cottage" concept that demands our attention now—the fundamental shape that this building type would take.

At the time that Davis designed the Blithewood gatehouse, American domestic architecture was dominated by two building types. The first was the rectangular block of the late colonial and early Neoclassical years,[35] which was always oriented lengthwise to the street and had its principal door in the center of the long side. In addition, the more formal examples frequently had a slightly projecting central pavilion, topped by a pediment. The second type was the classical temple of the Greek Revival.[36] Oriented short end to the street, and always crowned by a pediment, it was also graced in the larger houses by a full freestanding order. Sometimes, too, the temple form was flanked by balanced side wings, but these remained secondary to the main block.

The cottage, as first seen in *Rural Residences* and as later developed by Davis, was, in effect, a combination of these two earlier forms. By enlarging the projecting central pavilion of the late colonial type to an equivalent of a classical temple front, Davis created a new type of cross relationship in which the two blocks interpenetrated one another to form a two-directional system that in its spatial implications was not unlike the cruciform massing of the medieval church. Moreover, in Davis's scheme the depressed triangle of the classical pediment gave way to a steeply pitched, broadly projecting gable, open at the bottom, and ornamented on the sloping sides by a verge board carved in tracery-like patterns. Hooded Gothic windows, oriels, pinnacles, and clustered chimney stacks were added, too, and combined with high-pitched roofs they created both the vertical emphasis and the broken outline so characteristic of the architect's romantic vision. For convenience the cottage frequently remained symmetrical in its basic relationship of parts; it was nevertheless a lively, picturesque concept which rejected altogether the single rectangular block of the classical tradition in favor of the dynamic opposition of strongly directional units. Although Davis derived all aspects of the cottage form from the English house pattern books of the early nineteenth century, he was among the first to recognize its peculiar suitability to the American scene, and under his leadership, the cottage type—with refreshing variations—would become as ubiquitous in rural and suburban America during the 1840's and '50's as the classical type had been in the early part of the century. But before that would happen it would also play a fascinating role in the design of Davis's next major domestic work, Lyndhurst.

PART III

LYNDHURST

Paulding's Gothic Villa in Tarrytown

Lyndhurst is Davis's masterpiece in the field of domestic architecture and the finest surviving Gothic Revival house in America (Fig. 212). Designed originally in 1838 for General William Paulding and his son Philip, the house as it stands today is primarily the result of two major building campaigns. The first was carried out for the Pauldings and was begun in 1838. The other, begun in 1865, was for the second owner, George Merritt. The fact that there were two separate clients and a time span of almost thirty years between the campaigns might suggest that the final result was a patchwork of parts, particularly since the house was almost doubled in size. But, fortunately, Davis was the architect for both phases of the design, and as a result the building not only has a remarkable coherence of form, but also combines in a unique and expressive way both the vitality of his early Gothic manner and the sureness of his mature style. A third era of Lyndhurst began in 1880 when the house was purchased by Jay Gould, the railroad tycoon. Neither Gould nor his family made any significant changes in the architecture of the house, so that the building willed to the National Trust for Historic Preservation in 1964 by Gould's daughter, the Duchess of Talleyrand-Perigord, was essentially the house designed by Davis. Today it is preserved and maintained by the Trust as a National Historic Landmark.

The first phase of Lyndhurst began early in 1838 when General Paulding invited Davis to inspect his newly acquired property in Tarrytown.[37] Paulding's motive was to persuade Davis to design a house for the site. That he should have turned to Davis was a natural outgrowth of the architect's association with the men of the Hudson River Valley. Paulding was a close friend of Davis's patron and client, Robert Donaldson, and he shared with Donaldson both a love for the region and a driving desire to create for himself and his son a country seat that would be appropriate to their mode of living. Paulding was also a prominent member of one of the oldest and most prestigious families in the area. A public-minded citizen, he was well known in political circles, having served as a congressman from New York and twice been mayor of the City of New York. Equally important, Paulding was the brother of the remarkable James Kirk Paulding, who was co-author with Washington Irving in the writing of *Salmagundi,* a whimsical periodical that satirized contemporary American life and caused a considerable flurry in literary and social circles. James's professional association with Irving was sustained by a warm friendship as well, a friendship which extended to the entire family and made the

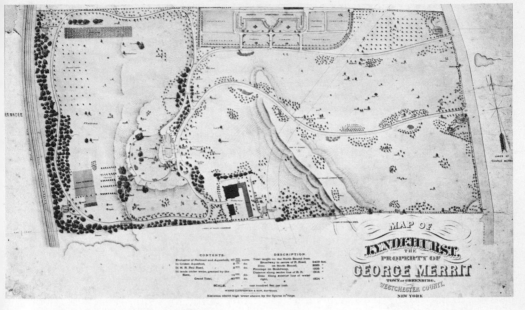

FIGURE 187. A. J. Davis. Lyndhurst,
Tarrytown, N.Y., plan of the grounds.

Pauldings an intimate part of that inner circle of romantics who not only
left their mark on the region but also helped to create in America a taste
for the Gothic style. That Davis's friendship with both Irving and Donaldson brought him into a special relationship with this group is confirmed by
the fact that General Paulding, along with Donaldson, was one of the early
sponsors for *Rural Residences*.[38] The two enthusiastic patrons obviously
sensed in Davis a creative mentality in tune with their own point of view,
and recognized in him an architect with those professional qualifications
necessary to gratify both their ambitions and their romantic attitudes.

In response to Paulding's summons, Davis made a visit to Tarrytown
in May of 1838 and by July of that same year had produced "a portfolio
of plans, sections, elevations . . . etc." for what he called "Paulding's
Villa."[39] The scheme was accepted, and by August work was in progress, although without Davis's supervision. By June of 1839, however, things were not going well at the house, and on the twenty-
ninth, General Paulding wrote Davis an urgent appeal asking him to
come to Tarrytown and help them out. There was a hint of frustration in
the client's summons: "We cannot proceed in erecting our house, without previously consulting you."[40] Davis responded immediately and during
the rest of the summer made several trips to Tarrytown. As he was later to
note in his journal, "the work had progressed without Mr. P's being sen-
sible of the value of professional services."[41] From the summer of 1839

on, Davis was in complete charge, although at this point the elder Paulding seems to have withdrawn from direct participation, and during the latter phases of construction the architect dealt entirely with the son, Philip. Under Davis's professional direction work seems to have progressed smoothly. Within two years the house was virtually finished and Davis was at work designing furniture for the interior.

Knoll: The Plan

The setting chosen by the Pauldings for their new house could not have been more appropriate to Davis's growing vision of the picturesque villa. The actual site was a bold promontory high above the Hudson River with views to the north of the Tappan Zee and Haverstraw Bay, and to the southwest of the towering stone face of the Palisades (Fig. 187). Close by, to the south, a steep wild ravine dropped precipitously to the river. In Davis's own words the general setting provided "an agreeable diversity,"[42] retaining all the untamed roughness of the American landscape, at the same time that the area immediately surrounding the house, with its rocky sub-structure, was open to the spacious view. Because of its hilltop location the house was named "Knoll" by the Pauldings, and to relate it to its setting the orientation was from north to south. The west side, therefore, overlooked the valley with a sweeping vista up and down the river. The main façade was to the east, looking toward higher ground, and was approached by a long gradually descending drive from the old Highland Turnpike.

The house which Davis designed for this romantic site was not large. In its over-all dimensions it was 92 by 75 feet, and this included the semi-enclosed spaces of its veranda system (Fig. 191). On the other hand, it was asymmetrical in massing and irregular in profile (Figs. 188–190). Paulding's villa was a house of sparkle and light, of weight and shadow, which reached out in its proliferous varied forms to embrace and enhance the landscape of which it was a part. At the same time, through the logic of its internal arrangements, it was responsive to the life style of the Pauldings. The house was practical as well as poetic, and part of its fascination lies in the workable complexities of its plan (Figs. 191, 192). Basically, it was a cruciform arrangement with a decisively articulated crossing unit, or transept, cutting laterally in an east-west direction through the main body of the house. On the ground floor this transept was made up of a sequence of spaces beginning with the open area of the porte-cochère on the east (Fig. 191 E), and progressing inward to the vestibule (D) and the saloon, or reception room, beyond (B). The latter terminated on the west end in a bay, made up of three sides of a dodecagon, the full-length windows of which looked out through an arcaded porch (A) toward the river. This porch was identical in its semi-enclosed character to the porte-cochère on the east, and together with the other transept spaces formed a self-contained continuum, from exterior to interior to exterior, which was clearly distinguished from the rest of the house.

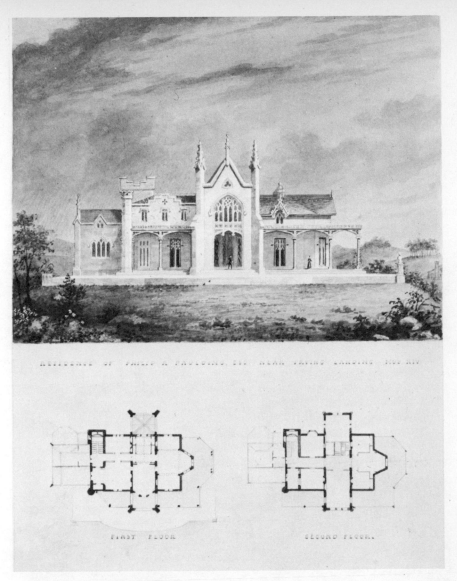

FIGURE 188. A. J. Davis. Knoll,
Tarrytown, N.Y., west façade and plans, 1838.
Original water-color drawing.

The main body of the house, although divided by the transept, nevertheless had internal coherence, its two parts being joined on the ground floor by an off-center hall (H) that ran north and south between the rooms in the north wing (G, I) and then passed through the vestibule to the drawing room to the south (F). The latter was the largest and most important room on the ground floor, and extended lengthwise, east and west, across the entire south end; it was therefore parallel to the transept. At the same time, it had an equally forceful southward thrust into a large hexagonal bay which projected prominently down river and formed

FIGURE 189. A. J. Davis. Knoll,
Tarrytown, N.Y., south and east façades, 1838.
Original water-color drawing.

the southern terminus of the entire plan. To the north of the transept the
main body of the house extended farther than it did to the south and was
marked on the northeast corner by a square tower containing the main
staircase (K). The rooms in this area were asymmetrically arranged
around the off-center hall. The larger, to the west, was the dining
room, which was almost square in plan (G). Because of a large alcove
in its north side (J), however, it was actually oriented north and
south, at right angles to the transept. The other room (I), to the east
of the hall, was an office.

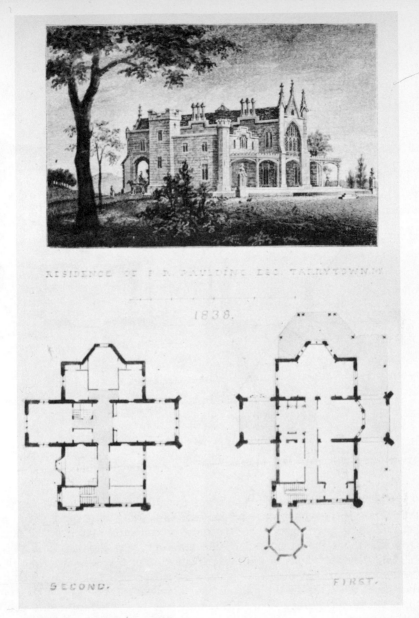

1838.

SECOND.   FIRST.

FIGURE 190. A. J. Davis. Knoll,
Tarrytown, N.Y., from the northwest, 1838.
Old print.

On the second floor (Fig. 192), the interior space of the transept extended its entire length over both the east porte-cochère and the west
porch. Thus its volume was almost double that of the first floor, and because of its size and its bold projections beyond the main body of the
house, it dominated the second-floor plan. At the same time, the north-
south hall, instead of being off-center as it was on the first floor, was
strictly aligned with the central axis of the house (h). It passed through
the transept, as it did on the first floor, but in this case divided the lat-

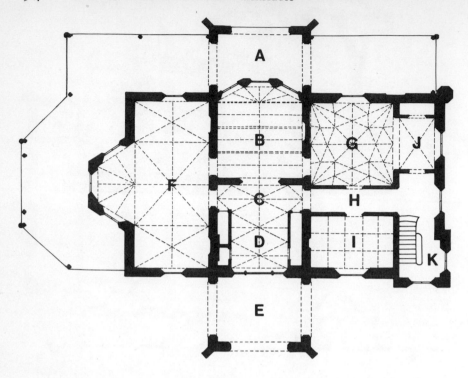

FIGURE 191. A. J. Davis. Knoll,
Tarrytown, N.Y., plan of the first floor, 1838.

ter equally down the middle. The space toward the river was given over to the library (a), which was the largest room on the second floor, and because of its lofty position was the most prominently placed in the house. Opposite it, at the other end of the transept, was the master bedroom (c). Because the vaults of the porte-cochère were 6 feet higher than those on the inside of the house they penetrated the second floor. To accommodate this, the floor of the master bedroom was raised four steps above the level of the library (Fig. 201), and was separated from the central hall by a utility area (Fig. 192 b) which contained a closet on one side and the stairwell to a music gallery on the other. The space to the south of the transept, above the drawing room, was divided into three bedrooms, one centered on the axis and culminating in the south octagonal bay (e), the other two matching each other left and right (g, i). To the north of the transept, the central hall created two bedrooms which were identical (d, f), except that the one on the east side had an oriel window. At the extreme north end of the house the stairway to the east (k) was balanced on the west by a bathroom (j).

In a recent, detailed analysis of this house, Davis's plan for Knoll has been called "symmetrical" with the east-west, or transept, axis sep-

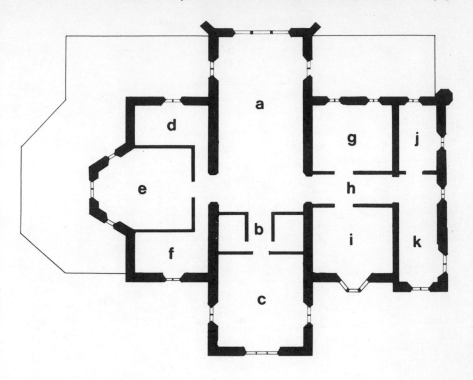

FIGURE 192. A. J. Davis. Knoll,
Tarrytown, N.Y., plan of the second floor, 1838.

arating "two identical designs and the second axis, running north to
south, also . . . balanced on both sides."[43] As we have just seen, however, this is not what Davis devised. There were, to be sure, symmetrical sub-units within the over-all design, as there were in Gothic architecture itself, and there was also a strong cross axis created by the
transept. In fact, so powerful was the crossing effect, that in its general
configuration the plan looked very much like a stubby cruciform medieval
church, with the wing north of the transept imitating the nave, and the
one to the south, with its octagonal bay, the choir. Except on the second floor, however, where the bedrooms were symmetrically disposed
for practical purposes, the interior spaces did not correspond left and
right of either the longitudinal or cross axis, nor did the plan of the second floor concede anything to that of the first. Each room was individually shaped, placed, and oriented in order to fulfill its specific function. Within his primary cruciform scheme, Davis arranged his interior
spaces with extraordinary subtlety, and because of the freedom assured
by the asymmetry of his picturesque concept, he was able to achieve a
fluid relationship of rooms which had no parallel in American domestic architecture up to this time.

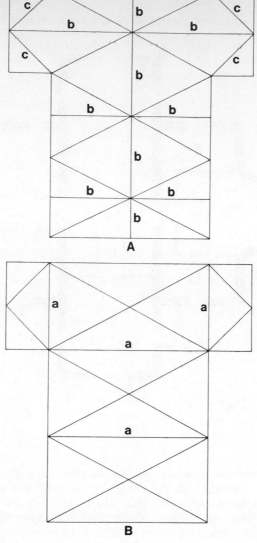

FIGURE 193. A. J. Davis. Knoll,
Tarrytown, N.Y., vestibule, 1838.
(A) Davis's rib pattern. (B) Rib pattern
of conventional four-part vault.

Knoll: Space and Function

In dividing and arranging the various spaces, Davis's first concern was their use. Thus the first-floor rooms, with the exception of the office, were entirely public rooms; those on the second floor were all private. Beyond this broad and obvious distinction, however, the spatial relationships were extremely complex. The pivotal space on the first floor was the vestibule (Fig. 191 D), and as in all well-planned entrance ways, the major rooms were immediately accessible from this point. The crucial problem which Davis had to solve, however, was not just one of ready access. It was rather the actual interlocking of the two major spatial components of the design, the transept on the one hand and the main body of the house on the other. As we have just seen, the dividing hall in the north part of the house crossed the transept to connect with the drawing room, thus providing a flow in a north-south direction. At the same time, however, the vestibule and reception room formed a continuous space, at right angles to the hall, which had a strong directional movement to the west. The transept and hall therefore actually crossed one another through an ambivalent rectangle of space (Fig. 191 C) which belonged simultaneously to both parts of the house.

Davis's clarification of this dual function was both imaginative and practical. He began by giving a special shape to the vestibule. This he did by placing a row of closets along each side, closets which began at the entrance end, on either side of the main door, and extended two thirds of the length of the vestibule. This narrowed the proportions of the entrance area and reinforced its east-to-west directional thrust. At the point where the closets ended, however, the vestibule broadened again to the full width of the transept itself. The result was a total space shaped like a stubby T (Fig. 193), the crossbar of which served both as the head of the vestibule and as the hall which connected the north part of the house with the south.

The two-directional dynamics of this spatial volume were further articulated by the architect through the rib pattern in the ceiling (Fig. 193). The main central area of the vestibule was divided into three vaulted bays, each one defined by a pair of diagonal ribs. These bays formed a continuous four-part vaulted ceiling, in typical Gothic manner, with its diagonal ribs springing from common corbels in the wall. One aspect of Davis's solution, however, did not conform with Gothic precedents. The lateral ribs which in a four-part Gothic bay characteristically ran directly across the vault, between opposing corbels (Fig. 193 B a), were eliminated altogether by Davis, and replaced by decorative ribs in the crowns of both the longitudinal and the cross vaults (Fig. 193 A b). This had the visual effect of generating a powerful directional line down the center of each of the two major components of the T-shaped vestibule, thus accentuating its two-directional character. Moreover, the innermost of the three bays, made longer by supplementary ribs at each end (Fig. 193 A c), corresponded exactly with the crossbar of the T. The result was a dramatic reinforcement of the heart of the design by a splay of ribs at the exact center of the crossing. From there, the spherical triangles which Davis's unusual and imaginative threading of the ribs created became a fluid network that moved as easily in the shape and direction of the hall as it did along the vestibule (Fig. 194). In other words, the space was not just another entrance way that opened conveniently into adjacent parts of the house. It was instead a vital core through which the space of the house flowed freely, thus giving to Davis's picturesque plan a living quality that not even his asymmetrical and irregular arrangements could altogether provide.

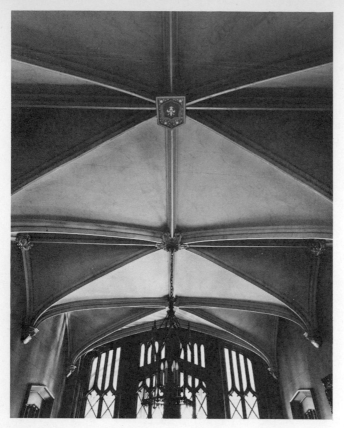

FIGURE 194. A. J. Davis. Knoll,
Tarrytown, N.Y., vestibule vaults, 1838.

The directional flow which Davis's design for the vestibule set in motion
had as its terminal objective the reception room at the west end of the
transept (Fig. 191 B). This room was not only on the same axis as the
vestibule, but opened from it through a wide Tudor-arched opening (Fig.
195) of the same shape and size as the entrance door on the east end. This
in itself encouraged a movement through to the reception room, but an
equally powerful attraction was the bay window at the far end. To be
sure, the reception room could be closed off by the sliding doors in the
archway, in which case the north-south hallway become the primary artery
of movement. But if these doors were open, one would have been irre-
sistibly drawn to the reception room as the natural point of arrival. From
here it would have been possible to move with equal ease to either the dining room to the north or the drawing room to the south, depending upon
the social occasion.

Like the vestibule, the principal public rooms on the ground floor of
Knoll were shaped and oriented to fulfill their function. The reception
room was the smallest and, in many ways, the least complicated (Fig.
191 B). It was a simple rectangle with a dodecagonal bay window occupying the entire west end; it also had an almost flat ceiling, the two planes

FIGURE 195. A. J. Davis. Knoll,
Tarrytown, N.Y., reception room
to bay window from vestibule, 1838.

of which pitched slightly upward toward the center. Here, the ridge was marked by a Gothic rib which extended from the vestibule wall to the window, where it flowered in a splay of ribs into the bay. Lateral ribs, alternately large and small, ran from the side walls to the ridge rib, creating a measured sequential rhythm which was in marked contrast to the strongly directional interlace of the vestibule vaults. This change in rhythmic character slowed the sense of movement impelled by the vestibule vaults, and finally brought it to rest in the luminous tracery patterns of the bay window. Because of its flattened angles the bay was a less assertive projection than was the hexagonal bay of the drawing room, and this, together with the lighter scale and more regular rhythmic pattern of the ceiling, made the reception room the least active of the public rooms.

In contrast to the relative simplicity of the reception room, the drawing room was complex and subtly fluid (Figs. 191 F, 196). Like the vestibule, it was two-directional with its east-west orientation along the end of the house countered by the spectacular southward thrust of the bay window. As in the vestibule, the room was completely vaulted in a system of ribbed bays, the pattern of which defined and reinforced the cross-directional plan. At the same time, the vaulting splayed dramatically into the

FIGURE 196. A. J. Davis. Knoll,
Tarrytown, N.Y., drawing room, 1838.

expansive 18-foot bay, urging the space toward the brightness of the full-
length windows, and evoking a promise of access through them to the
outdoor space of the veranda beyond. In the windows themselves (Fig.
197), the tracery and leaded glass had a vivacity which, when combined with the delicate patterns of ornament in the hood moldings over the
windows, gave a light and elegant touch to the brilliantly articulated
room.

It is important, of course, to recognize that the drawing room at
Knoll was absolutely balanced in a symmetrical arrangement of parts
around its short axis, an arrangement moreover which climaxed on the
inner wall, where identical fireplaces opposed one another either side of
the entrance doors. With all its visual animation, therefore, the room
still had an underlying formal dignity. On the other hand, that Davis understood the space as active more than static, is underscored by the way
he planned the entrances. Instead of a single door, on axis, facing the
center of the bay, he provided *two doors,* one opening from the vestibule, the other from the reception room. Because of this, it was impossible to enter from anything but an off-center position (Fig. 198). One's
first impression, therefore, was gained from an angle of vision which
suppressed the underlying symmetry of the scheme and evoked instead its

FIGURE 197. *A. J. Davis. Knoll,*
Tarrytown, N.Y., drawing room toward bay window
showing original tracery, 1838.

fascinating spatial movement. In every way, the drawing room was the liveliest on the first floor, and the one most conspicuously intended for urbane social intercourse.

On the north side of the reception room was the dining room, the most formal of the public rooms (Fig. 191 G). It was almost square in its proportions and was totally stabilized as a space by the absolute symmetry of a rib-vaulted ceiling (Fig. 199), which sprang from all four corners toward a dropped pendant in the center. As gracefully centripetal as a waterlily, in the converging pattern of its ribs, this remarkable composition of Gothic interlace hovered like a canopy above the space where the dining-room table once graced the room. The centralized balance thus established by the ceiling was reaffirmed by the distribution of other major components of the room. The door entering from the hall at the center of the east wall faced a full-length double window on the west. At the center of the south wall (Fig. 200) an imposing fireplace was flanked on the left by the door from the reception room, and to maintain symmetry Davis put an identical—but false—door on the right. The north wall (Fig. 199), in turn, was broken on axis by a large Tudor-arch opening which led to a deep alcove. This extended the dining room considerably into a secondary space directly opposite the fireplace, and gave the room

FIGURE *198. A. J. Davis. Knoll,*
Tarrytown, N.Y., from reception room entrance
into drawing room, 1838.

a positive line of orientation which ran from the fireplace to a window in
the alcove. Since the area of the dining room itself was only 2 feet
longer than it was wide, the alcove provided the increased sense of direction necessary to relieve the monotony of a squarish space and to accommodate more easily the long proportions of the dining-room table. It also
added a dynamic note of asymmetry to an otherwise completely symmetrical scheme.

Conceived by Davis as a related but self-contained spatial unit, the alcove had its independence assured by the positive frame of its Tudor-arch
opening, and by a four-part vaulted ceiling which took nothing from the
complex centripetal vault pattern of the dining room itself. Indeed, as
seen through the opening, the alcove recalls the continuity tempered by
separateness that we have already seen in the relationship of chancel to
nave in the Ecclesiological church (compare Figs. 199 and 126). The interesting fact is, however, that Davis was already at work building
Paulding's villa at least a year before Upjohn introduced this concept for

FIGURE 199. A. J. Davis. Knoll, Tarrytown, N.Y., dining room, 1838. *Original water-color drawing.*

FIGURE 200. A. J. Davis. Knoll, Tarrytown, N.Y., Paulding dining room *toward fireplace, 1838.*

FIGURE 201. *A. J. Davis. Lyndhurst, Tarrytown, N.Y., Paulding library (1838) after conversion to Merritt art gallery (1865), viewed toward screen.*

the first time into American church architecture at Trinity Church, New York (Fig. 114). Although the two architects must surely have developed the idea independently of one another, and for different reasons, its appearance in the work of both men at almost the same time points up the fact that the Gothic church was an ancestor of the Gothic Revival house as well as the Gothic Revival church.

To insure the privacy of the second-floor rooms at Knoll, the main staircase was isolated in the northeast tower, as remote from the entrance vestibule as it could possibly be. A means of access to the second floor, therefore, was neither apparent nor immediately available to the visitor. As well as being private, the bedrooms were basically practical rooms, and were all relatively the same size; for convenience they were symmetrically placed along the north-south hall (Fig. 192). By contrast, the master bedroom (c) and the library (a), each of which satisfied a special need, stood out conspicuously because of their larger size in the aggressive projections of the transept. At the same time, their removed position on the second floor, and their isolation in the sharply defined area of the transept, made them the most private rooms in the house.

Of all the rooms on the second floor the library was by far the most impressive, and because of the precisely defined nature of its function, it was also among the most direct in its design. It was a simple rectangle, enclosed at the hall end by a Gothic screen (Fig. 201). At the other end it came to a spectacular climax in a pointed-arch Gothic window (Fig. 202), the largest in the house, which ran from the floor well up into the ceiling area. The window terminated in an ogee-arched crown and a

FIGURE 202. *A. J. Davis. Lyndhurst, Tarrytown, N.Y., Paulding library (1838) after conversion to Merritt art gallery (1865), viewed toward great window.*

carved finial. Additional light came in through flanking windows on the side walls, left and right of the large window. The ceiling in the library was actually the underside of the roof, and in typical Gothic manner was made of wood with the rafters exposed (Fig. 203). Each pair of rafters was stiffened by a collar beam, with the triangle between the collar and the ridge filled by wooden tracery. Additional support came from five arched struts which sprang from corbels in the wall and crowned in a point at the height of the collar beams. Made of oak and darkened by stain, this ceiling at Knoll preceded Upjohn's truss ceiling in the Church of the Holy Communion in New York by several years, and at the time it was built, it was the finest open timber Gothic ceiling in America.

Davis's highly complex plan for Knoll was both ingenious and expressive, and certainly produced the most freely developed interior space yet to appear in America. Its provocative quality was in no small measure the result of his extraordinary architectural sensitivity and of his own highly developed concept of the villa and its role in American life. Even so, Knoll has fascinating points of contact with the *beau ideal* of an English villa as discussed in Loudon's *Encyclopaedia of Architecture.* Loudon touched upon every aspect of the villa and its grounds and much of what he had to say was relevant primarily to England. But Davis was quick to realize that some of Loudon's ideas were highly suitable to Knoll, and to throw another light on our evaluation of the house some of these are worth examining.

With respect to location, Loudon writes that the ideal villa "should be situated . . . in a beautiful country, within reach of a public road, and

FIGURE 203. A. J. Davis. Lyndhurst, Tarrytown, N.Y.,
Paulding library (1838) after conversion to Merritt art gallery
(1865), detail of trussed ceiling.

at an easy distance from the metropolis. Were I to select a situation for a
residence of this description, I should choose a country neither flat nor
mountainous; varied with hill and vale, and rather approaching to the
mountainous than the dull monotony of a level surface." This was precisely the situation at Knoll.

Loudon's lengthy discussion of the rooms in the ideal villa also includes
several observations that have a direct bearing on Davis's arrangements at
Knoll. Concerning the entrance hall, for example, he notes that "if the
apartments are small, and devoid of ornament, I would then substitute
for the hall a smaller kind of entrance, with a vaulted roof; and, moreover, rather gloomy, to increase the general effect of the rooms which
open into it." To this he adds that "the walls" should be "painted to imitate stone." His views concerning "the Saloon, which is generally a sort
of vestibule to the living-rooms" are equally interesting. As though in anticipation of Davis's saloon at Knoll he suggests that it "might be in form
either a square, a long parallelogram, an oval, or circle; but a parallelogram of good proportions is the most usual form," while opposite
the door by which you enter "should be two windows, with a glass door
between them, opening to the terrace and garden." On the other hand

"the drawing room, which being the sitting apartment of the ladies, should be distinguished by the elegance of its proportions, decorations, and furniture . . . [and] should be larger than the saloon." Not only that, but "entering our drawing room from the saloon, at the end opposite would be a square or circular bay window, commanding a view of the park and the distant country beyond it." And then one final observation: "in this room I would have a splendid white marble chimneypiece, . . . these are usually of stone or colored marble: but white is the most elegant."

With so many fascinating references to Loudon at Knoll it can hardly be coincidence that the two mantelpieces in the house which are white marble are those in the drawing room. All the rest, on the first floor at least, are colored marble. Obviously Davis had not only read Loudon with great care but was ready to quote him directly when it seemed appropriate. At the same time, Davis's internal plan at Knoll had a coherence and excitement that went far beyond Loudon's lengthy and sometimes involved descriptions. In spite of the suggestions which he frankly took from the *Encyclopaedia* Davis's imaginative and highly individual solutions to the problems which confronted him in Tarrytown were carried through with a keen sense of time and place, of how and why, and in the end the house became Paulding's Villa and not Loudon's *beau ideal*.

Knoll: The Exterior Massing

The same freedom of arrangement which characterized Davis's handling of the interior of Knoll was found on the exterior. The dominant feature of the design as seen from the outside was the transept, which thrust through the building from the land to the river side (Figs. 188–190). A half story higher than the rest of the house, it terminated on each end in a steeply pitched crocketed gable, and was marked at the corners by angle buttresses and tall pinnacles. But the most intriguing aspect of the transept was that it was open on the ground floor at both ends, where it projected beyond the main body of the building (Fig. 189, top). Thus the major second-floor rooms—the library over the west porch, and the master bedroom over the porte-cochère—appeared as assertive solids above the semi-enclosures of supporting arcades. The result was an inversion of structural logic, since there was a greater massing at the upper story than at the lower. In its daring exploitation of the arch as a means of support, Davis's treatment had plenty of Gothic precedents,[44] but in this country in 1838 the open wall on the first floor, where foundation support would instead have been expected, was a conspicuous denial of classical stability. It was a provocative scheme and because it was dynamic rather than static it set the tone for the underlying restlessness which characterized all of Davis's design, a restlessness which was natural to the Gothic system itself, but which flowered with particular force in Davis's imaginative use of the style. It was a restlessness, too, which was born of a sensitive opposition of occult forces, of the movement and countermovement of asymmetrically ordered parts, as major components of the house were poised and joined toward the off-center climax of the transept.

Although the main body of the house was lower in its profile than the transept, it was no less assertive. Seen from the land side (Fig. 189, bottom), the north end was two stories high and had a low-pitched roof screened behind a parapet. The gable of an elaborate oriel window on the second floor broke through that parapet to form a small dormer; this in combination with the other windows and the crenelated stair tower on the northeast corner produced a definite vertical emphasis which matched that of the transept. By contrast, the south end of the house was horizontal in effect. Here, the pitch of the roof was relatively steep and brought the eave line well down into the second-floor level; and instead of being cut off at the eaves by a parapet, the roof swept out to a wide overhang. Open gables with verge boards hooded the windows on all three sides, and to accommodate the projection of the octagonal south bay, the roof was hipped as well as gabled in a complex system of intersecting planes. At the ground-floor level a veranda embraced the entire south end, thus creating a stepped-down horizontal profile with the mass of the sweeping roof hovering over the veranda. At the same time, however, the two ends of the house were the same height and width and were thus seen as a coherent mass, continuous within itself, and interlocking with the transept. The descending horizontal shape of the south end, together with the multi-faceted roof above and around the octagonal bay, gave the impression that the main body of the house had somehow pushed its way through the transept to emerge on the south side with its edges blunted and its angles flattened out. The relationship between the two major components of the house, therefore, was not a static one, in which two blocks had been joined as wings to a third block. It was rather a vital union, in which all parts seemed to grow together as living components of the same organism.

There was yet another and extremely important point of contrast between the two ends of the building (Fig. 189, top; and Fig. 190). The north end, with its oriel window and battlemented tower on the east, and its stepped gable and turret on the west, was conceived in the castellated Gothic, a sturdy and authoritative form of the style, which Davis had already used at Donaldson's villa, and which, in his own words, he had "adopted" at Knoll "with minute attention to the genuine character of the buildings of the Tudor age."[45] The south end, on the other hand, with its steeply pitched roof, intersecting gables, and verge boards, had all the animated grace and simplicity of Davis's "cottage." That this smaller concept should have been combined with the formidable Tudor character of the rest of the house might seem incongruous. Yet Davis made it work. He made it work, first, because his refined sense of scale and careful handling of ornamental detail gave the design a subtle coherence. But he also made it work because he introduced, in the very improbability of the combination, an extraordinary element of surprise. The cottage form became a deliberate and dramatic point of contrast, a conscious intrusion into a dynamic and complex scheme, of a totally unexpected motif. It brought to the design an element of freshness in much the same way that the solo instrument in a concerto provides both surprise and contrast in the development of the musical form.

FIGURE 204. A. J. Davis. Knoll, Tarrytown, N.Y., west veranda looking north, 1838.

If Davis's mixture of "castellated" and "cottage" elements at Knoll gave picturesque variety to the house, his imaginative use of the veranda gave it its ultimate unity. At Blithewood (Fig. 182) the veranda had provided a semi-enclosed transitional space between the setting and the symmetrical block of the house itself. It was an adjunct, although a useful one, to an existing and fiercely self-contained house. The veranda embraced the house on three sides, and was open to it, but it never penetrated its inner spaces.

At Knoll, the veranda was conceived from the beginning as an organic part of the total design, and although only semi-enclosed, was regarded by Davis as an essential part of the architectural space itself. It began at the south end (Fig. 191), where it served both as a screen and as an outdoor extension of the inner space of the drawing room. To emphasize the latter role, Davis related it to the hexagonal bay. Accordingly, the veranda swept southward in the broader, somewhat flatter shape of an octagon, thus reducing slightly its relative projection, but at the same time facilitating its bending flow. It then turned the southwest corner at right angles, to continue northward along the entire west side of the house (Fig. 214). Here, however, it very quickly encountered the crossing bulk of the transept, where it moved into one of the most exciting and prophetic relationships of space in the entire design. Since the transept was cut away at the ground-floor level by the open arcade of the west porch, the veranda, which was the same height and width as the porch, was able to pass through the transept and continue to the northwest corner of the building (Fig. 204). The connection thus established

FIGURE 205. *A. J. Davis. Knoll, Tarrytown, N.Y., veranda ceiling, south, 1838*

between the veranda and the transept was the same kind of ambivalent space that we have just observed in the intersection of the hall and vestibule on the interior.

As in the case of the vestibule, too, the subtle spatial flow of the veranda at Knoll found its crowning expression in the treatment of the ceiling. Although the space contained by the veranda was completely continuous at floor level, the ceiling was divided into two quite distinct parts. The first was the section which sheltered the south wall and bay window of the drawing room. Here the ceiling (Fig. 205), with its sweeping octagonal shape, was a flat wooden surface pitched slightly downward away from the house. The open rafters were slender, and splayed outward from the wall toward the supporting line of posts. Both in scale and multiplicity of parts this fan-like pattern projected into the space of the veranda all the lightness and animation of the tracery in the bay window, and hovered over the immediate area of the drawing room like a giant umbrella.

The other part of the veranda which was articulated by the ceiling was the straight run which began as a continuation of the south veranda and extended along the west wall of the house to the northern end (Fig. 204). Here the flat closely-ribbed plane of the south ceiling gave way to a vault-shaped wooden ceiling which ran the entire length of the veranda. It was sharply separated from the drawing room area by a heavy beam (Fig. 205) which extended in a line from the west wall and connected it with the structural system of the outer posts.

FIGURE 206. *A. J. Davis. Lyndhurst, Tarrytown, N.Y., 1865, west front seen from the air.*

The shape of this ceiling was determined by the Tudor-arch opening of the porch at the west end of the transept (Fig. 204). At the same time, the ceiling was hipped and the end planes thus sloped inward at the same pitch and in the same curved configuration as the main ceiling they enclosed (Fig. 205). Both the pointed crown of the west veranda ceiling and the hips at the four corners were articulated by ribs similar in scale to the rafters of the south ceiling; widely spaced lateral ribs sprang from both sides to the crown rib in the center, forming a powerful regular rhythm from one end of the veranda to the other. The effect was that of a vaulted aisle which took its height and shape from the arched openings in the transept through which it was made to pass. Thus the west veranda, although performing precisely the same basic function as that which sheltered the drawing room, was nevertheless shown to stand in a different relationship with the house itself. The south ceiling was a canopy which was suspended above a specific area of space, the west was the crown of a vaulted passageway which penetrated the main building and connected the south end with the north.

Even the roof, seen from above, carried out this basic intent (Fig. 206). Over the south veranda, with its fan-like ceiling, the roof was made to slope upward in a concave curve which strengthened even further the effect of a canopy; over the west veranda the curved hipped roof mimicked exactly the shape of the ceiling beneath, and proclaimed the continuity of the aisle-like space which it protected. Although Davis never expected his roof to be seen from the air, the complex interlocking of masses, as the transept penetrates the veranda, is nowhere more forcefully revealed.

Taken as a whole, the two parts of the veranda at Knoll formed a malleable space, as involved in its configuration as it was complex in its function. It was molded exactly to the form of the house to become a sheltered enclave in which the space of nature was brought together with the space of the house: every room that it touched had full-length windows (Fig. 207) which, when closed, provided visual passage in both directions, and when opened permitted the two spaces to flow easily one into the other. The veranda also touched and molded nature. During periods of storm it absorbed the violence and reduced its impact on the house and its occupants; when the weather was serene, it was like a broad and friendly brow from beneath which the expansive landscape could be seen and savored (Fig. 208). Above all, it was the ultimate unifier, that belt of space which passed around or through the major components of the building, and enfolded them, in spite of their variety, in one coherent whole (Fig. 214). When seen against the precise separation of spatial units, so characteristic of the conventional methods of planning which had dominated American domestic architecture up to this time, Davis's fluid manipulation of mass and space at Knoll stands forth as a major innovation, for it introduced for the first time in this country the concept of interpenetration, a concept which would become increasingly important as the nineteenth century progressed, and which would reach a climax during the first decade of the twentieth century in the prairie houses of Frank Lloyd Wright.

Knoll and the Gothic Style

Paulding's Knoll was the first house in America in which those ingredients that the nineteenth century regarded as essential to a "villa" were crystallized for the first time. Asymmetrical in plan and irregular in outline, it was picturesque in its appearance and was designed and oriented in relation to a particular and highly romantic natural setting. It was an experience in light, shadow, atmosphere, and texture; it was filled with contrast and surprise; and it was conceived as a rural retreat for men of prominence and taste. Of all the houses built in America up to that time only one other, Jefferson's Monticello,[46] could be thought of in terms of a villa, and even that supremely poetic and intelligent house did not really qualify. For Monticello was a symmetrical composition of coherently related blocks which, in its geometric self-containment, remained apart from the irregularities of both its natural and its planned setting. More than that, it was a triumphantly classical building, as pure and chaste in its adherence to Neoclassical doctrine as any building of its time. Monticello was, in fact, a supreme example of a major predicament of Neoclassicism: it was impossible to reconcile the formality of its architecture with the irregularity and roughness of a picturesque landscape, both of which the movement championed. In its supreme self-containment, Monticello remained visually independent of the irregular gardens which Jefferson so carefully planned to encompass it, as quietly aloof from the drama of its mountain vista as the Parthenon was from the rugged cliffs of the Acropolis.

At Knoll Davis escaped this predicament by his choice of the Gothic, a style far more suitable to the development of picturesque forms than

FIGURE 207. A. J. Davis.
Knoll, Tarrytown, N.Y.,
west porch to reception-room bay,
1838.

FIGURE 208. A. J. Davis.
Knoll, Tarrytown, N.Y.,
view from west veranda to northwest,
1838.

Jefferson's classical mode. It was a flexible idiom, less encumbered by
the limitations of symmetry, and he used it freely, in an original way,
with a clear sense of its provocative relationships with the irregularities of
the natural world. Davis's first major encounter with the Gothic came at
Glen Ellen (Fig. 180), but there his efforts were muted by the underlying classicism of Town's design. At Knoll, on the other hand, there
were no such constraints. Because of Paulding's obvious enthusiasm for

the Gothic, Davis's own romantic preferences were given free rein, and the style was made to function for the first time in American domestic architecture as an organic picturesque medium rather than as a system of ornament.

By the time he designed Paulding's villa, Davis had gained considerable experience with the Gothic and was now able to handle it with increased skill and authority. His Gothic design for New York University was one of the most important commissions to come to the firm of Town and Davis during the early 1830's, and we will discuss it in greater detail in another context. But it also played a major role in the quality of Knoll, for the direct experience of a work of this magnitude helped to quicken Davis's knowledge of the style. It is important to recognize, however, that Davis's growing skill with the Gothic was not only the result of a command over archaeological data. Even though he and his clients were constantly poring over books on the Gothic, it is impossible to find in his work a direct application of any identifiable source. The truth is that he relied on the books for information about the specific visual characteristics of the style but then used that information with imagination toward his own ends. What he derived from his sources was a mastery of the shape, proportion, and scale of both the structural and decorative components of the Gothic, and of the special ways in which the Gothic builders put all these ingredients together. In examining Knoll in detail, therefore, it is easy to find molding profiles, window shapes, and tracery patterns which are similar to published examples. But the manner in which they were composed by Davis is uniquely his own. To be sure, by designing in the Gothic as well as the Neoclassical styles, Davis was performing as an eclectic. On the other hand, his awareness of his clients' attitudes and preferences, and his extraordinary sensitivity toward the peculiar qualities of the Hudson River Valley itself, led him to shape the medieval forms into a new style, uniquely suited to his time and place. Just as in the case of Jefferson's adaptation of Roman and French Neoclassical ideas at Monticello, Davis's design at Knoll found its ultimate truth not so much in its Gothicism as in the extraordinary way in which he made the style work for the Pauldings in Tarrytown, N.Y., in 1838.

Davis's commitment to the Gothic was complete, and it was this as much as anything else which gave Knoll its remarkable stylistic coherence. His innate feeling for the style was prompted in part by his intensely romantic temperament; he reveled in its shadowed vaults, its traceried windows, its dramatic contrasts of mass and space. But as an architect, he also sensed its deeply organic nature, and there was throughout Knoll a persuasive urgency which evolved in no small measure from the architect's realization that continuity was the life blood of the Gothic system. Space flowed into space, rib into rib, tracery bar into mullion as though compelled by some living force. Knoll, of course, was not a masonry building in the all-inclusive Gothic sense of the word. The main outside walls were, to be sure, of Sing Sing marble, warm soft gray in color and mottled with a delicate neutral yellow. The structural and decorative elements, however, such as moldings, mullions, tracery, crockets, and finials,

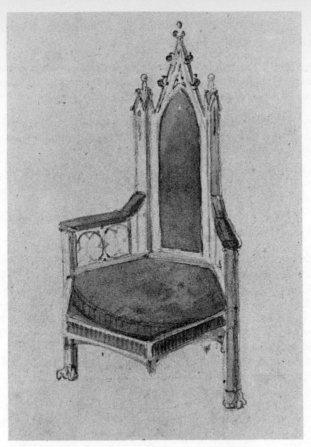

FIGURE 209. A. J. Davis. Knoll,
Tarrytown, N.Y., Gothic chair, 1838.
Original water color.

were wood on the outside and wood or plaster within, all carefully shaped and scaled by Davis and painted in imitation of stone. Even much of the furniture was designed by the architect himself in the Gothic style (Fig. 209). The result was a house which, in spite of its mixture of materials, was persuasively Gothic in detail, and visually, at least, had all the living vitality so characteristic of the style.

In assessing the Gothic quality of Knoll, it is also important to recognize that Davis's client, Philip Paulding, shared the architect's enthusiasm for the style and actually participated in the decision making which led to its authenticity. On September 16, 1839, he wrote to Davis:[47]

I called at your rooms and found that you would not be home for a few days. As soon as you return I wish to see you, and would thank you to drop a line in the post office that I may know when to come to town. My object in coming down is to look at some of your books, select some tracery for the window, and get you to make a drawing

of it. The carpenter is very anxious to commence the making of it. I
think it will be a great addition to the appearance of the house to add
some more detailing to the windows. . . .

The correspondence indicates that Paulding's involvement continued
throughout the construction of the house, and his faith in Davis's Gothic
taste remained constant. In another letter to the architect he wrote:[48]

You will much oblige me by calling at Underhill and Ferris as soon as
possible . . . and inspecting the mantels before they are sent up. If
you see anything offensive to your gothick eye . . . put your veto
upon it. They are extremely elegant and I wish them to be correct
specimens of the style. How the ladies will dote on them—

To Paulding the ultimate quality of Knoll obviously depended in part
on the discriminating selection of every detail, and in helping with this he
was able to assert his confidence in his own taste, as well as that of his
architect. He seems also to have welcomed the authoritative support of
others. In a particularly revealing comment in the last paragraph of the letter just quoted he says to Davis, "I received your letter and am delighted
to hear you have had such an able committee on taste to aid in your la-
bors." Although in this tantalizing statement we are not told who the
members of this committee were, we are nevertheless given an illuminating
glimpse into the working heart of the American Gothic Revival community.
In 1841, taste for the Gothic was new in this country and to the majority
of Americans it was still eccentric; for these were the years when the Greek
Revival achieved many of its greatest triumphs, including a number of
buildings designed by the firm of Town and Davis.[49] The enthusiasm for
ancient Greece was a national sentiment which touched broad areas of
American life, and typical of those caught up in it was the great New York
diarist, Philip Hone. In his biased view, Paulding's Knoll was "an immense
edifice of white or gray marble, resembling a baronial castle, or rather a
Gothic monastery, with towers, turrets and trellises; archways, armories
and air holes; peaked windows and pinnacled roofs, and many other
fantastics too tedious to enumerate, the whole constituting an edifice of
gigantic size, with no room in it; which if I mistake not, will one of these
days be designated as 'Paulding's folly.' "[50]

Undoubtedly, Hone's caustic remarks were motivated in part by the
intensity of his partisan feelings, for he and Paulding were political ene-
mies. On the other hand, what he had to say was also an expression of
the prevailing classical taste, and Knoll was in a style that was contrary
to that taste. The building was, of course, the first major American
house in which the Gothic emerged as a coherent style developed by men
who were beginning to understand its intrinsic qualities. They were men,
moreover, who were pioneers, men whose romantic fervor was taking
them away from the established certainties of the Greek style into the unfamiliar and still evasive world of the Gothic. Reliance upon one another, therefore, added a collective measure of security to their groping
efforts, and Davis's committee filled the same urgent need in the scheme

of things in Tarrytown as had Horace Walpole's "Committee" in his work at Strawberry Hill. Perhaps Davis was aware of Walpole's arrangement, and in bringing together his own committee he may have been emulating his great predecessor. In any event, there is no question that he and Walpole were reacting similarly to similar conditions. For neither Knoll nor Strawberry Hill was accepted by everyone in its day, yet each was the first of its kind in its own context, and both were seminal in the evolution of their respective Gothic Revivals.

The story of Knoll, or Lyndhurst, as it came to be called, did not end with the house designed for the Pauldings. Davis tells us that one of the reasons why he preferred the Gothic was the fact that in any given design it was "susceptible of additions from time to time."[51] In other words, Davis understood the Gothic, as the medieval builders did, as an organic style capable of proliferation and growth. This fascinating notion, which so boldly challenges the classical concept of the self-contained whole, would not have been possible without the greater freedom in architectural relationships assured by the picturesque mode, and it is a measure of Davis's understanding of the picturesque that he expressed the idea at all. But at Knoll he was able to do more than that. After the death of Philip Paulding in 1864 the house was purchased by George Merritt, who immediately hired Davis to enlarge it. The architect now had an unprecedented opportunity to develop his theory of extension in concrete architectural form.

Lyndhurst:
the Merritt Additions to Knoll

Like most of the men of means who lived in the Hudson River Valley, George Merritt was a prominent and influential New Yorker who achieved his success as a merchant. He was also the owner of a lucrative patent for a railroad car spring, and when he purchased Knoll in 1864 he brought to the region a level of wealth and ambition it had not known before. To make the house suitable for his more grandiose social aspirations, he almost doubled it in size. At the same time, he made it more elaborate, more glittering, more luxuriant. Indeed, Merritt represented an emerging breed of rich Americans for whom the house became not only a rural retreat but also a symbol of power and wealth. For him an extravagant taste could only be gratified by sensationalism and opulence of form. Even the name "Knoll," with its bucolic ring, was inappropriate to the new scheme of things; and so it was changed to "Lyndhurst" which had a more assuring, literary sound, suggestive in its clipped cadence of an ancient cultural heritage.

Along with his social ambitions Merritt had sound architectural judgment and was perceptive enough to realize that the only architect in America who could transform "Knoll" into "Lyndhurst" was the man who designed the building in the first place, Alexander Jackson Davis. Although by 1864, American architecture had already gone beyond its early Gothic phase into other equally romantic styles, the decision was made to enlarge Lyndhurst in the style in which it had been conceived. This Davis was particularly qualified to do. During the years that intervened between the two commissions, he had gained a national reputation as a gothicist through a number of important Gothic villas, both urban and rural, which he had been called upon to design and build.[52] These houses had all been variants on the Knoll theme, and together with other Gothic commissions had provided him with vast experience in the style. In fact, when Merritt called upon him to enlarge Knoll, Davis was the master in his field.

The changes which Davis was asked to make were conditioned by one important fact concerning his client: Merritt was an art collector. To have been an art collector in the late 1830's, when Knoll was built, would have been to be a pioneer. But by the 1860's when Merritt planned to enlarge the house, collecting was beginning to be the mark of the cultured gentleman,[53] and Merritt regarded himself precisely in these terms. At the time he bought Knoll, his collection of paintings and sculpture was already substantial enough to require a gallery. To provide this space, Davis used the most spectacular room in the original house, the library. Then to accommodate Merritt's books, which were as numerous as Paulding's, he converted the original dining room into a library, and furthermore added a second room (Fig. 210 L) beyond the dining alcove, thereby forming a continuous tri-compartmented space. In its entirety, the library now consisted of two almost identical rooms (G, L) connected through broad Tudor arches by the original alcove (J). A new dining room was then added to the north end of the house (N), and beyond that was built a smaller extension containing the kitchen and other service areas (O). The space east of the new library extension, and between the old tower and the new dining room, Davis made into a secondary entrance vestibule (M). This served as a second pivotal point at the other end of the original north-south hall, which now had entrances to the new library and the new dining room.

The resulting radical extension of the plan in a line upset the former balance of elements in each of the main façades—one facing the river; the other the road (Figs. 211, 212). To resolve this, Davis maintained the original configuration of the house, in its stepped build-up toward the transept. But he increased the height of the north and south wings and raised the whole profile toward a spectacular new tower, which ascended 76 feet above the ground (compare Figs. 188 and 211). Located in plan above the new library extension (Fig. 210 L), this tower was seen in its full length on the west façade where it became the climax of the entire design; from the east (Fig. 212) it appeared above the roof, behind and to the north of the old stair tower. From there the profile descended again through the new dining-room wing, with its octagonal cupola over the center, to terminate in the service wing at the extreme north end.

As well as extending the original house to the north, Davis also made a significant change in its east side. There he enclosed the porte-cochère (Fig. 210 E) to form a new vestibule in advance of the old one, which then became known as the hall. To make the entrance sequence complete, he added a new freestanding porte-cochère with turreted corners

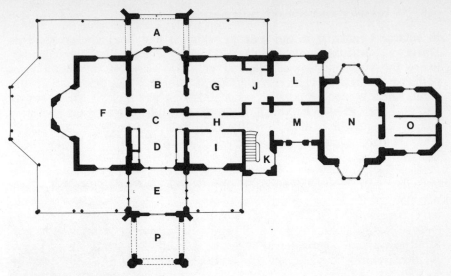

FIGURE 210. A. J. Davis. Lyndhurst,
Tarrytown, N.Y., plan, 1865.

and a crenelated top (Figs. 210 P and 212). It was at once more ornate
and more imposing than the original cave-like unit, and it extended beyond the walls of the transept, whereas the original one had receded. To
bind this new aggressive mass more closely to the house, Davis carried the
veranda along the east side in the same way he had done on the west,
passing it through the new vestibule and terminating it at the old northeast tower. This new stretch of semi-enclosed space had a ceiling and roof
similar to those on the west side, but it was glassed in to form a conservatory for plants (Fig. 213).[54] Finally, to compensate for the higher roof
line of the main body of the original house, the old northeast tower was
raised by a full story (compare Figs. 189 and 212).

As seen today, Lyndhurst (Fig. 212) in its outward appearance is essentially the same as when completed in 1866 for George Merritt (Fig.
213).[55] It is a much more complex and dynamic pile than the one designed for Paulding; it is also more elegant in its detailing. At Knoll, the
lower roof line of the main body of the house, together with the wide
overhanging eaves of the south end, held the house closer to the ground
and gave it a greater informality. The veranda, too, with its open horizontal stretch, made the house more accessible to both man and nature.
Against this the transept stood boldly, perhaps even awkwardly, as the
dominating Gothic motif of the design. Even the old northeast tower, so
essential to the asymmetrical balance, seemed subdued by its aggressiveness. In the new design, however, the transept not only became secondary
to the new tower in terms of height, but it was also reduced in importance
by the raising of the roof line of the old house.

On the west side, where it faced the river and the flat vertical cliffs of
the Palisades, Davis kept the façade of Lyndhurst relatively flat (Figs.
210, 211, 214). Only the transept projected significantly beyond the west
wall, and even this was muted in its effect by the powerful line of the veranda, which paralleled the plane of the wall in a second plane con-

FIGURE 211. A. J. Davis. Lyndhurst,
Tarrytown, N.Y., west front with plan,
c. 1865. Original water-color drawing.

FIGURE 212. A. J. Davis. Lyndhurst,
Tarrytown, N.Y., east façade, 1838 and 1865.

FIGURE 213. A. J. Davis. Lyndhurst,
Tarrytown, N.Y., east façade,
c. 1866. Old photograph.

FIGURE 214. A. J. Davis. Lyndhurst,
Tarrytown, N.Y., west façade, 1838 and 1865.

tinuous with the west front of the transept. Even the face of the new tower was in the plane of the main wall, its vertical shape visually articulated by corner turrets which ran its entire height. Moreover, to maintain further this sense of plane the new dining-room wing was made to recede rather than advance, with its boldly projecting bay never quite reaching forward to the plane of the wall. The dynamic balance of the west front, therefore, was resolved in the off-center opposition of the two major vertical components, the tower and the transept. They were poised against the bilateral build-up toward the center of the main part of the house, with the asymmetrical climax in the soaring tower, which on the west side was seen from ground to pinnacled top, without interruption.

On the other side (Figs. 210, 212), which faces the irregularities of the sloping land to the east, a dominating wall plane is impossible to find. Instead, the multiple components of the complex mass move forward and backward, as well as up and down, in a constantly shifting ascent toward the off-center tower. The easterly thrust of the transept, instead of being muted by the veranda, as on the west side, is here exaggerated by the new porte-cochère. The outer face of this bold unit is, in fact, the extreme point of projection. From here the massing moves back and up to the old tower, down and back to the wall of the secondary entrance, and finally back and up to the new tower on the other side of the roof. The new dining-room wing brings the movement forward again before it finally recedes to the service wing at the extreme end. The two entrances, the main one in the east transept, the secondary one centered beneath the tower, are conspicuously identified with the major climax points in the mass (Fig. 212). Yet each also retreats into the building, the main door beneath the cave-like arcade of the porte-cochère, the secondary door into the shadowed recess of the deepest funnel of the mass. As at Monticello, therefore, where the main door is recessed within a porticoed porch, Lyndhurst is made to invite and embrace the visitor as he is urged into its protective depths.

Within this subtly ordered and asymmetrically balanced scheme, the composition of internal parts is equally dynamic. In a splendid piece of occult opposition, the one-story projection of the porte-cochère is reflected on the other side of the tower in the smaller but more animated one-story prominence of the bay window in the new dining room. Here weight is set against multiplicity. Elsewhere (Fig. 215), window and door openings are not only rendered with a meticulous regard for Gothic proportion and scale, but they are infinitely varied in pattern, and are poised in relation to one another, even to the smallest part, with the same qualities of dynamic excitement that characterize the composition of the house as a whole. Here, too, a fascinating contrast can be drawn between the somewhat austere Gothic of the early house and the more urbane style of the Merritt additions. The system of window openings around the secondary entrance (Fig. 215), in contrast with the simple isolated windows of the early house (Fig. 216), is a complex pattern of shifting rhythms which animates the entire wall. Even the tracery, which in the original house was severely simple, is more involved, more dynamically rhyth-

FIGURE 215. A. J. Davis. Lyndhurst,
Tarrytown, N.Y., dining-room bay
and secondary entrance, 1865.

mic, and more elegantly shaped. The tracery in Knoll's great west window (Fig. 217) was distilled to the point of being awkward, especially
when compared either with that which Davis planned for the Merritt
modifications (Fig. 211), or to that which was actually built in the bay
windows of the new dining room (Fig. 222). Yet in spite of their greater
intricacy and variety, the Merritt parts of Lyndhurst all seem physically
consistent with the older parts. In some measure this is due to Davis's discreet control of scale. At the same time, each arch, each molding,
each tracery bar conveys the impression of being there as a result of natural growth. As is so often the case with various additions made to the great
Gothic cathedrals of England over a long period of time, the later windows of Lyndhurst seem to emerge from the substance of the older parts
as living organisms, capable of perpetual renewal, and appear more as
blossoms on a flowering tree than as cut flowers arranged for a special occasion.

For the most part, the interior spaces provided by Davis in the new
part of Lyndhurst are so much in character with those of the original
house that it is impossible to tell them apart. The new room which formed
the north end of Merritt's library was square in plan and had a centripetal

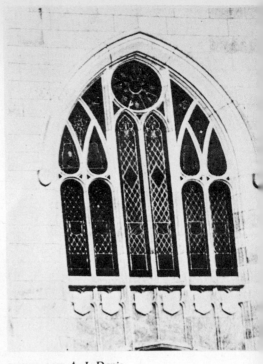

FIGURE 216. A. J. Davis.
Knoll, Tarrytown, N.Y.,
window in tower, 1838.

FIGURE 217. A. J. Davis.
Knoll, Tarrytown, N.Y.,
great west window, 1838. Old photograph.

ribbed ceiling springing from the four corners toward the center. It thus quietly mimicked its companion space, the old dining room to the south, and became an integral part of a coherent continuum of compartments, all given over to the same purpose. With one exception, the other rooms, too—from the small entry vestibule on the first floor to the new bedrooms on the second—were unified both in scale and ornamental treatment with the older part of the house.

The new dining room, on the other hand, stood apart in every way as a distinctive and separate room (Fig. 210 N). Oriented east and west, it was attached, off center, to the north end of the building as the counterpart of the drawing room on the south (Fig. 210 F). It was thus recessed behind the tower on the west façade, but projected on the east to form with the old northeast tower the small forecourt for the secondary entrance. The only access to the dining room was from the new entrance vestibule (M), through a sliding door, which was directly in line with the old north-south hall (H). At the same time, this door was also centered on the south wall of the dining room itself, so that the latter is firmly locked into the main axial scheme of the house. Indeed, the dining room stands as the northern terminus of a long cavernous passage which presses its way from the drawing room on the south through the original vestibule and the stair lobby to the secondary vestibule (Fig. 218). Here it passes, on axis, through the dining-room door to blossom in symmetrical splendor as the most extravagant room in the house (Fig. 219).

FIGURE 218. A. J. Davis.
Lyndhurst, Tarrytown, N.Y:,
view down north corridor
toward Merritt dining room,
1865.

Facing the door, directly across the room, is the centerpiece of the entire design, an elaborate Gothic fireplace (Fig. 220). Flanking it on either side, and symmetrically disposed, are two identical doorways which lead into the service wing still further to the north. On the east and west walls, the dining room opens up into broad deep hexagonal bays (Fig. 221), each of which is framed by marble colonnettes and a Tudor arch; splendid tracery with its original stained glass animates the windows. Because of their surrounding arches these bays are somewhat separated from the dining area itself. The effect is to emphasize the extension of the room, at both ends, into a different kind of space, and to establish unequivocal termini for the longitudinal axis. The room is therefore absolutely symmetrical around the fulcrum established between the entrance door on the south and the fireplace on the north; even the rectangular pattern of both the ceiling beams and the magnificent parquet floor reaffirm this symmetry. Fiercely contained by its emphatic cross-axis, and by its absolute balance, the dining room is by far the most formal room in the house.

It is also the most opulent. Its rich, sensuous color scheme and contrasting patterns take their theme from the marble mantel. The mantel shelf is a pink marble supported at the ends by heavy colonnettes of red-orange to black, grained marble. The chimney breast is also marble, this time, however, striated in richly varied patterns of brown and yellow-orange. Above the mantel, a large mirror is flanked by tall colonnettes

FIGURE 219. A. J. Davis. Lyndhurst, Tarrytown, N.Y., Merritt dining room, 1865.

FIGURE 220. A. J. Davis. Lyndhurst, Tarrytown, N.Y., Merritt dining-room mantel, 1865

FIGURE 221. *A. J. Davis.*
Lyndhurst, Tarrytown, N.Y.,
interior detail, Merritt dining-room
east bay, 1865.

FIGURE 222. *A. J. Davis.*
Lyndhurst, Tarrytown, N.Y.,
exterior detail, Merritt dining-room
east bay, 1865.

that are painted and grained to imitate the supporting colonnettes below; they in turn support an ogee arch of imitation oak. The plaster walls are of the dark neutral red of the fireplace and have a raised stencil pattern in glazed gold. The elaborate paneled ceiling is made of pine and plaster, but is skillfully painted and grained to imitate oak. Its heavy cross beams are carried on brackets, interspersed with tracery, which in turn are supported by colonnettes painted in imitation of the dark grained marble of the fireplace. As a subtle means toward unity, the tracery pattern between the brackets either side of the mantel is repeated almost exactly in the bay windows (compare Figs. 220, 221), and through the colorful, fleur-de-lis crowns of these windows, the abundance of Gothic energy which animates the entire room bursts forth to the outside in a flowering of ornamental proliferation unmatched anywhere else in the house (Fig. 222). The contrast between these sparkling windows and the austere exterior wall from which their vibrant patterns seem to grow is the same contrast which exists between the plain imitation stone walls of the original dining room (Fig. 199), and the sensational richness of the new one (Fig. 219). Even the tables and chairs were designed by Davis to participate in the display. As well as being formal, therefore, and suitable for high-style entertainment, the Merritt dining room was also exquisitely extravagant. Indeed, in the sequence of rooms that adjoined and sometimes flowed through the stretching corridor, it was the jewel box, the ultimate repository in which a typical American of means, with a growing taste for the opulent, could gather and display the fruits of his wealth.

The care with which Davis formalized the position of the great dining room by disposing it symmetrically at the end of the main longitudinal axis of the house is clear indication of the importance of the room as the climax of life in the Merritt household. Its very special character is also expressed in the subtle way in which he isolated it from the rest of the house. On the exterior, it stood out emphatically, receding on the west, projecting on the east, its bold bays, gables, and central cupola confirming both its symmetry and its independence as a unit in the massing. Even its corners were chamfered to establish a contrast with the square or turreted corners of the adjacent towers. Yet all of this was discreetly accomplished within the fabric of an immensely coherent scheme. Exterior wall textures were consistent throughout, and the new window openings, although more complex and more subtly composed, were handled with the same attention to a unifying scale as those in the older part of the house. Aside from the colorful flowering of the bay windows in the dining room, only an occasional proliferation of window tracery hints at the abundance concentrated in the new dining room.

The subtlety with which Knoll was transformed into Lyndhurst was made possible in no small measure by Davis's profound understanding of the Gothic style. Although he never saw Westminster Abbey in London, the dramatic burst of brilliance in the Merritt dining room, formally placed as it was amidst the involved and somber chambers of the older house, has a provocative kinship with that venerable monument of the English Gothic. Behind the austere four-part vaults in the choir of the great Abbey, and opening directly on axis from the ambulatory, the Chapel of Henry VII is suspended in shimmering translucent splendor. It is the most extravagant fan-vaulted interior in England, and no matter how familiar it may be, each time one enters from the older part of the cathedral the shift in style and mood comes as an exciting surprise. Yet it is a transformation which evolves without the slightest interruption of that underlying sense of organic continuity that is the mark of all great Gothic work. It was this quality which Davis perceived above all else, and although Lyndhurst has nothing directly to do with Westminster Abbey, the strategic placement of the Merritt dining room as a major focal point in the design and the extraordinary abundance of its architectural embellishment make it, too, come as both a surprise and as the logical climax to an organically developed scheme. Knoll flowed naturally and easily into Lyndhurst because Davis recognized in the flexibility and freedom of the Gothic style a way to gratify the extravagant taste of his client without destroying the roots from which he was called upon to make it grow. Lyndhurst, therefore, is not only a superb document of changing attitudes in America during the mid-nineteenth century, but when completed in 1866 it was the most profoundly intelligent and provocative house to be built in this country since Thomas Jefferson's Monticello.

CHAPTER VII

Andrew Jackson Downing
Villa, Cottage,
and Landscape

*The cottage is calculated for what, in countries having a
privileged aristocracy, are called the lower and middling
classes of society; but which in self-governed democracies,
like North America, or in newly-colonized countries, like
Australia, constitute nearly the whole rural population.*
                                    JOHN CLAUDIUS LOUDON

PART I

ANDREW JACKSON DOWNING,
AMERICAN ARCHITECTURAL CRITIC

Andrew Jackson Downing's Books on Architecture

The concept of the villa, tentatively set forth by Davis in *Rural Residences,* and shortly thereafter developed in specific architectural form at Knoll, was first fully discussed and defined in American architectural literature by Andrew Jackson Downing. Downing was the most articulate and literate architectural critic of his time. He was also a close friend and associate of Davis, and the ideas which he expounded in his various writings have such a direct relationship with those developed by the latter in his domestic architecture, that we cannot fully understand one man without taking into account the other. Their relationship was one of the most fascinating of the period and the direction that American domestic architecture would take between 1840 and 1875 was largely determined by these two men.

In assessing this relationship it is extremely important to recognize that throughout its course Downing was not an architect nor did he consider himself one. Only during the last two years of his life—when he went into partnership with the young English architect Calvert Vaux—did he make a positive move in that direction. By then, however, it was too late. Whatever promise his venture with Vaux may have held, it all came to an untimely and tragic end when in 1852, at the age of thirty-seven, Downing died in a steamboat fire on his beloved Hudson River. At the time, he was internationally known as a landscape gardener, horticulturist, and critic, and it was in the latter capacity, as a prolific and persuasive author, that his impact on American architecture was to be felt.

Downing was born on October 31, 1815, at Newburgh, New York, in the heart of the Hudson River Valley.[1] His father ran a nursery, and after his death Andrew and his brother continued to operate it. In 1837, the brother withdrew from the business and Andrew continued alone. His natural creative genius, however, soon took him into the more sophisticated world of landscape gardening, where he moved rapidly from success to success. By 1842 he had not only gained national recognition but had also been honored for his work by authorities in England, Holland, and Germany. A climax came in 1851, eighteen months before his death, when he was commissioned by President Fillmore to submit a proposal for the improvement of the Mall and White House grounds in Washington, D.C. Although never carried out, Downing's scheme was one of the important picturesque landscape designs of the century. But along with his skills as a practicing landscape designer, Downing was a philosopher at heart and actually gained his reputation through his writing. In 1845 his first important book, *The Fruits and Fruit Trees of America,* was widely acclaimed both in this country and abroad, and a year later he became editor of *The Horticulturist,* a monthly periodical which he had helped to found. A selection of the editorials which he had written for it was published in book form after his death under the title *Rural Essays.*

The earliest of Downing's books which dealt specifically with the subject of architecture was *A Treatise on the Theory and Practice of Landscape Gardening, Adapted to North America.* Published in 1841,[2] it was the first book in this country to treat the art of landscape gardening in both a scientific and a philosophical way. Throughout this discourse, Downing reveals his awareness of the fact that at the heart of every planned landscape is the house. To explore this notion, he devoted one section to "Rural Architecture" and to the general theme that *"architectural beauty* must be considered conjointly with the *beauty of the landscape or situation."* The important word here is "conjointly." Downing's arguments leave no doubt that he understood the relationship between the house and the landscape as reciprocal. It was not enough to plan the landscape to enhance and embrace a house; it was equally important that a house be designed to relate to the particular setting in which it was to be placed. In Downing's own words, "buildings . . . will be considered by the mind of taste, not only as architectural objects of greater or less merit, but as component parts of the general scene; united with the surrounding lawn, embosomed in tufts of trees and shrubs, if properly designed and constructed, they will even serve to impress a character upon the surrounding landscape . . . how much more likely to be successful are the efforts of him, who, in composing and constructing a rural residence, calls in to the aid of architecture, the genius of the landscape."[3]

Downing also realized that "architecture, either practically considered or viewed as an art of taste, is a subject so important and comprehensive in itself, that volumes would be requisite to do it justice." Accordingly, with his interest aroused by his reflections on architecture in his *Treatise,* he proceeded at once to write a book on that subject. *Cottage Residences, Rural Architecture and Landscape Gardening,* published in 1842, was intended to encourage the building of rural residences which would "harmonize with our lovely rural landscape." As the title implies the emphasis placed on gardening over architecture in the *Treatise* was here reversed. Downing begins *Cottage Residences* with a theoretical discussion in which he sets forth the basic principles of architecture. He then presents fourteen designs for houses, with a brief discussion of each. Only at the end, in a short concluding section, does he consider the question of gardens and grounds.

Downing's third and final book, *The Architecture of Country Houses,* was published in 1850, two years before his death. This is a larger, more searching endeavor and represents the maturation of his thinking about architecture. The ideas which were loosely expressed in the earlier books are here synthesized, enlarged, clarified, and refined, and his examples are more systematically presented. In this book, moreover, there is no section on gardening at all. The subject is entirely architecture, with chapters devoted to interiors, furniture, and heating and ventilation. Both the *Treatise* and *Cottage Residences* remained extremely popular and influential books, but it is *The Architecture of Country Houses* which provides the most comprehensive statement of Downing's views on architecture.

Downing and A. J. Davis

The association between Downing and Davis began with Downing's books. In preparation for his work Downing traveled extensively up and down the Hudson River Valley, visiting all the country residences and studying carefully both the houses and their grounds. He thus met and came to know many of the most prominent residents of the area, among them Robert Donaldson. Blithewood, in fact, was one of the estates which attracted Downing most, and it was through Donaldson that he and Davis were brought together. On December 12, 1838, Downing wrote to Davis:[4]

Dear Sir—

I am at present busily engaged in preparing a work for the press on Landscape Gardening and Rural Residences with the view of improving if possible the taste in these matters in the United States.

My friend, R. Donaldson, Esq., has informed me that he has mentioned my name to you and that you were so kind as to offer to show me any work, views or plans in your possession which might be of any service to me.

I shall probably be in town on Saturday morning next when I shall have the pleasure of calling upon you and will be glad to avail myself of your very kind offer.

Yours truly
A. J. Downing.

That first meeting must have been satisfactory to both men, for from that point on Davis worked with Downing in the preparation of his books. He visited buildings and sketched them, he helped the author judge what houses should be included, and he made the finished drawings for the illustrations directly on the end-grained wooden blocks which were then turned over to a master engraver for cutting.[5] Downing's attention was apparently first drawn to Davis by the latter's architectural illustrations in *The New York Mirror,* and by his *Rural Residences.* Downing may first have seen *Rural Residences* at Blithewood, although he later purchased a copy of his own. At the same time Downing was quick to recognize Davis's skills as an architect. Among the houses illustrated in the first edition of the *Treatise* were several designed by Davis, including Paulding's Knoll; in addition, Downing even recommended Davis, along with the Philadelphian John Notman, as "successful American architects."[6] As the association between the two men grew, it became both warm and professional, and although the pressure of work kept Davis from doing very much on *The Architecture of Country Houses,* Downing wrote him a friendly letter at the time of its publication, and before departing for England in July of 1850, sent him an advance copy.[7] The Downing-Davis friendship was cemented by a powerful kinship of interests and a common commitment to upgrade American taste in matters of living and the environment, matters in which both the landscape and the house were central issues of concern. The two men complemented one another at many levels, and each was supported and nourished in his own work by the enthusiasm of the other.

The most important fruit of the Downing-Davis relationship was the formulation, in theoretical and practical terms, of the cottage and the villa. These two building types would free American architecture from its time-worn classical tradition and open the way for wholly new relationships between the house and its environment: they would also serve an ever-widening spectrum of American society. Although Downing makes frequent reference to both the cottage and the villa in his first two books, he makes no formal attempt to define either. In his third book, however, *The Architecture of Country Houses,* he has a whole section given over to each. His definition of the cottage, and its subsequent important role in the evolution of American society, we will deal with later; Downing's ideas about the villa, however, bear so directly on what we have already seen developed by Davis in his architecture, that we will examine them now in some detail.

Downing and the Villa

In the United States, according to Downing, a villa "is the country house of a person of competence or wealth sufficient to build and maintain it with some taste and elegance. Having already defined a cottage to be a dwelling so small that the household duties may all be performed by the family, or with the assistance of not more than one or two domestics, we may add, that a villa is a country house of larger accommodation, requiring the care of at least three or more servants . . . The villa, indeed, may be as simple and chaste as a cottage."[8] Although important, size is not the only criterion of judgment; another is the matter of life style. "The villa . . . is the most refined home of America—the home of its most leisurely and educated class of citizens. Nature and art both lend it their happiest influence. Amid the serenity and peace of sylvan scenes, surrounded by the perennial freshness of nature, enriched without and within by objects of universal beauty and interest—objects that touch the heart and awaken the understanding—it is in such houses that we should look for the happiest social and moral development of our people." In other words, if the villa is more complex than the cottage, it is so to accommodate and express the more complex demands of its educated occupants.

"And what should the villa be, architecturally?" Downing asks. He summarizes: "It should, firstly, be the most convenient; secondly, the most truthful or significant; and thirdly, the most tasteful or beautiful of dwellings.

"The villa should, indeed, be a private house, where beauty, taste, and moral culture are at home . . . while in the arrangement of spacious apartments, especially in the devotion of a part to a library or cabinet sacred to books, and in that elevated order and system of the whole plan, indicative of the inner domestic life, we find the development of the intellectual and moral nature which characterizes the most cultivated families in their country houses."

With respect to convenience Downing is very specific. "The . . . highest rule of utility is that which involves convenience. In all architecture, adaptation to the end in view is important; in domestic architecture it is a principle which, in its influence on our daily lives, our physical comfort and enjoyment, is paramount and imperative. . . .

"This practical part of architecture involves, more particularly, what is called the plan of a building—providing apartments for the various wants of domestic and social life; adapting the size of such apartments to their respective uses, and all other points which the progress of modern civilization has made necessary to our comfort and enjoyment within-doors . . . [but] no absolute rules for guidance can be laid down here. Domestic life varies not only in different countries, but even in different portions of a territory so broad as that of the United States. Even different families have somewhat various habits, and therefore require different accommodations. The ingenuity and talents of the architect must therefore be put in full activity, even to meet the requirements of this humblest platform of his art. . . . To the majority of mankind the *useful* is the largest satisfaction derived from architecture."

Convenience by itself, however, is inadequate to fulfill the life of the mind and the spirit. "Beauty must be united to convenience and comfort, or at least must never be opposed to it. Instead of following the example of those who are always striving to make dwellings resemble temples and cathedrals," the architect should "bestow on windows and doors, roofs and chimneys, porches and verandas—those truly domestic features—that loving, artistic treatment which alone raises material forms from the useful to the beautiful."

The villa must truthfully express the man who is to live in it. His villa may be built "in any one of a dozen styles—convenient and comfortable in its accommodation; and yet, if there is no real fitness in the form and expression of the thing chosen, if it is foreign to the habits, education, taste, and manners—in short, the life of the proprietor," then it will be empty of any meaning or truth. "There is . . . something wonderfully captivating in the idea of a battlemented castle, even to an apparently modest man, who thus shows to the world his unsuspected vein of personal ambition, by trying to make a castle of his country house. But, *unless there is something of the castle in the man,* it is very likely, if it be like a real castle, to dwarf him to the stature of a mouse."

"The villa . . . should above all things, manifest individuality. It should say something of the character of the family within," and here the choice of style enters the picture in a very real way. Downing concedes that a certain type of person, one who is rational and well-organized, will prefer and need a house of classical design. A "man of common-sense views . . . will naturally prefer a symmetrical, regular house, with few angles, but with order, and method, and distinctness stamped upon its unbroken lines of cornice and regular rows of windows."

Although Downing admits that there are those for whom the classical styles would be appropriate, his continuing arguments make it clear that these styles were not his taste, nor did he see them as expressive of either American society or the American landscape. For this he prefers the picturesque and irregular. "The man of sentiment or feeling will seek for that house in whose aspect there is something to love. It must nestle in, or grow out of, the soil. It must not look all new and sunny, but show secluded shadowy corners. There must be nooks about it, where one would love to linger; windows, where one can enjoy the quiet landscape leisurely; cozy rooms, where all domestic fireside joys are invited to dwell." Downing's vision of the new men of America is as moving as his vision of the villa. They are, he says:

> men of imagination—men whose aspirations never leave them at rest —men whose ambition and energy will give them no peace within the mere bounds of rationality. These are the men for picturesque villas —country houses with high roofs, steep gables, unsymmetrical and capricious forms. It is for such that the architect may safely introduce the tower and the campanile—any and every feature that indicates originality, boldness, energy, and variety of character. To find a really original man living in an original and characteristic house, is as satisfactory as to find an eagle's nest built on the top of a mountain crag.

In this passage Downing appeals directly to the heart of a dynamic, expanding, restless America.

Downing and Thomas Jefferson

The concept of the villa as developed by Downing was not based on any particular style or, indeed, upon any particular shape of building. It was a concept in which the house grew freely in response to a way of life and found its kinship with a particular natural setting, just "as a tree expands which is not crowded by neighbors in a forest, but grows in the unstrained liberty of the open meadow."[9] Seen as architectural values, Downing's arguments derive conspicuously from the writings of Loudon,[10] but in adopting the English ideas he subjects them to the modifying fires of his own romantic, practical, and nationalistic notions, and tempers them to the American scene. Downing sees the freely developed form of the villa as expressive of certain conditions peculiar to American society, and in the end he arrives at conclusions that are quite different from Loudon's. Like Loudon, Downing was a landscape gardener, but the focus of his attention was not a countryside worked and reworked by the farmer, or formalized by great landed estates. Rather, it was a countryside much of which was still unspoiled wilderness, and into which man had made only minor inroads. In many instances, therefore, sites chosen for new houses were either farmlands surrounded by wilderness tracts, or parts of the actual wilderness itself, all of them free of encumbrances and potentially spectacular as visual settings. Indeed, Downing made unspoiled nature a basic condition of landscape design. He advises someone about to build a country residence "to choose a site where there is *natural wood,* and where nature offers the greatest number of good features ready for a basis upon which to commence improvements."[11] In this way, it would be possible, by judicial cutting, not only to achieve imaginative "ornamental" effects, but also to retain something of the quality of nature itself. He continues: "There is another most striking advantage in the possession of considerable wooded surface, properly located, in a country residence. This is the seclusion and privacy of the walks and drives, which such bits of woodland afford. Walks, in open lawn, or even amid belts of shrubbery, are never felt to have that seclusion and comparative solitude which belong to the wilder aspect of woodland scenes. And no contrast is more agreeable than that from the open sunny brightness of the lawn and pleasure-grounds, to the retirement and quiet of a woodland walk."[12]

As we have already seen, Downing was not the first American to be aware of the special qualities of his native landscape. Men like Bryant, Cole, and Davis were already celebrating its wonder, each in his own way. Indeed, the first American architect to pick a site for a house because of its romantic relationship with the natural environment was Thomas Jefferson at Monticello. Placed on top of a mountain, it commanded a sweeping view across unbroken forest to the Blue Ridge Mountains, prompting Jefferson to ask, "Where has nature spread so rich a mantle under the eye? mountains, forests, rocks, rivers. With what majesty do we there ride above the storms! How sublime to look down into the workhouse of nature, to see her clouds, hail, snow, rain, thunder, all fabricated at our feet! and the glorious sun, when rising as if out of a distant water, just gilding the tops of the mountains, and giving life to all nature!"[13]

As an admirer of the English irregular garden, Jefferson was fully aware that it was the wilderness quality of the setting at Monticello which distinguished his plantation from the landed estates of England, and he saw clearly the unique advantages that the wild American landscape offered the gardener. As early as 1788 he wrote that in this country "the noblest gardens may be made without expense. We have only to cut out the superabundant plants."[14] This is precisely what he did at Monticello. Leveling the mountaintop for the house and lawn, he nevertheless kept the irregular edge of the forest as the embracing frame, with the endless stretch of wilderness beyond. In reflections upon Monticello he sees "a flower here, a tree there; yonder a grove, near it a fountain; on this side a hill, on that a river. Indeed . . . I know nothing so charming as our own country."[15]

If Downing agreed with Jefferson about the American countryside, he also had similar views about life in the country. It is here "that the social virtues are more honestly practiced, that the duties and graces of life have more meaning, that the character has more room to develop its best and finest traits than within the walls of cities." Indeed, he continues, "In this most cultivated country life, everything lends its aid to awaken the finer sentiments of our nature . . . Happy is he who lives this life of a cultivated mind in the country!"[16]

This notion that life in the country was more beneficial to man than that in the city, and that it was conducive to the intellectual life lies at the heart of Jefferson's Monticello. More than that, educated persons at the time apparently associated this idea with Jefferson. In Davis's collection of quotations,[17] for example, is found the following: "And it seemed as if from his youth he had placed his mind, as he had done his house upon an elevated situation, from which he might contemplate the universe." Unfortunately Davis does not identify the author of this statement. He indicates only that it was said "of Jefferson." But the fact that Davis included it at all leaves no doubt that Downing's generation had not forgotten either the man of Monticello or his view of life.[18]

In a very real sense, Downing's vision of the good life, indeed, of America itself, had much in common with Jefferson's. Downing believed, as Jefferson had before him, in an aristocracy of the mind, in a society of intellectuals of means and taste who could live a refined life among their books and selected objects of beauty in the detached serenity of the incomparable American landscape. Just as Jefferson built Monticello on an elevated site with the Blue Ridge Mountains at his feet, so Downing placed his villa "Highland Gardens," on a hill above the Hudson River where sunlight and shadow, lush forests and gleaming water were seen across a lawn sloping to the mountains beyond. Here, as Jefferson had been before him, he was removed from the city where he could carry out his work as a nurseryman, and live a life of reflection among his books and friends.

Like Jefferson, too, Downing designed his own house and its grounds. The famous Swedish writer, Fredrika Bremer, who visited the Downings in October of 1849, tells us what it was like:

> Mr. Downing's carriage awaited to convey us up the hills to a beautiful villa of sepia-colored sandstone, with two small projecting towers, surrounded by a park: lying high and open, it has a free view over the beautiful river and its shores . . . he has built his house himself. It was himself who planted all the trees and flowers around it; and everything seems to me to bear the stamp of a refined and earnest mind. It stands in the midst of romantic scenery, shadowy pathways, the prettiest little bits of detail and splendid views. Every thing has been done with design—nothing by guess, nothing with formality. A soul has here felt, thought, arranged. Within the house there prevails a certain darkness of tone: all the wood-work of the furniture is brown; the daylight even is dusk, yet nevertheless clear, or, more properly, full of light—a sort of imprisoned sunshine, something warm and deep; it seemed to me like a reflection of the man's own brown eyes. . . . The only things which are brilliant in the rooms are the beautiful flowers in lovely vases and baskets. For the rest, there are books, busts, and some pictures.[19]

Downing's notion of life in the villa was anti-industrial in its sentiment. He saw agriculture as "the mother of all the arts, all the commerce, and all the industrial employments that maintain the civilization of the world."[20] Jefferson had a similar faith in the farmer. "Cultivators of the earth are the most valuable citizens," he wrote, "they are the most vigorous, the most independent, the most virtuous."[21] Had he known of it Downing would have applauded this statement, for he expressed the same idea in very similar language: "The cultivators of the soil constitute the great industrial class of this country; they may well be called its 'bone and sinew.' "[22]

There is no question that both the villa and the cottage, as functions of rural and suburban life, were not entirely romantic notions to Downing. He shared Jefferson's love of the country, and the two architectural types were, in part at least, reactions against the congestion and tensions of life in the cities. More than that, they were also a response to those threats to the individual, and to what men like Downing and Davis would regard as civilized society, which were contained in the dehumanizing trends of the growing industrial communities of the Northeast. Young women in particular were being lured away from the farms to the boardinghouses of Lowell and Lawrence, Massachusetts, and Manchester, New Hamsphire. There they lost their identity in the mass activity of a mass community. The villa and the cottage both offered a freedom of architectural form which could be expressive of the individual, and the individual in turn, happily situated in a house designed only for him, could then further develop and assert his own individuality. Although Jefferson never went as far as Downing in projecting his ideas about architecture to all levels of American society, he would surely have agreed.

Downing and Ralph Waldo Emerson

If the roots of Downing's theories about the relationship between the house and its environment are found in Jefferson, then several aspects of his mature reasoning, with all their debt to Loudon, are also nourished in no small measure by the greatest American philosopher of his time, Ralph Waldo Emerson. It is very apparent that Downing had a lively interest in Emerson, kept current with his published essays,[23] and even collected his works. It is with considerable delight and interest, therefore, that we read Miss Bremer's account of her evenings spent with the Downings at "Highland Gardens," evenings during which both host and hostess read to their guest from Emerson;[24] and it is with even greater interest that we read through the early essays themselves[25] and find there the rich clusters of thought which, filtered "through the alembic" of Downing's own abundant mind, emerge again as sustaining sinew in the body of the young author's thoughts.

Nature and beauty are conspicuous concerns of both authors. Emerson states that "the simple perception of natural forms is a delight . . . I see the spectacle of morning from the hilltop over against my house, from daybreak to sunrise, with emotions which an angel might share. The long slender bars of cloud float like fishes in the sea of crimson light. From the earth, as a shore, I look out into that silent sea. I seem to partake its rapid transformations; the active enchantment reaches my dust, and I dilate and conspire with the morning wind."[26] Downing is similarly moved: "We beget a partiality for every copse that we have planted, every tree which has for years given us a welcome under its shady boughs. Every winding path throughout the woods, every secluded resting-place in the valley, every dell where the brook lives and sings, becomes part of our affections, friendship, joy, and sorrows."[27]

For Emerson, however, beauty is more than simple experience. He states that "the presence of a higher, namely, of the spiritual element is essential to its perfection. The high and divine beauty which can be loved without effeminacy, is that which is found in combination with the human will. Beauty is the mark God sets upon virtue. . . . Beauty, in its largest and profoundest sense is one expression for the universe. God is the all-fair. Truth, and goodness, and beauty, are but different faces of the same All. But beauty in nature is not ultimate. It is the herald of inward and eternal beauty, and is not alone a solid and satisfactory good. It must stand as a part, and not as yet the last or highest expression of the final cause of nature."[28] Downing's views have an identical ring: "We may also add that the Beautiful is an original instinct of the sentiment of our nature. It is a worship, by the heart, of a higher perfection manifested in material forms.

"To see, or rather to feel how, in nature, matter is ennobled by being thus touched by a single thought of beauty, how it is almost deified by being made to shadow forth, even dimly, His attributes, constitutes the profound and thrilling satisfaction which we experience in contemplating the external works of God.

". . . Although beauty and truth are not synonymous in art, all beauty, to be satisfactory, must be based upon truth."[29]

In his vision of the artist and his environment, Emerson is emphatic: "Beauty, convenience, grandeur of thought and quaint expression are as near to us as to any, and if the American artist will study with hope and love the precise thing to be done by him, considering the climate, the soil, the length of the day, the wants of the people, the habit and form of the government, he will create a house in which all these will find themselves fitted, and taste and sentiment will be satisfied also."[30] Downing's expressed convictions are equally direct: "The highest merit of a villa or country house, after utility and beauty of form and expression, is, that it be, as much as possible, characteristic of the country in which it was built. In the Eastern and Northern states, high roofs, thick walls, warm rooms, fine stacks of chimneys—in the Middle and Southern, broad roofs, wide verandas, cool and airy apartments. But everywhere, and in all parts of the country, in planning a country house, let the habits, and wants, and mode of life (assuming them to be good and truthful ones) stamp themselves on the main features of the house. It is thus that our domestic architecture will always be growing better, more truthful, more individual, and therefore more rational and sincere, rather than more foreign and affected."[31]

There are other interesting points of empathy: the theme of self-reliance, for example, that runs through Emerson, and the constant assertion of the sanctity of the individual. "Insist on yourself; never imitate. Your own gift you can present every moment with the cumulative force of a whole life's cultivation."[32] For Downing, the individual is equally important, indeed, the *raison d'être* of all domestic architecture. When complete, a house "ought to be significant of the whole private life of man—his intelligence, his feelings, and his enjoyments." If a house "plainly shows by its various apartments, that it is intended not only for the physical wants of man, but for his moral, social, and intellectual existence; if hospitality smiles in ample parlors; if home virtues dwell in cozy, fireside family-rooms; if the love of the beautiful is seen in picture or statue galleries; intellectuality, in well stocked libraries; and even a dignified love of leisure and repose, in cool and spacious verandas; we feel, at a glance, that there we have reached the highest beauty of which Domestic Architecture is capable—that of individual expression."[33]

There is also a high moral tone in Downing's various notions about Beauty and Truth in architecture contributing to the intellectual and spiritual well-being of man, notions which have a strong Ruskinian ring but which were, in fact, expressed by Downing in his *Treatise* eight years before the publication of Ruskin's *Seven Lamps of Architecture*. Possibly some of these ideas may have been suggested by Loudon, some may even have been born in the high moral character of Downing himself; whatever their origin, there is no doubt that they were warmly nurtured by the disciplined thinking of Emerson, by his conviction that "all things are moral; and in their boundless changes have an unceasing reference to spiritual nature."[34]

PART II

THE PROLIFERATION OF THE VILLA

Davis, Downing, and the Gothic Villa

All of Downing's philosophical probing had as its ultimate objective the house, and in the progress of his travels in preparation for his books he came to know many of them intimately, not just as the homes of neighbors, but as works of architecture in the most sophisticated sense of the word. As he made his way from house to house in the valley, each came alive for him as a living object, each with its own individuality, and each feeding something of itself into the development of his ideas.

In spite of these personal experiences with the actual buildings themselves, Downing's most important link with the world of architecture was Alexander Jackson Davis. When the two men met in December of 1838, Davis had just published *Rural Residences* with its illustration and description of Donaldson's villa; he had also just submitted his designs for Paulding's villa, and work on that house had already begun. The only two villas in the Hudson River Valley which were in anything like a coherent form of the Gothic style, and which Downing could have known, were these two houses. It is possible, of course, that through Davis he was also familiar with Glen Ellen, and we know that he visited Irving's quasi-medieval renovation at Sunnyside. Other than that, all the houses that he saw while preparing his book must have been Dutch and English colonial works, plus Federal and Greek Revival buildings of fairly recent vintage. In view of this, it is of considerable interest that the buildings he chose to use as illustrations in the first edition of the *Treatise* were almost without exception in some form of the picturesque mode. Moreover, in the chapter on Rural Architecture he criticizes those who would transplant what he called city architecture into the country, he decries the Greek Revival as anti-nature, and he develops in detail his theme of a close relationship between the house and the landscape. Indeed, all the attitudes expressed are thoroughly romantic and he emerges as an anti-classical rebel, with a strong taste for the Gothic.

In reading Downing it is more than apparent that his preoccupation with the house in relation to the landscape was primarily the result of his life and training as a landscape gardener. But it is also obvious that the depth of his understanding of picturesque architecture, particularly the Gothic, resulted from his association with Davis. The most important evidence of this is found in his own house, "Highland Gardens," which he designed and built himself in 1840 (Fig. 223). It was Tudor Gothic in style, and cruciform in plan. Its high gabled central pavilion had a porch and was flanked by turrets. Elsewhere in the building Downing combined stepped gables, bay and oriel windows, and clustered chimneys in a manner remarkably similar to that already developed by Davis in Donaldson's villa and Knoll. Indeed, Davis's concept of the Gothic villa appears in Highland

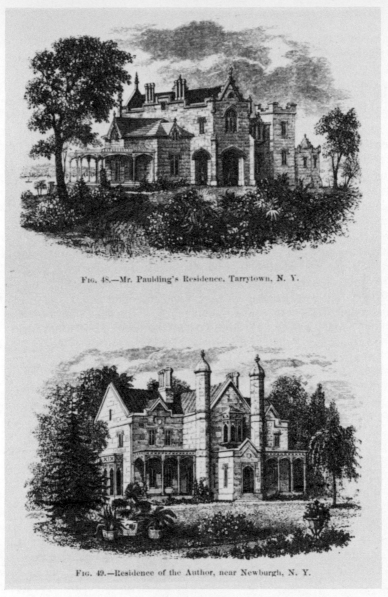

FIG. 48.—Mr. Paulding's Residence, Tarrytown, N. Y.

FIG. 49.—Residence of the Author, near Newburgh, N. Y.

FIGURE 223. TOP: *A. J. Davis, Knoll, Tarrytown, N.Y., 1838.*
BOTTOM: *A. J. Downing, Highland Gardens, Newburgh, N.Y., 1840.*

Gardens in such a comprehensive form, if not in specific detail, that there can be no question of where Downing turned to for inspiration. Moreover, ideas already developed by Davis are found throughout Downing's *Treatise*. Not only was the book enriched by the architect's skill as a draftsman, but several of his works were among the illustrations, including Knoll. Together, Davis and Downing were responsible for the flowering and climax of the Gothic villa in American domestic architecture of the nineteenth century, Davis as the creator and master of its form, Downing as its propagator; and it was perhaps deliberately symbolic of their creative association that in later editions of the *Treatise,* Knoll and Highland Gardens are illustrated, one above the other, on the same page (Fig. 223).

The concept of the villa, once established in architectural form by Davis, and critically defined and philosophically explained by Downing, was quickly taken up, and soon came to dominate the American architectural scene. The particular Gothic form of the villa developed by Davis, however, did not become characteristic of the type. There were, of course, various architects who did design villas in the Gothic style, and Downing illustrated a few examples, including his own house, but for the most part the high style Gothic villa remained the domain of Alexander Jackson Davis.

One reason for this was that the Gothic as it developed in American domestic architecture of mid-century was an elitist style. It had powerful literary overtones, especially those harking back to the medieval world of Sir Walter Scott. There were a number of ambitious pragmatists among the rising class of wealthy Americans, however, who had little interest in Scott's chivalrous knights or, for that matter, Downing's life of the mind. To them fantasy and philosophical reflection were out of touch with reality, and to celebrate their increasingly aggressive life style they demanded levels of grandeur for which the profoundly organic Gothic style was inappropriate. For them, the "Italian villa" offered far more options. Its Renaissance detailing carried a potential for a more respectable formality; and its classical roots also made it attractive since the sentiment for classical forms never completely died out in nineteenth-century America. At the same time, the campanile tower, the most dramatic feature of the Italianate style, combined with bold asymmetrical massing, made possible a dynamic and robust form of the picturesque, which was far more expressive of the largeness, the energy, and the ambition of industrial America than the more intricate and mysterious Gothic. Davis himself was deeply involved in both the introduction and the development of the Italianate style in this country (to be discussed in the next volume of the series). But with all his versatility Davis never forsook his preference for the Gothic, and those romantics in the American cultural community who still read their Scott turned to him almost exclusively for their villas. Indeed, Davis was the first domestic architect in America to become identified so emphatically with a particular segment of American society.

During the years between Knoll and Lyndhurst, Davis designed scores of houses of which a significant number were variants on the theme of Knoll. Of these one of the most interesting and one of the most completely documented is the Harrel House in Bridgeport, Connecticut.[35] It has been destroyed, as have most of the others, but it will suffice to illustrate the type (Fig. 224). Designed in 1845, for the leather dealer H. K. Harrel, it was an asymmetrical scheme, conceptually very similar to Knoll, although somewhat different in detail. As seen in Davis's drawing, it was a rambling house and had a prominently projecting section

FIGURE 224. A. J. Davis. Harrel House, Bridgeport, Conn., 1845.
Original water-color drawing.

with a high gable which was open on the first floor in an arcaded porch.
The right corner of this section was marked by an octagonal crenelated
tower rising to a height well above the roof line and providing the most
important vertical accent in the house; a smaller octagonal tower opposed
it on the left corner. Behind and to the right of the larger tower, an aggressive wing extended at right angles and ended in a steep gable similar to
that on the main façade (Fig. 225). Beneath the gable, on the second
floor, a pointed-arch window with a Tudor hood molding matched the
large window beneath the gable of the façade. On the first floor a bold octagonal bay window with an elaborate Gothic crown, prophetically similar in character to the bay window in the new dining room at Lyndhurst,
formed the terminus of the right wing; on the second floor of the adjacent
wall a smaller oriel window imitated the larger bay below.

To the left of the entrance unit (Fig. 226), the emphasis was more
horizontal, as it was at Knoll (Fig. 189). Here, the lower roof line of
the wing was accentuated by the horizontal movement of the veranda,
which extended from the open arcade of the entrance porch and then
turned at right angles, thus embracing two sides of the left wing. The
windows on this side were smaller than those on the right, and their related gables were less prominent. The total effect of the scheme, therefore, was not unlike Knoll: a lighter horizontal side balancing a heavier
vertical side, and the whole system asymmetrically poised around the
vertical thrust of the entrance unit and its two towers.

Although the arrangement of the towers in the Harrel House differed
from that at Knoll, and although there were a number of differences in
the plan, the broad relationships with the earlier house are obvious,

FIGURE 225. A. J. Davis.
*Harrel House, Bridgeport, Conn.,
oriel window and bay, 1845.*

FIGURE 226. A. J. Davis. *Harrel House, Bridgeport, Conn.,
entrance façade, 1845.*

FIGURE 227. A. J. Davis. Harrel House,
Bridgeport, Conn., bedroom, 1845.

and leave no doubt as to the conceptual origin of the design. On the interior, however, there were some interesting variances. Most of the house had Gothic detailing (Fig. 227), and some of the furniture was designed especially for the house in the Gothic style. In the parlor, which was to the left of the entrance and behind the veranda, the ornamental features were Gothic in scale and proportion but Renaissance in specific detail (Fig. 228). The effect was almost Rococo in its lightness and elegance.

This mixture of stylistic features on the interior, which seems to contradict the Gothic coherence of the exterior, was not uncommon in Davis's work, and was consistent with the growing eclectic taste which marked American interior decoration during the second half of the century. Indeed, in many instances, as we shall see, the interior design was regarded as something quite separate from the exterior. In the hands of Davis, differences in interior decorative style were coherently related, as they were in the Harrel House, through inventive ingenuity and controlled scale. As knowledge of historical styles increased, however, and as a taste for the opulent led to more and more extravagant forms, the interiors of many of the houses of the period became virtual showpieces of decorative virtuosity. We have already seen the impact of this trend on Davis in the later dining room at Lyndhurst.

The exact number of Gothic villas designed and built by Davis may never be known, although surviving drawings and entries in his various journals indicate at least a dozen major examples and a greater number of minor ones.[36] There is good evidence, too, that still others were designed by architects who had been influenced by Davis. For the most part, however, the Gothic villa seems to have remained the special province of Davis, and Lyndhurst was his greatest masterpiece in that style.

Variations on the Gothic Villa:
Richard Upjohn's Kingscote and the Cottage Orné

Quite apart from the direct influence that Davis's actual Gothic villas may have had on the architecture of his time, there is no question that both the simple force of his creative personality and the enormous volume of his work were powerful factors in the dissemination and solidification of the Gothic style in mid-century America. Davis was simply too outspoken and too aggressive to be ignored, and together with Upjohn, and to a lesser degree with Renwick, he may be said to have created the Gothic in this country. There is no evidence to prove that the three men ever communicated with one another, and if the antagonism between Davis and Renwick[37] is any indication of their relationship, professionally they may not even have been on speaking terms. But they surely knew of one another, and there is always the probability that, in spite of their competitive independence, they were much more aware of one another's work than they might wish to admit.

An unusual example of this, which has fascinating connections with Davis, is Richard Upjohn's Kingscote in Newport, Rhode Island (Fig. 232). This highly original and important house was designed by Upjohn in 1839 for George Noble Jones, a wealthy planter and speculator from Savannah, Georgia. It was intended as a summer home for Jones, and as a year-round residence for his mother and sister. The fact that it was a summer residence is in itself significant. As early as the eighteenth century Newport was a popular summer resort for wealthy Southerners, primarily from the Carolinas and Georgia. The cool climate of the Rhode Island shore offered relief from the oppressive summer heat of the South, and the location was also regarded as healthy, particularly for those who were ailing. In fact, in the eighteenth century the town was referred to as the "Carolina hospital." At first the visitors to Newport generally stayed in boardinghouses, but by the 1840's large resort hotels made their appearance and began to function as the center of the summer social activities. Moreover, by the mid-1830's some families had begun to build their own summer "cottages," and it was in this development that the future of Newport as an exclusive resort for the rich was born. Kingscote was among the first and certainly the most important of those early summer houses: it was also the predecessor of the fabulous summer palaces—whimsically called "cottages"—which by the end of the century were unmatched anywhere in the land for size and opulence.

Kingscote received its name from William Henry King, who purchased the house in 1864. In 1881 it was more than doubled in size from designs by the talented young architect Stanford White. The rooms which he added, particularly the new dining room, are of immense architectural

FIGURE 228. A. J. Davis. Harrel House,
Bridgeport, Conn., parlor, 1845.

interest, but they belong to a wholly different age in American architecture and for the present we will concern ourselves only with the original
Upjohn house, most of which still survives. Kingscote is now owned by
the Preservation Society of Newport County, and is open to the public.

At the time he was commissioned to design the Jones House, Upjohn
was just beginning his work on Trinity Church in New York, and had
not yet gained national recognition. He had already done a number of
houses in Maine, however, and it was through one of these that he
came to the attention of the young Georgia planter. In 1834, Jones had
married Delia Tudor Gardiner, the daughter of Robert Hallowell Gardiner of Gardiner, Maine. The following year Upjohn was commissioned
by Gardiner to design a new house, Oaklands (Fig. 234), to replace an
older one which had been destroyed by fire in 1834. While this new building was in progress Jones and his bride visited Gardiner, and during
their stay the young son-in-law took a lively interest in the construction of
the house. He thus came to know and admire Upjohn, and after deciding to build his own summer residence in Newport he wrote to the architect, on September 6, 1839, seeking his "assistance in planning a cottage." Upjohn responded immediately, sending some drawings, and a
week later Jones wrote again, this time giving specific instructions. Because of the valuable information this letter contains it is worth quoting in
full:[38]

Newport, September 13th, 1839

Mr. Richard Upjohn

Sir:

I yesterday received your letter of the 7th with a plan of a cottage & front elevation. It is very pretty, but it is not sufficiently large for my purpose. You will oblige me by sending a plan of a cottage containing eight chambers, besides two or three sleeping apartments for servants.

I recollect a plan of a cottage—two stories in front—which you showed me some time ago, which with a few alterations I think will suit my views. I will thank you to send that plan to me and any others you can spare. I shall be in New York in a fortnight when they will be returned to you. The lot upon which I propose building is at the corner of two streets, containing in front 200 feet in depth 400. The sooner you can send me the plans the more agreeable it will be to me. If your parcel was put on board the I. W. Richmond the day of the date of your letter, there must have been great neglect on the part of the agents in not sending it to me sooner.

The largest parlours of my cottage I should like to have 18 by 20. As I have plenty of room I do not care to have a very extensive basement. Let the water closets be in the house—also a bath. I will thank you to mention in your next letter your address.

Very respectfully
yours
Geo. Jones

The most intriguing part of Jones's letter is his reference to "a plan of a cottage—two stories in front" which Upjohn at one time had shown him. What was this cottage? Unfortunately there are no drawings or other documents among the Upjohn papers which provide an answer to this question. There is, however, an extremely important illustration for a two-storied cottage in Davis's *Rural Residences* (Fig. 230), and a comparison between that design and the east façade of Kingscote (Fig. 229) leaves little doubt as to where Upjohn got his idea. Upjohn arrived in New York shortly after *Rural Residences* was published, and as an architect the book must surely have come to his attention. Indeed, he may even have seen it before he went to New York, and it is highly probable that the plan he showed to Jones was Davis's cottage orné.

This cottage orné shown by Davis is a completely symmetrical building, and in his illustration is even seen to have classical details. In contrast, Upjohn's over-all design is Gothic and asymmetrical (Fig. 231). Even so, the east front of Kingscote is an unbroken plane, with strong horizontals at the eave line and in the veranda. It is also absolutely balanced with part matching part left and right of center, and in the original drawing (Fig. 229) there are trellised posts instead of clustered colonnettes supporting the veranda roof. All of this constitutes a degree of

FRONT.

FIGURE 229. *Richard Upjohn. Kingscote,*
Newport, R.I., east façade, 1839.
Original water-color drawing.

similarity between the Upjohn design and the cottage orné that makes it difficult not to conclude that Davis's scheme was the source for Upjohn's east façade.

In view of the serene stability of the east façade of Kingscote it comes as a surprise to encounter on the south side an asymmetrical arrangement with a broken cornice, irregular roof lines, steep pointed gables ornamented with verge boards, and a dynamic forward and backward movement of the mass (Fig. 232). Except that they are united by Upjohn's control of scale and by the repetition of certain decorative forms, the two façades of the building would seem to have little to do with one another. Yet they in fact have a common source, for the principal ingredients of the south façade can also be traced to *Rural Residences*. The projecting pavilion with its steep ornamented gable, and the rectangular hoods over the double windows, are found in Davis's illustration for the Blithewood gatehouse (Fig. 186). Thus what seems to have happened at Kingscote is that Upjohn combined two of Davis's most important ideas in the same design. All this suggests the very real possibility that the architect's first proposal, which Jones rejected because it was too small, was for the picturesque cottage which makes up the main part of the south façade, and further, that he met his client's wishes for more room and two stories simply by incorporating the cottage orné into his preliminary scheme.

VILLA, DESIGNED FOR DAV. CODWISE, ESQ.– BY A.J. DAVIS, ARCT.

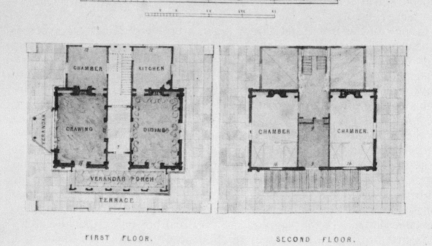

FIRST FLOOR.   SECOND FLOOR.

FIGURE 230. *A. J. Davis. Villa for David Codwise, 1837.*

FIGURE 231. *Richard Upjohn. Kingscote, Newport, R.I.,
south elevation, 1839. Original water-color drawing.*

FIGURE 232. *Richard Upjohn. Kingscote, Newport, R.I.,
south façade, 1839.*

FIGURE 233. *Richard Upjohn. Kingscote, Newport, R.I.,*
southeast corner, 1839.

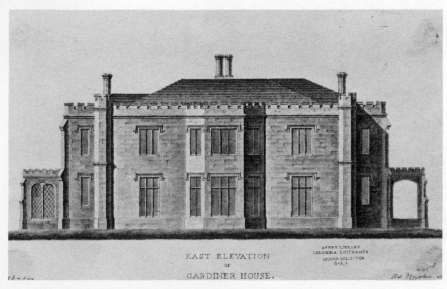

FIGURE 234. *Richard Upjohn. Oaklands, Gardiner, Me.,*
1835–36. Original water-color drawing.

FIGURE 235. *Richard Upjohn.*
Kingscote, Newport, R.I., veranda, 1839.

FIGURE 236. *Richard Upjohn. Kingscote,*
Newport, R.I., detail of entrance, 1839.

In spite of the diverse character of the main components, Upjohn has joined the two in a fascinating integrated design. Actually, because of its location on a corner, the house was only meant to be seen from two sides, and in the total sweep from east to south there is only one point at which the cottage orné motif asserts it symmetry, and that is when seen, on center, directly from the east. Even here, however, Upjohn has softened the severity of the balance by making the south end octagonal from ground to roof, while on the north end he has used a rectangular bay window on the ground floor only. The two ends, therefore, do not exactly match. Seen toward the southeast corner (Fig. 233) the cottage orné motif immediately becomes dynamic. Its rhythmic parts are seen in the dramatic perspective of a diagonal, and the octagonal end together with the profile of the veranda became participating units in the irregular composition of the entire south façade (Fig. 232).

Upjohn's mastery of asymmetry, which we have already seen in a somewhat restrained form in his churches, is highly spirited at Kingscote. This was unusual for the sober Englishman. Unlike his design for Oaklands (Fig. 234), which is a heavy stone pile in the castellated Gothic style, with a crenelated roof line, and corner turrets, all devoid of ornament, Kingscote is light and open. An elegant veranda (Fig. 235) is carried on slender clustered colonnettes, with curved and tapered rafters sweeping in a concave profile from the house to the eaves. The effect is more that of a sagging awning than a solid roof, and that Upjohn had such an idea in mind is borne out by the fact that in the original draw-

FIGURE 237. *Richard Upjohn. Kingscote, Newport, R.I.,*
perspective view, 1839. Original water color.

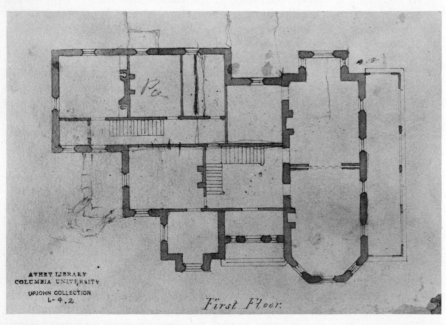

First Floor.

FIGURE 238. *Richard Upjohn. Kingscote, Newport, R.I.,*
original plan of the first floor, 1839.

FIGURE 239. *Richard Upjohn. Kingscote, Newport, R.I., parlors, 1839.*

ing (Fig. 231) the veranda roof is shown with alternating light and dark stripes.[39] The rhythmic sweep of the supporting posts, and the scalloped line of the dropped fleur-de-lis along the eaves all add to the impression of a lively shelter for outdoor living. In a similar vein on the south side of the house, the undulating wave-like pattern in the verge boards evokes the rhythms of the sea (Fig. 236).

The house is made of wood, not stone, which makes possible a very light scale, even though the siding is tightly drawn, matched boards coated with paint mixed with sand to imitate a stone surface. A watercolor perspective by Upjohn (Fig. 237) shows the house originally to have been a light neutral yellow, a kind of warm stone color, with its projecting and receding masses boldly modeled by the light, and with its elegant veranda and intricate Gothic detail sparkling against the pockets of shadow. Situated on relatively open land, and high enough so that the ocean was visible in three directions, the house was conspicuously designed as a summer cottage, and was open to the sun and the sea. At the same time, it was a substantial house—indeed, on one side, aggressively formal—and could easily serve Jones's mother and sister as a year-round residence.

FIGURE 240. *Richard Upjohn. Kingscote, Newport, R.I.,*
parlor fireplace, 1839.

An interesting feature of the interior, and one that would later become
a mark of distinction in the nineteenth-century house, was the double
parlor. Jones had called for "parlours" rather than a single living room,
and in filling this request Upjohn used the entire ground floor space of the
east end (Figs. 238, 239). This he divided down the center by sliding
doors so that for special occasions the two rooms could be thrown together
as one. Because of the octagonal bay which occupied the entire end of the
room, the south parlor was more spacious than the north. Here, instead
of the broad opening of the octagon, the room terminated in a wall from
which a conventional bay window opened through a Tudor arch similar to
that which separated the two rooms. Otherwise the rooms were identical,
with a corresponding fireplace in each centered on the inner wall (Fig.
240).

Except for this one formal sequence, the first-floor plan was completely asymmetrical, with the other major rooms, a library, a dining
room, and an office, all opening off the entrance hall. In many ways
this hall is the most dynamic room in the house (Fig. 241). The main entrance, which is sheltered beneath a canopied porch (Fig. 236), opens
into a small vestibule, a space which is separated from the main hall by a
partial screen of Tudor arches carried on two clustered colonnettes. Al-

FIGURE 241. *Richard Upjohn. Kingscote, Newport, R.I., hall, 1839.*

though the paneled ceiling in both the hall and vestibule does not seem to
be original, the Gothic wainscoting is, and together with the heavy
staircase, it creates a sense of the Gothic that is more persuasive here
than in any other room in the house. Elsewhere, the Gothic detailing,
especially in the door paneling, is authentic but simple, much like that
which we have already seen in Upjohn's splendid church interiors.

Since Kingscote was designed and built at the same time that Upjohn
was working on Trinity Church in New York, it is an early work, and
its fresh exuberance suggests something of the excitement that Upjohn
must have felt at this opportunity to explore the Gothic in a new direction.
Kingscote is a joyous house, designed as a summer residence for a man
in the first years of marriage. Although the young bride died before she
could ever move into the house, this in no way affected the ultimate outcome of the house. Kingscote has a lightness of touch which we will not
encounter again, for Upjohn's work became more severe in his mature
years. The house, in addition, is superbly picturesque, not only affirming
Upjohn's natural feeling for the mode, but above all demonstrating his
keen awareness of the ideas that were taking shape elsewhere in America.
Measured against the architectural values of his time, Kingscote was a
villa in much the same sense that Knoll was a villa; it was asymmetrical,
irregular in massing, rich in color and texture, and it was built as a
pleasure house for a man of wealth and taste. It was also situated in a
small but spectacular natural setting. But since it was constructed of wood

FIGURE 242. *John S. Norris. Green-Meldrim House, Savannah, Ga., 1856.*

rather than stone, it was also more closely related than Knoll to the main-line tradition in American domestic architecture. At the same time, deriving as it did from cottage and villa concepts developed by Davis, it pointed toward the future. Whereas Knoll was transformed into Lynd-hurst to glorify the achievements of wealth and privilege, Kingscote remained modest and accessible even after it was doubled in size in 1881. Built as the first important Newport "cottage," prior to the publication of Downing's *Treatise* in 1841, it was an imaginative and superbly designed predecessor to the wide proliferation of the Davis-Downing cottage which, as we shall see directly, would reach the heart of middle America.

The Green-Meldrim House

One other extremely interesting and important Gothic Revival house that seems either directly or indirectly to have had a connection with Davis's cottage orné is the Green-Meldrim House built in Savannah, Georgia, in 1856 (Fig. 242). It was designed by John S. Norris of New York for Charles Green, who was a wealthy cotton merchant and the grandfather of the novelists Anne and Julien Green. It was largely con-structed of imported materials at a cost of $93,000, which probably made it the most expensive house in Georgia at the time. Architecturally the Green-Meldrim House is important for two reasons: it is a rare surviving example of an elaborate mid-century Gothic mansion in an urban set-ting, and its extensive verandas and entrance portico are of cast iron. The latter feature we will discuss in detail in the next volume of this series; here we are concerned with the intrinsic qualities of the house as a Gothic Revival work, and its apparent relationship with Davis.

FIGURE 243. *John S. Norris.*
Green-Meldrim House, Savannah, Ga.,
detail, cast-iron portico, 1856.

The Green-Meldrim House is not a wholly picturesque design. It is a conventional rectangular block, with its entrance on the long side; it has a low hipped roof, partially concealed behind a parapet, with windows and door openings symmetrically disposed on its principal sides. All details on the exterior, however, are Gothic. The chimneys are clustered, the parapet is crenelated. The south, or main, façade is dominated by a cast-iron portico having turrets at the corners and a double-arched screen-like top (Fig. 243). A deep bay window above the portico has tall slim traceried windows in the Perpendicular style; the other windows on the entrance side are square-headed with Gothic hood moldings. On the east façade, the windows on the second story are prominent polygonal oriels (Fig. 244). Like the large bay over the entrance portico, they are crenelated and have Perpendicular lights with finely scaled tracery. Below, on the ground floor, an elegant shallow veranda, with a concave roof, extends along both the east and south sides, and is supported by extremely delicate cast-iron trellises and posts, all fashioned with intricate Gothic detail.

It is the east façade of the Green-Meldrim House which suggests an ultimate source in Davis's "cottage orné" (Fig. 230). Although Savannah might seem too remote from the Northeast to make such an influence possible, the connection could, in fact, have been very easily established. The architect of the house, John Norris, was from New York, and in 1856 could hardly have been a stranger to the work of either Davis or Upjohn. But even more important, George Noble Jones, the man who built Kingscote, was a prominent member of the business and social circles of Savannah; thus he might well have known Green, and perhaps even

FIGURE 244. *John S. Norris. Green-Meldrim House,
Savannah, Ga., east façade, 1856.*

FIGURE 245. *John S. Norris. Green-Meldrim House,
Savannah, Ga., drawing room, 1856.*

FIGURE 246. John S. Norris.
Green-Meldrim House, Savannah, Ga.,
dining room, 1856.

talked to him about his summer house in Newport. In any case, the appearance of the cottage orné motif in Savannah, although surely possible without any connection with Davis, does raise some intriguing questions about discourse which took place between architects in the nineteenth century. Although in regard to the Green-Meldrim House the matter cannot be resolved because of the total lack of supporting documents, it is kept alive by the persuasive implications of the physical evidence.

Both Kingscote and the Green-Meldrim House were highly individual designs, each in its own way remaining well above the general level of the Gothic Revival as it developed in this country. One was rural, and the other urban; the Green-Meldrim House, too, was more precious and ornamental, and more delicate in scale, than the organic and integrated Kingscote. Its oriel windows stand out in fussy isolation against the bland stretch of the unbroken stucco wall, and in its ornamental lavishness the interior of the house has little to do with the exterior. The detailing in the drawing room (Fig. 245) is quasi-Gothic in form but is mixed with Baroque elements, the result being an excessively lush scrambling of architectural and floral devices. The dining room, in the eclectic manner of mid-century interiors, is a mixture of Baroque and Rococo (Fig. 246). In contrast to Upjohn's restraint at Kingscote, the Green-Meldrim House is one of the more flamboyant eclectic showpieces of the period. It was spectacular in its time and place and prophetic of things to come.

FIGURE 247. *Afton Villa, West Feliciana Parish, La.,*
Gothic detailing added in 1849.

Other Manifestations:
The Gothic Hybrids

The strong individuality of Kingscote and the Green-Meldrim House is
symptomatic of all American domestic architecture of the Gothic Revival.
Not even those houses derived from the plates of Downing were all cut
from exactly the same pattern. The Gothic designs varied—sometimes
dramatically—from region to region, and there were even differences
within particular regions. Above all, there was always a special touch of
the individual patron, designer, and builder. Although much more
needs to be done at the local level before this intriguing phase of American building can be properly evaluated, those fragments which are visible
are sufficient to hint at the general character of the movement, and to
evoke some of these could enliven and broaden our understanding of the
period.

One important general observation which can be made is that the
Gothic does not seem to have made major inroads into the Deep South.
The Greek Revival had functioned with supreme success for the great
plantation houses; furthermore, there was no urban development with a
burgeoning industrial base to upset the serene and self-contained life of
the Southern planter. There was, therefore, no serious challenge to the

FIGURE 248. John E. Johnson. Staunton Hill, Charlotte County, Va., 1848.

established architectural ways, and when the Gothic did appear, it was generally as an intruder. Such was the case of Afton Villa in West Feliciana Parish, Louisiana (Fig. 247). This house—tragically destroyed by fire in 1963—was in its day one of the most elaborate Gothic confections in the country, although it was not initially designed in the Gothic style. Its profuse and ornate Gothic detailing was all added in 1849, during a rebuilding of an older house. According to local legend the owner, David Barrow, remodeled the house for his Kentucky bride, a young woman who had acquired a taste for the Gothic through her reading of Sir Walter Scott. With all its medieval splendor Afton Villa was unique among the great southern houses of the mid-nineteenth century. Elsewhere the classical portico, so eminently appropriate to life on the plantation, maintained its rule.[40] Nevertheless, there were a few instances where the Gothic was permitted to join with the Greek to form some curious hybrids, and two of these are worth examining briefly.

Staunton Hill in Charlotte County, Virginia, is an impressive building (Fig. 248). Designed by John E. Johnson for Charles Bruce, and built in 1848, it is a severe weighty house executed in what Davis would have called the castellated style. A dominating central three-story block, with corner turrets, is flanked by identical two-story wings. This central pavilion has a large Tudor arched window on the top floor; the other windows are square-headed and double hung, with the upper mullions crossing to form pointed tops. In contrast with this austere, fortress-like symmetrical pile is the more lightly scaled veranda, which stretches across the entire main façade. With its clustered colonnettes and fussy detailing, it is the most Gothic part of the house. Like the building itself, it has three sections: a large central one which corresponds to the three-story block, plus two balancing sections which, like the wings, are carried through at a lower level. The main façade, therefore, is absolutely symmetrical, with a dominating central pavilion, much in the manner of a conventional Greek Revival house. The impression which the house conveys is mixed, with the reasonably authentic and solid Gothic details subdued by the overriding classical massing.

More hybrid, and at the same time more characteristic of the conventional large houses of the deep South, is Errolton in Columbus, Mississippi (Fig. 249). In an unabashed combination of Greek and Gothic forms, which is found elsewhere in the Columbus area, the house has a full colonnade across the front in the manner of a typical ante bellum mansion. Instead of classical columns, however, the main supports are heavy octagonal piers, paneled to look like Gothic clustered colonnettes; the capitals have Gothic rather than Greek profiles. The entablature, which is pure Greek in its detailing, does not rest directly on the capitals. Instead, it is lifted above them by impost blocks, which are interspaced with Tudor arches. The resulting spandrels are filled with lace-like, quasi-Gothic ornament. Because of the rhythmic force of the colonnade and the persistent horizontal of the full entablature, and because of the symmetry and classical proportions throughout the building, the anemic Gothic details are made to participate fully and without concession in what is predominantly a classical scheme.

In the North, in contrast to the South, a restless society in a rapidly expanding urban scene opened the way for more dynamic solutions. We have already seen the results of this in the industrial communities of New England, and in the flowering of the Gothic church and villa. Beyond this world of technology and high profession, the Gothic houses in the North before the Civil War were as heterogeneous, and in many instances as hybrid, as the American churches designed by architects outside the circles of Upjohn and Renwick. After 1840, from Bath, Maine, to Marshall, Michigan, the Gothic house appeared and stood side by side with the Greek temple on the streets of almost every American town. Often built contemporaneously with the Greek, its character varied with location and individual whim, and the Gothic forms were almost always used in a decorative rather than an organic sense. Nevertheless, the Gothic house changed the face of the American town, and shattered forever the simplicity and stylistic coherence of a deeply rooted classical tradition.

The pure Gothic cottage which would be developed by Davis and Downing constitutes a special phase of the domestic Gothic in America, and we will later consider it in detail. Here we are concerned with an adul-

FIGURE 249. *Errolton, Columbus, Miss., c. 1850.*

terated form of the style, for a stubborn classical taste persisted in the
North just as it did in the South, particularly in provincial areas, and
the result was a variety of regional hybrids. The Milan Walter Harris
House, in Harrisville, New Hampshire (Fig. 58), which we have already discussed, is typical, but the Hall-Tosi house in Northfield,
Massachusetts, is more interesting (Fig. 250). It was built about 1846
and like a number of others in the central New England region was designed from the beginning to combine Greek and Gothic forms. Basically,
the house is a Greek temple type with its short end to the street. The pediment is very high in pitch however, and thus seems more like a Gothic
gable, and all the windows are topped by tall pointed arches. Even the
Palladian motif in the gable is crowned by pointed arches. At the same
time, two identical cut-away porches, one on either side at the front of
the house, are supported by Greek Doric columns, correctly proportioned and replete with flutings and a full entablature. Yet there is no con-
ceivable relationship between the heavy scale of these classical inserts,
and the delicate moldings which mark the pointed arches over the windows; nor does the entablature continue across the entire end façade,
which would have completed the thin horizontal line of the closed pediment. Throughout the house, the Greek elements are handled with a far
greater sense of authentic detail than the more primitive Gothic elements,
so that the hybrid form is a matter not only of styles, but of the degree to
which those styles were understood. The Gothic, here, is conspicuously
the awkward newcomer.

FIGURE 250. *Hall-Tosi House,*
Northfield, Mass., c. 1846.

An even more outrageous mixture of Gothic and classical forms is
found in one of the most famous and also one of the finest examples of the
provincial Gothic Revival in America, the Wedding Cake House at Kennebunk Landing, Maine (Fig. 251). Built in 1826 by George W.
Bourne, a Kennebunk ship builder, it was originally a conventional but
very elegant Federal style house with a superb elliptical fanlight over the
central door and an equally fine Palladian window above it on the second
floor (Fig. 252). The house is brick, painted yellow, with stone lintels
over the windows, and a classical balustrade. All of this can still be seen
beneath the semi-transparent skin of Gothic ornament which Bourne
himself later applied to his house. The bizarre transformation began early
in the 1850's, when Bourne redecorated his barn with Gothic detail (Fig.
253). This pleased him so much that in 1855 he also gave his house a
new suit of Gothic clothes. The results are charmingly naive. Though it
fits snugly, and divides the house logically into vertical and horizontal
components, the Gothic ornament has absolutely nothing to do stylistically with the original house; nor does it pretend to, and perhaps this is
what is so disarming and attractive about it. To be sure, the delicate
Gothic interlace does have an empathy with the elegant linear character
of the Neoclassical ornament, but in terms of style each shuns the other
with almost arrogant indifference.

FIGURE 251. *Wedding Cake House, Kennebunk Landing, Me., 1826,*
Gothic detailing added in 1855.

FIGURE 252. *Wedding Cake House,*
Kennebunk Landing, Me., 1826;
main entrance with Gothic
detailing added in 1855.

FIGURE 253. *Wedding Cake House,*
Kennebunk Landing, Me.,
barn and pump house, 1850's.

The American architect Leopold Eidlitz once defined American architecture as "the art of covering one thing with another thing to imitate a third thing, which, even if genuine, would not be desirable." In one sense, Eidlitz's cynical view aptly fits the Wedding Cake House, and hundreds of others like it throughout the land. But what it overlooks is the utter innocence with which folk architecture is conceived and executed. In fact, the Wedding Cake House is perhaps one of the earliest and most dramatic examples in this country of the impact not of style but of fashion on architecture. George Bourne brought his house up to date simply by applying to it all the visual paraphernalia of the new and fashionable Gothic. Moreover, in cutting and carving much of the ornamental detailing himself, he gave it a special individual flavor. The house, therefore, is an eloquent testimonial to the aggressive independence of the average American seeking to keep up to date. As architecture, the Gothic barn comes off better than the house, both because it is simpler and because it is wood applied to wood. The house, on the other hand, consists of a wooden lace garment wrapped around a brick building, with no attempt whatever to integrate the two. Reassuring in its utter frankness, and in its own way joyously beautiful in detail, it is a masterpiece of folk architecture, and a superb document of the changing popular taste of America in mid-century.

PART III

HOUSES
FOR THE MIDDLE CLASS

Davis, Downing, and the Cottage

With all the pleasure and good humor to be had from the Wedding Cake House, such architectural fantasies, and there were many others like it, did not represent the mainstream of American domestic architecture during the first half of the nineteenth century. Nor, for that matter, did the elitest villa, although the villa did speak, and very eloquently, for the nation's growing ambitions. On the contrary, that development which touched the lives of the greatest number of Americans, and had the greatest impact on the architectural character of the nation, was the cottage. During the colonial years a single basic form, the simple rectangular block, had served for all houses, large and small. In the late 1830's, however, a specific kind of house, the cottage, designed to function for the ever-growing middle segment of American society, appeared in this country for the first time.

The cottage, of course, was not an American invention, nor did those responsible for its development ever claim that it was. English architectural publications from the 1820's onward, such as Robinson's *Rural Architecture,* published in London in 1823, are filled with examples of such cottages (Fig. 254). It was these books which provided the essential information for the American cottage builders. On the other hand, the cottage, as even the English were aware, was a house form that was particularly appropriate to the United States, and it was the Americans who tapped its potential and made it a national type.

The first American architect to see the possibilities of the English cottage as appropriate to life in his own country was A. J. Davis; the first articulation of the idea in architectural form was the Blithewood gatehouse. Although this tiny building was intended for a specific function rather than general use, Davis was clearly aware in his design of the enormous potential which the cottage form held, and when he published the Blithewood gatehouse in *Rural Residences* in 1837 he identified the building as one in "the rustic cottage style."

He states his case in the Preface:

The bald and uninteresting aspects of our houses must be obvious to every traveler; and to those who are familiar with the picturesque Cottages and Villas of England, it is positively painful to witness here the wasteful and tasteless expenditure of money in building.

Defects are felt, however, not only in the style of the house but in the want of connection with its site.

FIGURE 254. *Design for a cottage by P. F. Robinson, 1823.*

We have already seen Davis's lively response to these ideas in his intelligent and impassioned development of the Gothic villa, and his feelings with respect to the cottage were no less strong. The very fact that he chose to illustrate and describe a house that in the larger world of architectural ambition would seem of no consequence indicates both his awareness of an urgent need and his deep conviction that something should be done about it. Although the purpose for which he proposes the cottage in *Rural Residences* is specific on the one hand, and rather vague on the other, he does list what he thinks to be the prominent features of the style. They are, he says, "the rustic porch, bay, and mullioned windows, high gables, with ornamental carved verge-boards, and the chimney-shafts." All of these are features which give the cottage its picturesque vitality and help to integrate it into the landscape. To aid in this he also proposes board-and-batten construction.

In carrying out his ideas Davis did not stop with the Blithewood gatehouse, nor with its publication in *Rural Residences*. He began at once to design and build other small houses in the cottage style, and to develop the original scheme into one of more substance, particularly "by enlarging the porch and windows." In this way, he quickly arrived at a form of modest dwelling which, with subtle and individual variations, became ubiquitous throughout the United States except in the South, and even there an occasional example could be found. By the time he met Downing, the concept of the cottage was a crystallized fact. For that matter, one of the earliest cottages designed by Davis, the Sheldon

House in Tarrytown, New York, would be illustrated by Downing in the first edition (1841) of his *Treatise* as an outstanding example of the type (Fig. 255).

What Davis achieved in his own designs became the primary source for Downing's theory of the cottage. In his *Treatise* he discusses in general terms the "English cottage style," which he calls "rural Gothic," and like Davis, he points to such features as high gables, chimney stacks, and verandas as characteristic of the mode. It is not, however, until his *Architecture of Country Houses,* in a full section entitled "What a Cottage Should Be," that he develops in detail his concept of the form. There his primary definition is functional and clearly directed toward the average American.

> What we mean by a cottage in this country, is a dwelling of small size, intended for the occupation of a family, either wholly managing the household cares itself, or, at the most, with the assistance of one or two servants. The majority of such cottages in this country are occupied, not by tenants, dependents, or serfs, as in many parts of Europe, but by industrious and intelligent mechanics and workingmen, the bone and sinew of the land, who own the ground upon which they stand, build them for their own use, and arrange them to satisfy their own peculiar wants and gratify their own tastes.[41]

In these lines by Downing a special architectural type—conceived and developed by Davis—became identified with, and expressive of, the core of American democratic society. This was the first time in American architectural literature that such a notion was so emphatically proclaimed.

But Downing also had some specific things to say about the character of the cottage. He pleads first for simplicity, stating that it ought "to pervade every portion of cottage architecture. . . . There should be . . . simplicity of arrangement . . . simplicity of construction . . . simplicity of decoration." Indeed, the cottage "should avoid all pretention to what it cannot honestly and faithfully be." He then makes an extremely significant observation:

> Regularity, uniformity, proportion, symmetry, are beauties of which every cottage is capable, because they are entirely consistent with the simple forms of the cottage, while irregularity and variety are usually possible, with good effect, in a dwelling of larger size, and consisting of a great number of parts. Small cottages can scarcely be very irregular in form and outline, unless they are built in highly picturesque situations, such as a mountain valley, or a wooded glen, when they form part of the irregular whole about them, rather than single objects, as is usually the case.

This tells us why, rather than having the irregularity of the villa, the American cottages, both as designed by Davis and as recommended by Downing, were symmetrical buildings. Because they were small they did not lend themselves in a practical sense to irregular arrangements. Their picturesque appeal had to come from other aspects of their form:

When the means of the builder enable him to go beyond these simple beauties of form, his first thought, on elevating the expression of the cottage, should be to add ornament to the most important parts of the dwelling. These are the entrance door, the principal windows, the gables, and the chimneys. The front door and the principal or first floor windows should be recognized as something more than mere openings, by lintels, hoods, or borders (dressings); the gables by being very simply moulded or bracketed about the junction of the roof; the chimneys, by a pleasing form or simple ornaments, or merely by having the usual clumsy mass lightened and separated into parts.

After this, the next step is to add something to the expression of domestic enjoyment in cottage life—such as a simple porch, or veranda, or simple bay window.

Finally, as in the case of the villa, Downing made clear that the cottage must always be thought of in relation to its natural setting. "The effect of Rural Architecture is never a thing to be considered wholly by itself, but, on the contrary, as it always depends partly upon, and is associated with, rural scenery."

In his definition of the cottage, Downing sees it as distinct from the villa in that it serves the average workingman rather than the man of wealth and privilege. This, of course, is a social distinction which to modern ears has an anti-democratic ring, and because of his views Downing has, with some justification, been called a reactionary. But Downing was facing the realities of the society which he saw taking shape around him, and was trying within the limits of his available means to find solutions that were sufficiently flexible to accommodate them. It is certainly true that he identified himself, intellectually and emotionally, and perhaps even financially, with the men who built the villas—the Donaldsons, the DeWitts, the Pauldings, the Verplancks—but the fact that he was concerned at all about the ordinary American, and sought to open his eyes to the grace and wonder of the world around him, makes Downing a man of vision in his day. To him the cottage differed from the villa only in the restraints that were imposed upon it by the more modest means of its owner. It was still an object susceptible to the same principles of excellence as the larger houses. "I am still more anxious," he wrote, "to inspire in the minds of my readers and countrymen livelier perception of the BEAUTIFUL in everything that relates to our houses and grounds. I wish to awaken a quicker sense of the grace, the elegance, or the picturesqueness of fine forms that are capable of being produced in these by Rural Architecture and Landscape Gardening—a sense which will not only refine and elevate the mind, but open to it new and infinite resources of delight."[42]

The Gothic Cottages
of Alexander Jackson Davis

Davis shared Downing's idealism. Although he was impetuous and irascible as compared to the gentle and well-mannered Downing, he was no less sensitive and he treated the problem of the cottage with the same dedication and purpose that he gave to the great villas. No other American architect of his time served so wide a segment of American society, nor did it with the same ferocity of purpose. The evidence of the scope of his work is all in his various journals and drawings. The number of cottages designed by him which still survive is in itself remarkable, and makes it possible for us to understand as no other evidence could the sheer creative force of the man. With this in mind we will examine three of his cottages in some detail. To see them in proper relationship with the entire body of Davis's work, however, we must go back briefly to the Blithewood gatehouse, and examine its immediate impact on both the work of Downing and that of Davis himself.

Subsequent to the actual building of the Blithewood gatehouse, and its publication in *Rural Residences,* Davis seems to have started at once to develop what he had tentatively conceived at Blithewood into a firm and workable architectural form, the cottage. In considering that form, we must emphasize again that neither Davis nor Downing ever claimed to have been its inventor. Their sources in English architectural literature are obvious; both men were frank to admit them, even to call attention to them. The important point is not so much where they got their ideas as what they did with them to make them function in relation to American society and the American scene. The evidence makes it clear that Davis arrived very quickly at firm solutions. The basic cruciform scheme introduced at Blithewood was enlarged and strengthened, with much greater emphasis on bold projection; and because of the smaller size of the cottage, and the difficulty of composing asymmetrically with the limited number of workable units, a symmetrical arrangement became the rule. Gables and gabled dormers, all open at the base were increased in pitch and strengthened by carefully designed tracery-like ornament. Dynamic spatial elements, such as bay windows, oriels and chimney stacks, added essential elements of movement and irregularity, and above all the veranda became the primary link between the house and its surroundings. For those houses made of wood, the board-and-batten siding animated the surface, gave the design a lively verticality, and added a refined note of scale that was in keeping with the smaller and more delicate increments of the natural environment.

That all of this had materialized for Davis by 1840, before Downing published his *Treatise,* is made clear by "Millbrook" (Fig. 255), which was designed by Davis in the late '30's for Henry Sheldon. It was built in Tarrytown, New York, not far from where Davis was working at Paulding's Knoll. The house was illustrated by Downing in his *Treatise,* along with the Blithewood gatehouse. Together they became the first visual

"MILLBROOK," RESIDENCE OF HENRY SHELDON, Esq.

DAVIS, ARCH.

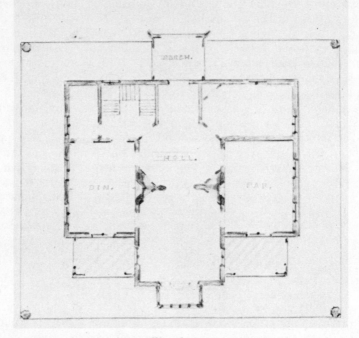

FIGURE 255. A. J. Davis. Millbrook, Tarrytown, N.Y.,
late 1830's. Old engraving with plan added by the architect.

presentation of the American cottage, a concept which Downing would
define with some care, and which Davis would make one of the specialties
of his work. Davis was called upon to design a considerable number of
cottages in the '40's, especially after the publication of "Millbrook" by
Downing, and three of them in particular, because they survive with so little change, provide us with a revealing picture of the variety and sureness
of Davis's treatment of the theme.

FIGURE 256. *A. J. Davis. Rotch House, New Bedford, Mass., 1845.*

The Rotch House,
New Bedford, Massachusetts

One of the best-known and surely one of the finest of its type is the Rotch House in New Bedford, Massachusetts. It was designed early in 1845 for William J. Rotch. The date is confirmed by an entry in Davis's office book made on May 20 of that year, which shows a small plan and elevation, and lists the drawings which the architect submitted for the project (Fig. 170). Five years later it was illustrated and described by Downing in *Architecture of Country Houses.* The caption called it a "Cottage-Villa in the Rural Gothic Style" (Fig. 256). It is interesting that Downing, perhaps even after discussion with Davis, was equivocal as to whether this house was a cottage or a villa. On the one hand it was larger than he would have liked for a cottage "with strong aspirations after something higher than social pleasures." At the same time, it was a masterpiece of the cottage form. In the first place, the house is absolutely symmetrical. The plan, therefore, is extremely efficient, with room balancing room around a central hall (Fig. 258); and Davis's original elevation (Fig. 257),[43] rendered without any landscape references, confirms the unyielding balance. Yet the house is remarkable in its picturesque animation. As Downing points out in his description, "the high pointed gable . . . has a bold and spirited effect," which is intensified by "the equally bold manner in which the chimney tops spring upwards." Unfortunately, Davis's original clustered stacks have been rebuilt as single chimneys, thus changing their scale and robbing them of their lightness and elegance. The house was in-

FIGURE 257. A. J. Davis. Rotch House, New Bedford, Mass., 1845.
Original water-color drawing.

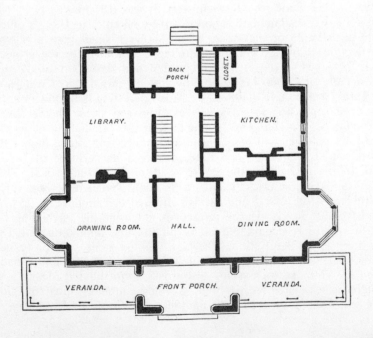

FIGURE 258. A. J. Davis. Rotch House, New Bedford, Mass.,
plan of the principal floor, 1845.

FIGURE 259. A. J. Davis. Rotch House, New Bedford, Mass., 1845.

FIGURE 260. A. J. Davis. Rotch House, New Bedford, Mass., hall, 1845.

FIGURE 261. *A. J. Davis. Rotch House, New Bedford, Mass., living room, 1845.*

FIGURE 262. *A. J. Davis. Rotch House, New Bedford, Mass., into library from living room, 1845.*

tended to be built in stone, but was actually carried out in matched boards, painted a stone color. Seen in the sunlight (Fig. 259), as Davis conceived it in his drawing the façade with its splendid verge board and elegant veranda is one of the dramatic climaxes in Davis's cottage work, and a memorable moment in the American Gothic Revival.

Another imaginative touch in the Rotch house, which is characteristic of a number of Davis cottages, is the interpenetration of the veranda and porch. Just as at Knoll, the original porch was open on all three sides. This permitted movement through the frontal arched opening toward the main door to the hall within; at the same time, the space of the veranda passed easily through the porch in a right-angle direction. Inside the hall (Fig. 260), the symmetry of the house asserts itself in the placement of identical motifs on either side of the entrance door, with the Gothic molding and details kept extremely simple though elegant and light in scale.

In spite of their symmetrical arrangement the interior spaces also have their dynamic interest. The movement in the living room, for example, from larger space into the crystal splendor of the all-glass bay window (Fig. 261), or that from the living room into the more quiet bay of the library (Fig. 262), adds a welcome excitement to what could otherwise have been a coldly static interior. The effect is a discreet combination of vitality and restraint, which conveys with uninhibited directness both the conservatism and aggressiveness of William Rotch and his times. Today the house belongs to descendants of the original owner; appreciative of nineteenth-century architecture, they are keeping the house alive as it was originally conceived by Davis in 1845.

The Wood House, Mount Kisco, New York

Similar in its high gabled vertical massing and symmetrical arrangement, but smaller in size and more limited in intent, is the Wood House in Mount Kisco, New York (Fig. 263). Known as "Bramblewood," it was designed in 1846, and was built largely by Wood himself.[44] Davis's drawings, three elevations and a plan, still survive and are in the possession of the present owner; they show that except for an addition to the rear, the exterior of the original house is virtually unchanged. The existing house followed almost exactly Davis's drawing (Fig. 264). It is a simple rectangle, one story high with a steep hipped roof. It is oriented with its long dimension parallel to the street and an open gable penetrates the roof at each end. Cutting through at right angles, from front to rear and on center, is a bold projecting mass with a steeply pitched roof. It is 10 feet higher than the lateral roof of the house and is gabled at both ends. The system of roof planes, therefore, although symmetrical is extremely complex, with pitched and hipped roofs intersecting at three different levels. Over the crossing a clustered chimney stack rises another 9 feet into the air.

FIGURE 263. *A. J. Davis. Wood House, Mount Kisco, N.Y., 1846.*

FIGURE 264. *A. J. Davis. Wood House, Mount Kisco, N.Y., 1846.*
Original drawing.

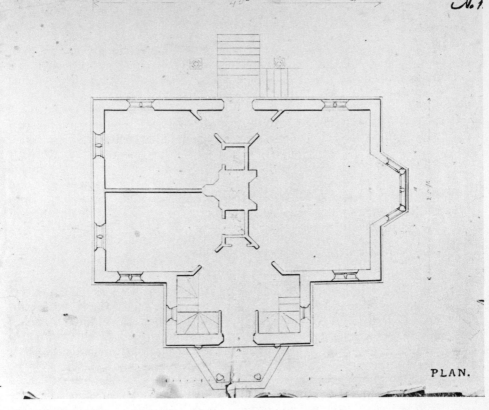

PLAN.

FIGURE 265. *A. J. Davis. Wood House, Mount Kisco, N.Y.,
original plan, 1846.*

In contrast to the Rotch House, Bramblewood is made of a gray local stone laid up in random ashlar. Heavy stone sills and uncarved hood moldings articulate the windows and a three-sided porch, with Tudor arches between the posts, is centered beneath the steep gable. Except for a hint of tracery in the spandrels of the porch, the only other ornament on the building is the bold flowing pattern of the verge board. With its filigree of Gothic cusps, it hangs like a strip of lace in sharp contrast with both the rough texture of the masonry and the baldness of the hood moldings which break in decisive steps over the four-part central window.

As a result of later alterations the interior deviates from Davis's original plan (Fig. 265) in two significant ways: the winding stairs which went down into the cellar from just to the right of the main door have been eliminated; the partition which once separated the two rooms to the left of the entrance hall has been removed, thus creating one large room, which is now used as a dining room. This makes the dining room and the original living room identical in shape, except that the living room has a bay window. The latter is the only serious concession to asymmetry in the house. The space in both the main rooms on the first floor is livened by the fact that the doors through which entrance is gained to the front and rear halls are cut into walls which are set at 45-degree angles (Fig. 265).

This makes all the rooms polygonal rather than rectangular, and most noticeably so in the living room, where the diagonal interior walls are imitated in the diagonal sides of the bay windows. Against this dynamic handling of the space, ornamental enrichment occurs only in the delicate turnings of the balustrade of the main staircase, and in the grained black marble Tudor fireplace (Fig. 266). Elsewhere, the moldings of the cornice and the door surrounds have simple profiles. Altogether the house conveys a sense of restrained energy both inside and out; the simplicity imposed by convenience and limited means is brought alive by the innate vitality of the Gothic forms. "Bramblewood" must surely have been one of the most successful of Davis's small cottages, and must have been regarded by Downing as a superb example of precisely what he thought the cottage should be.

The Delamater House, Rhinebeck, New York

The third example, which relates to Downing as well as Davis, is the Delamater House in Rhinebeck, New York (Fig. 267). Davis did several houses in Rhinebeck in the early 1840's, and of these the Delamater House, designed in 1843, is by far the most important. This is so for two reasons. First, owing to the specific nature of its design, it is the one cottage by Davis through which we can enlarge our understanding of the relationship between him and Downing. Second, it is a board-and-batten house, and thus provides an unusually fine example of Downing's theories with respect to structure and form.

One of the most intriguing questions to come out of the Davis-Downing association is the degree of influence that the two men had on one another. It is certainly obvious that the primary sources of architectural ideas for Downing were the English architectural literature on the one hand, especially the writing of Loudon, and the work of A. J. Davis on the other. What Loudon provided in the way of theoretical doctrine was given flesh and bones by Davis. It was Davis who provided the living data for both the villa and the cottage, and he made that data available to Downing for the preparation of his books. The two men corresponded and talked with one another and it is apparent that they saw things in very much the same terms. It is inconceivable, therefore, that the determined and persuasive Downing should not also have left his mark on Davis, and the Delamater House is fascinating proof that indeed he did.

In a letter written to Davis on March 16, 1842, Downing presented a design for what he called an "English cottage" which he intended to include in his forthcoming book *Cottage Residences*.[45] He included a sketch of the house, along with plans and a detail of the porch and veranda (Fig. 268). There is nothing in this sketch which had not already been carried out by Davis in numerous villas and cottages that he had designed and built; nothing, that is, except the specific arrangement of the parts. In this respect, the most intriguing thing about Downing's proposal is his articulation of the porch, which he shows in detail. Instead of an arcaded porch such as that which Davis had already used at Knoll, Downing had

FIGURE 266. A. J. Davis. Wood House,
Mount Kisco, N.Y., living room, 1846.

FIGURE 267. A. J. Davis. Delamater House,
Rhinebeck, N.Y., 1843.

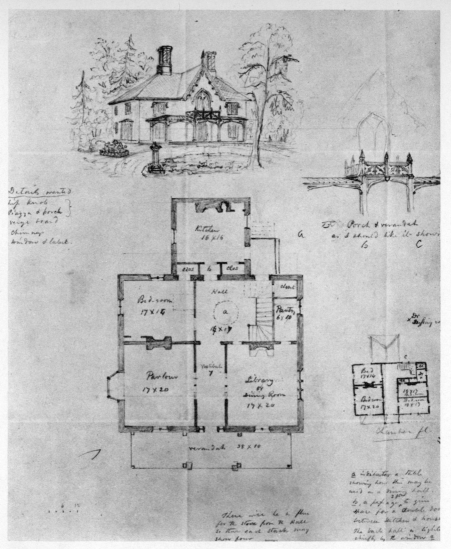

FIGURE 268. A. J. Downing.
Sketch and plans for English Cottage, 1842.

sketched a wooden frame technique, raising it above the level of the veranda, and giving it an open lattice parapet. In his letter, he asked
Davis to draw the design on the block for the illustration. This he did,
following very carefully Downing's scheme, even to the surrounding
landscape. At the same time he refined the details (Fig. 269).

It is precisely this form of the cottage, as it appears in the Downing illustration, which Davis used for the Delamater House (compare Figs.
267 and 269). He seems to have added only two touches of his own, but
they are important ones: he raised the central gable to a more dramatic
height, and he added a bay window to the library, a modification which
balanced the bay in the parlour thereby strengthening the symmetry of the
over-all design. The Gothic details, on the other hand, are derived
from those suggested in Downing's original sketch. In keeping with the

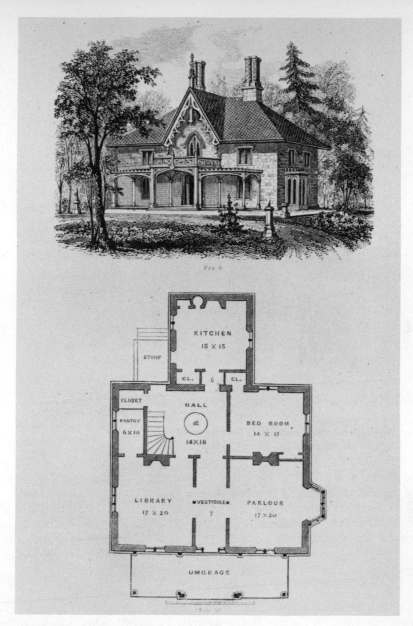

FIGURE 269. *Design for a cottage by Davis.*

more delicate scale imposed by the board-and-batten siding, they are much lighter and more intricate than those which we have seen in the Rotch House.

The plan of the house is also similar to that published by Downing. In spite of the splendid Gothic exterior, however, the detailing on the inside of the house is rather simple and entirely Greek. Although such a mixture of styles was not unusual during the period, or sometimes even in the work of Davis himself, it seems incongruous here and was not designed by Davis. All the major rooms are crowned by deep Greek en-

FIGURE 270. A. J. Davis.
Delamater House, Rhinebeck, N.Y.,
window viewed from interior, 1843.

tablatures, and all the trim is Greek, with the characteristic dog ears at
the corners of door and window frames (Fig. 270). The only concession
to the Gothic exterior is the slightly pitched headers over the doors and
windows which coincide, in basic profile, with the Tudor-arched windows on the outside.

Downing
and Board-and-Batten Construction

The most significant deviation from Downing's illustration is that Davis
constructed the Delamater House entirely of wood, using board-and-batten siding. Downing's illustration shows the house in stone, and we will
discuss this in detail below. But Davis's pragmatic and highly effective use
of this type of wood siding impressed Downing and helped stimulate his
own views on its nature and appropriate use. By 1850, eight years after
the Delamater House was built, Downing's ideas on board-and-batten
were fully developed, and his presentation of them in his book *The Architecture of Country Houses* is of immense importance. In that publication he has a section given over to materials and modes of construction,
which is a fascinating account of those familiar to him. His discussion of
what he calls "vertical boarding" is as follows:

There are two modes of constructing the exteriors of wooden houses, now generally practiced. The most common mode is that of covering the frame on the outside with boards or narrow siding in horizontal strips; the other is, to cover it with boards nailed on in vertical strips (up and down). In the *horizontal boarding,* the weather is kept out of the joint by the upper board overlapping the under one; in the *vertical boarding,* it is kept out by a narrow strip, called a *batten,* about two inches wide, which is nailed over the joint formed by the meeting of the two boards. . . .

We greatly prefer the vertical to the horizontal boarding, not only because it is more durable, but because it has an expression of strength and truthfulness which the other has not. The main timbers which enter into the frame of a wooden house and support the structure, are vertical, and hence the vertical boarding properly signifies to the eye a wooden house; in the same manner, the main weight of a stone or brick house is supported by walls laid in courses, and hence the truthfulness of showing horizontal courses in brick or stone buildings. It is as incorrect, so far as regards truthfulness of construction, to show horizontal lines on the weatherboarding of a wooden house, as it would be to mark vertical lines on the outside of a brick or stuccoed wall.[46]

This particular passage in Downing has been widely discussed and pointed out for its remarkable insights into the nature of material and form in architecture.[47] The idea that every material should be used in such a way as best to express itself was not new to Downing nor, for that matter, was it new to American architectural literature. We remember that Arthur Gilman, in his evaluation of Upjohn's Trinity Church in New York, objected strenuously to its plaster vaults, and there were other instances of such observations before Downing's *Architecture of Country Houses.* But Downing was certainly the first critic to be so specific in defining the relationship between a structural method and the visual effect it creates; and on the basis of his reasoning he was also the first to challenge the horizontal clapboard, which was not only universally accepted but had been in use in this country since early colonial times. Neither Davis nor Downing invented vertical siding, but Davis was the first American architect to use and define it. He was also the first to exploit it, not only because it was practical and expressive of itself, but also because its visual qualities made it more in keeping with the vertical emphasis of the Gothic style. What Davis made workable and meaningful in his actual buildings, Downing developed into a persuasive doctrine which he then delivered with sufficient breadth and impact to change the whole course of American architecture.

Downing's sensitivity for materials did not stop with the self-expressiveness of board-and-batten. He was also aware of its aesthetic qualities. "There is not only greater economy in vertical boarding," he wrote, "but, being a bolder mode of construction, it better expresses the picturesque—a kind of beauty essentially belonging to wooden houses."[48] More than that, Downing was convinced that the use of material should be truthful. "The principle which the reason would lay down for the government of the architect . . . is the simple and obvious one, that the material should *appear* to be what it is. To build a house of wood so exactly in imitation of stone as to lead the spectator to suppose it stone, is a paltry artifice, at variance with all truthfulness.

"When we employ stone as a building material, let it be clearly expressed: when we employ wood, there should be no less frankness in avowing the material."[49]

Downing's response to materials was also highly pictorial, taking into consideration not only the integument and texture of a structure but also its color.

> The *color* of buildings may very properly be made to increase their expression of truthfulness. Thus a barn or stable, being regarded entirely in a useful point of view, may have a quiet, unobtrusive tone of color, while a cottage or villa should be a cheerful, mellow hue harmonizing with the verdure of the country. A mansion may very properly have a graver color than a cottage, to be in unison with its greater dignity and extent. There is one color, however, frequently employed by house painters, which we feel bound to protest against most heartily, as entirely unsuitable and in bad taste. This is *white,* which is so universally applied to our wooden houses of every size and description. The glaring nature of this color, when seen in contrast with the soft green of foliage, renders it extremely unpleasant to an eye attuned to harmony of coloring . . . buildings introduced by the great masters have uniformly a mellow softened shade of color, in exquisite keeping with the surrounding objects.
> . . . drab or fawn color, . . . will be found pleasing and harmonious in any situation in the country.[50]

Downing's aversion to white and his predilection for colors that would harmonize with nature is one of the keys to the taste of the period. Although Neoclassical doctrine would never completely die out in this country, and white would always be favored by those with classical taste, by mid-century the picturesque preference for warm dark colors had impressed a new tonality on the architectural face of America, a tonality which would dominate the second half of the century and lead Lewis Mumford to characterize the period as *The Brown Decades.*[51] This development will be discussed in depth at a later point. As a matter of historical interest, it is worth noting now that under the influence of the academic classicism which swept American architecture at the turn of the twentieth century, many of the mid-nineteenth-century houses which had originally been painted in the rich colors prescribed by Downing were sterilized and rendered clean by dense coats of fresh white paint. Many that survive are still that way today, and stand in embarrassing nakedness, stripped of their original vitality and warmth.

FIGURE 271. *Queset, Oakes Angier Ames House,*
North Easton, Mass., 1854.

The Permeation of the Davis-Downing Cottage

Along with the picturesque aesthetic doctrine which Downing proposed, he also offered his readers specific examples of a vital new concept of the house. The cottage as he defined it was both suitable and appealing to an aggressive middle-class society. More than that, as the country expanded westward and settlements became towns the demand for new houses increased accordingly. Downing's books, therefore, through many editions, fell into the eager hands of a people on the move and the impact of these works was felt not only in the old and established regions of the country, but also in the most remote parts of the newly settled lands.

In many instances the cottages that were built followed the Downing plates very closely, even to the use of materials. One of the finest is Queset in North Easton, Massachusetts (Fig. 271). It was built in 1854 for Oakes Angier Ames by an unknown architect. The building has been considerably added to over the years, and except for the main stairway the interior has been almost completely changed. On the exterior, however, the front part of the house still retains much of its original character.

The source for Queset was obviously the design in Downing's *Cottage Residences* (Fig. 269) for which Davis made the drawing and which he later used as the model for the Delamater House in Rhinebeck. At Queset, however, the builder adhered even more closely to Downing's

FIGURE 272. *Queset,*
Oakes Angier Ames House,
North Easton, Mass.,
main staircase, 1854.

intentions by constructing the house of stone rather than wood. He used a local granite that is warm pink in tone and has variegated patterns of rust color formed by filtrations of iron oxide. It is laid in rock-faced random ashlar with dressed quoins of gray granite bonding the corners; the door and window openings on the first floor are also of gray granite. On the second floor, the openings are framed in brick, but were originally covered with stucco. Generally, the treatment of all the openings is simpler than that in Downing's illustration: the hood moldings shown by the author are eliminated, and the clean-cut door and window surrounds are held flush with the wall. The wooden verge board, on the other hand, is more lightly scaled and more lace-like than Downing's, although the flat arches and clustered colonnettes of the veranda structure are virtually identical. In its present state the veranda differs from Downing's in that its central section, namely the porch, has no parapet. The effect is unfinished and awkward, particularly so in the central section, which, because it has no crown molding, looks truncated. This suggests the strong probability that there was once a parapet over the porch, as there is in the Delamater House, but that it has since deteriorated and been removed.

Queset is a classic Downing type house. It has the prescribed shape and massing; it is built of a colorful stone which has been permitted to assert its true nature; its veranda is lightly scaled in a manner consistent with its wooden structure and is painted a soft brown to harmonize with the stone; and the setting is park-like and picturesque.[52] Altogether, there were not many Gothic cottages built in this country during the middle years of the century which conformed more happily to Downing's prescription. At

FIGURE 273. *Surgeon's Quarters, The Dalles, Ore., 1857.*

the same time, Queset has certain very special qualities which provoke the tantalizing notion that Davis may have been involved. Although there is not a single reference to the house in the Davis papers, the building has a solidity and authority, especially in the handling of details, that are strongly reminiscent of his work. This is apparent not only on the outside, but also in the one fragment of the original interior which still survives, the main staircase (Fig. 272). Here the bold scale and fine detailing suggest something other than a pattern-book origin. But whether it was designed by Davis or not, Queset is an unusually impressive house which established the picturesque firmly in North Easton as a prelude to the dramatic decade of the late 1870's and early 1880's when the gigantic figures of Henry Hobson Richardson and Frederick Law Olmsted would transform the town.

In 1850, when Downing first published his *Architecture of Country Houses,* Fort Dalles on the Columbia River in Oregon was a newly established outpost in the northwestern frontier. Yet seven years later, when the original log cabins and tents of the fort were replaced by buildings of sawed lumber, a copy of Downing's book seems to have made its way into the area. The Surgeon's Quarters (Fig. 273), built in 1857 by Louis Scholl, comes directly from a plate in *The Architecture of Country Houses* (Fig. 274). As in the case of Queset, the builder followed the Downing model with great care. From the center of the main block of the

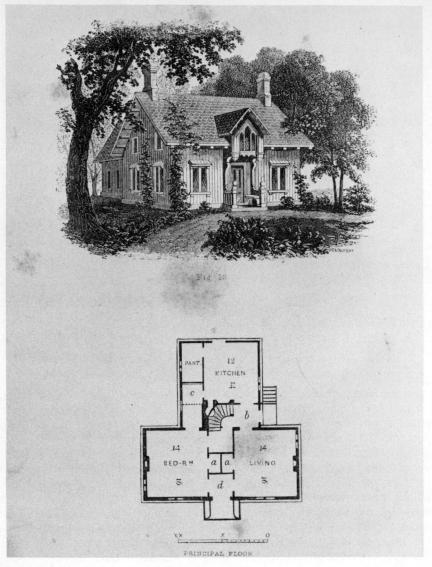

FIGURE 274. *Design for a cottage by Downing.*

house, a second-story pavilion projects boldly on supporting brackets to form a shelter over the main entrance door; beneath the deep gable of this pavilion is a pointed compound window, consisting of a tall central light and two shorter side lights. On the first floor, balancing left and right of the central door, are identical bay windows, each hooded by a short sloping and bracketed roof. The construction of the house is board-and-batten. There are, to be sure, a few interesting differences between the Surgeon's Quarters and the plate from which it derives. In the house the

FIGURE 275. *Joseph C. Wells, Roseland Cottage, Woodstock, Conn., from the southeast, 1846.*

brackets holding the pavilion have been simplified, and those which appear under the eaves and on the gables in the illustration have been eliminated altogether. Moreover, because of the sloping site, the porch is approached by a long flight of steps while the main door, with its pointed headers and side lights, is more elaborate than the one shown by Downing. Otherwise the similarities between the two are obvious. Such a detail as the continuation of the wall batten pattern onto the sloping roofs of the bay windows leaves no question that Downing's model cottage was the source for the Oregon builder. But whatever the relationship between the house and Downing's book might be, the remarkable fact about the Surgeon's Quarters is that there was someone in that remote outpost who knew enough about the Hudson River critic to turn to him for help.

Queset and the Surgeon's Quarters in The Dalles can be taken as typical of the scores of houses built in this country during the mid-nineteenth century which were directly inspired by specific illustrations in Downing's books. In addition, there were a considerable number of houses, designed by known architects, which showed the influence of Downing but were not directly derived from his books. Of these, one of the finest survivors is Roseland Cottage in Woodstock, Connecticut (Fig. 275). Designed in 1846 by Joseph C. Wells as a summer residence for Henry C.

FIGURE 276. *Joseph C. Wells. Roseland Cottage,
Woodstock, Conn., east façade, 1846.*

Bowen of Brooklyn, New York, it is a house of unusual architectural interest. It is preserved virtually intact, including the outbuildings, gardens, and fences, and it still retains its original pink wall color with dark red trim. The architect's plans and specifications also survive. At the same time, the house has important historical associations. Bowen was a prominent silk merchant who gained special renown as the publisher of the *Independent,* a weekly journal with strong anti-slavery leanings. He was also a man with powerful political connections and it is recorded that during his occupancy of the cottage its exotic pink walls were privileged to shelter four Republican Presidents of the United States. The house is now owned by The Society for the Preservation of New England Antiquities and is open to the public during the summer months.

Specific examination of the architectural features of Roseland Cottage reveals at once the importance of both Davis and Downing in its conception. The east end, facing the street (Fig. 276), is a characteristic cottage façade, having a prominent central pavilion flanked by verandas on either side. The scheme is symmetrical, although extremely vertical in proportion with a steep open gable and carved verge boards as the crowning motif. In a manner similar to Davis's treatment of the south wing at Knoll, particularly as published by Downing (Fig. 223), smaller ornamental gables break the eave lines above each of the second-story windows. In the pavilion itself, the second-floor window is an aggressive octagonal oriel crowned by a Gothic fleur-de-lis; on the first floor is a broad full-length window of Perpendicular design which, on the inside of the

FIGURE 277. Joseph C. Wells.
Roseland Cottage, Woodstock, Conn.,
interior window, 1846.

pavilion, runs from floor to ceiling (Fig. 277) and extends across the entire width of the room. The verandas, which are short, are carried on
trellises ornamented with quatrefoil tracery, and are crowned by a running
crest of fleur-de-lis.

On the south side of Roseland Cottage, which is the main façade (Fig.
275), the dominating feature is a projecting vestibule. Extending in a
continuous line with the top of this unit is a deep bracketed hood which
shelters the main entrance door and reaches sufficiently toward the drive-
way to form a small porte-cochère. This is an unusual feature, vigorous
in its outward thrust, awkward and tenuously poised in its radical unsupported extension into space. This unbalanced projection, however, is
the mainspring for the animated, perhaps even fussy, nature of the
over-all design. There are many small lively parts to the house—the repe-
titious open gables, the fleur-de-lis crests, the traceried trelliswork,
the bays, the oriels, the varied windows, the hoods, the pinnacles—
all etched sharply against sky and house by the strong contrasts of the
pink walls and the red trim. Where both Downing and Davis in their work
plead for harmonious, organic relationships, Roseland's multiple components stand in sparkling isolation, each reveling in its own decorative
lace, the whole animated by the rapid linear accents of the board-and-
batten siding. Although the sources of Roseland Cottage are conspicuous, it is an original and joyous house, singing of its independence in
a brilliant convoluted line against the subdued tones and slower rhythms
of the gentle Connecticut countryside.

Amid the proliferation of the Davis-Downing cottage forms, Roseland proclaimed its individuality, as did numerous other architect-designed houses of the period. The personal touch of each designer made each cottage a unique structure, and together these professionals brought new levels of variety and excitement to the growing heterogeneity of domestic architecture in rural and suburban America. By far the most numerous and varied of the Downing-inspired cottages were those built by the local carpenter working with Downing's books but vitalizing what he found there through his own special skills and preferences. Here all the personal and regional idiosyncracies of the folk artist had free play. The theoretical concerns of men like Downing and Davis—for the cottage as an architectural object and for the picturesque as an aesthetic mode of expression —gave way to the uninhibited outpouring of the individual craftsman. Sometimes the results were crude and primitive, yet in a surprising number of instances they show an inspired originality. Although Downing's ideas are clearly discernible in the over-all fabric of American carpenter Gothic, the varieties within the idiom were as numerous as the men who built the houses, and as far-reaching as the land in which it all took place. To cover this fascinating phase of American architecture in depth would require a careful examination of all the parts of the country that were settled and growing during the middle decades of the century. This is a specialized story which has no place in this book. On the other hand, the major characteristics of the development can be illustrated by a few select examples, each chosen from an area in which the Gothic cottage flourished.

The first is an anonymous house in Peterborough, New Hampshire, which was built about 1850. New England is particularly rich in provincial forms of the Gothic cottage and the one in Peterborough is thoroughly typical (Fig. 278). In its basic form it follows the Downing type rather faithfully. The central pavilion with its high gable and verge board, the end gables, also with verge boards, and the veranda, all are familiar elements properly arranged in relation to one another; and the construction is board-and-batten. The verge boards and the drop molding along the eaves, however, are not carved; they are cut out instead with a jigsaw. The most conspicuous deviation from Downing's principles is the veranda, which is in a scale completely unrelated to the rest of the house. Instead of the clustered posts prescribed by Downing, the vertical supports are heavy piers more Greek than Gothic in proportion, and the horizontal eave of the veranda roof is a classical entablature. Only the pointed-arch tops of the recessed vertical panels in the piers hint at a Gothic origin. The house, therefore, is a Downing cottage in hybrid dress, shaped largely by the builder's unwillingness or inability to cope with the more complex configuration of Gothic posts, and his reluctance to forsake altogether the Neoclassical forms which were still very much a part of his idiom.

In both *Cottage Residences* and *The Architecture of Country Houses* Downing prescribes a variety of forms for farmhouses, and in several rural areas, especially in prosperous farming sections of eastern and

FIGURE 278. *Gothic cottage, Peterborough, N.H., c. 1850.*

FIGURE 279. *Meadowbank, Hillsdale, N.Y., 1845–50.*

central New York State, numerous examples of the Downing type farm-house are still to be found. Characteristic is Meadowbank just north of Hillsdale (Fig. 279), in the mid-Hudson River Valley. Built in the early 1840's for Norton S. Collin, it derives indirectly from a type which Downing called "an ornamental farmhouse."[53] For this type of dwelling Downing insisted upon a simpler form than he did for the cottage: the projecting pavilion of the cottage was eliminated, although the frontal gable was retained, and the combination porch and veranda was replaced by a simple continuous veranda. All this is clearly seen in the Hillsdale house, yet there are also differences. Downing's model has a pitched roof with end gables; the Hillsdale house has a broad hipped roof which gives it a truncated, block-like character, and eliminates altogether the dynamic opposition of the Gothic crossing system. A characteristic high central gable, with a simple jigsaw-cut verge board, dominates the façade, and the construction is the familiar board-and-batten. The continuous veranda is carried on trellised supports but here there is a jarring note. The open balustrade which presently crowns the veranda is so totally different in scale and character from the rest of the house that it would seem to have been a later addition. The simplicity of the Hillsdale house is in keeping with Downing's proposal for a farmhouse. As in the Peterborough house, however, a shadowy reminder of a persistent classical preference is still apparent in the emphasis upon heavily proportioned block-like forms.

The Gothic Cottage
and the Jigsaw

A superb Gothic cottage of a wholly different kind is the Neff Cottage in Gambier, Ohio (Fig. 280). Built in 1845, it has a vivacious extravagance that portrays a significant and exciting development in the Downing-inspired Gothic cottage. In contrast to the provincial awkwardness and simplicity of the Peterborough and Hillsdale houses, the Neff Cottage is complex and elegant in the extreme. To be sure, certain aspects of the house are clearly inspired by Downing: the intersection of masses, the open decorated gables, the bay windows, and the veranda, these are all familiar components, although disproportionate here in their relationships to one another. The decorative elements, however, and even some of the structural parts, which in most folk Gothic buildings are so bluntly handled, are here multiplied, divided, and subdivided to the point where they finally evolve into proliferous patterns of delicate, fine-lined lace. Instead of the few broad flat arches which generally spring from post to post in a typical Downing veranda, the span in the Neff Cottage is compounded into multiple small arches, four on each side and six across the front. The arches next to the house, and those forming the two corners, are carried on clustered colonnettes of extraordinary thinness; those in the center, are totally unsupported and left hanging in the air as pendants. This partial denial of structure in favor of a fanciful multiplicity of parts gives the entire system a curious ambivalence. The

FIGURE 280. *Neff Cottage, Gambier, Ohio, c. 1845.*

verge boards, the panels in the balustrades over both the veranda and the
bay windows, the spandrels in the veranda arches, the elaborate
brackets under the eaves are all thin and flat, and appear as paper decorations stamped out by stenciling knives rather than carved wood ornaments. The truth is they were made with a jigsaw, a tool which was one
of the major advances in building technology during the nineteenth century. Its high-speed, flexible cutting capacity made possible the mechanical reproduction of shapes in an inexhaustible variety and in any amount
of repetition. By the 1840's the jigsaw had become the prime tool of carpenter Gothic—that ubiquitous folk phase of the Gothic Revival—and the
Neff Cottage, in which a refined sense of pattern was combined with the
versatility of the saw, is a masterpiece of the style.

The impact of the jigsaw on the Gothic cottage cannot be overes-
timated. Because of the sinuous nature of Gothic tracery and ornament,
the jigsaw's ability to cut curves made it a natural tool for the Gothic Revival housebuilder. This was particularly true in this country, where so
much of the domestic architecture was made of wood. At the same time,
the jigsaw left its peculiar mark on all the ornament it was called upon to
produce. Along with its capacity to fashion curves in endless variety, the
cut which it made through any piece of wood was at right angles to its sur-

face. Consequently, all the curved shapes were revealed by sharp edges. This is an extremely important point because medieval Gothic tracery and ornament, in spite of their linear character, are molded and rounded, and Downing was aware of this. When he refers to an ornamental verge board in his writing he describes it as "carved," not "cut," thus affirming both its Gothic three-dimensionality and its origin in a handcraft. The jigsaw, in contrast, was a machine which made the complex Gothic forms easy to turn out, especially as far as their outline was concerned, and it opened the way for an unlimited exploitation of two-dimensional linear pattern. Indeed, the complex lace of the Gothic cottage represents the first instance in this country in which technology, in the form of a power-driven tool, had a major effect on the visual character of the American house; and it was through the jigsaw more than anything else that the more weighty and organic Gothic proposed by Downing was transformed into a sparkling folk art.[54]

The jigsaw affected almost every phase of folk Gothic in every part of the country. The ornament of both the Peterborough and Hillsdale houses was cut by a jigsaw, and in the Wedding Cake House in Kennebunk Landing, Maine (one not inspired by Downing's books), the decorative overlay of Gothic lace represents the ultimate achievement of the jigsaw, together with the chisel, in the hands of an imaginative and resourceful workman. It was this combination of tools plus Downing's books which created the Gothic cottage style, and as it spread throughout the land, in houses of infinite variety, it brought a new vitality to the streets of American towns and to the American countryside. We have seen the Gothic cottage style in its contrasting modes in the houses already discussed, but to show the extreme limits of its permeation we will conclude by examining two examples built in unusual geographical settings.

The first is the Bishop Gilbert Haven Cottage (Fig. 281) in Wesleyan Grove, a Methodist camp meeting ground at Oak Bluffs on the island of Martha's Vineyard. The initial shelters in this remarkable religious settlement were tents, and it has been shown that the houses which replaced them during the late 1860's were influenced in part by the elaborate and ornamental canvas structures which once made up the community. In some of the houses, on the other hand, the Downing cottage also hovers in the background, especially in the spreading verandas and the high gables with their ornamental verge boards. The lively, abundant details, however, were primarily shaped by the jigsaw.

Of the more than one thousand cottages which, at the turn of the twentieth century, were packed shoulder to shoulder on this site, approximately three hundred remain. Together they constitute one of the most remarkable concentrations of folk architecture anywhere in the country. The cottages appear in a variety of picturesque styles and therefore provide a fascinating summary of American architecture during the second half of the nineteenth century. The majority, however, are in some form of the Gothic, and the Haven Cottage, although one of the more elaborate, is in many ways typical. It is a tiny building, the central pavilion of which reflects its origin in the earlier tents; at the same time, the

FIGURE 281. *Bishop Gilbert Haven Cottage, Oak Bluffs, Martha's Vineyard, Mass., late 1860's.*

FIGURE 282. *The Lace House, Black Hawk, Colo., c. 1860.*

intersecting massing along with certain other details suggests the influence of Downing. The Gothic features, themselves, are elaborate and in some instances surprisingly authentic, but they are also awkward and inconsistently scaled, and in general seem to belong to a much larger building. Heavy hood moldings compete with the undulating openwork of the verge boards; delicate drop moldings, looking more like lace aprons than architectural ornament, are coupled with heavy classical balustrades. The sum of all the parts is charmingly incoherent, and in its uninhibited and joyous exhibitionism it is American folk architecture in its most exuberant form.

Far removed from the quiet groves of the Wesleyan campground, and high in the mountains west of Denver, Colorado, is an equally fascinating reminder of the extraordinary degree to which the Gothic cottage permeated this country during the mid-nineteenth century. "The Lace House" (Fig. 282) stands in Black Hawk, one of many mining towns which burgeoned in the Rocky Mountains of Colorado during the heyday of gold and silver, and it is a superb survivor of the numerous Gothic cottages which once formed the pretentious façade of this raw boisterous community. In its own primitive way the Lace House is as elegant as the Neff Cottage, and is eloquently expressive of the aggressive ambitions which gave it life. At the same time, perhaps by pure accident more than design, it stands in unruffled harmony with the rugged mountainside to which it clings. Because it was a dynamic form, susceptible to both extravagant display and infinite flexibility, the Gothic cottage was happily functional for the Colorado mining towns, just as it was for any number of different areas within the growing nation. Its natural affinity with the land was felt wherever it was placed, and because of its potential for ornamental proliferation it became the ideal folk idiom. The Gothic cottage, in the hands of the local builder, was also the primary vehicle through which Downing's notions of the house in America achieved their most popular destiny.

Downing, Davis, and Llewellyn Park

Although both Downing and Davis would have been appalled by the playful extravagance of the Neff Cottage, they would have rejoiced in the extraordinary affinity between the irregular, sharply angled Lace House and its tumbled mountain setting. Throughout the careers of both men the relationship between the house and its surrounding landscape remained a compelling issue. To be sure, in approaching the matter, Downing began with the landscape, whereas Davis began with the house, but in the end both arrived at the same conclusion: the house and the landscape were inseparable. Because this conviction was so absolutely central to their creativity, it is impossible to conclude an analysis of their work without at least brief discussion of one of the most important fruits of their thinking, Llewellyn Park in West Orange, New Jersey.[55]

Llewellyn Park was the first instance in this country of a residential park deliberately designed to have a picturesque natural setting. Located beneath the rugged cliffs of Eagle Rock on the eastern slopes of Orange

FIGURE 283. *View from Eagle Rock,*
Llewellyn Park, Orange, N.J.

Mountain (Fig. 283), it was an imaginative and intensely romantic
scheme which was conceived by a successful drug importer from New
York City, Llewellyn S. Haskell. An ardent lover of nature and a close
friend and disciple of Downing's, Haskell was deeply involved during
much of his adult life with various landscaping projects. Among these was
Central Park in New York, an effort to which he gave his determined
and influential support. He was also associated in a more active way with
the development of two estates on the Passaic River, actually participating in their landscape planning. He thus brought to his project for
Llewellyn Park practical experience as well as natural enthusiasm.

Like all the landscapes that were planned for the great country estates
of the period Llewellyn Park was intended as a pleasure ground for living, but unlike the landscapes of such places as Blithewood and
Lyndhurst, it was designed to embrace not one house but many. Downing held that the smallest house was susceptible to sympathetic landscaping even if the property was limited. Haskell's objective was to combine this notion with that of the large estate, and make an extensive park
available as a common holding to a community of people, all of whom
would live within its bounds. It was an enlightened if snobbish concept,
but if it did not exactly throw the property open to the general public, as
Central Park in New York City would do, it did provide all the advantages of an immense and dramatically beautiful natural setting for a group
rather than an individual. To the extent that it broadened the base of participation, and made available to many what would normally have been

FIGURE 284. A. J. Davis. Gate Lodge,
Llewellyn Park, Orange, N.J., 1857.

the privilege of a man of wealth, it approached Downing's ideal of a cottage and garden for all "industrious and intelligent mechanics and workmen."

Downing was dead before work was seriously begun at Llewellyn Park,
but surely his doctrine and his practical experience must have figured
largely in the formation of Haskell's preliminary plans. The two friends
were both enamored of the forest, and saw there, as Downing put it, the
unique "seclusion and privacy of the walks and drives" and the "solitude
which belongs to the wilder aspect of woodland scenes." This is precisely
what Haskell strove for and achieved in Llewellyn Park and it is perfectly
obvious that the vision if not the hand of Downing left its mark upon the
plan.

In contrast to Downing, Davis was directly involved throughout the
history of the park. He, too, was a close friend of Haskell's, and by
the time planning began he had already done some architectural work for
him, including the remodeling of the old farm house on the property
which Haskell purchased in 1853 on Eagle Rock. Moreover, it was from
Haskell that Davis acquired the twenty-five acres on Eagle Rock where he
built his own country retreat, Wildmont (Fig. 171). Although Davis
seems to have had nothing to do with the landscape planning of the
park, he did do a number of the houses which were ultimately built
there, including the gate lodge (Fig. 284). There can be no question,
therefore, that he was very much a part of any architectural discussions
concerning the park, and he may even have been influential in Haskell's
decision to develop it in the way he did. Beyond that, it was Haskell who
directed the planning, with assistance from two landscape gardeners,

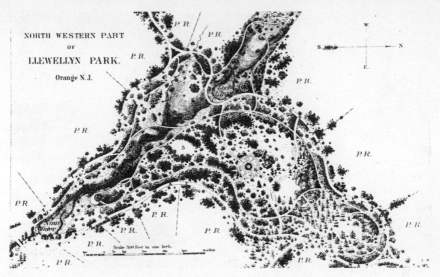

FIGURE 285. *Llewellyn Park, Orange, N.J., plan in 1859.*

the European-trained Eugene A. Baumann and the American, Howard Daniels.[56] Davis's connection with the development of the park, however, remained very real and personal, and much of what was actually done there has his signature on it.

After his first purchase of forty acres on Eagle Rock in 1853, Haskell continued to acquire land, and by 1857 had increased his holdings to about three hundred and fifty acres, all on the south slope of the mountain. By this time the shape of the park was clear. At the heart was a fifty-acre piece that followed a tumbling mountain stream. This was retained very much in its natural state with paths cut through to make it accessible, and to connect it with the cliff walk along the ridge of the mountain. It was this section which was originally known as Llewellyn Park, but as the residential community developed the name was transferred to the entire tract and the wilderness core became known as "the Ramble." The rest of the land was divided into building lots, all of substantial acreage, and connected by winding roads which followed the contours of the land. The area around each house was landscaped according to the owner's taste, but on the whole every effort was made to harmonize each house with its site, and to retain as far as possible the natural fall and character of the land.

A plan of the northwest corner of the Ramble, and the residential lots immediately around it, was made by Baumann and was published by Henry Winthrop Sargent in his supplement to the sixth edition of Downing's *Treatise on Landscape Gardening* (Fig. 285). Here it is easy to see the enormous impact of contours on the curvaceous outline of the Ramble and the arabesque design of the pathways. This preoccupation with undu-

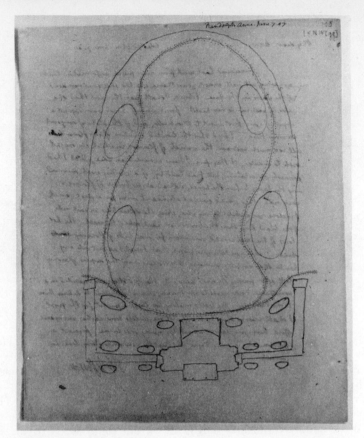

FIGURE 286. *Thomas Jefferson.*
Monticello, Charlottesville, Va.,
plan for the gardens, 1807.

lating curvatures may be traced to the picturesque gardens of England, whose winding paths were first introduced into this country by Thomas Jefferson in his plan for the gardens of Monticello (Fig. 286). At the same time, it represents a fascination with certain basic qualities of nature, particularly as seen in the organic surging of the earth itself, a fascination which also lies at the heart of Downing's doctrine. It was his advice in choosing a site "to select, always, if possible, a surface varied by gentle curves and undulations."[57] In proclaiming this, Downing was also reflecting a point of view which characterizes much of the landscape painting as well as the landscape gardens of the period, and helps to clarify in part the attraction which the curvilinear Gothic style had for a man like Davis. When Davis turned his attention to the landscape garden in his many water-color sketches, as he did in a view of the Ravine Walk at Blithewood (Fig. 287), his evocative handling of texture, light, and color was coupled with an extraordinary response to contour, to the swelling curves of the land mass, which he sought out and even exagger-

FIGURE 287. *A. J. Davis. View of the grounds, Blithewood, Barrytown, N.Y. Water color.*

ated in his search for the controlling energies of the scene. It is this sense of organic growth and movement, of the timeless rhythms of nature, which lies beneath the reasoning and intuitive responses of both Downing and Davis and vitalizes both their work and that of their contemporaries.

Some of the Davis houses at Llewellyn Park still survive. Two are especially revealing of his role in the grand scheme of things. One of these is the Gate Lodge (Fig. 288), the first building that one encounters on entering the park at the lower end of the Ramble. Built in 1857, it is a rustic, irregular building. The dominating feature is a round tower with a sweeping conical roof. The structure is fieldstone, laid without cutting in a rough random pattern. Its texture therefore is that of the stones along the bottom of the stream; its immobile walls are the rocky sides of the ravine. Its round and concave shapes are the swelling contours of the mountain land that lies ahead. The building rises out of the earth like a natural outcropping, eternally solid yet carefully shaped and pressing upward as an eloquent prelude to the park and to the houses which it shelters within its forest walls.

The second is farther up the mountain, on the edge of the Ramble, and is one of Davis's simplest and most expressive small cottages. It was designed in 1859 for the landscape painter Edward W. Nichols, and was originally intended also to have been built in stone (Fig. 289). Subsequent modifications, however, changed the fabric to wooden siding and eliminated the verge boards and the ornamental crests on the veranda eaves

FIGURE 288. A. J. Davis. Gate Lodge,
Llewellyn Park, Orange, N.J., 1857.

FRONT.

0   10   20   30   40

FIGURE 289. A. J. Davis. Nichols Cottage,
Llewellyn Park, Orange, N.J., 1859.
Original water-color drawing.

FIGURE 290. A. J. Davis. Nichols Cottage, Llewellyn Park, Orange, N.J., 1859.

(Fig. 290). Thus stripped of its decorative elegance, the house became more rustic and was made to settle more quietly into the seclusion of its setting—a sunlit clearing surrounded by the deep oak forest of the inner park. Here, its soaring pointed outlines, tall chimney stacks, and sheltered veranda all gesture sympathetically toward the towering limbs and shadowed verdure of the enveloping forest. The vertical threads of the board-and-batten siding lift its tapered shapes toward the treetops; they also paint on the surface of the buff-colored walls a fragile linear pattern which sharpens and retreats as the shifting shadows of the foliage swing and turn with the wind. Because of its angular varied shapes, which carry to the interior as well as the exterior (Fig. 291), and because of the sharp differentiation of parts accorded by the dark brown trim, the house never loses its individuality as a work of architecture. At the same time, it accepts and is enfolded by its environment. The other houses designed by Davis, which vary in size and style, are equally integrated with the park.[58] But of all of them, none expresses more vividly the es-

FIGURE 291. A. J. Davis. Nichols Cottage,
Llewellyn Park, Orange, N.J., interior, 1859.

sence of the Davis-Downing association. The creative energies of both
men poured into Llewellyn Park as a triumphant climax to one of the dramatic episodes in American architectural history, and Davis's simple cottage and its unspoiled mountain setting represent better than any other
combination of house and park in America the full and undefiled flowering
of picturesque doctrine in this country.

Llewellyn Park was a suburban community intended, as advertised in
its day, to provide "country homes for city people."[59] Within one hour of
New York City by railroad and ferry, it offered the harried businessman
an escape from the tensions and pressures of the city in the tranquility of a
forest retreat. At a somewhat snobbish level, it provided an ambience,
as Downing put it, "where one can enjoy the quiet landscape leisurely
. . . where all domestic fireside joys are invited to dwell," and where it is
possible to find "that intellectual and moral nature which characterizes the
most cultivated families in their country houses." Llewellyn Park was a
friendly moderator, designed to remove the frustration, feed the ambitions, and confirm the self-assured morality of the successful American.

It reached out with poetic urgency to stir that instinct which lies at the bottom of every human heart to return to its origin in the earth. The conception was both romantic and practical and it was a success in its day.

On the picturesque banks of the Merrimack River, the industrial towns of Lowell (Fig. 32) and Lawrence, Massachusetts, and Manchester, New Hampshire, stood in stark contrast. They too were planned communities, they too were practical, and in their own way even romantic; but the motive which brought them into being was not the escape of the individual into nature from the mass pressures of the city, but rather the concentration of many individuals in a man-made environment to serve the will of the machine. The mills, the housing, and the related utility buildings were all laid out in a regular manner calculated to serve the technology of the textile industry. If reflecting water added an ingredient of visual animation to the architectural scene, it was the placid water of the canals, man-directed in regular channels toward the water wheels, which provided the mirror. The rocky torrent of the great river itself, always so close at hand, was screened from the inner regions of the community by the continuous line of mills that shouldered their way, one after the other, along the riverbank. Nature in its untouched state was kept at arm's length in these communities, and far from attracting people to the seclusion and tranquility of the country, they drew young women from the country to the mills, putting them together in the mass living of the boardinghouses, and committing them to the mass activity of the manufacturing process. Although for a period at least these communities were models of correctness as far as the moral life of the young women was concerned, and although a unique social structure catered to their welfare and personal needs, the ever-present and awesome autonomy of the machines dominated life in both the mills and the boardinghouses, and except for the pots of geraniums which the young women kept in their windows, nature was excluded from their living and working environments.

The idealistic romanticism which produced the Gothic cottage and Llewellyn Park, and the ruthless technology which led to the corporate boardinghouses and mills of the Merrimack Valley, were both clearly and honestly portrayed in these two remarkable and thoroughly American achievements. That they were so different was the nature of the time and place. Each in its own way was the outgrowth of those powerful forces that were shaping this country during the first half of the century. Each passed out of adolescence about 1850 to compete against, blend into, and be absorbed by the complex, dynamic conglomerate of American society which followed the Civil War.

CHAPTER VIII

The Board and Batten
and the Gothic Revival Church

The leading idea of Gothic architecture is found in its up-
ward lines . . . upward, higher and higher, it soars . . . in
spires, and steeples, and towers, . . . in the vaulted aisles,
and the high, open, pointed roofs in the interior of a fine
Gothic church.

ANDREW JACKSON DOWNING

Richard Upjohn
and the Board-and-Batten Church

Board-and-batten siding, because of its verticality, was recognized by
both Davis and Downing as the most expressive structural technique in
wood for the Gothic style. By mid-century, largely through their influence,
it was used for the majority of wooden Gothic cottages in this country. The
board and batten was, in fact, the most important mark of distinction
which set American cottages apart from their equivalent in England and
closely tied them to the traditional use of wood in American domestic
architecture. Because of their deeply rooted sensitivity for wood, American
builders were quick to recognize and exploit the advantages which the
board and batten offered over the traditional clapboard, and to make it
uniquely their own idiom.

Downing knew that the character of the Gothic style, as "found in its
upward lines," had its ultimate origin in the medieval church, and it
was through the board and batten that not just the Gothic Revival cottage
but also the Gothic Revival church achieved its uniquely American form.
The vertical thrust of the Gothic, which in the cottage was limited to the
peak of the highest gable, was not only heightened in the taller walls and
gables of the church, but came to a dramatic climax in the soaring flanks
of the tower. Applied to the joints of the vertical matched boards, the
sharp and closely spaced battens generated a positive upward movement.
At the same time, they functioned in the tower as directional multipliers
in an already firmly established vertical mass. Here the effect was not
unlike that in the classical column where the expression of the vertical
support function is so clearly intensified by the fluting. In the board-and-
batten church it was the gothicism that was emphasized. Except for the
fluid patterns of tracery produced by the jigsaw, no other technological
development of the century contributed more to the Gothic character of
the wooden churches of America than the board and batten.

The first American architect to understand and take advantage of board-and-batten construction in his churches was Richard Upjohn. Born with the Gothic in his blood, and gifted with an inordinate feeling for the nature of materials, Upjohn realized at once the close affinity between the technique and the Gothic style. Although he preferred to work in stone or brick, as did both Downing and Davis, he accepted the American preference for wood as a condition of the American environment, and went on to use the material with a sensitivity and imagination which was unsurpassed by any other architect of his time, including Davis.

Upjohn could have known about the board and batten from either Davis's early works or his *Rural Residences.* By the time Upjohn first used the technique in a church, Davis had already built at least two board-and-batten cottages, both of which were illustrated by Downing. Just as the bell-cote type church, after it appeared in this country—especially in St. James-the-Less in Philadelphia, was quickly recognized by Upjohn as particularly appropriate to rural America, so, too, the board and batten was seen by him as a building method remarkably suitable for the same end. During the 1840's he was to put the technique to practical use in a number of wooden churches, and by 1852 many requests for plans were coming in from small parishes, more in fact than he could possibly accommodate. To meet this need he published a book, *Upjohn's Rural Architecture,* which gave plans and specifications for a small wooden church and an even smaller chapel. Each called for board-and-batten siding.[1] Largely as a result of Upjohn's initiative, the technique which originated in domestic architecture became ubiquitous as well for the small Gothic church; as in the case of the cottage, too, it was the principal feature which distinguished the small Gothic Revival churches in America from those in England.

First Parish Congregational Church, Brunswick, Me.

Upjohn's first major church constructed with board-and-batten siding was the First Parish Church in Brunswick, Maine (Fig. 292).[2] Built for a group of Congregationalists, and designed early in 1845, it was one of the few churches by Upjohn that was not Episcopal in denomination. Moreover, it was one of the architect's very early churches, coming immediately after the Church of the Holy Communion in New York, and just before St. Mary's, Burlington; and like the others it was in the Gothic style. This in itself is of considerable historical interest, for the Brunswick church was one of the first—if not *the* first—major Congregational churches of the nineteenth century in New England to be built in an authoritative form of the Gothic. Upjohn was already known in Maine for earlier Gothic works, particularly St. John's Church in Bangor (Fig. 109), and it may have been this which motivated the Congregationalists in nearby Bath to build the Winter Street Church, a delightfully naive hybrid of Gothic and Greek forms (Fig. 293). It was erected in 1843, two years before Upjohn's Brunswick church. It is therefore an important early indicator of the changing attitudes within the Congregational Church toward architectural style.

FIGURE 292. *Richard Upjohn.*
First Parish Congregational Church,
Brunswick, Me., from the southwest, 1845–46.

Upjohn's First Parish Church, Brunswick, is not a hybrid. It is a fully developed Gothic building, both in massing and detail, designed by an architect who understood the complex nature of the style. At the same time, it
has characteristics, particularly in its internal arrangements, which accommodate its thoroughly Gothic character to the demands of the Congregational service.

The fascinating relationship between Gothic form and Congregational
function which Upjohn achieved in Brunswick was compounded by yet
another influential consideration. Although the church was built for the
oldest Congregational parish in Brunswick, a great many of its leading
members were in one way or another associated with Bowdoin College,
and it was intended from the beginning as a place of worship for students
and faculty as well as the people of the town. It also played a special role
in the life of the college itself, serving as the auditorium where commencement was held each year. Even Upjohn's natural preference for the Gothic
style may have been encouraged by the strong presence of the Bowdoin

FIGURE 293. *United Church of Christ,*
Winter Street, Bath, Me., 1843.

faculty in the congregation. In fact, William Smyth, a professor of mathematics, was actually the supervisor of construction. All of this created for
Upjohn some very special requirements which he had then to accommodate to this over-all Gothic scheme.

In its basic form the church is a conventional cruciform arrangement
but as originally designed by Upjohn it had a tall square frontal tower
topped by a parapet (Fig. 294). This feature was apparently viewed by
the Building Committee as less "popish" than a spire,[3] and was described, while still under construction, as "a great ornament to our village." When it was finally in place, however, its unusual height and

FIGURE 294. *Richard Upjohn.*
First Parish Congregational Church, Brunswick, Me.,
1845–46. Detail from an old print showing Bowdoin College.

square top made it seem awkward and overbearing, even to those who had
conceived it. In fact, so general was the adverse reaction that in 1848,
only two years after its completion, the decision was made to change it.
To reduce its impact and temper its bluntness the square top was removed
and the next stage down was remodeled to form a belfry, which in turn
served as a base for a tall octagonal spire (Fig. 295).[4] The church stood
in this form until 1866. In that year the spire was blown down in a hurricane and never replaced. Today the church thus stands stripped of one of
its most Gothic features.

As originally painted the building was a warm stone-like color, such as
that prescribed by Upjohn in his *Rural Architecture,* but as is so often the
case with early Gothic Revival churches in New England, it is now white.
Its present color, together with its single frontal tower may hint faintly of
the traditional Wren-Gibbs formula. Actually, the church is anything but
that. The tall tower has well-proportioned corner buttresses which rise unbroken from the ground to their pinnacled tops. Between these pinnacles
steeply pitched crowning gables terminate in applied tracery patterns and
imitate the pointed-arch compound louvered openings which grace all four
sides of the upper tower. Through the height of the tower, from the
water table to the peaks of the gables, the closely spaced ribbons of
shadow cast by the battens multiply and confirm the Gothic verticality. At
the crossing, the aggressive right-angle thrust of the transept, together

FIGURE 295. *Richard Upjohn. First Parish Congregational Church, Brunswick, Me.,
1845–46. Old photograph.*

with the lively upward sweep of the double-pitched roof obliterate any lingering suggestion of the conventional New England meetinghouse. Although the main body of the church is austerely simple (Fig. 296), with
expansive stretches of wall sparsely punctuated by unadorned but superbly proportioned lancet windows, the building is Gothic down to the last
detail; and to break the monotony of the flat walls the rapid, delicate accents of the battens texture the surface and carry the vertical theme of the
tower to every part of the building.

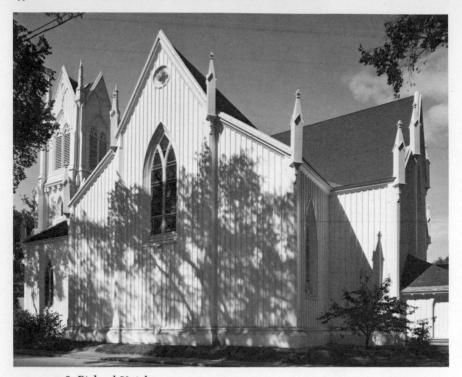

FIGURE 296. *Richard Upjohn.*
First Parish Congregational Church, Brunswick, Me.,
from the southeast, 1845–46.

In spite of both its convincing gothicism and the canonical implications
of its cruciform plan, the Brunswick church was intelligently manipulated
by Upjohn to accommodate both its Congregational and collegiate functions. The south porch, for example, was eliminated altogether. The main
doors instead are in the west and front sides of the tower (Fig. 302), with
entrance into the auditorium through a single door in the center (Fig.
299). The transepts project boldly from the nave, but the chancel, which
for canonical reasons should be equally deep, is extremely shallow, extending from the crossing only half the distance of the transepts. At the
same time, both the transepts and chancel are broader than Gothic precedents call for. The reason for this can be read in the relationship between
the upper and lower planes of the double-pitched roof. In a conventional
Gothic church the lower roof plane covers an area only about half that beneath the main roof of the nave (Fig. 134). In the Brunswick church it
covers an area on either side which is as wide as that in the center (Fig.
296).

To understand this adjustment of the basic Gothic relationship it is necessary to go inside the church (Fig. 297). Here there is not the expected
triple division of a narrow nave and side aisles which lead to the chancel

FIGURE 297. *Richard Upjohn.*
First Parish Congregational Church, Brunswick,
Me., interior, toward pulpit; 1845–46.

(Fig. 127), but rather a broad and open space which extends in three directions from the pulpit as an unencumbered listening area. Instead of containing an altar the shallow chancel is completely occupied by a raised platform which functions both as a dais for the pulpit and a stage for commencement and other special events.[5] In addition, the deeper but equally open transepts have balconies along their entire width, placed there by Upjohn to provide seating for the students at church services. The organ and original choir loft, in typical Congregational fashion, are over the main entrance facing the pulpit (Fig. 299).

The most ingenious part of Upjohn's unusual interior spatial arrangement is the way in which he was able to achieve it within the Gothic system. The key to his solution is the open timber truss that supports the roof. This remarkable piece of carpentry has been criticized for its confusing complexity by everyone who has written about the church, including Upjohn's great-grandson Everard M. Upjohn.[6] Complex it is, and its forest of beams, struts, braces, and purlins, when seen from certain points, *is* confusing. When considered as a solution to the problems Upjohn was called upon to solve, however, it is eminently logical.

FIGURE 298. *Hampton Court Palace, Middlesex, England, hall, 1531–36.*

In a conventional Gothic interior the ratio of the width of the nave to that of the side aisles is generally about 1:2:1, with the three spaces separated by the two rows of piers. If a double-pitched roof is used, the line of intersection of the two roof planes is carried on a plate directly above the piers (Fig. 135). In the Brunswick church the ratio is 1:4:1, a broad open relationship which Upjohn accomplished by using a hammer-beam truss (Fig. 299). This made it possible to move the line of piers very much closer to the outer walls so that they define an area which is little more in width than that necessary to provide access down either side of the blocks of pews. In this position the piers then become the fulcrum from which the hammer beams are cantilevered. From their hinge above the piers the beams then reach toward the center of the church to a point beneath the intersection of the two roof planes. The plate to carry this critical intersection in turn is supported on pointed arches and posts all of which spring from the ends of the hammer beams. With the aisles thus compressed to the minimum possible within the limits of the truss system, the space that in a Gothic church would be the nave becomes instead a wide auditorium which turns easily into the transepts (Fig. 297) and provides an unbroken view of the pulpit from virtually every pew in the church.

FIGURE 299. *Richard Upjohn.*
First Parish Congregational Church, Brunswick, Me.,
interior, toward front entrance, 1845–46.

Upjohn's combination of a hammer-beam truss with the nave and side aisles structural system of a cruciform church was as unorthodox as it was imaginative. The hammer-beam ceiling was one of the most original inventions of the English Gothic builders and was used as a means of roofing large rectangular interior spaces such as the great hall of Richard II in the palace of Westminster, London, or the one at Hampton Court Palace (Fig. 298). By using the hammer-beam truss in a cruciform church, which Upjohn obviously did to increase the size of the auditorium, it was necessary for him to turn the truss at the corners of the crossing. This added considerably to the number of truss members, and by retaining the aisle it also became necessary to cantilever the hammer beams over the piers. In Gothic times by contrast the hammer beam was bracketed directly from the masonry wall where its leverage action was contained either by the wall itself or by a wall buttress on the outside. In Upjohn's solution the hammer beam is balanced on the pier and the leverage motion is exerted as a vertical stress at that point where the beam is anchored in the frame of the outside wall. It was a completely open wooden system, but the numerous truss members necessary to contain the tensions, stabilize the pressures, and carry the weight caused the inordinate visual complex-

FIGURE 300. *Richard Upjohn.*
First Parish Congregational Church, Brunswick, Me.,
south flank, 1845–46.

ity of the structure. This was particularly true at the crossing (Fig. 297), where some of the force generated had ultimately to be held in check by iron tie rods. Upjohn's eccentric exploitation of Gothic structure made it possible to provide the kind of auditorium space required by the conditions of the commission and fortunately, to do so without sacrificing the intrinsic visual qualities of the Gothic style itself.

Upjohn's command of materials and structure, as revealed in this complicated truss, can further be demonstrated by comparing a flank of the wooden Brunswick church (Fig. 300) with one at St. Mary's, Burlington, a stone structure that he began the following year (Fig. 301). The manner in which the details of the stark lancet windows in Brunswick are worked out with total respect for the capabilities of the carpenter's tools, while those at St. Mary's give way to the mason's chisel, and the contrast between the attenuated linear character of the wooden siding and the block-like appearance of the rough stone wall, all point to his sympathetic probing of the innate qualities of materials. In each church the scale, the shapes, the textures all speak exclusively for either wood or stone, and in neither instance does Upjohn attempt to make one material look like the other.

Early evidence of Upjohn's compositional genius is also apparent in the Brunswick church. The proportions and the placement of the simple lancet windows (Fig. 300), in relation to the wall itself and to the spacing of

FIGURE 301. *Richard Upjohn.*
St. Mary's Church, Burlington, N.J.,
south flank, 1846–48.

the vertical battens, have extraordinary qualities of rightness; with equal directness the dynamic contrast between the bold pointed shapes of the window surrounds, and the regular rhythm of the battens, all evoke the dynamic vitality of the Gothic style in the simplest possible terms, without a single extraneous element. The south door (Fig. 302)—cut into the thickness of the frame wall in an almost primitive manner, and yet poised with infinite subtlety between the tiny lancets that flank its frame—is one of the inspired moments in American Gothic Revival architecture. It represents an interpretation of the Gothic in wood by a man who not only knew and loved the style, but who also sensed in New England a deeply rooted tradition in wooden architecture and then joyously made it his own. Above all, it is vibrantly simple and in its taut, poised purity it is prophetic of that distilled essence which characterizes the work of those great twentieth-century masters of the minimal, Mies van der Rohe and Philip Johnson.

In turning to the Gothic style, Upjohn was performing as a revivalist and to a certain extent even as an eclectic. But the Gothic forms are so transformed by his own genius that the style which emerges is nineteenth-century Upjohn and not medieval English. The uniqueness of Upjohn's work stems in no small measure from the fact that his interpretation of the Gothic was organic. Because of his keen architectural sense the style for him was not a system of ornament applied to structure, but rather a

FIGURE 302. *Richard Upjohn.*
First Parish Congregational Church,
Brunswick, Me., south door, 1845–46.

flowering organism of forms which takes its life from the practical and structural necessities which brought it into being. This is the essence of all great architecture, and in Upjohn's case is dramatically demonstrable in a comparison between his bold solution on the interior of the Brunswick church and that of another and more radically eclectic Gothic Revival church of the period, the Unitarian Church in Charleston, South Carolina (Fig. 303). This building was designed and built during 1852–54 by Francis D. Lee, an eclectic architect of Charleston who worked in a variety of styles and became one of the pioneers in that area in the use of cast iron. The commission for the Unitarian Church was actually a remodeling in which Lee was called upon to transform an existing church into a Gothic building. The squarish proportions of the interior, therefore, were imposed on the architect.

In contrast to Upjohn's daring use of trussing to provide an auditorium space, Lee's interior was divided into a conventional relationship of nave and side aisles. Then, through an ingenious use of lath and plaster, he hung from the roof trusses a fanciful imitation of the spectacular fan vaults and pendants of the Chapel of Henry VII in Westminster Abbey in London. The result is an exquisite masterpiece of fakery which is visually delightful but structurally illogical. Lee's solution in the Unitarian Church is typical of that trend already observed in American eclectic architecture of mid-century toward an increasing opulence of interior decorative treatment, and it stands in revealing contrast to Upjohn's structural approach. It is true that Upjohn used plaster vaults in Trinity Church, New York,

FIGURE 303. *Francis D. Lee.*
Unitarian Church, Charleston, S.C.,
interior, toward front entrance, 1852–54.

but he did so against his better judgment, and in all of his subsequent church work he employed wood for the ceilings.

The First Parish Church in Brunswick was Upjohn's largest board-and-batten church. Since it posed the most complex problems, it was also his most experimental. But more than anything else, the experience seems to have convinced him of the profound affinity between the board and batten and the Gothic style. From that point on he was to become a chief proponent of a movement, either through his commissions or his book *Upjohn's Rural Architecture,* that would carry the small wooden Gothic church to every corner of the settled land. Two examples will illustrate the variety and vitality of Upjohn's direct contribution to that movement.

Through his reputation within the Episcopal Church itself, Upjohn

FIGURE 304. *Richard Upjohn. Church of St. John Chrysostom, Delafield, Wis., view from the west, 1851–53.*

was called upon to submit designs for a number of remote churches. Of these, one of the most unusual is the Church of St. John Chrysostom at Delafield, Wisconsin (Fig. 304). It was built between 1851 and 1853 during that same missionary thrust into the frontier which created the Chapel of St. Mary the Virgin at Nashotah. Situated on the top of a knoll in a lovely wooded grove, St. John's is a simple nave-type church with a chancel and south porch.[7] Although the roof pitch is extremely steep, there is no bell tower of any kind immediately associated with the church. Instead, in an unusual and provocative arrangement, the bell is contained in a freestanding bell house located a short distance from the southwest corner of the church.

Structurally the church is rough-cut planks with heavy battens over the joints (Fig. 305). The planks vary in size and width so that the battens are laid on with irregular spacing, and are not always strictly parallel to one another. Moreover, the large and simple patterns of the verge boards are built up rather than cut out, thus are more the product of conventional carpenter's tools than of the jigsaw. This is consistent with the roughness of the planks and battens, some of which still show the texture of the circular saw cuts. St. John's is also one of the few Gothic Revival churches in America which still retain their original color; its variegated surfaces are warmed by a deep red stain. Because of its remote location Upjohn did not supervise the construction. As a result, the crude execution, together with the loose spacing of the heavy battens, creates an

FIGURE 305. *Richard Upjohn.*
Church of St. John Chrysostom,
Delafield, Wis., south porch and flank, 1851–53.

awkward, primitive effect which recalls the limited means and skills of
the frontier. St. John's is a marvelously vital mutation of a simple but subtle conception by a master church designer and in its diminutive size and
bold rendition contrasts poignantly with the Chapel of St. Mary the Virgin
only a few miles away. It is also a high point in the reach of the board-
and-batten church into the fringes of nineteenth-century America.

Exactly the opposite in its charming elegance is the tiny church of St.
Luke's in the settled countryside of Clermont, New York (Fig. 306). As
originally built in 1857 it was a simple nave-type church with a frontal
porch and open wooden bell cote. The small vestry which now appears on
its south-west side was a later addition. It is listed among the small rural
works of Richard Upjohn, but may have been influenced in part by his
son Richard M. Upjohn, who was then with the firm.[8] In spite of its
diminutive size, St. Luke's is extremely refined, with the delicately
scaled battens rhythmically placed. Its soaring bell cote is intricately constructed in a fascinating basket of open woodwork. This in turn is laced to
the gable and verge boards by means of exquisite segments of jigsaw
tracery. Such an extravagant piece of structural and ornamental finery
might seem pretentious on so small a building, but it is made compatible
by the superb harmony of scale between its many intricate parts and the
delicate lines of the battens. Indeed, it was Upjohn's sensitivity to scale
and proportion more than ornamental virtuosity which transformed a simple box into a building of extraordinary grace.

The Proliferation
of the Board-and-Batten Church

The box-like type of church with a frontal porch and bell cote, which is represented in St. Luke's, Clermont, became extremely popular for rural churches throughout the country. Although frequently used by small Episcopal parishes such as St. Luke's, it was free of the canonical implications of the chancel and south porch, and was thus useful for other denominations as well. Typical is the Community Presbyterian Church in Fairplay, Colorado (Fig. 307). The town lies in South Park, a breathtaking mountain meadow land which stretches for 75 miles at 10,000 feet above sea level between the flanking peaks of the Rocky Mountains. Here the church was built in 1872 by Dr. Sheldon Jackson, the pioneer missionary who founded the Presbyterian Church in Fairplay. Today it is known as the Sheldon Jackson Memorial Chapel. Although the heavy detailing of its bell tower and its bracketed eaves betray its later date, it is a classic example of the continuing force of that utterly simple form of the board-and-batten church which is typified at St. Luke's. Standing crisp and luminous against the fleeting clouds and blue-black sky of its high-altitude setting, the Fairplay church is another of the many reminders that it was the Gothic style above any other which maintained the image of an established church tradition and brought an element of grace to even the most isolated pioneer town.

FIGURE 307.
Sheldon Jackson Memorial Chapel,
Fairplay, Colo., 1872.

FIGURE 308.
Tualatin Plains Presbyterian Church,
North Plains, Ore., c. 1876.

The variations on the small Gothic board-and-batten church were as numerous as the locations in which they were built. A particularly interesting one which was even further removed in time and place from the epicenter of the Gothic board-and-batten movement, is the Tualatin Plains Presbyterian Church near North Plains, Oregon (Fig. 308). It was built around 1876. The setting is the lush fertile plains between the Columbia River and the Coast Range, in the northwest part of the state, an area abundant in tall fir trees whose pointed tops shatter the immediate skyline as the sawtoothed backbone of the distant mountains breaks the horizon. The church, as though in imitation, is tall and bold, sharp vertical lines of the battens rising precipitously through walls and central tower to the multiple sharp open gables and tapered top of the spire. There is no applied ornament to break the upward flow, no wooden tracery to seduce the eye; even the proportions, the steeply pitched roof, and the clean sharp lancet windows conspire to celebrate the landscape. There is throughout the building a reliance upon essentials boldly conceived and cleanly cut, which is a mark of its frontier origin; at the same time, there is an immense strength which proclaims the breadth and sharpness of the land in which it has been set. When compared with the gentle elegance of little St. Luke's, Clermont, set as it is in the soft rounded hills of the Hudson River Valley, the Oregon church seems like a pointed outcropping in the slanting snow fields of Mount Hood.

FIGURE 309. *Edmund B. White. Church of the Cross,*
Bluffton, S.C., 1854.

Nor was this sympathetic response to the environment entirely acci-
dental. In many of the remote Gothic churches of America there is some
hint of the immediate surroundings. Far from Oregon, on the coastal plains
of the Carolina low country, for example, the Church of the Cross in
Bluffton, South Carolina, presents yet another image (Fig. 309). Located in an area where the roots of Anglican tradition were still strong, it
is a conventional cruciform scheme. Designed by the Charleston architect
Edmund B. White, and built in 1854, it is austerely simple, with no ornament whatsoever to elaborate its pointed-arch windows or to interrupt
the quiet rhythms of its board-and-batten walls. Nor is there a bell cote or
steeple to disturb its serene acceptance of an isolated site on a broad
marshy inlet only a few miles from the sea. Here its unpainted walls,
browned and softened by the salt-laden air, join in sympathetic harmony
with the silver gray shawls of Spanish moss which shroud the surrounding
trees.

The Board-and-Batten Church:
A Rural Masterpiece

If the diversity of the countless small board-and-batten churches of
America reflects a heterogeneous people moving through a varied land,
so the small wooden churches of Richard Upjohn comprise one of the few

FIGURE 310. *Richard Upjohn.*
Church of St. John in the Wilderness,
Copake Falls, N.Y., from the southwest, 1851–52.

focal points of the country's genius. Of all the Gothic churches of America none is more subtly conceived and more expressive of the religious tone of America in the nineteenth century than Upjohn's magnificent little Church of St. John in the Wilderness in Copake Falls, New York (Fig. 310). Only twenty-six miles from his masterpiece in brick, the Church of St. Thomas in Amenia Union (Fig. 128), St. John's was designed for the Episcopal parish of a small but prosperous iron mining community in the Taconic hills. It was begun in 1851, the year St. Thomas's was completed, and was finished the following spring. Upjohn also designed the adjacent rectory. The man in charge of the work was W. L. Pomeroy of Copake.

St. John's is an Ecclesiological church in the purest sense of the word. As seen from the outside, it is a simple nave-type structure with articulated chancel, south porch, and bell cote. On the interior (Fig. 311) the chancel is separated from the nave by an austere chancel arch. The chancel itself terminates in a triplet of simple lancet windows cut into the wall without molded surrounds. The stained glass in these windows is original, but the gilt inscription around the chancel arch and the stenciling on the splayed inner surfaces of the window surrounds are not. Like the interior of St. Thomas's, that of St. John's seems originally to have been unadorned. The simple timber ceiling is carried on bold pointed-arch

FIGURE 311. *Richard Upjohn.*
Church of St. John in the Wilderness,
Copake Falls, N.Y., interior, toward chancel, 1851–52.

struts elegantly curved in their tapered sweep toward the crown. A simple molding pattern cut in profile at the lower end of each strut gives the slightest hint of a line of wall brackets down each side of the church from which the entire truss system springs. There is no tracery in either the truss or the windows. To sustain the scale and character of this simple interior, even the church furniture[9] was designed by Upjohn.

As a work of architecture, the building is a masterpiece of distilled grace. There is not a single redundancy or a single over-statement, yet nothing is neglected. In spite of its austerity, the building is elegant in proportion and infinitely refined in scale. Indeed, all of the promise found in certain passages of the earlier experimental church in Brunswick, Maine (Fig. 296), here matures to permeate the entire design; and the church is structurally without flaw. The taut strings of the battens are closely spaced to accentuate the vertical movement; the west façade, broken only by a single lancet window in the center, climaxes in the sharp pitched roof of the bell cote. This simple but exquisite open-tim-

FIGURE 312. *Richard Upjohn.*
Church of St. John in the Wilderness,
Copake Falls, N.Y., south porch and bell cote, 1851–52.

bered tower is among the most subtly composed to be found in the small Gothic Revival churches of America. Far simpler than the bell cote on St. Luke's, Clermont (Fig. 306), it is unsurpassed in the way that its structural elements are logically combined toward both canonical and aesthetic ends. Here the stone bell cote of the medieval English parish church as typified by St. James-the-Less in Philadelphia (Fig. 123) is translated into wood—but not in a manner imitating stone, rather in an uncomplicated system of framing which has its own excitement and its own identity.

The principal structural elements of St. John's bell cote are rectangular posts, three on each side. The center posts of each pair of three, which are slightly wider than the others, break through the overhanging eaves of the front gable and continue down the façade, as engaged pilasters, to the water table at the foundation. This establishes a visual extension of the bell cote from ground to peak and embraces the central lancet window; it also strengthens the general vertical emphasis of the façade, in much the same way that the stone buttresses did at St. James-the-Less. The two rear posts of St. John's bell cote rest on the roof; the two front ones pass downward clear of the building to be carried on short hammer beams about 8 feet below the peak of the roof. They thus overlap the façade and terminate in dropped pendants at their bottom ends. They are braced by horizontal beams at the bell platform, and by a pair of diagonal braces crossing one another in the lower stage. The angle of these braces parallels the pitch of the eaves thus repeating in the wooden frame the basic angle of the peak of the roof. There are only two concessions to Gothic curves in the entire bell-cote structure. The first is the two cusps which fill the angles formed at the lower connections between the diagonal braces and the front vertical posts; the second is an ogee arch with a fleur-de-lis top which is cut in outline into the tympanum of each of the bell-cote gables. Elsewhere in the building, the only pointed-arch shapes are the main door in the south porch (Fig. 312) and the three lancet windows in the chancel (Fig. 311). All the other windows are brought to points by planes that are straight-pitched rather than arched; there is no tracery and there are no verge boards anywhere in the building.

The similarities between St. John's in the Wilderness and St. Thomas's, Amenia Union, are pronounced. They are almost the same size, and except for the hooded west door of St. Thomas's are virtually identical in layout; they have similar trussed ceilings and similar furniture. Indeed, they are so much alike that it is impossible to think of one without the other. Yet, they are very different. They are different because they are constructed of different materials; they are different, too, because Richard Upjohn had such a profound sense of structure that it was impossible for him to conceive the two buildings, one in brick and the other in wood, in anything but their own terms. Each in its own way stems from a long-established American building practice and is therefore firmly rooted in its place of origin. At the same time, by making the board and batten function so logically as a vehicle of the Gothic style, Upjohn created something without precedence in this country, something which by its very uniqueness was expressive of a new and ever-changing America.

The board-and-batten cottages and churches of Davis, Downing, and Upjohn together spoke of a restless people moving ever farther into the wilderness and taking with them as they went, not the established certainties of a familiar building tradition, but rather the ingredients of a new architecture, flexible and varied in form, but simple and attainable in structure. Together they became the most eloquently American architectural forms yet produced in this country. If the industrial towns of the Northeast spoke of the nation's technological genius, if St. Patrick's Cathedral spoke of the growing strength and size of its institutions, if the villas and gardens of Davis and Downing spoke of its romantic idealism, the wooden cottage and the small wooden church spoke of both the vitality and ambitions of the enormous and ever-growing heart of middle-class

America, in town, village, and farm throughout the country. More than that, the changing attitudes toward architecture which encouraged the board-and-batten cottage and church became the seeds of a dynamic architectural growth, large in conception, experimental in its search for new forms, and probing in its efforts to identify with the American way of life. Both Upjohn and Davis continued to play creative roles in broadening the foundations of that movement before turning the leadership over to a new generation of professional and demanding men.

Notes

CHAPTER I

1.1 For a full account of Robert Mills and the Greek Revival in the United States see Volume I in this series: William H. Pierson, Jr., *American Buildings and Their Architects; The Colonial and Neoclassical Styles,* Garden City, N.Y., Doubleday & Company, Inc., 1970, hereafter referred to as Pierson, Volume I.

1.2 Talbot Hamlin, *Greek Revival Architecture in America,* London, New York, Toronto, Oxford University Press, 1944.

1.3 See Pierson, Volume I, Chap. X.

1.4 Fiske Kimball, "Romantic Classicism in Architecture," *Gazette des Beaux-Arts,* XXV (1944), pp. 95–112.

1.5 *The American Journal of Science and Arts,* Vol. XVII, January 1830, pp. 99–110, 249–73; Vol. XVIII, July 1830, pp. 11–26, 212–37.

1.6 See Pierson, Volume I, Part II, "Neoclassicism in America."

1.7 For a general discussion of the picturesque, see
Christopher Hussey, *The Picturesque; Studies in a Point of View,* New York, Putnam's, 1927.
Nikolaus Pevsner, "The Genesis of the Picturesque," *Architectural Review,* London, Vol. XCVI, July–December 1944, pp. 139–46.

1.8 For detailed discussion of Price on the picturesque, see
John Steegman, *The Rule of Taste from George I to George IV,* London, Macmillan, 1936, pp. 59ff.
"Price on Picturesque Planning," *Architectural Review,* London, Vol. XCV, February 1944, pp. 47ff.

1.9 See Pierson, Volume I., pp. 111ff.

1.10 See *ibid.,* pp. 216–17.

1.11 Pevsner, "Genesis of the Picturesque," p. 146.

1.12 See Pierson, Volume I, pp. 112–13.

1.13 For a complete discussion of Stourhead, see
"The Gardens at Stourhead, Wilts," *Country Life,* Vol. LXXXIII, No. 2160, pp. 608–14.
"Stourhead—II, Wiltshire," *Country Life,* Vol. LXXXIII, No. 2161, pp. 638–42.
Christopher Hussey, *English Gardens and Landscapes, 1700–1750,* London, Country Life Ltd., 1967, pp. 158–64.

1.14 Nikolaus Pevsner, "Richard Payne Knight," *Art Bulletin,* Vol. XXXI, No. 4., December 1949, p. 296.

1.15 The description is by John Josselyn of the view from Sugarloaf Mountain in Connecticut as seen in the late seventeenth century. Quoted by Hans Huth, *Nature and the American,* University of California Press, 1957, p. 5.

1.16 Josselyn, quoted by Huth, *Nature,* p. 7.

1.17 *Notes on the State of Virginia* was compiled in 1781 for the benefit of the Secretary of the French legation, François de Marbois, and thus served as a guidebook in one sense of the word. A private edition of two hundred copies was printed in 1785; the first public edition, published in Philadelphia, appeared in 1788. I have used the second American edition: Philadelphia, 1794.

1.18 Jefferson, *Notes,* Query XIX, pp. 239–40.

1.19 *Ibid.,* Query IV, pp. 23–24. In his vivid account of the confluence of the Potomac and Shenandoah rivers, Jefferson relates all that he sees to geological time, and reflects on the great forces which have brought it into being. His sensitive response to the visual qualities of the scene suggests a thorough and sympathetic reading of Burke's discourse on the Sublime and the Beautiful. Moreover, in his fascination with the wild and irregular, he even anticipates Price and the picturesque.

1.20 Bryant set the stage for his new vision of nature in a highly original poem, "Thanatopsis," first published in the *North American Review* in 1817.

1.21 James Fenimore Cooper, *The Last of the Mohicans,* 2 Vols., Philadelphia, H. C. Carey and I. Lea, 1826, Vol. I, p. 216. *The Pioneers,* the first of Cooper's famous *Leatherstocking Tales,* was published early in 1823 and sold 3,500 copies the first day.

1.22 Ralph Waldo Emerson, *Nature,* Boston, James Munroe and Company, 1836, pp. 5f.

1.23 Henry David Thoreau, *The Maine Woods,* Boston and New York, Houghton Mifflin and Company, The Riverside Press, 1894, p. 95.

1.24 Thoreau, *Walden, or Life in the Woods,* Boston, Ticknor and Fields, 1854, p. 126.

1.25 The roller spinning machine invented by Lewis Paul was first tried in a warehouse in Birmingham in 1741. A year later, Paul installed his device in a water mill in Northampton, and by 1759 John Kay, inventor of the flying shuttle, had converted an old fulling mill at Keighly into a weaving factory.

1.26 In making this statement I am aware of the similarity between the late eighteenth-century factory and many earlier warehouses. However, there are several marked differences. First, the warehouse was not always rectangular in plan. In fact, it tended toward the square. Its dimensions varied more in accordance with the nature of the site than with the requirements of function. In the case of the factory the opposite was true. Its long, narrow and high proportions were determined by its use. During the nineteenth century these proportions became standardized according to certain structural modules which were based upon the size and operation of the machinery and upon the structural strength of materials.

The second difference between the types relates to their interior spaces. The factory required relatively unobstructed space, hence a minimum of columnar support. The warehouse, because of the great weights involved, frequently had closely spaced vertical supports. The third difference is in the fenestration. To provide interior light for workers, the factory tended to have more windows.

1.27 Figure 5, which shows sections of Strutt's North Mill at Belper, was published by Jennifer Tann in her splendid book *The Development of the Factory,* London, Cornmarket Press, 1970, p. 136. I am indebted to Miss Tann for her help in obtaining a photograph of this and Fig. 10.

1.28 Sir William Fairbairn, *Treatise on Mills and Millwork,* London, Longmans, Green, 1863, p. 334.

1.29 Even after the introduction of metal millwork, which made possible an enormous increase in the length of the mills, their width remained relatively the same. The lateral dimension of the working area did not appreciably increase until the sawtooth system of overhead lighting was introduced by Sir William Fairbairn in the first half of the nineteenth century.

1.30 Sigfried Giedion, in *Space, Time and Architecture* (Harvard University Press, 1941 [12th printing, 1959], p. 182), suggests that the utilization of the multi-storied form depended upon the introduction of the cast-iron pillar sometime in the early 1780's. Concerning a "typical late eighteenth-century factory at Bolton," he remarks that "at first the machinery was installed only in the attic; the timber roof trusses . . . soon to be replaced by trusses of cast iron . . . left enough space down the center for the installation of the long spinning frames. Later on, the use of cast iron pillars made it possible to install machinery on all floors."

In view of the number of multi-storied factories that were built prior to 1780 it is impossible to accept this theory. The early machines were light and small. There was no question of the prevailing structural systems being capable of carrying their weight or providing adequate space for them. Even if an increase of span had been necessary it could not have been achieved by the iron column because the wooden column was already supporting the maximum span possible with the wooden beam. In fact, after the introduction of the cast-iron beam the number of columnar supports was not at first greatly reduced. In New England, wood remained the principal material for the interior construction of factories throughout the nineteenth and into the twentieth century. In these interiors some of the heaviest spinning frames ever built were carried on a minimum of wooden columnar support. Iron began to replace wood in the last decade of the century not because of any structural weakness in wood but because iron was less combustible.

1.31 Victor S. Clark, *History of Manufactures in the United States,* Washington, D.C., Carnegie Foundation, 1916, Vol. I, p. 180.

1.32 The most notable instance is the so-called merchant mills, which appeared primarily in the middle colonies. They were considerably larger in size and productive capacity than the country grist mills and produced flour for the large city markets. At one time the manufacture of flour became one of the most speculative American industries. See Clark, *History of Manufactures,* p. 179.

CHAPTER II

2.1 For a complete analysis of Monticello, see Pierson, Volume I, Chap. VIII.

2.2 Letter to John Jay, August 23, 1785. See Julian Parks Boyd (ed.), *The Papers of Thomas Jefferson,* Princeton University Press, 1950–74, Vol. 8, p. 426.

2.3 Hamilton's *Report on Manufactures,* submitted to Congress December 5, 1791. See H. C. Syrett (ed.), *The Papers of Alexander Hamilton,* Columbia University Press, 1966, Vol. X, December 1791–January 1792, p. 291.

2.4 Letter to David Humphreys, June 23, 1791. See Syrett, *Hamilton,* p. 5.

2.5 Letter to Benjamin Austin, January 9, 1816. See Paul Leicester Ford (ed.), *The Writings of Thomas Jefferson,* New York, Putnam's, 1892–99, Vol. X, p. 10.

2.6 Ford, *Thomas Jefferson,* Vol. III, p. 269, n. 1.

2.7 The company which Hamilton helped to promote was the Society for the Establishment of Useful Manufactures, chartered by the New Jersey legislature on November 22, 1791. In May 1792, it decided to locate at the Great Falls of the Passaic River where a 104-foot head provided sufficient power for 247 wheels. The site was called Paterson after William Paterson, governor of the state. Although the initial efforts failed because of bad management, the company was revived in 1807 and by 1822 had twelve cotton mills and three woolen mills. See William R. Bagnall, *The Textile Industries of the United States,* Cambridge, Riverside Press, 1893, Vol. I, pp. 178ff.

2.8 As early as 1787 a multi-spindle jenny was put into operation in Beverly, Mass. but because of its inadequate design it failed to work. A year later, in Providence, R.I., Moses Brown was also experimenting with jennies, but the quality of the yarn was so poor, and the production rate so slow, that they, too, were abandoned. Moreover, none of these early spinning machines could be made to operate from a water wheel. At this point in the development of American textile machines only the slow-moving carding machines could be powered by water.

2.9   Recent research indicates that the machinery developed by Almy and Brown was, in fact, producing cloth at the time of Slater's arrival. There were difficulties, however, and Slater was brought into the partnership, because of his experience to improve this machinery. Although Slater actually worked with the existing machines, it was his knowledge and skill which made them operate efficiently. Equally important to the success of the undertaking was the high level of artisan skills available to Slater in the Providence area.

2.10 George S. White, *Memoir of Samuel Slater,* Philadelphia, 1836, p. 89; Syrett, *Alexander Hamilton,* Vol. X, pp. 330–31.

2.11 John Winter, *Industrial Architecture, A Survey of Factory Building,* London, Studio Vista, 1970, pp. 24–25.

2.12 Alfred P. Wadsworth and Julia Mann, *The Cotton Trade and Industrial Lancashire,* Manchester University Press, 1931, p. 305, nn. 4 and 6.

2.13 H. W. Dickinson and H. P. Vowles, *James Watt and the Industrial Revolution,* Science in Britain Series, London, 1943, p. 492.

2.14 See Winter, *Industrial Architecture,* fig. 14.

2.15 Figure 10 reproduces a water-color drawing, archived in the Derbyshire Record Office, which Jennifer Tann (*Development of the Factory,* p. 158) identifies as Arkwright's "Old Mill" at Cromford, built in 1771. According to Richard Candee, however, who reviewed Miss Tann's book (*Journal of the Society of Architectural Historians,* Vol. XXXI, No. 4, December 1972, pp. 336–37), the water color is one of several made in the 1780's as designs for Derbyshire pottery, and represents Arkwright's second, or lower, mill at Cromford, which dates from 1777.

2.16 For recent photographs of the New Lanark mills and housing, see Winter, *Industrial Architecture,* pp. 34–35.

2.17 It is of some interest how the partnership of Arkwright and Owen broke up: they quarreled over the location of the cupola and agreed to part. G. D. H. Cole, *The Life of Robert Owen,* London, 1930, p. 85.

2.18 A number of other interesting and important textile mills built during the late eighteenth century had the same basic form but with varying degrees and quality of architectural embellishment. Of particular interest is Samuel Oldknow's mill at Mellor, built in 1790. It was a large rectangular block of brick and stone, six stories high, with ranges of twenty-five windows along its major side. Like the New Lanark mills, it had a center pavilion with a pediment and cupola. For an informative summary of the mills of this period see Winter, *Industrial Architecture,* pp. 7–43.

2.19 In 1768, the year Arkwright took out his first patent, the whole cotton trade of Great Britain did not return more than £200,000 to the country; twenty years later the gross return exceeded £7,000,000. James Butterworth, *The Antiquities of the Town, and a Complete History of the Trade of Manchester,* Manchester, 1822, p. 90.

2.20 Alfred Freihernn von Wolzogen, *Aus Schinkels Nachlass, Reistagebucher, Briefe, und Apkorismen, Mitgetheilt und einem Verzeichniss sammtlicher Werke Schinkels versehen,* Berlin, 1862, 4 vols., Vol. 3, p. 124.

2.21 Quoted by John Gloag, *Industrial Art Explained,* London, George Allen and Unwin, 1934, p. 56.

2.22 I am indebted to Mr. Paul Rivard, then Director of the Old Slater Museum, for the information concerning the additions.

2.23 Not too many years ago two were still standing: Hope's Mill in Brimscombe and Bentley's Piano Factory in Woodchester. Unfortunately, the latter has since been destroyed by fire.

2.24 If the monitor window was used in other early mills in the United States, it most likely appeared in such ambitious schemes as that sponsored by Alexander

Hamilton in Paterson, N.J. No examples of it survive, however, and early descriptions of the buildings do not indicate such treatment of the roof.

2.25 Theodore Anton Sande, "The Architecture of the Rhode Island Textile Industry 1790–1860" (Ph.D. diss., University of Pennsylvania, 1972, p. 212). Professor Sande was kind enough to give me a copy of this work, which includes much new and important information about Rhode Island's industrial architecture.

2.26 Caroline F. Ware, *The Early New England Cotton Manufacture, a Study in Industrial Beginnings,* Boston and New York, Houghton Mifflin, 1931, p. 34. Profits from cotton manufacture were modest but steady.

2.27 Ware, *Cotton Manufacture,* p. 19.

2.28 See Pierson, Volume I, pp. 137ff.

2.29 Joseph Brown died in 1785.

2.30 Ware, *Cotton Manufacture,* pp. 7f.

2.31 Sande, "Rhode Island Textile Industry," p. 190.

2.32 *Ibid.,* p. 212. The clerestory monitor seems to have been used first in this country by the machine shop of the Hope Manufacturing Company in Hope, R.I. The date is 1806–7, the same time as the trap-door monitor in Samuel Slater's mill in Slatersville. Since the dating of both of these structures is approximate, it is impossible to say which one was used first. Nor is it known for certain whether or not there were earlier examples of each. English derivation of both, however, does remain a high probability.

2.33 As it stands today, the Lippitt Mill has a thick double-planked floor on heavy timber, a type not generally used in American mills until after 1830. But this is not the original floor. When first built, this part of the structural system was the same as that in the Slater Mill, joist floors on timber frame. When the new floors were put in the Lippitt Mill, sometime in the nineteenth century, the joists were removed altogether and the original horizontal timbers were encased in 1-inch dressed lumber. Since the old beams were hand-hewn this was unquestionably done to give them a smoother surface for better resistance to fire. In places where this later covering has been taken off it is possible to observe the original joist slots in the beams. The original siding of the building is vertical plank covered with lath and plaster on the inside and clapboard on the outside.

2.34 Henry Russell Hitchcock (*Rhode Island Architecture,* Providence, R.I., Museum Press, 1939, p. 41) gives the date of this mill as 1813. In 1853, however, the mill was purchased by Zachariah Allen of Providence, and among his papers are several references to the Nightingale Factory which indicate that the date was 1812. The papers include several plans for the mill, some of them made in 1828 when the first addition was built.

2.35 In 1828 an addition 80 feet long was made to the east end of the old mill, bringing the total length to 160 feet. It is this form of the building which is illustrated in Figure 14. Already in an advanced state of decay in the late 1940's, this fascinating early building has since been torn down.

2.36 Ware, *Cotton Manufacture,* p. 56.

2.37 According to Allen's own account (Zachariah Allen Papers, Memoranda, p. 159) the original mill was a stone building 60 feet by 36 feet. Precisely when it was enlarged is not clear. The same memoranda mention additions to the mill in 1825, additions of sufficient magnitude to require stagings. Moreover, Allen's application to his insurance company in 1834 for a reduction in rate, because of fire-prevention improvements, seems to relate to the enlarged mill. On the other hand, Richard Candee, who has done more work on the Allendale Mill than any other scholar, believes the additions were not made until 1839 at the time of the refitting for the manufacture of cotton. A decision on this must wait until Candee publishes his findings.

2.38 The cupola was destroyed in the hurricane of 1938 and has never been replaced.

2.39 The fire door was one of many devices developed by Zachariah Allen. Those first installed in the Allendale Mill were made of heavy wood. They were later replaced by wood doors covered with roofing tin. See Wilfred E. Stone, "Schemes from the Fertile Brain of Zachariah Allen," *Providence Sunday Journal,* June 2, 1935.

2.40 Proceedings of the New England Cotton Manufacturers Association, No. 27, October 29, 1879, p. 63.

2.41 See Pierson, Volume I, pp. 386–94.

2.42 Slow-burning construction and the role of the insurance companies in the development of industrial architecture in the United States will be discussed in greater detail in Vol. II B.

2.43 Robert Rogerson was a Boston merchant, and his keen awareness of his cultural heritage is manifest in the naming of his two mills: "Crown" reflects his roots in the English past; "Eagle," his active and aggressive citizenship in the new republic.

2.44 The granite Sears House on Beacon Street in Boston was designed by Parris and was certainly known to Rogerson. It was finished in 1816 and exemplifies the austere rational qualities that were beginning to characterize a number of Neoclassical buildings in Boston, including the later work of Charles Bulfinch. Parris's Quincy Market, one of the most impressive commercial buildings in Boston, was finished just before the Crown Mill was begun. See Pierson, Volume I, pp. 417–30.

2.45 The total length is 273 feet, not 320 as given by some writers. (See Robert Vogel and Theodore Sande, "The New England Textile Mill survey," *Historic American Buildings Survey, Number Eleven,* National Park Service, Washington, D.C., 1971, p. 81.) The error seems to have come from William Bagnal's unpublished history of the textile industry in the United States. A manuscript copy is in the Baker Library, Harvard University.

2.46 Where the connector spans the river the exterior walls are supported on massive segmental granite arches; the interior columns are carried on timber and iron Pratt trusses. See Vogel and Sande, "Textile Mill survey," p. 79.

2.47 Jeremiah Spofford, *Gazetteer of Massachusetts,* Newburyport, Mass., 1828. See also *The Architectural Forum,* Vol. 135, No. 1, July–August 1871, p. 64.

2.48 For the plans of the University of Virginia and Union College see Pierson, Volume I, pp. 316–25; for the city of Washington see Pierson, Volume I, pp. 395–98.

2.49 See Pierson, Volume I, pp. 325–34.

2.50 For further discussion of the early Rhode Island mill villages see Hitchcock, *Rhode Island Architecture,* pp. 36ff.

It could be argued that the slave quarters of Southern plantations during the eighteenth century represented a form of company housing. Architecturally, however, these buildings were marginal at best and represented such a different sphere of social and economic values that they are hardly comparable; most certainly they had no influence whatever on the growth of industrial housing in New England.

An especially interesting multiple housing enterprise of the eighteenth century is Bulfinch's Tontine Crescent in Boston (see Pierson, Volume I, pp. 244–48). It was the first planned housing of its kind in America and was both important and influential in its day. But it was urban and not rural, along with being a real estate speculation and not a company-planned and -controlled project. Although it had no direct bearing on the mill villages of Rhode Island, it had substantial influence on the industrial housing in the Merrimack Valley.

2.51 John Wood, *A Series of Plans for Cottages, or Habitations of the Labourer either in Husbandry, or Mechanic Arts, Adapted as Well to Towns as to the Country,* London, 1806.

2.52 Entries in Allen's diary for February 1822. Zachariah Allen Papers, Rhode Island Historical Society Library, Providence, R.I.

2.53 Ware, *Cotton Manufacture*, p. 60.

2.54 For a full discussion of this fascinating episode in American history, see Ware, *Cotton Manufacture*, Chap. IV.

2.55 The Waltham system of industrial organization was social and economic as well as technical. The factory was now visualized as the nucleus of a planned community in which everything was devoted to one objective, mass production. For an excellent discussion of the social and economic factors in this new concept, see John Coolidge, *Mill and Mansion, a Study of Architecture and Society in Lowell, Massachusetts, 1820–65,* New York, Columbia University Press, 1942, pp. 12–17.

2.56 Members of the corporation of the Boston Manufacturing Company at Waltham included some of Boston's most prominent citizens. Besides Francis Cabot Lowell and Nathan Appleton were E. Brooks, U. Cotting, Warren Dutton, John Gore, Benjamin Gorham, Charles Jackson, P. T. Jackson and James Lloyd. All of them were business and cultural leaders in the splendid changing city of Boston, so much of which was the result of the creative genius of Charles Bulfinch.

2.57 Coolidge, *Mill and Mansion,* pp. 18ff.

2.58 See *ibid.,* Chap. III, for a full discussion of the early planning of Lowell. For a more recent account of the canal system see Patrick M. Malone, *The Lowell Canal System,* Lowell, Massachusetts, The Lowell Museum, 1976.

2.59 Ware, *Cotton Manufacture,* Appendix A.

2.60 Charles Dickens, *American Notes for General Circulation,* London, Chapman and Hall, 1842, Chap. 4.

2.61 In the United States during the first half of the nineteenth century, the characteristic water wheel was the pitch-back type, which only developed about three quarters of the applied power. In 1840 at Lowell, for example, the mills of the Merrimack Company were still powered by eight pitch-back wheels, 30 feet in diameter with 12-foot buckets. And the new Bay State Mills, when built in Lawrence, Massachusetts in 1846, were also equipped with high breast wheels. Use of this type of wheel kept the individual factory units limited in size.

2.62 The first building in Harrisville which can be regarded as a factory was built in 1822 by Bethuel Harris and his eldest son Cyrus. A small brick building, it was used at first for carding and fulling wool. It may also have had a simple spinning machine, and is known to have had primitive power looms. Because of its location between the later "Upper" and "Lower" Mills it was known as the "Middle Mill." It was torn down in 1866 by Milan Harris to make way for the larger "New Mill."

2.63 The Cheshire Mill was built by Cyrus Harris in 1847. In 1849 a member of the Colony family from Keene purchased an interest in the mill and by 1850 the Colonys owned it entirely. After that they shared the industrial activity of Harrisville with the founding family until 1881, when the Harris's New Mill burned down. This ended the Harris enterprise and in 1887 the Colonys purchased the remaining Harris properties. From that point on they continued to operate the mills until October 1970 when bankruptcy forced them to shut down. The one hundred and twenty years of continuous ownership by the same family, however, has been the principle factor in the remarkable preservation of the town. Following the bankruptcy, a group of concerned citizens formed an organization, Historic Harrisville, Inc., which purchased core buildings of the Harris Company; the Cheshire Mills were purchased by Filtrine, Inc., a new light industry which is now the main employer in the town. Historic Harrisville, Inc., has rehabilitated the historic buildings and they are now all in use for a number of light industrial, business, and domestic purposes. The historic character of the community has thus been preserved not as a museum but as a living, working community. The entire community is now a National Historic Landmark.

For the historical data on Harrisville I have relied almost entirely on the definitive work of John Borden Armstrong, *Factory Under the Elms: a History of Harrisville, N.H.*, 1774–1969, Cambridge, Mass., MIT Press, 1969.

2.64 There is one exception to this. In 1922 a large wing was added to the Cheshire Mill. Its stark twentieth-century ugliness is an unhappy backdrop to the town but does not intrude to the point where it disturbs the visual homogeneity of the earlier community.

2.65 See Pierson, Volume I, pp. 54f.

2.66 See Pierson, Volume I, Chapter VII.

2.67 This idea was suggested to me by Professor Theodore Sande while he was at Williams College. He is now with the National Trust for Historic Preservation.

2.68 Hoxie Neale Fairchild, *The Romantic Quest,* New York, Columbia University Press, 1931, p. 251. I am indebted to Mrs. Hart Moore for this quote and for the conclusions which follow.

CHAPTER III

3.1 Pierson, Volume I, pp. 16–21.

3.2 "Philosophy of Gothic Architecture," *The English Review; or, Quarterly Journal of Ecclesiastical and General Literature,* Vol. II, October–December 1844, p. 419.

3.3 Pierson, Volume I, pp. 34–45.

3.4 *Ibid.,* pp. 61–65.

3.5 John Summerson, *Architecture in Britain, 1530–1830,* Pelican History of Art, Baltimore, Penguin Books, 1954, Chap. 10.

3.6 Wren's London churches built in the Gothic style were St. Dunstan's-in-the-East (1698), St. Mary Aldermary (1702), St. Michael, Cornhill (1721), St. Alban's, Wood St. (1721, completed by Hawksmoor), and St. Christopher le Stocks (originally a Gothic church, restored in 1671, and further beautified in 1696).

3.7 While working on the towers of Westminster Abbey, Hawksmoor also produced a remarkable, if ponderous, Gothic design of his own: one entire quadrangle at All Souls College, Oxford, completed in 1734. Although heavier in scale than Wren's Gothic, it is similarly classicized.

3.8 Pierson, Volume I, pp. 111–13.

3.9 The screen in Gloucester Cathedral, erected in 1742, is typical. See Summerson, *Architecture in Britain,* pp. 239–40.

3.10 See Nikolaus Pevsner, "Richard Payne Knight," *Art Bulletin,* Vol. XXXI, No. 4, December 1949, p. 295.

3.11 Horace Walpole was the fourth son of the famous Whig Prime Minister, Sir Robert Walpole; he was educated at Eton and King's College, Cambridge, and for a while served in Parliament. But in spite of his family background, he had little enthusiasm for politics, and turned instead to writing. The main bulk of his work was in the form of letters, which fill more than thirty volumes, but he was also a dramatist, an essayist, and a novelist.

3.12 William Robinson, who had recently been appointed Clerk of the Works at Greenwich Hospital, was put in charge of construction, and was probably responsible for the main fabric of the house.

3.13 For an interesting and detailed account of the building of Strawberry Hill see Wilmarth Sheldon Lewis, *Horace Walpole,* New York, Pantheon Books, 1960, Chap. IV.

3.14 Pierson, Volume I, pp. 205–11.

3.15 See J. Mordaunt Crook, "John Britton and the Genesis of the Gothic Revival," *Concerning Architecture,* John Summerson, ed., London, Penguin Press, 1968.

3.16 Quoted by Lewis, *Horace Walpole*, p. 101.

3.17 Walpole's "Committee" included, beside the architect William Robinson, John Chute and Thomas Pitt. Toward the end James Essex took Robinson's place as architect a few years after the latter died.

3.18 In a letter to Mann, Walpole explained that "one has a satisfaction in imprinting the gloomth of abbeys and cathedrals on one's house." Quoted by Lewis, *Horace Walpole*, p. 116.

3.19 The exception is in medieval domestic architecture, which developed in response to practical rather than formal design intents and displayed a variety of interior space arrangements.

3.20 Pevsner, "Richard Payne Knight," p. 294.

3.21 *Ibid.*, p. 295, gives quotation.

3.22 See Chapter I.

3.23 Pevsner, "Richard Payne Knight," p. 296, gives quotation.

3.24 *Ibid.*

3.25 One room from Lee Priory is preserved in the Victoria and Albert Museum in London.

3.26 See Pierson, Volume I, pp. 360–72.

3.27 Figure 74 shows an enlargement of the original church of 1698 after it was completed in 1737. In both its enlarged and its original form, the building was of stone, had a Gothic-like tower and spire, and Gothic-like vertical windows with central brick mullions. See Isaac Newton Phelps Stokes, *The Iconography of Manhattan Island*, New York, R. H. Dodds, 1915–28, Vol. IV, pp. 445, 493, 542. Although the enlarged church was remarkably similar in form to the New Dutch Church, built in 1731 (*ibid.*, Vol. I, p. 28), an engraving of First Trinity made about 1780, after the fire, clearly shows pointed Gothic-like window construction (*ibid.*, Vol. III, p. 868 and pl. 8).

3.28 See Pierson, Volume I, pp. 34–45.

3.29 The church is defined in a description of 1827 as "plain Gothic." See Stokes, *Iconography*, Vol. V, entry July 14, 1827, p. 1,668.

3.30 See Pierson, Volume I, p. 362.

3.31 St. Pauls Church, Alexandria, Va., still stands but in a drastically altered condition. Latrobe's Bank of Philadelphia, completed in 1808, was destroyed less than two decades after its completion. See Talbot Hamlin, *Benjamin Henry Latrobe*, New York, Oxford University Press, 1955, pp. 344–46.

3.32 See Pierson, Volume I, fig. 164.

3.33 The Sullivan Dorr House (1809) at 109 Benefit St. has a freestanding Gothic portico which is superbly integrated into the otherwise Neoclassical design.

3.34 See Pierson, Volume I, Chap. X, *passim.*

3.35 John Holden Green's Gothic St. John's Church (1810) was followed in 1816 by the First Congregational Church, a conventional Federal style building. It was also designed by Green and is only a few blocks away from St. John's.

3.36 "Architecture in the United States," *The American Journal of Science and Arts*, Vol. XVIII, July 1830, p. 20.

3.37 See Pierson, Volume I, Chap. IV.

3.38 See Pierson, Volume I, pp. 205–9.

3.39 Town apparently did not like the painting, and he and Cole had an unpleasant exchange of correspondence on the matter. In a letter to his friend Asher B. Durand, Cole reports on this exchange, and at one point says, "I have written to him (Town), saying that I would rather give him his books back, and consider the commission as null." See Louis Legrand Noble, *The Life and Works of Thomas Cole*, Cambridge, Harvard University Press, 1964, pp. 212–13.

3.40 See Pierson, Volume I, Chap. VIII.

3.41 The term "revival" has been used by architectural historians to identify that mode of design which derives its inspiration from a single style in the past, thus, Jefferson's *Roman Revival*, the *Greek Revival*, the *Gothic Revival*, and later the *Romanesque Revival*. Yet within any one of these large style concepts there are frequently many sub-styles which, except for certain pervasive characteristics such as the pointed arch of the Gothic style, are sometimes as different from one another as two parent styles. An example would be the disparity between the Early English Gothic with its austere lancet windows (Salisbury) and the English Perpendicular Gothic with its spectacular fan vaults (King's College Chapel). The fact is that each of the revival movements of the nineteenth century was based on selectivity within one particular style and was as eclectic in method as the more overt forms of eclecticism which made their choice between two wholly different historical styles.

3.42 The water color is signed H. C. Curtis and is dated May 13, 1864. It is in the possession of the Trinity Parish.

3.43 James Gibbs, *A Book of Architecture*, London, 1728, pl. 25. The tower of All Saints, Derby, is the only Gothic building shown by Gibbs, and he shows it not because he had any special interest in the Gothic, but because he was commissioned to add a new church body to the existing tower. This he did in 1725, and in spite of the splendid Perpendicular Gothic of the tower, he rendered his addition in his own heavily classical style. The 210-foot tower was built during 1509–27. Gibbs's beautiful engraving of it was the most important and readily available source of the Gothic for American church builders of the early nineteenth century. Another possible source for Town at Trinity was Joseph Halfpenny, *Gothic Ornaments in the Cathedral Church of York*, London, 1775. This may have provided details for both the open crenelation and the original chancel window.

3.44 Published in its entirety by J. Frederick Kelly, *Early Connecticut Meeting Houses*, New York, Columbia University Press, 1948, Vol. II, pp. 28–31.

3.45 See Pierson, Volume I, pp. 235–39, 268–85, 429–32.

3.46 See S. N. Dickinson, *The Boston Almanac for the Year 1843*, Boston, Thomas Groom, p. 79. Trinity Church was located at the corner of Summer and Hawley streets in downtown Boston. Its destruction in the great Boston fire of November 9–10, 1872, led to the building of H. H. Richardson's Trinity Church on Copley Square. The Church of the Messiah on Broadway in New York (also destroyed) was built shortly after the 1829 Trinity in Boston, was almost identical in character to it, and in all probability was directly influenced by it. See "New York Church Architecture," *Putnam's Monthly*, Vol. II, No. IX, September 1853, pp. 240, 246.

3.47 See Pierson, Volume I, pp. 434ff.

3.48 An engraving of 1829 shows that the towers were also at one time crenelated. See George B. Tatum, *Penn's Great Town*, Philadelphia, University of Pennsylvania Press, 1961, fig. 81.

3.49 See Tatum, *Penn's Great Town*, fig. 74.

3.50 See Tatum, *Penn's Great Town*, fig. 73.

3.51 The Riverton Union Church is now the Hitchcock Museum. Recently purchased by the Hitchcock Chair Company, it has been carefully restored and is now one of the most interesting examples of the adaptive use of historic buildings in New England. Although the interior has been modified to make it suitable for a museum, this has been done with great taste. The Hitchcock furniture and other related objects on display are both beautiful and fascinating. It is well worth the trip to Riverton, which is itself a charming town, to see this collection.

3.52 See Pierson, Volume I, p. 442, fig. 316.

3.53 At St. Paul's, Troy, the original wooden mullions have been covered with an outer protective window, but the double lancet divisions can just be seen behind the newer window in Figure 100.

3.54 Trinity, New Haven, is 103 feet long and 74 feet wide; St. Paul's, Troy, is 103 by 70 feet. The lancet windows at Trinity are 25 feet high and 8½ feet wide; at St. Paul's they are 25 by 8. The tower at Trinity is 25 feet square; at Troy it is 24.

3.55 The altar window at Trinity, New Haven, was 22 feet wide; at St. Paul's, Troy, it was 20.

3.56 *The Troy Sentinel,* August 15, 1828.

3.57 The interior of St. Paul's, Troy, was completely rebuilt during 1892–93, and nothing remains of the original arrangement.

3.58 Records in the Town Clerk's office in Arlington indicate that a William Passman was paid $58 for forty-six and one-half weeks of board, and was given $50 with which to return to England. If Passman was, indeed, the "architect" of the building, nothing in its style indicates that he had any professional knowledge of the Gothic. What seems most probable is that Passman was the builder, and that just like American architects and builders he relied on local sources of architectural information.

3.59 For an illustration, see Kate M. Schutt, *The First Century of St. Stephen's Parish,* 1830–1930, Pittsfield, Mass., Eagle Printing and Binding Co., 1930, p. 8.

CHAPTER IV

4.1 For a highly readable summary of the writings that influenced the Gothic Revival, see Kenneth Clark, *The Gothic Revival,* London, Constable, 1928, Chap. 4. Now available as a Pelican Book.

4.2 For a detailed account of Britton's writings, see Crook, "John Britton," in Summerson, *Concerning Architecture,* 1968.

4.3 The functional point of view expressed by Pugin embraces all architecture, not just that in the Gothic style, and in propounding his theories he shows himself to be very much a part of his time. Indeed, his ideas, except for their narrow Gothic application, were precisely those already developed by the rational Neoclassicists of the late eighteenth and early nineteenth centuries. See Pierson, Volume I, pp. 338ff.

4.4 For a full account of Pugin's life and work, see Phoebe Stanton, *Pugin,* London, Thames and Hudson, 1971. For a discussion of Pugin as a church architect, see Henry Russell Hitchcock, *Early Victorian Architecture in Britain,* New Haven, Conn., Yale University Press, 1954, Chap. III.

4.5 See Pierson, Volume I, pp. 55–58.

4.6 *Ibid.,* pp. 94–105, 131–40, 235–39.

4.7 For a full account of the Ecclesiological movement, see James F. White, *The Cambridge Movement: The Ecclesiologists and the Gothic Revival,* Cambridge University Press, 1962.

4.8 "Rubrically ordered" means ordered according to church doctrine. "Rubrical" was a favorite term of the Ecclesiologists and occurs frequently in their writings.

4.9 Hitchcock, *Early Victorian Architecture in Britain,* p. 74.

4.10 This article was the first of two by Pugin published in *The Dublin Review* in May 1841 and February 1842. They were presented in book form in 1843 under the title *On the Present State of Ecclesiastical Architecture in England,* London, Charles Dolman. Reprinted by St. Barnabas Press, Oxford, 1969.

4.11 Perhaps the best example is the Church of All Saints, Margaret Street, London. Designed by the leading Ecclesiological architect, William Butterfield, and finished in 1849, it drew the highest praise from the Ecclesiologists and is one of the most original and exciting works of the Ecclesiological movement. Its tall, completely asymmetrical massing, orthodox interior arrangements, and rich polychrome decoration exemplify better than any other church of the period the complex doctrine of Ecclesiology. For a provocative discussion of this unusual building, see John Summerson, *Heavenly Mansions,* New York, W. W. Norton, 1963, Chap. VII.

4.12 Pugin, *Present State of Ecclesiastical Architecture,* p. 8.

4.13 See Everard M. Upjohn, *Richard Upjohn, Architect and Churchman,* New York, Columbia University Press, 1939. Reprinted by DeCapo Press, New York, 1968.

4.14 For Latrobe, see Pierson, Volume I, pp. 337ff.

4.15 For a full account of the building of Trinity Church, see Upjohn, *Richard Upjohn,* Chap. 4.

4.16 The Isaac Farrar House (1833) and the Samuel Farrar House (1836), both in Bangor, Me. See Upjohn, *Richard Upjohn,* p. 35.

4.17 That the longitudinal section shown in Figure 113 was one of the drawings submitted in 1839 is borne out by the fact that it shows an open timber ceiling and an articulated chancel, both of which the church records make clear were objected to by the Committee.

4.18 Gilman was only twenty-three when he wrote the article. On the whole it is a vigorous rebellion against the Neoclassical revivals and a passionate defense of the Gothic. We will encounter Gilman again in the designing of the Boston City Hall in 1862.

4.19 Gilman was obviously aware of both Britton and Pugin, and he reiterates Pugin's contention that it is only in Gothic architecture "that the great *aesthetical* principles of building have been fully carried out." *North American Review,* Vol. LVIII, 1844, p. 465.

4.20 *Ibid.,* p. 463.

4.21 *Ibid.,* pp. 477–78.

4.22 Upjohn owned all five volumes of Britton's *Architectural Antiquities* by 1836. See Upjohn, *Richard Upjohn,* p. 36.

4.23 Phoebe B. Stanton's *The Gothic Revival and American Church Architecture* (Baltimore, Johns Hopkins Press, 1968) is the definitive study of the Ecclesiological movement and its impact on American church architecture. I have relied on it heavily in my development of the theme. Stanton was the first modern critic to point out (pp. 60–61) the relationship between Upjohn's Trinity Church and Pugin's ideal church as shown in *True Principles.*

4.24 A. Welby Pugin, *True Principles of Pointed or Christian Architecture,* London, 1841, p. 42 and pl. H, fig. I.

4.25 In the Pugin drawing the church is assumed to be oriented with the chancel to the east, which would make the porch on the south side. At Trinity, however, this traditional orientation is reversed, much to the distress of the *Ecclesiologist* (Vol. X, 1850, p. 195), so that the porch is actually on the north side.

4.26 The stained glass was designed by Upjohn and was manufactured on the site. See Upjohn, *Richard Upjohn,* pp. 54–55.

4.27 Pugin, *True Principles,* p. 31, states that *"Wooden groining* is decidedly bad, because it is employing a material *in the place and after the manner of stone, which requires an entirely different mode of construction."*

4.28 On February 3, 1808, Benjamin Latrobe gave his young assistant Robert Mills the first two parts of Britton's *The Architectural Antiquities of Great Britain.* See Hamlin, *Benjamin Latrobe,* p. 345.

4.29 "On the Architecture of America," *American Museum,* Vol. VIII, Philadelphia, October 1790, p. 174. Talbot Hamlin (*Greek Revival Architecture in America,* London, Oxford University Press, 1944, p. 359) says that the article "contains a good description of Gothic architecture."

4.30 Silliman, one of the leading intellectuals of his day, was a friend of Ithiel Town, the architect of Trinity Church. It is tempting to suggest that either Town or Alexander Jackson Davis, who joined him as a partner in 1829, had something to do with the articles, if they did not actually write them. They are too "architectural" in tone and substance not to have been done by someone in the profession.

4.31 *The American Journal of Science and Arts*, Vol. XVIII, No. 2, July 1830, pp. 220–29.

4.32 *North American Review*, Vol. XLIII, October 1836, pp. 356–84. The article is a review of James Gallier, *The American Builder's General Price Book and Estimator*. The review says nothing about Gallier's book. It does, however, say a good deal about American architecture in the early 1830's.

4.33 Cleveland describes a building on the Harvard campus in some detail (Bulfinch's University Hall?) but does not precisely say why he dislikes it so much, except that its portico is too light. *North American Review*, Vol. XLIII, p. 362.

4.34 Illustrated in Hopkins's *Essay on Gothic Architecture*, pl. 5.

4.35 It has added a special dimension to my work on this book to realize that many of the books and documents that I have been privileged to use at the Boston Athenaeum were also used by Bishop Hopkins and by other writers and architects of his time such as A. D. Gilman and A. J. Davis.

4.36 For Hopkins's activities as an architect in Vermont, see Lawrence Wodehouse, "John Henry Hopkins and the Gothic Revival," *Antiques Magazine*, Vol. CIII, No. 4, April 1973, pp. 776–83.

4.37 Stanton, *Gothic Revival*, pp. 56ff.

4.38 For a full account of this church, see Sarah E. Rusk, "Hezekiah Eldridge, Architect-Builder of St. John's Church, Cleveland Ohio," *Journal of the Society of Architectural Historians*, Vol. XXV, No. 1, March 1966, pp. 50–58.

4.39 *The New York Ecclesiologist* was first published by the New York Ecclesiological Society in 1848. The first issue contained a review of Trinity Church which criticized it for its liturgical faults. See Stanton, *Gothic Revival*, p. 183.

Trinity also came under fire from other critics than the Ecclesiologists. A letter to the editor of the *United States Magazine and Democratic Review* (Vol. XX, 1847, pp. 139ff.) finds Trinity "solid and truthful," but at the same time sees "the portico more ambitious than the house," and protests that the nave "should have forty feet *at least* more length, and fifteen more breadth." Five years later an article entitled "New-York Church Architecture," which appeared in *Putnam's Monthly* (Vol. II, September 1853, No. IX, pp. 233ff.), was also critical of Trinity. While admitting that "the present 'Trinity Church' is every way a more beautiful building than the old dingy stone edifice, with a wooden spire, which it has displaced," it nevertheless finds the spire of the new church "clumsy and wanting in lightness," and "the body of the church . . . poor, and decidedly wanting in character." Although it says that "the interior of the church is, at first glance, very fine," it protests "the evident insincerity of the whole affair. The side walls, the whole roof, and the chancel are of *plaster, colored to imitate stone.*"

4.40 Stanton, *Gothic Revival*, pp. 225ff., discusses several examples.

4.41 *The United States Magazine and Democratic Review*, Vol. XX, 1847, p. 144.

4.42 See Upjohn, *Richard Upjohn*, fig. 35 and p. 87.

4.43 Robert Dale Owen, *Hints on Public Architecture*, New York, Putnam, 1849, pl. 2 and p. 71.

4.44 J. M. Neale and B. Webb, *The Symbolism of Churches and Church Ornaments*, Leeds, 1843, is a translation of Book I of the *Rationale divinorum officiorum* of Durandus. Here it is stated that doors in transepts are generally on the west (or short side) of the transept to avoid confusion between the transept and the south porch (p. cii).

4.45 My analysis and evaluation of St. Mary's was based on observations and notes made before the fire (April 16, 1976) and thus represents the building in nearly its original form. My photographs were also made before the fire.

4.46 *Elevations, Sections, and Details of Saint John the Baptist Church at Shottesbrooke Berkshire* (Oxford, London and Cambridge: for the Oxford Architectural Society, by J. B. Parker, Rivington's and Stevenson, 1846).

4.47 Quoted by Stanton, *Gothic Revival*, p. 44.

4.48 "New Churches," *Ecclesiologist*, Vol. V, February 1846, p. 80.

4.49 Upjohn, *Richard Upjohn*, p. 89.

4.50 See Pierson, Volume I, pp. 404–12.

4.51 Stanton, *Gothic Revival*, Chap. III.

4.52 *Ibid.*, p. 91.

4.53 The other two were All Saints, Teversham, Cambridgeshire, and St. Mary's, Arnold, Nottinghamshire. Stanton, *Gothic Revival*, pp. 91–92.

4.54 *Ibid.*, pp. 98ff.

4.55 *Instrumenta Ecclesiastica, A Series of Working Designs for the Furniture, Fittings and Decorations of Churches and their Precincts,* London, Van Voorst, 1847. The book appeared in twelve parts and was prepared for the Cambridge Camden Society by William Butterfield.

4.56 Carver was a contractor who called himself an "architect" (see Stanton, *Gothic Revival*, p. 112, n. 33). He cannot, however, be regarded as on a par with such nationally known professionals as Upjohn, Latrobe, Mills, Strickland, Town, and Davis.

4.57 See Pierson, Volume I, p. 42.

4.58 Stanton, *Gothic Revival*, p. 103. All my information about St. James-the-Less comes from Stanton.

4.59 Stanton discusses a number of these (*Gothic Revival*, Chap. VI). One small bell-cote type church which she mentions, the Church of the Ascension in Westminster, Md., was built circa 1845, thus before St. James-the-Less. It was designed by architect Robert Cary Long, Jr. (*ibid.*, fig. VI–14). Long designed two other small churches in Maryland in 1845 (*ibid.*, p. 248). As Stanton points out, they were probably based on English examples, St. Anne's, Keighley, and St. Mary's, Southport, which were illustrated by Pugin in his *Present State* and are reproduced here in Figure 125.

4.60 See Upjohn, *Richard Upjohn*, fig. 39.

4.61 The interior of St. Mary's, Nashotah, has been radically changed and thus does not tell us much about Upjohn's original intentions.

4.62 Robert Payne Bigelow, *A Sketch of the History of St. Paul's Church in Brookline*, Brookline, Mass., 1949, pp. 1–3. St. Paul's was the first Episcopal church in Brookline, although there were three earlier churches in the town. Before the fire St. Paul's was the oldest surviving church in the community.

4.63 In making my photographs of St. Paul's I was not as fortunate as I was at St. Mary's. Although the exterior shots had all been made before the fire (January 1976), the interior had not. My photograph for Figure 135, therefore, was made a few days after the fire before the badly burned ceiling trusses were all removed.

4.64 The two early drawings are in the possession of St. Paul's parish. The third is in the Upjohn collection at Avery Architectural Library, Columbia University.

4.65 The "triforium" at St. Paul's was planned by Upjohn but was not completed until 1883. Bigelow, *History of St. Paul's*, p. 9.

4.66 "Church Roofing," *Ecclesiologist*, Vol. III, 1844, p. 102.

4.67 *Ibid.*

4.68 See p. 157.

4.69 For a discussion of this unhappy episode in Upjohn's life, see Stanton, *Gothic Revival*, pp. 183ff.

4.70 Two of Wills's most important and interesting buildings were St. Anne's Chapel and Christ Church Cathedral, both done for Bishop Medley in Fredericton, New Brunswick, Canada. Wills came to New York before completion of the cathedral and the designs necessary to finish both the building and some of its furnishings were sent to Canada by William Butterfield. See Stanton, *Gothic Revival*, Chap. IV.

4.71 For a full account of St. Mark's, Philadelphia, see Stanton, *Gothic Revival*, pp. 115ff.

4.72 Like Upjohn, both Frank Wills and Henry Dudley were from Exeter; John Notman was a Scotsman.

4.73 For the full development of this story, see Pierson, Volume I, Chap. VI–X.

4.74 *New York Ecclesiologist*, Vol. III, September 1851, p. 141. Quoted by Stanton, *Gothic Revival*, p. 185, n. 76.

CHAPTER V

5.1   See Pierson, Volume I, pp. 235–39, 440–44.

5.2   See *ibid.*, Chap. V.

5.3   See *ibid.*, p. 269.

5.4   The Reverend Monsignor James F. Rigny, in a speech entitled "A History of the Cathedral" delivered before the Society of the Friendly Sons of St. Patrick, March 2, 1970. The speech was published in its entirety in *The Yearbook of the Society of the Friendly Sons of St. Patrick*, 1970, pp. 21–30. The quotation is from p. 23.

5.5   The letter is dated May 29, 1858. Hughes Papers, Archives of the Diocese of New York, Box A–2.

5.6   See Pierson, Volume I, pp. 360–72.

5.7   The fourth see was Bardstown, Kentucky; it served an enormous frontier territory but very few people.

5.8   In Philadelphia, the Church of St. Augustine (1799–1801), on Fourth Street near Vine, served as the cathedral until the Cathedral of SS. Peter and Paul was dedicated in 1864. In Boston, Charles Bulfinch's Church of the Holy Cross (1803), in Franklin Street near the Tontine Crescent, became the Cathedral of the Holy Cross in 1808, and continued as such until the new Cathedral of the Holy Cross, at Washington and Waltham streets, was dedicated in 1875. Both St. Augustine's and the Bulfinch church were conventional Federal style buildings.

5.9   Mangin was a French aristocrat who apparently came to this country to escape the Revolution. His main activity in New York was as an engineer, but he was also the designer of the New York City Hall (1811), a handsome classical building with strong overtones of the style of Louis XVI. For an illustration of old St. Patrick's, see John M. Farley, *History of St. Patrick's Cathedral*, New York, Society for the Propagation of the Faith, 1908, facing p. 51.

5.10 However, old St. Patrick's Cathedral (120 ft. long) was smaller than Latrobe's Baltimore Cathedral (170 ft. long).

5.11 The letter is dated June 14, 1858. Quoted by Farley, *History of St. Patrick's*, p. 120. Unless otherwise noted all my historical data about St. Patrick's are taken from Farley.

5.12 How Renwick happened to get the commission is not exactly clear, but according to one verbal account it was Renwick's maid who alerted him to the fact that a new cathedral was under discussion, and motivated him to seek the commission. I am indebted to Walter Knight Sturges for this attractive piece of intelligence.

5.13 *New York Times,* October 30, 1854.

5.14 Sarah Booth Conroy, "The Restoration of James Renwick," the Washington *Post,* January 30, 1972, p. 18.

5.15 Letter from the Archbishop Hughes to leading members of the archdiocese, dated June 14, 1858. Quoted by Farley, *History of St. Patrick's,* p. 119.

5.16 Letter from Archbishop Hughes to Renwick and Rodrigue, undated. Hughes Papers, Archives of the Diocese of New York, Box A–7.

5.17 Preliminary contract, dated September 1865. Archives of the Diocese of New York, Box A–27.

5.18 Unidentified newspaper clipping, dated September 6, 1885. Archives of the Diocese of New York, Box K–3. Contract was believed to be for $190,000.

5.19 For an interesting account of Renwick and Grace Church, see Carl Carmer, *The Years of Grace, 1808–1958,* New York, Grace Church, 1958, pp. 16–22.

5.20 In May of 1842 the architectural firm of Town and Davis at the request of Mr. F. Sheldon submitted a variety of plans for Grace Church, and according to Davis these "were the first made, and served in the getting up of the plan finally adopted." See Davis's Office Book, in the Print Department of the Metropolitan Museum of Art, p. 73.

5.21 Effingham P. Humphrey, Jr., "The Churches of James Renwick," Master of Arts thesis, New York University, 1942, p. 6.

5.22 Robert Dale Owen, *Hints on Public Architecture,* New York, George P. Putnam, 1849, pp. vi–vii. I shall discuss Owen's relationship with Renwick in Part B of this volume.

5.23 This drawing is in the collections of the New-York Historical Society and will be reproduced in Part B of this volume.

5.24 Renwick's twin-tower façade was not the first in America, nor even the first among the many revival churches of his day. The twin-tower façade first appeared in this country during the eighteenth century in the Spanish mission churches of the Pacific Southwest (see Pierson, Volume I, Chap. V), and it was used by Latrobe during the first decade of the nineteenth century in the Baltimore Cathedral (*ibid.,* p. 361). During the 1820's it appeared, as already mentioned, in St. Stephen's Church, Philadelphia, designed by William Strickland. The twin-tower façade was also used by a number of European-trained architects working in the United States at the same time as Renwick. Of these the most important was Leopold Eidlitz. His St. George's Episcopal Church in New York, designed with Otto Blesch in 1846, was Romanesque in style and had matching towers with open-work masonry spires. It will be discussed in Part B of this volume.

5.25 Stanton, *Gothic Revival,* p. 69.

5.26 Illustrated in Hitchcock, *Early Victorian Architecture in Britain,* Vol. II, pl. III, 10.

5.27 Stanton, *Gothic Revival,* p. 61.

5.28 The drawing is one of eighteen sketches and thirty-three ink drawings contained in a box of Renwick papers in the Lienau Cabinet at the Avery Library. The early sketch is framed and has a description attached which says in part:

"These original drawings made by James Renwick, architect of St. Patrick's Cathedral, were done shortly after he was selected for the undertaking by Archbishop John Hughes of New York in 1853. . . .

"These pencil sketches were among several early designs for the Cathedral made by James Renwick. They were found among the private papers and drawings of the architect and handed down through several generations of the Renwick family."

5.29 The length and width given by Renwick are slightly greater than those given two months earlier by Archbishop Hughes.

5.30 Renwick Papers, Lienau Cabinet, Avery Library.

5.31 I am indebted to Selma Rattner for pointing out to me the existence of the date in the watermark. I have since re-examined the drawings myself and have found that ten bear the watermark J. WHATMAN 1876, and five the watermark J. WHATMAN TURKEY MILL. I would also like to add that Mrs. Rattner is currently working on a definitive study of James Renwick and has generously shared with me her extensive knowledge of the architect and his work.

5.32 *Building: A Journal of Architecture.* Volume V, no. 7, August 14, 1886, shows the façade, the longitudinal section, the plan, and the side elevation. Volume V, no. 10, September 4, 1886, shows a perspective view (not one of the Avery drawings); and on a double spread it shows the reredos on the left (an Avery drawing), the pulpit on the right (not an Avery drawing), plus two cross sections of the nave as built, one looking east, the other west, and the rear elevation.

5.33 The best account of the continental Gothic Revival is George Germann, *The Gothic Revival in Europe and Britain: Sources, Influences and Ideas,* Cambridge, MIT Press, 1972. I have relied heavily on this splendid book for my own development of the subject.

5.34 I have used Sulpice Boisserée, *Vues, plans, coupes et détails de la Cathédrale de Cologne, avec des restaurations d'après le dessin originale,* Stuttgart and Paris, 1821.

5.35 For an illustration see Henry Russell Hitchcock, *Architecture of the Nineteenth and Twentieth Centuries,* Baltimore, Penguin Books, 1958, pl. 55B.

5.36 *Allgemeine Bauzeitung,* 1858; plates 164–66 show plan, elevation, and cross section.

5.37 *The Ecclesiologist,* Vol. XII, 1851, p. 272; quoted by Germann, *The Gothic Revival,* p. 113.

5.38 Allen Nevins and Milton Halsey Thomas, eds., *The Diary of George Templeton Strong,* New York, Macmillan, 1952.

5.39 National Archives. Letter from Major William Wade to Colonel R. Lee, dated May 13, 1830, regarding the use of iron columns in a new arsenal building at the Springfield Armory, states that Mr. Cyrus Alger of Boston "has made many [iron columns] of late for churches in Boston."

5.40 All measurements reported in this section were made directly from the drawings themselves, using the scale provided by Renwick.

5.41 This fascinating document is in the possession of the Cathedral. It not only dates exactly the beginnings of the plaster vaults but also provides interesting information about the Powers family and the Company.

5.42 Quoted in full by Humphrey, "The Churches of James Renwick," Appendix D. The first three paragraphs of this description are repeated word for word by Fred H. Allen, *The Great Cathedrals of the World,* Boston, Haskell and Post, 1886, Vol. II, pp. 301–2, and again by Farley, *History of St. Patrick's,* pp. 153–54.

5.43 *New York Times,* August 16, 1858.

5.44 *Ibid.,* April 5, 1868.

5.45 *The American Architect and Building News,* Vol. III, no. 108, January 19, 1878, pp. 20–22.

5.46 Stained-glass windows are, of course, a coherent and spectacular feature of the Gothic church and quite apart from their didactic role were regarded as part of the architecture and absolutely essential to the consummation of the interior visual effects. Although called for by Renwick, the windows installed in St. Patrick's at the time it was opened in 1879 were all of French design and manufacture. The glass, for the most part especially fine, adds enormously to the splendor of the interior, and made a very great impression in its day. Several of the windows were exhibited at the Philadelphia Centennial Exposition of 1876 before their installation in the church.

5.47 In 1853, the year in which Renwick received the commission for St. Patrick's, the Congregational Churches of America published *A Book of Plans for Churches and Parsonages,* which showed eighteen designs for churches all of which were in some form of medieval style. Among the architects represented were Renwick and Upjohn. I shall discuss the impact of the picturesque movement on the Congregational Church in Part B of this volume.

5.48 *New York Times,* April 5, 1868.

5.49 In *American Architect and Building News,* January 19, 1878, p. 21, the author substitutes Exeter for Lincoln, a change which points to an interesting relationship with St. Patrick's.
   Recently, Walter Knight Sturges has pointed out to me the similarity between the aisle windows and buttresses at St. Patrick's and those at Beverly.

5.50 *New York Times,* May 18, 1879.

5.51 To be discussed in Part B of this volume.

5.52 Renwick kept a scrapbook of sketches and photographs, the bulk of which is in the possession of Mr. Winslow Ames. The contents are listed by Humphrey, *Churches of James Renwick,* Appendix A.

5.53 *Ibid.,* pp. 53ff.

5.54 Daniel Van Pelt, *Leslie's History of Greater New York,* New York [c. 1898], Vol. I, p. 476.

5.55 This unusual arrangement was first pointed out to me by Walter Knight Sturges.

5.56 The critic was the architect Alfred Darcel, who frequently reviewed architectural exhibitions for the *Annales archéologiques.* See Germann, *Gothic Revival,* p. 144.

5.57 *Annales archéologiques,* Vol. XV (1855), p. 246.

5.58 John Coolidge, "Gothic Revival Churches in the United States, 1823–1892," thesis, Harvard Architectural School Library, Cambridge, Mass., p. 186.

5.59 *Ibid.,* p. 182.

5.60 Charles P. Dwyer, "Ecclesiastical Architecture," *Sloan's Architectural Review and Builders' Journal,* September 1868, p. 198.

5.61 *New York Times,* May 18, 1879.

5.62 The wooden vaults of York Minster were destroyed by fire in 1849 and restored, again in wood. It is not impossible that Renwick knew about the fire and subsequent restoration from his visits abroad, and thus was aware of the unorthodox use of materials in the English cathedral.

5.63 See Pierson, Volume I, pp. 221–28.

5.64 The only other major Roman Catholic cathedral begun before the Civil War was the Cathedral of SS. Peter and Paul in Philadelphia. It was designed in 1846 and finished in 1859. The architect was John Notman, working in collaboration with two Catholic prelates. Like Latrobe's Baltimore Cathedral, it was classical rather than Gothic in style. With its tall central dome and porticoed façade, it was reminiscent of the churches of the sixteenth-century Italian architect Palladio in Venice. It was about 100 feet shorter than St. Patrick's. The central dome that was originally planned had to be reduced in size and built in wood rather than stone.

5.65 I am indebted to Robert T. Murphy of Brooklyn, N.Y., for sharing with me his extensive knowledge of Keely. Mr. Murphy is currently engaged in a comprehensive study of Keely; when published, it should make a substantial contribution to the history of the architecture of the Catholic Church during the nineteenth century.

5.66 See William Jordy, *American Buildings and Their Architects,* Vol. III, *Progressive and Academic Ideals at the Turn of the Twentieth Century,* pp. 3f.

5.67 George B. Post's Western Union Telegraph Building was ten-and-a-half stories high, but, because of its shorter tower, rose only 230 feet.

5.68 Renwick's final drawings for the lady chapel were made in a very interesting way. In 1886, when the illustrations of St. Patrick's were published in *Building* (see p. 222 above), proof prints seem to have been sent to the architect, and it was two of these, the plan and the rear elevation, which were used in the preparation of the lady chapel drawings. Fresh paper was pasted over the relevant parts of the prints and the new scheme was drawn thereon.

CHAPTER VI

6.1 See Pierson, Volume I, pp. 419ff.

6.2 Published in 1834, Dunlap's history was the first book of its kind to appear in this country. Since much of it is based on first-hand accounts provided by men who were alive, it is a document of primary historical value.

6.3 Quoted from Davis's manuscript copy, which is in the Avery Architectural Library. Almost without exception the information about Davis in this chapter comes from the large collections of his papers held by the Avery Architectural Library at Columbia, the Metropolitan Museum of Art, the New-York Historical Society, and the New York Public Library—identified in subsequent footnotes as Avery, MMA, NYHS, and NYPL.

6.4 Published in London, 1735. Davis edited the quotation slightly. In Blackwell's book, the full passage occurs on pp. 148f.

6.5 Quoted from the Avery copy of the biographical manuscript which Davis wrote for Dunlap.

6.6 In *The North American Review,* Vol. LVIII, April 1844, pp. 436–80.

6.7 John Claudius Loudon (1783–1843) was a prominent British landscape gardener and writer on horticulture and architecture whose published works were of central importance in the United States between 1835 and the Civil War. His *An Encyclopaedia of Gardening* (1822) and *Encyclopaedia of Cottage, Farm and Villa Architecture and Furniture* (1833) directly influenced the writings of Downing and the thinking of Davis.

6.8 Gilman, "Architecture in the United States," p. 461. The original may be read in J. C. Loudon, *The Architectural Magazine,* Vol. I, June 1834, p. 147.

6.9 See Pierson, Volume I, p. 374.

6.10 Roger Hale Newton, *Town and Davis, Architects,* New York, Columbia University Press, 1942, p. 93. Newton quotes the letter in full and identifies it as being among the Ithiel Town papers in the New Haven Colony Historical Society. Actually, the letter is among the Ithiel Town papers preserved in the print collections of the Metropolitan Museum of Art.

6.11 Newton quotes this passage twice (in *Town and Davis,* pp. 60, 95) and says each time that it is an entry made in Davis's diary on February 1, 1829. Unfortunately, he does not give the location of the document he saw, nor does he specifically identify which of the numerous records among the Davis papers he regards as the "diary." A search of all possibilities in the four major repositories has turned up no such entry. I am convinced, however, that Newton did see and record a document of some kind which, because of his careless methods of acknowledging his sources, we have not yet been able to identify. I have therefore taken his quotation as authentic and am using it as it appears in his book.

6.12 NYHS, Davis Papers, *Fragments, Scraps, Etc.* Davis copied the quotation exactly except in one instance. Instead of "Drawing has now become an essential part of polite education," Loudon had written, "We again recommend our readers to attempt to realize these improvements on paper. The benefit they will derive from so doing, is far greater than may at first sight appear" (*Encyclopaedia of Architecture,* p. 94).

From this it is obvious that the first sentence in the quotation, as it appears in the Davis papers, was the architect's own introduction to the ideal expressed by Loudon. It provides an interesting insight into one aspect of American education in the second quarter of the nineteenth century.

6.13 Several European-trained architects other than Latrobe came to this country during the late eighteenth and early nineteenth centuries, all of them highly skilled in the water-color medium. Among them was the Neoclassicist George Hadfield (1763–1826), who was Latrobe's predecessor as architect to the Capitol. Hadfield was also the brother of Jefferson's friend Maria Cosway. As a water-colorist he was among the best of his time, and together with the English-born John Haviland (1792–1852), who settled and worked in Philadelphia, exerted a considerable influence in the development of architectural rendering in this country. Latrobe, however, remained the central figure of the group and his water-color renderings are the most varied and interesting.

6.14 The term "architectural composer" occurs in various places in the Davis papers, but its most notable use is on Davis's professional calling card, which reads: Alex. J. Davis, Architectural Composer, New York, No. 34 Merchants' Exchange, Wall Street. Office Hours from 12 to 2 o'clock.

6.15 *Architectural Magazine,* Vol. I, No. 6, August 1834, p. 222.

6.16 NYPL, Davis, Day Book, p. 85.

6.17 *Ibid.,* p. 93.

6.18 *Ibid.,* p. 129.

6.19 *Ibid.,* p. 135.

6.20 Avery, Davis Collection, M–4. A list of "Davis Firsts" written in the hand of Davis's son.

6.21 Batty Langley, pl. LII. For other very early examples of the Gothic see Loth and Sadler, *The Only Proper Style,* Boston, New York Graphic Society, 1975, pp. 11–41.

6.22 Wollaton Hall in Nottinghamshire, designed by Robert Smythson and built in 1580–88, is one of the best examples of the corner-pavilion type of plan (see Summerson, *Architecture in Britain,* fig. 16). An interesting survival of this type of plan in colonial America is Mulberry (1714) on the west branch of the Cooper River in the South Carolina low country (see Hugh Morrison, *Early American Architecture from the First Colonial Settlements to the National Period,* New York, Oxford University Press, 1952, p. 173).

6.23 The verge board, also known as a barge board, is a tracery-like ornament, carved or sawn in wood, on the raking cornice of a Gothic gable. It became a favorite device of the Gothic Revival domestic architect in both England and America.

6.24 See Pierson, Volume I, Chap. X.

6.25 Davis himself was an avid reader of Scott. A particularly appropriate entry in his Day Book for February 1, 1830, reads: "Rainy, sloshy day, passed mostly reading Scott's 'Talisman.' "

6.26 See Hitchcock, *Early Victorian Architecture in Britain,* Vol. I, Chap. VIII, especially pp. 245–46.

6.27 There are a number of Scottish names in the area of the Glen Ellen site.

6.28 The designs for the Gothic details and other working drawings were listed by Davis in his Day Book on January 15, 1833. Unfortunately none survives.

6.29 Five hundred copies of *Rural Residences* were printed in the original edition and all of them were hand-colored by three artists other than Davis (see Day Book [NYPL], pp. 27–28). There seems also to have been a number printed that were not colored. The original edition contained a frontispiece, advertisement (preface), and nine plates, each of which was accompanied by a description. Davis intended to add regular supplements from time to time, but none was ever issued. He did produce several hand-made enlarged copies of the book. Each one is unique and includes additional buildings, most of them illustrated with water-color drawings. I have seen three of these, one in the Avery Library, one in the Metropolitan Museum of Art, and one in the possession of the Sleepy Hollow Restorations, Inc., in Tarrytown, N.Y. There are untouched and uncolored copies in the Metropolitan Museum of Art and in the American Antiquarian Society in Worcester, Mass. Sleepy Hollow Restorations, Inc. owns an untouched colored copy inscribed to Washington Irving, while the Boston Athenaeum has an incomplete uncolored copy. The New-York Historical Society has one complete colored copy and three incomplete copies. These are all that I have seen.

6.30 *Encyclopaedia of Architecture,* Book III, No. 1620, p. 763. Davis bought Loudon's *Encyclopaedia* on Sept. 8, 1835 (NYPL: Day Book, p. 172).

6.31 NYPL, Davis, Day Book, p. 157.

6.32 In the Avery Library.

6.33 Margaret Henderson Floyd has called to my attention a fascinating mid-century development that lends support to this theory. The German architect and writer Gottfried Semper (1803–79) and the British architect, industrial artist, and writer Owen Jones (1809–74), who were closely associated during the early 1850's, were strong advocates of the use of color in architecture. In the course of their studies, each of them concluded that both fabrics and the tent were primary sources for architecture. Jones in particular, in a work on *The Alhambra* (1841), observed that "the Arabs, in changing their wandering for a settled life —in striking the tent to plant it in a form more solid" achieved a new form by "changing the tent-pole for a marble column, and the silken tissue for gilded plaster."

Although these ideas were published too late to have directly influenced the development of the veranda in America, the very fact that they were published indicates an interest of the period in the tent as a potential architectural source.

6.34 The quotation is found in Davis's description of the Blithewood gatehouse as it appears in *Rural Residences,* where it is called "Gate-House in the Rustic Cottage Style."

6.35 Pierson, Volume I, pp. 66ff.

6.36 *Ibid.,* pp. 445ff.

6.37 MMA, Davis, Office Book, p. 59.

6.38 NYPL, Davis, Day Book, p. 20.

6.39 MMA, Davis, Office Book, p. 59.

6.40 Avery, Davis Collection II, 17–6. Paulding to Davis, letter dated 27 June 1839.

6.41 MMA, Davis, Office Book, p. 59.

6.42 Avery, Davis Collection II, 17–8. Description of Knoll in Davis's own hand which was the basis for that published by Downing in his *Treatise on Landscape Gardening,* first ed., 1841.

6.43 Joan R. Olshansky, "Lyndhurst, Historic Structures Report," 1973, Chap. II, p. 4. The document is in the files at Lyndhurst.

6.44 P. F. Robinson's *Rural Architecture,* pl. 1, for example, shows a cruciform plan with an upper story supported on an arched opening. Medieval market buildings were also frequently open on the ground floor, with heavy enclosed second stories carried on either timber or arched supports.

6.45 Avery, Davis Collection II, 17–8, Davis's description of Knoll.

6.46 Pierson, Volume I, pp. 310ff.

6.47 Avery, Davis Collection I, N–13–g.

6.48 Avery, Davis Collection I, N–13–f. Paulding to Davis, letter dated November 10, 1841.

6.49 Newton, *Town and Davis,* figs. 26–28, 31, 33, 37. See also Pierson, Volume I, pp. 422–23.

6.50 Allan Nevins, ed., *The Diary of Philip Hone, 1828–1851,* New York, Dodd, Mead, 1936, p. 550.

6.51 Davis, *Rural Residences,* Advertisement (Preface).

6.52 Among the Gothic villas which Davis designed between the two campaigns at Lyndhurst were the following: 1842, the Joel Rathbone house, near Albany, N.Y.; 1844, the W. C. H. Waddell house, New York City; 1845, "Belmead" for George Cocke on the James River, Va.; 1845, the Charles Alger house, Berkshire, Mass.; 1847, Phelps Villa, near Springfield, Mass. Of these only "Belmead" still survives, but drawings are in existence for all of them.

6.53 Russell Lynes, *The Tastemakers,* New York Harper, 1949, Chap. IV. It is also of interest that in a later addition to Blithewood Davis planned a picture gallery for Robert Donaldson. See Avery, Davis Collection, Cl–4–b.

6.54 Davis also included conservatories at Glen Ellen and Donaldson's Villa, which indicates the growing interest in them. Later they appeared in the works and writings of Downing.

6.55 The photograph reproduced in Figure 213 was apparently taken just at the time of the completion of the Merritt additions. Workmen can be seen, as well as construction debris.

CHAPTER VII

7.1 For a full account of Downing's life, see George B. Tatum, *Andrew Jackson Downing, Arbiter of American Taste,* Ann Arbor, Michigan, University Microfilms, 1950. A moving and personal image of Downing as a human being may be found in *Rural Essays,* New York, George Putnam, 1853. This is a collection of editorials written by Downing for *The Horticulturist,* and published after his death. The introduction includes a memoir written by the editor, George William Curtis, and a letter to Downing's friends by Fredrika Bremer. Written by literate observers who knew Downing well, both give fascinating insights into his nature.

7.2 Downing's *Treatise* was published in New York and London (sixteen issues of eight editions to 1879). His other works include: *Cottage Residences; or, A series of designs for rural cottages and cottage villas, and their gardens and grounds, adapted to North America,* New York and London, 1842 (thirteen issues to 1887); *The Architecture of Country Houses, including designs for cottages, farm houses and villas, with remarks on interiors, furniture, and the best modes of warming and ventilating,* New York, 1850 (nine issues to 1866); and *Rural Essays* (George W. Curtis, ed.), New York, 1853 (seven issues to 1881).

7.3 Downing, *Treatise on . . . Landscape Gardening,* pp. 320–21.

7.4 The letter is in the possession of Mr. Anthony Garvan.

7.5 The most important of the engravers who worked on Downing's books was Alexander Anderson. He worked in the so-called "white-line" technique of wood engraving which Thomas Bewick had popularized in England at the end of the eighteenth century. Anderson was the ablest wood engraver in America at mid-century, and from his skill, as well as Davis's architectural genius, derives the quality of Downing's illustrations. See Tatum, *Downing,* pp. 55ff.

7.6 Downing, *Treatise on . . . Landscape Gardening,* p. 361.

7.7 Avery, Davis Collection II–52–3. Downing to Davis, letter dated July 3, 1850.

7.8 Unless otherwise noted, this and the following quotations relevant to the villa come from Downing's *Architecture of Country Houses,* Section IX, pp. 257–70.

7.9 Downing, *Architecture of Country Houses,* pp. 22f.

7.10 J. C. Loudon, *Encyclopaedia of Architecture,* Book II, is devoted to the designing of villas. We have already (Chapter VI) seen its impact on Davis at Lyndhurst; its influence on Downing was equally great and frankly acknowledged.

7.11 Downing, *Rural Essays*, p. 161.

7.12 *Ibid.*, p. 163.

7.13 H. A. Washington (ed.), *The Works of Thomas Jefferson*, Vol. II, pp. 35–36. This is part of Jefferson's famous "The Head and the Heart" letter which he wrote to Maria Cosway. See also Pierson, Volume I, p. 314.

7.14 Travelling notes for Messrs. Rutledge and Shippen, June 1788. Quoted by Eleanor D. Berman, *Thomas Jefferson among the Arts*, New York, Philosophical Library, 1947, p. 150.

7.15 Berman, *Thomas Jefferson*, p. 150.

7.16 Downing, *Architecture of Country Houses*, p. 258. The last part of the Downing quotation recalls a passage from Horace which begins:
Happy is he who far from business,
like the first race of man,
can till inherited lands with his teams. . . .
It is interesting to note that Jefferson had copied the poem containing those lines some years before he began planning Monticello. From his broad knowledge of classical literature he was familiar with the Roman farm, and it was among the many sources of inspiration for his own house. See Pierson, Volume I, pp. 310–11.

7.17 NYHS, Davis Collection.

7.18 There is no doubt that Downing was familiar with Jefferson's views on architecture. In an editorial entitled "A Few Words on our Progress in Building," which appeared in the *Horticulturist* for June 1851, he begins by referring to a famous line from Jefferson's *Notes on Virginia* (see Pierson, Volume I, p. 289). His opening sentence reads: "The 'Genius of Architecture,' said Thomas Jefferson, some fifty years ago, 'has shed its malediction upon America.' "

7.19 Fredrika Bremer, *The Homes of the New World; Impressions of America*, translated by Mary Howitt, 2 vols., New York, Harper, 1853, Vol. I, pp. 19f. Miss Bremer was a Swedish novelist whose works were extremely popular in this country at mid-century.

7.20 *The Horticulturist*, Vol. II, January 1848, p. 297. Quoted by Tatum, *Andrew Jackson Downing*, p. 32.

7.21 Letter to John Jay dated August 23, 1785. Julian P. Boyd, ed., *The Papers of Thomas Jefferson*, Princeton, N.J., Princeton University Press, Vol. 8, p. 426.

7.22 *The Horticulturist*, Vol. II, January 1848, p. 297.

7.23 Downing, *Rural Essays*, p. xxxii. George William Curtis, in a memoir of Downing which introduces the book, notes, "I remember the conversation . . . touched an essay upon 'Manners,' by Mr. Emerson, then recently published."

7.24 Bremer, *The Homes of the New World*, p. 27.

7.25 The early Emerson essays which are particularly relevant to Downing are "Nature," 1836; "The American Scholar," 1837; "Thoughts on Art," 1841; "Self-Reliance," 1841.

7.26 Ralph Waldo Emerson, *Nature*, Boston, James Munroe and Company, 1836, p. 20.

7.27 Downing, *Architecture of Country Houses*, p. 258.

7.28 Emerson, *Nature*, pp. 24, 30.

7.29 Downing, *Architecture of Country Houses*, pp. 9, 31.

7.30 Emerson, *Essays*, Boston, James Munroe and Company, 1851, "Self-Reliance," p. 67.

7.31 Downing, *Architecture of Country Houses*, p. 264.

7.32 Emerson, *Essays,* "Self-Reliance," p. 68.

7.33 Downing, *Architecture of Country Houses,* pp. 22f.

7.34 Emerson, *Nature,* p. 51.

7.35 For another point of view on the Harrel House see Wayne Andrews, "A Gothic Tragedy in Bridgeport?" *Antiques Magazine,* Volume 72, July 1957, pp. 50–53.

7.36 See note 6.52 above.

7.37 Davis charged, for example, that Renwick's design for Grace Church was based on drawings submitted earlier by Town and Davis. MMA, Davis Collection, Office Book, p. 73.

7.38 All the information about Kingscote and the Jones family comes from an extensive preliminary report on the house in the files of the Preservation Society of Newport County. The copy of Jones's letter to Upjohn also comes from this source.

7.39 In *Rural Residences,* Davis shows a design for a villa in "the Oriental Style" in which the top of the veranda is painted in broad stripes like an awning. This is one more indication that Upjohn was familiar with the book and drew from it at Kingscote.

7.40 See Pierson, Volume I, pp. 452–60.

7.41 Unless otherwise noted all Downing quotations relevant to the cottage come from Section II, "What a Cottage Should Be," of his *Architecture of Country Houses.*

7.42 Quoted by Michael Hugo-Brunt in his introduction to the Library of Victorian Culture edition of Downing's *Cottage Residences* (1967), p. xvi.

7.43 Davis apparently added the date 1836 to his drawing of the Rotch House long after the fact, confusing this house with one he designed for Charles H. Roach in 1836.

7.44 The Wood House is recorded in Davis's Office Book (MMA, Davis Collection) p. 86, on April 6, 1846.

7.45 MMA, Davis Collection.

7.46 Downing, *Architecture of Country Houses,* pp. 50f.

7.47 The first and most penetrating discussion of the philosophical implications of board-and-batten siding, and of Downing's role in the matter, is by Vincent J. Scully: "Romantic Rationalism and the Expression of Structure in Wood," *The Art Bulletin,* Vol. XXXV, No. 2, June 1953, pp. 121–43. Scully not only points up the importance of Downing's observations about the relationship between the board and batten and the vertical character of the frame which it covers up, but he also suggests that the balloon frame, with its multiple vertical studs, was analogous to the board-and-batten technique. This whole question is pursued in a comprehensive study by Robert Jensen: "Board and Batten Siding and the Balloon Frame: Their Incompatibility in the Nineteenth Century," *Journal of the Society of Architectural Historians,* Vol. XXX, No. 1, March 1971, pp. 40–50.

7.48 Downing, *Architecture of Country Houses,* p. 52.

7.49 *Ibid.,* pp. 35–36.

7.50 Downing, *Cottage Residences,* pp. 13–14.

7.51 Lewis Mumford, *The Brown Decades, A Study of the Arts of America 1865–1895,* New York, Harcourt, Brace, 1931.

7.52 Much of the landscaping at Queset today was designed by Frederick Law Olmsted in 1892. I shall discuss Olmsted's work in North Easton in greater detail in Part B of this volume.

7.53 Downing, *Cottage Residences,* pp. 79–87.

7.54 The lace-like ornament produced by the jigsaw was to flower into even more intricate and gracious form after mid-century when cast iron came into use for architectural ornament. I shall discuss this development in Part B of this volume.

7.55 The most recent and definitive account of Llewellyn Park and of Davis's role in the project is by Jane Davies: "Llewellyn Park," *Antiques Magazine,* Vol. CVII, No. 1, January 1975, pp. 142–58. This beautifully written and superbly illustrated article gives a fascinating and solidly documented account of the development of the park. See also John W. Reps, *The Making of Urban America,* Princeton University Press, 1965, Chap. 12.

7.56 Daniels was among the landscape architects who competed for the design of Central Park in New York City and he actually won fourth place.

7.57 Downing, *Rural Essays,* p. 109. From "The Beautiful in Ground," an editorial in the *Horticulturist* for March 1852.

7.58 Among the houses designed by Davis which still survive are the following: "Arcade Cottage," a house in the Italian villa style; "Castlewood," a massive fortress-like Gothic villa built of local stone; "Tyrdyn Terrace," a highly formal and extremely elegant Italianate house with a large conservatory wing with walls mostly of glass; the Byerly-Kerr House, a later work (1868) in the French Mansard style.

7.59 From an undated promotional leaflet published at the time. Quoted by Davies, "Llewellyn Park," p. 143; for the full citation see p. 155, n. 7.

CHAPTER VIII

8.1 Richard Upjohn, *Upjohn's Rural Architecture, Designs, Working Drawings and Specifications for a Wooden Church, and other Rural Structures,* New York, George P. Putnam, 1852. As well as designs for a church and chapel, there are designs for a schoolhouse and parsonage. All are in wood.

8.2 Upjohn came to Brunswick on September 5, 1844, at the invitation of President Leonard Woods of Bowdoin College. The purpose of his visit was to present plans for a new college chapel. This remarkable building was among the earliest Romanesque Revival churches in America and will be discussed in detail in Part B of this volume.

While Upjohn was in Brunswick to consult with the college authorities, he was commissioned to do two other churches in the town, First Parish Congregational Church and St. Paul's Episcopal Church. St. Paul's still exists; like the First Parish Church, it is a small board-and-batten church; and it was begun at almost the same time as its larger and more imposing neighbor. Because of its more modest size it was finished several months sooner and is thus an even earlier example of the board-and-batten type which Upjohn's *Rural Architecture* would later make so popular.

8.3 The decision on the part of the Brunswick congregation to build in the Gothic style drew sharp criticism from the more conservative elements in the Congregational Church. A letter entitled "Popery in Maine" appeared in the Boston *Recorder* (foremost publication of the Congregational churches in New England) on February 20, 1845, which clearly singled out three offensive aspects of First Parish Church; its cruciform plan, its "chancel," and what the writer assumed to be the sign of the cross on the steeple. In a reply to this attack, the Reverend George Adams, minister of the church, said regarding the tower: "We shall have no steeple, and therefore . . . shall not have 'the sign of the Cross on the steeple.' Instead of the steeple. . . . we propose to have a square, high tower, which, we think, will be a great ornament to our village."

Dr. Adams's letter is quoted in full by Thompson Eldridge Ashby, *History of the First Parish Church in Brunswick, Maine,* Brunswick, 1869, pp. 187–89.

8.4 The designer of the remodeled tower and spire appears to have been the supervisor of construction, Professor William Smyth of Bowdoin College. Himself a gothicist of some distinction, Smyth corresponded with Upjohn continually during the building of the church and even made several trips to New York to consult with him. It is possible, therefore, that Smyth discussed the problem of the tower with Upjohn, but there are no extant documents to prove this. Local tradition ascribes the new tower to Smyth, not to Upjohn.

8.5   That the shallow chancel with its platform was intended to serve both the Congregational service and the Bowdoin College commencement is borne out by Dr. Adams's letter to the *Recorder,* mentioned in note 8.3 above. His rebuttal with respect to the chancel is as follows:

"We shall *not* have 'a chancel behind the pulpit,' but, after having a cartload of boards and joists brought into our House every year for forty years for a Commencement stage, we are weary of the system, and propose, until otherwise ordered, to occupy all that part of the new House east of the Cross, being forty-eight feet by twelve, by a permanent platform on which will be seated on Commencement occasions, the Trustees and Overseers of the College, the Magnates of the State, and 'pilgrims' of distinction who may be present from Massachusetts or elsewhere.

"We shall *not* 'have the Pulpit on one side of the transept and The Reading Desk on the other side,' . . . The Pulpit, a moveable one, will stand on ordinary occasions, at the front of the platform, aforesaid, and the Reading Desk . . . will occupy the *identical space* occupied by the pulpit!"

8.6   Upjohn, *Richard Upjohn,* p. 73.

8.7   The present west porch on St. John's is a later addition. The original entrance was through the south porch, thus in Ecclesiological terms the church as built was simpler and purer than it is today.

8.8   Upjohn, *Richard Upjohn,* p. 209.

8.9   Avery, Upjohn Collection, Plan Book, p. 121. Included were the communion table, chancel rail, faldstool, lectern, sedilia, and stalls.

Glossary of Terms

ADAMESQUE. Having qualities of style which derive from the work of the late eighteenth-century Scottish architects Robert and James Adam. The Adamesque mode is characterized by slender proportions, delicate scale, graceful curves, and linear compartmented ornamentation held flat to the wall or other architectural surface. In its American form the style is typified by the work of Charles Bulfinch and Samuel McIntire.

AMBULATORY. A sheltered passageway, generally in a church, intended for walking about.

ANTEFIX. A small decoration running vertically at the eaves of a roof to hide the ends of the tiles.

APSE. A semi-circular or polygonal projection of a church, usually at the east end.

ARCADE. A row of arches supported on piers or columns; a covered passage having an arched roof and arches on one or both sides.

ARCH. A curved support over an opening in a wall, formed by a series of wedge-shaped parts which are held in place by the weight of the wall above pushing them together and against the vertical supports on either side of the opening.

ARCHITRAVE. See ORDER.

ASHLAR. Building stone which has been "squared" (cut and shaped so that the edges of the blocks form accurate rectangles) and then "dressed" (its visible surfaces rubbed smooth and true). See also RANDOM ASHLAR.

ASYMMETRY. An occult and dynamic balance achieved by the irregular distribution of weights and forces around an off-center fulcrum.

BARGE BOARD. See VERGE BOARD.

BAROQUE. A style of architecture which flourished in Europe during the seventeenth and eighteenth centuries. Although based on the architecture of the Renaissance, it was more dynamic, with circles frequently giving way to ovals, flat walls to curved or undulating ones, and separated elements to interlocking forms. It was also a monumental and richly three-dimensional style with elaborate systems of ornamental and figural sculpture.

BATTEN. In building siding, a thin narrow strip of wood applied over the joint between vertical boards to seal it from the weather.

BAY. A principal space which occurs between such repeated elements as columns or windows.

BELFRY. A cupola, turret, or room in a tower where a bell is housed.

BELL COTE. A shed-like structure designed to house a church bell.

BLIND LANCET. A lancet-shaped recess that has no actual window opening. See also LANCET.

BRACE. A member placed diagonally within a framework or truss to make it rigid.

BRACKET. A supporting member projecting from the face of a wall. In American architecture it is frequently used for ornamental as well as structural purposes.

BROACHED SPIRE. In nineteenth-century Gothic Revival usage, an octagonal spire sprung from a square base. The uncovered triangles which remain at the corners of the square base are covered by low lean-to roofs.

BUTTRESS. A localized thickening of a wall which forms a vertical projection on the exterior and is designed to strengthen the wall against structural pressures such as those generated by arches, vaults, roofs, or beams. See also FLYING BUTTRESS.

CAMPANILE. In Italian, a bell tower. Freestanding in its original form, it became a popular device of the Italianate styles of the nineteenth century, where it was incorporated as a climactic unit in the general massing of a building.

CANTILEVER. An overhanging horizontal member which is supported at only one end and carries a load beyond its point of support.

CAPITAL. The moldings and carved enrichment which form a finish to the top of a column, pilaster, pier, or pedestal. See also ORDER.

CASTELLATED. Ornamented with battlements like a medieval fortified castle.

CENTRIPETAL. Characterized by a visual gathering toward the center or axis.

CHAMFER. The surface formed by cutting off a square edge at an equal angle to each face.

CHANCEL. That part of a church containing the altar, seats for the clergy and, often, the choir.

CHEVET. The rounded end of a choir in a church, especially characteristic of the Gothic churches of France.

CHOIR. That part of a church in which the singers and participating clergy are accommodated.

CINQUEFOIL. In tracery, a circular shape divided into five tangential circular or nearly circular parts.

CLERESTORY. That part of a building which rises above the roof of another part and which has windows in its walls.

CLERESTORY MONITOR. A form of roof fenestration, in which a section of the roof plane on either side of the ridgepole is lifted to a higher level, and in the space thus created a continuous range of windows is extended the entire length of the building; in character something like the clerestory windows in medieval churches.

COLLAR BEAM. A horizontal tension member in a pitched roof connecting opposite rafters, generally halfway up or higher. Its function is to tie the angular members together and thus prevent them from spreading.

COLONNADE. A series of regularly spaced columns usually supporting the base of a roof structure.

COLONNETTE. Any diminutive column.

COLUMN. An upright, supporting member, usually cylindrical in form. See also ORDER.

CONTRAPUNTAL.   Marked by interlocking or opposition of movement. An architectural passage in which two or more differing rhythmic sequences meet or pass through one another at common points.

CORBEL.   A strong supporting member built into but projecting from a wall to carry a heavy load such as a roof truss; in appearance similar to a bracket, it is, however, stronger. Also, to build outward, by projecting successive courses of masonry beyond those below.

CORNICE.   The crowning group of moldings in a wall or entablature. See also ORDER.

CORPORATE STYLE.   That architectural style which developed in the early industrial communities of the Merrimack Valley of New England during the first half of the nineteenth century. It is an austere but graceful mode of red brick and white stone lintels derived from the Neoclassical architecture of early nineteenth-century Boston. It is characterized by the same elegant proportions, cleanly cut openings, and simple but refined detailing.

COTTAGE ORNÉ.   A rustic building of romantic or picturesque design, noted for such features as bay windows, oriels, ornamented gables, and clustered chimneys.

COVED CEILING.   A ceiling where the junction of wall and ceiling is disguised by a large hollow or concave curved molding.

CRENELATION.   A form of embellishment on a parapet consisting of indentations alternating with solid walling. See OPEN CRENELATION.

CROCKET.   A small stylized ornament consisting of bunched curved foliage placed at intervals on the sloping edge of gables, spires, etc.; primarily a feature of the Gothic style.

CROWN.   The central, or highest, part of an arch or vault.

CROWN MOLDING.   The highest in an arrangement of moldings.

CRUCIFORM.   Arranged in the shape of a Latin cross.

CUPOLA.   A small open domed structure built on top of a building, usually for ornamental purposes.

CUSPS.   Small roughly triangular projections from the ribs or mullions into the enclosed area of traceried windows, screens, or panels.

DENTIL MOLDING.   A type of molding composed of a row of small rectangular blocks.

DIAPER WORK.   A diamond-shaped pattern or design on a flat surface.

DODECAGON.   A polygon of twelve sides and twelve angles.

DOG EARS.   Slight projections of the vertical and horizontal members at the upper corners of a door or window casing.

DORIC.   The simplest of the three orders of classical architecture developed by the Greeks.

DORMER WINDOW.   A window in a sloping roof, with vertical sides and front.

DOUBLE-HUNG WINDOW.   A window consisting of a pair of frames, or sashes, one above the other, arranged to slide up and down. Their movement is stabilized by a system of cords and counterbalancing weights contained in narrow boxing at each side of the window frame.

DRIP MOLDING.   A molding which is designed to divert rain water from the window or door below it and which follows the shape of the arch over the opening it protects.

ECLECTICISM. That method of design in architecture which selects elements from a variety of stylistic sources and combines them in a new and original way.

ELEVATION. A geometrical drawing which shows the right line projection of any vertical plane of a building. It is drawn to scale and without perspective.

ENCAUSTIC TILE. A tile decorated by a painted pattern in polychrome which is fired into the tile by the application of heat.

ENTABLATURE. See ORDER.

EYEBROW MONITOR. See TRAP-DOOR MONITOR.

FAN VAULT. A type of Gothic vault in which the ribs all have the same curve and radiate in a half circle around the springing.

FASCIA. A flat continuous band with a vertical face that projects slightly from adjacent members such as a stringcourse or belt.

FINIAL. An ornament placed at the apex of an architectural feature, such as a gable or turret.

FLYING BUTTRESS. In Gothic vaulting a spanning member, usually in the form of an arch, which reaches across the open space from an exterior buttress column to that point on the wall of the church where the thrusts of the interior vaults are concentrated. Because of its arched construction it exerts a counterthrust against the pressure of the vaults and is contained by the vertical strength of the buttress column.

FOUR-CENTERED ARCH. See TUDOR ARCH.

FOUR-PART VAULT. See QUATREPARTITE VAULT.

FRAMED CEILING. A ceiling in which the framing members are exposed.

FRIEZE. See ORDER.

FULCRUM. That part of a design around which other elements are balanced visually.

GABLE. A triangular-shaped piece of wall closing the end of a double-pitched roof.

GAMBREL ROOF. A roof which has a double pitch. The lower plane, which rises from the eaves, is rather steep; the upper plane, which spans from the lower to the ridgepole, has a flatter pitch.

GROIN. The curved edge formed by the intersection of two vaults of the same height and configuration.

HAMMER BEAM. A short cantilevered beam securing the foot of the principal rafter to the brace, strut, or tie. It is usually horizontal and forms part of at least two of the triangles of construction, namely the one above, connected with the principal rafter, and the other below, connected with the wall piece.

HAUNCH. The part of the arch between the crown or keystone and the springing.

HEADRACE (sometimes called penstock or millrace). A narrow opening or canal through which a large amount of water passes in a strong current, providing a source of power to drive the mill wheel. Also the water itself.

HIPPED ROOF. A roof which pitches inward from all four sides. The external angle formed where an end plane and side plane meet is called the hip.

HOOD MOLDING. A type of molding which forms a small projecting canopy of roof over a doorway, window, fireplace, etc.

IMPOST. The top part of a pier or wall upon which rests the springer or lowest wedge-shaped component (voussoir) of an arch.

JOIST. Any horizontal beam intended primarily for the construction or support of a floor or ceiling.

LANCET. A window generally tall in proportions and topped by a sharply pointed arch; characteristic of early English Gothic.

LATH. Thin narrow strips of wood nailed to rafters, joists, or studding with open spaces between to serve as a base or cleat for the plaster surface of a wall or ceiling.

LIERNE (also called a tertiary rib). A short ornamental rib connecting the tiercerons and ridge ribs in a Gothic vault.

LIGHT. A window or the main subdivisions of a window.

LINTEL. The horizontal structural member which supports the wall over an opening, or spans between two adjacent piers or columns. See also ORDER.

MODILLIONED. Having a series of small ornamental brackets under the projecting top moldings. Such brackets are common to the Corinthian and Composite orders in classical architecture.

MOLDING. A plane surface given the appearance of stripes of light and shade by the addition of combined parallel and continuous sections of simple or compound curves and flat areas.

MULLION. An upright post or similar member which divides a window into two or more units, or lights, each of which may be further subdivided into panes.

NAVE. The main part of a church, or that part between the side aisles and extending from the chancel or crossing to the wall of the main entrance.

OCULUS. A circular opening in a ceiling or wall.

OGEE ARCH. A pointed arch formed by a pair of S-shaped curves.

OPEN CRENELATION. Wood crenelation that imitates medieval stone crenelation but has tracery-like perforations in the solid units. Used along the crowns of raking and horizontal cornices, it especially occurs in early American Gothic Revival buildings.

ORIEL. A bay window located at an upper floor level and supported upon corbels or by a pier attached to the main wall below.

ORDER. The most important elements of classical architecture are the orders, first developed as a structural-aesthetic system by the ancient Greeks. An order has two major components, a *column* with its *capital;* together, they form the *post,* or main vertical supporting member. The principal horizontal member is the *entablature,* or *lintel.* The entablature consists of three horizontal parts. The lowest one is the *architrave,* an unbroken horizontal element which rests directly on the capitals and forms the principal part of the lintel. Above this is a second horizontal area called the *frieze,* which is generally decorated with sculptural ornament. The top member is the *cornice;* made up of various combinations of moldings, it overhangs the rest of the entablature and becomes the crowning motif. On the gabled end of a building, the cornice is continued up along the edge of the roof (now called a *raking cornice*) to form an enclosed triangle, or *pediment.* In classical architecture, the roof planes were pitched at a moderate angle, making the pediment a low, wide equilateral triangle. The Greeks developed three different types of orders, the Doric, Ionic, and Corinthian, each distinguishable by its own decorative system and proportions (see Pierson, Volume I, Figs. 1, 4, and 5). All three were taken over and modified by the Romans, who added two orders of their own, the Tuscan, which is a simplified form of the Doric, and the Composite, which is made up of elements of both the Ionic and the Corinthian. The Romans often used the orders as a structural system in the same manner as the Greeks. Unlike the Greeks, however, they also applied them as decoration to the surfaces of walls that were supported by other means.

PALLADIAN. Architecture based on the theories of the sixteenth-century Italian architect, Andrea Palladio (1508–80), whose famous work, *I quattro libri dell' architettura,* was published in Venice in 1570. Translated into several European languages, including English, it became the basic doctrinal work for several phases of post-Renaissance architecture in Europe and America.

PARAPET. A low wall, at the edge of a roof or balcony, sometimes formed by the upward extension of the wall below.

PAVILION. An isolated building for ornamental purpose in a park or garden. Also a wing which projects from a larger architectural unit and is usually accented by special decorative treatment.

PEDIMENT. See ORDER.

PICTURESQUE. The aesthetic doctrine, developed in England during the late eighteenth century, which added to Edmund Burke's definitions of the sublime and the beautiful a third category of experience, one characterized by such qualities as irregularity, roughness, and variety.

PIER. A freestanding vertical element, usually rectilinear in shape, supporting one side of an arch or one end of a beam, lintel, or girder. A thickening of a wall in the form of a vertical strip to strengthen it or to carry a heavy load for which the wall alone would not be strong enough.

PILASTER. The projecting part of a square column which is attached to a wall; it is finished with the same cap and base as a freestanding column. Also a narrow vertical member in a similar position.

PINNACLE. A small turret-like Gothic structure, usually slender and pointed, forming an ornamental finish to the highest part of a buttress, gable, roof, etc.

PITCHED ROOF. A roof in which the two planes slope equally toward one another.

PORCH. A roofed structure supported by posts or columns to shelter an entrance. A similar space formed within a building by recessing the entrance.

PORTE-COCHÈRE. A projecting porch offering protection to vehicles and to pedestrians entering a building.

PORTICO. A porch consisting of a low-pitched roof supported on classical columns and finished in front with an entablature and pediment. Any open structure consisting of a roof supported on columns.

POST. See ORDER.

POST AND LINTEL. A structural system in which the main support is provided by vertical members, or posts, which carry the horizontal members, or lintels.

PROSTYLE. Having a columnar portico in front, but not on the sides and rear.

PUDDING STONE. A conglomerate; a rock consisting of round pieces of stone of various sizes.

PURLIN. A horizontal beam which supports the rafters in a roof. Also referred to as a purlin plate.

QUATREFOIL. A type of Gothic tracery generally formed by four circles or near circles, each tangential to the next around a center.

QUATREPARTITE, or FOUR-PART, VAULT. A vault divided into four triangular sections by a pair of diagonal ribs. See GROIN.

QUOIN. The bricks or stones laid in alternating directions which bond and form the exterior corner angle of a wall.

RAFTERS. Structural timbers rising from eaves to ridge which support the covering of a pitched roof.

RAKING CORNICE. See ORDER.

RANDOM ASHLAR. The type of masonry where squared and dressed blocks (see ASHLAR) are laid in random fashion rather than in straight horizontal courses.

RAYONNANT. A phase of Gothic architecture characterized by radiating patterns of tracery.

REFECTORY. A dining hall, especially in medieval architecture.

RIB. A narrow projecting member supporting or strengthening a panel or surface such as a vault or ceiling. The term is also used to describe an architectural feature which appears to have this use but is in reality an ornament.

RIDGEPOLE. The board or plank at the apex of a roof and against which the upper ends of the rafters abut.

ROCOCO. A late phase of the Baroque style; marked by elegant reverse-curve ornament, light scale, and delicate color.

ROMANESQUE. A style of architecture developed in Italy and western Europe (c. 1000 A.D.) and characterized by round arches and vaults, piers rather than columns, and the decorative treatment of arcades. In the medieval architecture of Europe the Romanesque was the precursor of the Gothic.

ROOD SCREEN. An ornamental screen which serves as a partition between the nave and the chancel or choir of a church.

ROSETTE. A geometric circular floral ornament similar to an open rose.

RUBBLE WALLS. Walls made of uncut or roughly shaped stone.

SACRISTY. A room in a church where the sacred vessels, vestments, and so on are kept.

SECTION. A drawing done to scale and with no perspective which shows the appearance of a building as if it were cut through by an intersecting plane.

SEDILIA. A set of seats, along the south wall of a church, where the clergy may sit when not officiating during a service.

SEGMENTAL CURVE. An arch formed of a segment of a circle or an ellipse.

SHAFT. The tall part of a column between base and capital.

SPANDREL. The quasi-triangular space formed by two adjoining arches and a line connecting their crowns.

SPLAY. The slanting surface formed by cutting off a right-angle corner at an oblique angle to one face.

SPRING.   The lowest point of an arch or vault where the inside curve begins.

SQUARE HEAD.   The squared-off upper part of a door or window.

STEPPED GABLE.   A gable in which the wall rises in a series of steps above the slopes of the roof.

STRINGCOURSE.   A narrow horizontal band of masonry which projects slightly from the wall. Usually occurs at floor level.

STRUT.   In a truss, a rigid member which acts as a brace or support. It differs from a post in that it is commonly set in a diagonal position and thus serves as a stiffener by triangulation.

SURROUND.   The border or casing of a window or door opening.

SYMMETRY.   A balance achieved by having an exact correspondence in size, shape, and relative position of parts on each side of a center or axis.

TABERNACLE.   An ornamental container for the consecrated bread of the Eucharist. A canopied framed niche or recess.

TAILRACE.   The lower millrace, which carries the water discharged from the waterwheel back into the stream.

TERTIARY RIB (also called a lierne).   In Gothic vaulting, a third, ornamental rib inserted between the main rib and the tiercerons.

TERMINUS.   The end point, and sometimes the climactic point, in a design.

THRUST.   The continual pressure of one member against another, such as of a rafter against a wall.

TIE BEAM.   A horizontal member in a pitched roof or truss placed low down to tie together the opposing angular members and keep them from spreading outward.

TIE ROD.   A metal rod which performs the function of a tie beam.

TIER.   A row or rank of architectural elements arranged horizontally.

TIERCERON.   A secondary rib which rises from the springing to an intermediate position either side of the diagonal ribs of a Gothic vault.

TRACERY.   Openwork stone decoration formed by curvilinear lines or narrow bands and fillets or more elaborately molded strips which supports stained glass in a Gothic window or opening; when imitated in wood, used in a screen or applied to a door or panel.

TRANSEPT.   The part of a cruciform church which is at right angles to the nave.

TRANSVERSE RIB.   In a rib vault, a rib at right angles to the ridge rib.

TRANSVERSE BEAMS.   Beams at right angles to the main longitudinal axis of a building.

TRAP-DOOR, or EYEBROW, MONITOR.   In a sloping roof, a large section which is raised to a flatter angle as though it were a trap door hinged at the top, and having a window inserted in the opening. Unlike a clerestory monitor, it does not run the entire length of the roof.

TREFOIL.   In tracery, a shape which is divided into three parts by cusps.

TRIFORIUM.   In a Gothic church an arcade in the wall which appears above the arches of the nave, choir, or transept and below the clerestory window.

TRUSS.   A rigid triangular framework made up of braces, struts, and ties and used for the spanning of large spaces.

TUDOR ARCH. A flat arch characterized by two pairs of arcs, one pair at the spring, the other at the apex or crown.

TURRET. A small tower-like structure built against the side or in an angle of a building.

UMBRAGE. A term used by A. J. Davis as a synonym for the veranda, the implication being a shadowed area.

VARIEGATED. Given variety by subtle differences in color, shape, and texture.

VAULT. An arched roof or ceiling constructed in masonry; sometimes simulated in wood and plaster. An arch or a combination of arches used to cover a space.

VERGE BOARD (also known as barge board). A wide board fastened on edge below the slope of the roof on the gable end. A popular device of the Gothic Revival, it was either carved or sawed in ornamental tracery-like patterns.

VESTIBULE. A hall between the outer door and the main part of a building.

WATER TABLE. A steeply inclined surface at the top of a projecting member, such as a stone buttress or a foundation board, and designed to throw off rain water.

Index

Italicized figures refer to illustrations